River of Blood:
Serial Killers and Their Victims

By

Amanda Howard and Martin Smith

River of Blood: Serial Killers and Their Victims

Copyright © 2004 Amanda Howard and Martin Smith
All rights reserved.

Universal Publishers/uPUBLISH.com
Boca Raton, Florida
USA • 2004

ISBN: 1-58112-518-6

Cover photography by Stephen Bendeich

*"The river of blood, where all those wretches boil
Whose violence filled the earth with pain and fear"*

Dante Alighieri - The Divine Comedy - 1. Hell Canto XII lines 47-48

The journey to the completion of this first volume has sometimes been dark, we wrote about the murder of innocents on every page. I once held a draft copy of the book in my hand and the thickness of the book shocked me, knowing that on almost every page at least one innocent victim was murdered, raped, dismembered, maimed, or tortured. People that were loved and missed by those closest to them. That realisation comes at a price; it is something that I carry with me and something that is sometimes hard to deal with alone.

I have spent thousands of hours talking with killers, as well as surviving victims and their families and we have only scraped the surface of the tragedy that murderers wreak.

Had I not the loving support of my parents Brenda and Gordon, nor the devotion of my husband Steve and my family, I am not sure that I would have been able to continue on the journey. I am sincerely grateful to them all for their support.

I want to thank Martin, my co-author, together our ideas have become a huge project resulting in the first of several volumes pertaining to serial killers and their victims. To Chris Edwards, my IT expert, I thank you for teaching me that it is always good to do a backup before the hard drive crashes. Had it not been for you, the manuscript would have been lost forever. I would also like to thank Professor Paul Wilson, my mentor, for his guidance and encouragement.

Amanda

I have been studying serial killers for approximately 20 years and as a subject, it continues to fascinate and intrigue me, as I am sure it does so many other people. While researching this book, hardly a day went by without coming across new information about this type of criminal. New serial killers entered the arena at an almost regular occurrence; even as I write this, Pakistan authorities in Muridke are hunting the serial killer of five children, and man in South Korea has confessed to twenty-six murders. In Kenya, a pair of killers are responsible for twenty murders and remain at large, while in the USA an arrest has been made following a series of deaths in Port Salerno, Florida. Investigations continue in the cases of Derrick Todd Lee; Sean Vincent Gillis; Charles Cullen and Richard White. The Marc Dutroux case, in Belgium, recently ended with a guilty verdict and so the list goes on.

We must always remember that this book would not exist if it was not for the heinous crimes of these killers and as such, the victims should never be forgotten, despite how infamous their killers become. My thanks go to Phil Smith who gave me the confidence to write, to Phil Rouzel for keeping my head straight and to Amanda whose enthusiasm made this book happen. Finally, I dedicate this to my mother, Margaret, who may have since left this world, but shall continue to inspire us.

Martin
July 2004

Finally, we would both like to thank Brenda, our Editor, who made a good book great.

Table of Contents

Defining the Serial Killer	*3*
The Serial Killer	*3*
The Thrill Killer	*4*
The Spree Killer	*5*
The Black Widow and Bluebeard	*5*
Baby Farmers and Child Killers	*6*
Killer Kids	*6*
Poisoners	*6*
Medical Killers and Angels of Mercy/Death	*6*
Sex/Torture Killer	*7*
Tandem/Group Killers	*8*
A	*9*
Abdallah Al-Hubal	*9*
Wolfgang Abel and Mario Furlan	*10*
Howard Allen	*12*
Beverley Allitt	*14*
Marcelo de Andrade	*24*
Richard Angelo	*25*
Ann Arbor Hospital Murders	*26*
Ramiro Artieda	*27*
B	*28*
Bai Baoshan	*28*
Marcel Barbeault	*29*
Donald Bashor	*32*
Elizabeth Bathory	*33*
Dieter Beck	*36*
Mary Bell	*37*
Manuel Bermudez	*39*
Kenneth Bianchi and Angelo Buono	*40*
Bible John	*43*
Andreas Bichel	*44*
Arthur Bishop	*45*
Bernd Bopp	*47*
William Burke and William Hare	*50*
Jerome Brudos	*56*
Butcher of Kingsbury Run	*63*
C	*68*
Ricardo Caputo	*68*
Douglas Clark and Carol Bundy	*70*
Liao Chang-Shin	*78*
George Chapman a.k.a. Severin Klosowski	*79*
Richard Chase	*82*
The Chicago Rippers	*84*
Hadden Clark	*86*
Rory Conde	*90*
Dean Corll	*91*
Juan Corona	*98*
Antone Costa	*100*
Mary Ann Cotton	*101*
Dr Thomas Cream	*104*
D	*108*
Andonis Daglis	*108*
Jerome Dennis	*109*
Martin and Marie Dumollard	*110*
Theodore Durrant	*111*
E	*112*
Marti Enriquetta	*112*
F	*114*
Albert Fish	*114*
Kendall Francois	*127*
G	*131*
John Gacy	*131*
Luis Gavarito	*145*
Ed Gein	*146*
Guy George	*148*
John Glover	*153*
Anatoly Golovkin	*162*
Klaus Gossman	*163*
Harrison Graham	*164*
Dana Gray	*165*
Cleo Green	*167*
Samuel Green	*168*
Richard Grissom	*170*
Edson Guimaraes	*171*
H	*172*
William Heirens	*172*
Johann Hoch	*177*
Dr Herman Holmes	*178*
Fritz Honka	*182*
I	*183*
Javed Iqbal	*183*
Colin Ireland	*184*
J	*186*
Jack the Ripper	*186*
Jack the Stripper	*192*
Delfina and Maria de Jesus Gonzales	*195*
Matthew Johnson	*196*
Russell Johnson	*197*
Harold Jones	*198*
K	*199*
Yasutoshi Kamata	*199*
Edmund Kemper	*200*
Bela Kiss	*205*
L	*207*
Donald Lang	*207*
Posteal Laskey	*208*
Fernando Leyva	*209*
Wendall Lightbourne	*210*
Michael Lockhart	*211*
M	*212*

Name	Page
Maoupa Cedric Maake	212
Ronald Macon	213
David Mahlanga	214
Simon Majola and Themba Nkosi	215
John and Sarah Makin	216
Martha Marek	218
Richard Marquette	220
Kenneth McDuff	221
Michael McGray	224
Gennadiy Mikasevich	225
Ivan Milat	226
Zola Jackson Mqomboyi	230
Bilal Musa	231
N	232
Arnfinn Nesset	232
Dennis Nilsen	234
Robert Nixon	241
Gordon Northcott	242
O	243
Mohammed Omar	243
Anatoly Onoprienko	244
P	249
Carl Panzram	249
Eusebius Pieydagnelle	251
Dr Marcel Petiot	252
Thomas Piper	256
Rudolf Pliel	257
Jesse Pomeroy	258
Madame Popova	261
Dorothea Puente	262
Q	269
Thomas Quick	269
R	270
Gilles De Rais	270
Richard Ramirez	273
Sid Resala	287
Angel Resendiz	289
Sjef Rijke	291
John Robinson	292
S	300
Heriberto Seda	300
Robert Shulman	304
Peter Stubbe	305
Ahmad Suradji	306
T	308
Bobbie Sue Terrell	308
Sipho Thwala	309
Daniel Troyer	310
Tylenol Case	311
U	313
Andrew Urdiales	313
V	315
Hans Van Zon	315
Marie Velten	316
W	317
Hu Wanlin	317
Eugen Weidmann	318
William Wells	319
Zhou Wen	320
Werewolf of Chalons	321
Ronald West	322
Chris Wilder	326
Aileen Wuornos	332
X	336
Yang Xinhai	336
Y	337
Robert Yates	337
Huang Yong	343
Ma Yong and Duan Zhiqin	344
Graham Young	345
Z	352
Christopher Zidoke	352
Anna Maria Zwanzinger	353
Bibliography	355
Index	360

Defining the Serial Killer

The Serial Killer

When defining the serial killer, there is dissent amongst criminologists as to which killers should be included in the classification.

The varying theories differ greatly and it is to this extent that we have attempted to, firstly show that the term serial killer per se is too vague to encapsulate the range of killers, before secondly providing sub-categories that are more definitive.

According to editors Ronald and Stephen Holmes (1994)[1] a serial killer murders at least three victims; the victims are killed separately and in different places. Between each murder, there is a cooling off period. Though a good theory, such killers as John Gacy would not be included as all of his victims were killed in the one place, his home.

Steven Eggar in *The Killers Among Us* (1998)[2] gives a more definitive description. Eggar states that "a serial murder occurs when:
  (1) one or more individuals (in many cases, males) commit(s) a second murder and/or subsequent murder;
  (2) there is no general prior relationship between victim and attacker (if there is a relationship, such a relationship will place the victim in a subjugated role to the killer);
  (3) subsequent murders are at different times and have no apparent connection to the initial murder; and
  (4) are usually committed in a different geographical location. Further,
  (5) the motive is not for material gain and is for the murderer's desire to have power or dominance over his victims.
  (6) Victims may have symbolic value for the murderer and/or are perceived to be prestigeless and in most instances are unable to defend themselves or alert others to their plight, or are perceived as powerless given their situation in time, place or status within their immediate surroundings, examples being vagrants, the homeless, prostitutes, migrant workers, homosexuals, missing children, single women (out by themselves), elderly women, college students and hospital patients."

Eggar's definition covers the classic type of serial killer, the sexually motivated murderer; however, his classification does not lend itself to other sub-groups of the serial killer category. He also does not discuss the 'cooling-off' period between murders that separates the serial killer from the mass murderer. The cooling off period is, however, part of the FBI's classification. The Crime Classification Manual defines serial murder as "three or more separate events in three or more separate locations with an emotional cooling off period in between the homicides." Many criminologists however tend to disagree that three or more murders are required for a killer to be categorised as a serial killer. Oftentimes two murders are sufficient to see a pattern and signature and the propensity for further violence emerging.

When the term "serial killer" was penned in the 1970's by the FBI's then-called Behavioural Science Unit, there had been a spate of sexually motivated multiple homicides that, until that time, were quite an uncommon, though not an unheard of, event. It was only after the capture and study of Ted Bundy that Robert Ressler came up with the term serial killer.

---

[1] Ronald M Holmes and Stephen T Holmes (1994)
[2] Egger, Stephen A, *The Killers Among Us*, Prentice-Hall 1998

The FBI then began a study of many incarcerated serial killers and compiled a list of common traits. At the time, nearly all of the killers were white men. Many were aged between 20-35 and most of them had some form of sexual dysfunction.

The victims numbered from 2-3 onwards. Throughout history, some killers have claimed over 600 victims, yet on average, the victim count is around 7-10. Victims are usually females, with prostitutes as the most likely and easily accessible victims.

A three-point checklist was compiled as a common thread between most of the killers interviewed. Now called the "serial killer triad" it consisted of three childhood indicators that may have lead to the person becoming a serial killer. The three common points were:

>   Cruelty to Animals
>   Enuresis -bed wetting beyond the age of 12
>   Pyromania- the lighting of fires

People that have any or all of these traits do not necessarily go on to become killers, however the serial killers studied, such as John Gacy, Ted Bundy, Henry Lee Lucas, Ed Kemper, David Berkowitz all possessed the triad indicators, making the traits a common theme.

Since the 1970's and even more so now, as we head further into the 21st century, the serial killer per se is beginning to metamorphasise and many recent killers, though still classed a serial killer, require a more defined genus.

The differences in the cooling down periods, motives, signatures, and modes of murder of serial killers are becoming rather diversified. Where such killers as Jeffrey Dahmer, Lee Malvo and Harold Shipman would once have all been classified as serial killers, today the labels are outdated and need to be further refined.

Following, we have compiled a list of recognised types of serial killers.

The Thrill Killer

The Thrill Killer is a term used to cover the "grey area" between serial killers and mass murderer.

However, the difference of the thrill killer from the broader serial killer term is that there is no functional need to kill. Their actions are based on the high of the kill itself, similar to the feeling an extreme sports enthusiast may experience.

The thrill killer murders his/her victims for the death alone; there is usually neither prolonged attack nor sexual interference. The killer seeks the adrenalin rush from the hunt and kill. Robert Hansen in Alaska would fly his victims to a secluded area where he would set them free, before hunting them and killing them.

The thrill killer can in fact be able to abstain from killing for long periods. The killer is fully aware of his actions and often becomes more professional and more successful over time as he continues to refine the method of murder.

Many thrill killers attempt to commit the perfect crime, and assume they will not be caught.

The lack of a solid motive (in terms of sexual, robbery etc), the thrill killer can be harder to catch, and often is only caught after they make an error.

An example of the thrill killer is the 2002 Washington Sniper case. Lee Malvo and John Muhammad baffled police for weeks. They chose their victims at random, often those at petrol stations, shooting them from a 'safe' distance before leaving the scenes unnoticed. The men modified their car so the shooter could fire shots from the trunk of the car through a hole made in the rear of the sedan.

Until the men were found, police believed that they had been pursuing a Caucasian male in a white van. Instead, they captured two black men in a blue sedan. The case highlights the evolution of the serial killer. Serial killers can no longer be personified as a sexually motivated white male.

The Spree Killer

Many experts believe that the spree killer has their own unique classification, separate from both the serial killer and mass murderer, yet instead they actually lend themselves to both categories.

The spree killer is similar in the style of the mass murderer in that the time between killings generally covers a shorter span of time. Where the mass murderer has no emotional cooling down due to the continual assault on his victims in a populated area, for the spree killer, the emotional cooling down only happens because of a lack of access to victims.

The spree killer, like the thrill killer often does not have any contact with the victim. The murders occur quickly and the killer leaves the scene immediately such as the case of Charles Starkweather. The young man and his teenage girlfriend went on a shooting spree across the United States leaving many people dead in their wake. Most of the murders were opportunistic and were of little gain to the couple.

The victims are usually chosen at random, usually due to locality and opportunity. The spree killer will cross racial and social barriers. The ongoing spree prevents any long emotional cooling down.

The difference between the spree and thrill killer is that the spree is often compelled to murder, whereas the thrill killer is more in control of their desires.

The Black Widow and Bluebeard

Black Widow killers are named after the Black Widow spider found in North America. The female of the species is extremely toxic whereas the male and juveniles are completely harmless.

Contrary to popular belief, the Black Widow female spider rarely kills and consumes the male after mating. Yet it is a legend that has seen the spider lend its name to the female serial killers who murder their husbands or lovers, children and relatives, often for financial gain.

The use of the term "Bluebeard" is based on the 1697 story of the same name by Charles Perrault. The fairy tale is about a man who murders his wives, one after the other, consolidating a vast wealth until he is finally murdered by the brothers of his last wife.

Bluebeard serial killers are those who murder their wives, usually for financial gain. George Joseph Smith in England and Henri Landru of France both murdered several wives after milking them of their wealth or insuring them for large sums of money.

Both the Bluebeard and Black Widows are extremely patient killers. The murders they commit can take years, some victims are slowly poisoned, others are dispensed of quicker, but these killers will bide their time before they kill. Regardless of their close relationship with the victim. Bluebeard and Black Widow killers rarely show true remorse for their crimes. They can calmly watch a family member die in agony, only feigning concern to elude suspicion.

Baby Farmers and Child Killers

We usually see the serial killer as choosing his victims among the adult community; however, a small group of these killers use children to satisfy their murderous needs.

Similar to black widows murdering for insurance money, the Baby Farmers use children as a means to make money. Parents would pay the baby farmers cash to find a home for unwanted children, usually newborn babies, the children would be killed and the money taken, the parents being none the wiser.

The worse category of serial killers, if there is such a thing, are the child predators. Child Killers usually prey on children for sexual gratification and the murders are often an attempt to conceal the sex-crime. Killer such as Arnold Sodeman in Australia and Robert Black in England are examples of this type of serial killer. Each killer lured their victims away from safety for the sole purpose of sexually assaulting them.

The subsequent death is to prevent the victim identifying the killer.

Killer Kids

Killer Children such as fifteen-year-old Jesse Pomeroy and seventeen-year-old William Heirens are examples of the heightened escalation in murders exhibited in children who kill. Young killers are often more brutal and cruel than their adult counterparts. Their crimes are usually indirectly sexually motivated, the killer child knows they want to experience sexual pleasure but their actions are misdirected, often resulting in murders of victims younger than themselves.

Poisoners

Today killers are loath to use poisons as a tool for serial murder for two reasons,
1. The change in laws making poisons increasingly difficult to purchase
2. The advancements in forensic science and the ability to detect the smallest trace amount of most toxins in post mortem examinations.

From the late 1800's through to the early 20th century however, poisons were used often by killers wishing to dispatch of cheating or wealthy spouses, children, or anyone else that got in their way, often revelling in the agony the victim suffered.

Another type of serial killer poisoner is the product tampering cases such as the still unsolved Tylenol Killer case in Chicago in 1982 where seven people died after consuming Tylenol laced with cyanide.

Regardless of scientific advancements, Mass Murderers have continued to use poisons and toxins in widespread murders, such as the subway attack in Tokyo in 1995 and the infamous Jonestown Gatorade-cyanide mass suicide twenty-five years ago, where detection is not of concern to those who mastermind such killings.

Medical Killers and Angels of Mercy/Death

The only killers who continue to use poisons as their means of murder are Medical Killers and "Angels" who have the medical knowledge and ability to conceal their crimes.

Medical Killers such as Dr Harold "Fred" Shipman murdered at least 15 victims with large doses of drugs. The number of victims however may be as high as 300. Most of the doctor's victims were his own patients, some leaving him money in their wills. He would go to see them at their houses and inject them with high doses of various drugs, killing them quickly.

Shipman would then sign the death certificate himself, ensuring that no autopsy was done. He was able to elude detection for several decades before the family of one of his victim's question the validity of the deceased's will.

Beverley Allitt was a typical Angel of Death, whenever she was on duty she was surrounded by trauma and often death. Allitt worked as a paediatric nurse at a hospital in England and began her murderous career appearing as a hero rather than killer. She would often inject a child with drugs, before reviving the child to the praises of hospital staff and parents. The praise fuelled the psychological disorder she suffered, Munchausen's Syndrome by Proxy (MSP). MSP is the disorder where the sufferer inflicts pain on another to gain attention themselves. Parents and carers have been known to poison or injure children in their care so they can then nurse them back to health, being seen as the good mother/father or carer/lifesaver. Yet, as in the case of Allitt, the disorder can be deadly for those around them.

At the opposite end of the spectrum to Angels of Death are the Angels of Mercy. These killers are often advocates of euthanasia. They often assist the elderly or terminal patients in taking their own lives. The killings are often done with the permission of the victim, and not at the pleasure of the killer. Dr Kevorkian in America and Dr Nitschke in Australia are both famous euthanasia campaigners and have both assisted in many medically assisted deaths.

Other Angels of Mercy are less vocal and lurk in the greyer area of the genus. Often victims die unexpected and the killer may be a nurse or doctor known to them. The killer may claim the murder was to "ease the pain" of the victim, yet the victim may not have given permission nor made a suicide request to others.

Often health professionals are investigated when a large number of patients in their care die. The media often pounces on such cases of victims dying at the hands of a caregiver.

Sex/Torture Killer

The Sexual Killer is the most common type of serial killer. Many of these killers will derive some form of sexual pleasure from the murder, or from the attack of the victim pre or post mortem.

Andrei Chikatilo, the serial killer dubbed the Red Ripper, in Russia murdered at least 52 victims during a reign of terror lasting almost 15 years. The first murder in 1978 was committed almost by accident. He attempted to rape a young girl, but could not achieve an erection. He stabbed the victim out of anger and found that the blood on the girl's body aroused his sexual appetite. The epiphany changed him into a sadistic sexual murderer.

There are two different strains of sex serial killers. Those who are organised and those who are not.

The organised sex killer will spend time with the victim, sometimes stalking them before striking. Often they will take the victim to their residence or another place where the killer knows he will not be disturbed. Jeffrey Dahmer, Robert Berdella, and John Gacy all hunted for victims. When a suitable one was found, they were taken back to the killer's home. It was there that the killer's demeanour would suddenly flip into 'kill mode'. The victims are drugged and confined and the killer then takes their time commit the murder, often taking photos or records of the event as it unfolds. The killer often brings his own tools as part of the plan.

Charles Ng and Leonard Lake, took the organised serial killer definition to its extreme. The men bought a secluded home in Wileysville, California and built a large underground bunker in which to incarcerate young women. The killers found victims through various means including classified ads. Once the victims and their families were at the Wileysville house, Lake and Ng would kill the children and husbands quickly, leaving the women alive and chained up in the dungeon, filming them as they were sexually abused and tortured for long lengths of time. The women were ultimately murdered when they no longer excited the men. Most of the victims were interred in the grounds surrounding the house.

The organised sex killers often kill for years before they are caught.

The unorganised sex killers are generally arrested at an earlier stage of their rampage than their organised counterparts. The victim choice is usually opportunistic and the killer is liable to strike at any moment. Just as the organised killer is aware of the consequences of his actions and will take steps to prevent discovery of the victim, the disorganised killer does not. The victim is found at the murder scene or dumpsite, often having suffered more extreme injuries both pre and post mortem. The killer has little thoughts for his own safety and will regularly leave obvious clues that expedite their arrest.

The signature of the serial killer, the unique brand of the individual, often helps authorities link the sex murders and frequently helps the media dub the case with a nickname.

The Hillside Strangler was such a case. Although the case nickname was in the singular, there were in fact two killers, cousins Ken Bianchi and Angelo Buono. The men picked up young women around California during 1977-1978. The women were sexually tortured before being murdered and dumped. Often their naked bodies were thrown from the killers' car on roads and highways onto banks and hills, hence the moniker. The bodies were found quickly and the escalating torture and the way in which they were dumped linked the murders of the women. Bianchi, alone, also murdered several more women in Washington, and the signature of the murders allowed police to also link these murders to those in California.

There is another less significant strain of sex killers, those who murder to avoid detection. These killers murder their victims after violently sexually assaulting them. The victims are mutilated or hidden; the murder is used to prevent the victim from telling anyone about the attack, rather than the murder itself being the act in which the killer is interested.

Many of these killers began their 'career' with rape.

Tandem/Group Killers

The most interesting and least understood type of serial killer is the tandem killers, those killers who work in pairs or in groups. The term Tandem Killers was penned by Professor Paul Wilson in 2002 in his excellent book, *Tandem Killers.*

The ability to commit murder in the company of another requires a great deal of trust and accord and often the reason that Tandem Killers are caught.

In most cases of tandem killings one of the killers is the dominant partner and seduces the other into his or her murderous fantasies. The dominator rarely concerns himself or herself with the state of the victim after death, the follower is generally left to deal with the aftermath.

However, the follower usually brings the team to justice. The weaker partner will confess if pressured and will identify the main killer.

Tandem Killers rarely continue a friendship/relationship beyond their apprehension and incarceration. Most Tandem killers, such as Ian Brady and Myra Hindley in England become enemies once in prison.

A

Abdallah Al-Hubal

Police gunned down Forty-three-year-old Abdallah Al-Hubal on August 16, 1998 during his arrest for the murders of twelve people.

Yemen police closed in on the serial killer in the town of Beit al-Fakieh near Sanaa when he opened fire, shooting a police officer dead in cold blood and severely wounding three others before he was brought down in a hail of bullets.

Al-Hubal had already served a prison term for the murders of seven people in 1990 in Aden. The last five victims were killed in the weeks leading up to his own murder on August 16, 1998.

The killer was a wealthy oil baron before he took to murder in the turbulent political climate of the Arab Emirates.

Wolfgang Abel and Mario Furlan

In August 1977 in Verona, the murderous campaign of Wolfgang Abel and Mario Furlan began. The two sons of wealthy families began a crusade against homosexuals, gypsies, and others they believed to be degenerates of society.

Eighteen-year-old Abel and seventeen-year-old Furlan chose a drug-addicted gypsy as their first victim. The two young men callously set the man alight, as he slept in a car.

Abel and Furlan ran from the scene as the victim attempted to escape the flames that burned into his skin. People passing by helped the man, dousing the fire as emergency services arrived. The gypsy was taken to hospital, where he told police two, but possibly three young men had attacked him. He died shortly after making the statement.

Police found a note at the scene. The letterhead on the note said "Ludwig", a swastika, and Nazi eagle were below it. The letter contained Nazi propaganda quotes. It would become part of the killers' signature at each subsequent murder. The men would leave similar letters filled with slogans from Nazi Germany at each scene, making it easy for police to link the murders to one set of killers.

The next victim, a casino worker from Padua was stabbed to death. The killers believed the man was a homosexual.

Abel and Furlan next stabbed and bashed to death a gay waiter in a side street in Venice. The victim had been stabbed at least thirty-four times.

Victim number four was a prostitute. Believing she was a disease carrier, the two young men used axes to hack her to death.

In Vicenza, Abel and Furlan used hammers to kill two priests. The padres were found with their heads crushed from multiple blows to the head with the killers' hammers.

Abel and Furlan next murdered a hitchhiker. The victim had been sleeping at a rest stop in Verona when the two thrill killers attacked him. The men set the hiker alight before watching him burn to death.

The men enjoyed the torturous deaths to which they subjected their victims. The next victim's murder was particularly brutal. Abel and Furlan tortured a priest who was a homosexual before hammering a nail into the man's forehead as he screamed in pain. When that did not kill him, the men next hammered a chisel into his face. The chisel's handle was in the shape of a cross.

Abel and Furlan's continued fascination with fire, fuelled by Furlan father's job as a plastic surgeon specialising in burns, saw them torch a pornographic cinema in Milan. Inside the theatre was a small group of people. Five people died in the inferno as the killers watched.

The conflagration was so successful that the men decided to set fire to another building. The fire was lit at a disco in Milan. One young woman died and many others were maimed and burned.

Again, the men were impressed by their efforts and on March 3, 1984, partygoers in Mantua caught them as they were dousing another disco with flammable liquid. Inside the club, over 400 people were unaware of how close they had come to death that night.

A "Ludwig" letter was found at the scene once again, and though the men denied they were the killers from the other murders, police found Nazi propaganda at their homes and officials charged the men with the string of brutal murders across Italy.

The trial of Abel and Furlan opened on December 1, 1986. A total of twenty-seven charges of murder were presented in the case. The trial lasted until early February 1987 when the men were found guilty of ten of the murders, but a question was made of their sanity. Both were given thirty-year sentences for their crimes, a light sentence considering the barbaric crimes they had committed.

However, neither man spent thirty years in prison. Both Abel and Furlan were released after three years, their sentences reduced to house arrest under the guidance of their wealthy and politically influential families.

Howard Allen

Howard Allen was born on February 10, 1949 in Indianapolis and remained close to his home when murdering his victims in later years.

The first murder committed by Howard Allen was in August 1974 and was unplanned. While robbing the home of Opal Cooper, the elderly woman disturbed the twenty-five-year-old black man. Panicking, Allen bashed the woman to death.

The killer was arrested soon after the murder and sentenced to 21 years in prison on a charge of manslaughter during the act of a robbery. By January 1985, less than ten years after being incarcerated the man was released back into Indianapolis society.

Yet the man was far from rehabilitated and decided to kill again.

On May 18, 1987, a woman survived an attack by Allen and was able to give the police a description of the black man who had bashed her.

On May 20, 1987, Howard Allen broke into the home of eighty-seven-year-old Laverne Hale. Laverne's house shared a boundary fence line with that of Allen.

When she disturbed Allen searching for items of value she was bashed savagely. Laverne was found near death the next morning by neighbours and rushed to the local hospital, where her life hung in the balance for nine days before she expired, the brutality of her assault was too much for her frail body.

By this time, Howard Allen had a taste for robbery and murder. He had staked out another elderly resident to be the next victim and decided to pounce on June 2, 1987. When Allen entered the home, he was furious at finding the victim not home. The killer took out his frustration through the house. He left nothing untouched, items were torn and smashed. In one final act of anger, Allen set the house on fire.

Six weeks later Allen struck again. On July 13, 1987, Howard Allen knocked on the door of Ernestine Griffin in Indianapolis. The killer had come to the house to enquire about a car he had seen for sale. Allen however had inadvertently gone to the wrong house. He had meant to go next door to the surgery of Dr Victor Seaman, a dentist and friend of seventy-three-year-old Ernestine. Dr Seaman was not at the office that day and Mrs Griffin told the man that she would get the dentist to call Allen the following day.

Allen wrote his name and phone number on a piece of paper and gave it to the elderly woman.

Later that evening, Ernestine left the name and telephone number of Allen on Dr Seaman's answering machine. The dentist attempted to ring the man on his return and spoke to Allen's sister. She did not, however, pass the message on to her brother.

At lunchtime the following day, Dr Seaman went to the house next door to see Ernestine, he found the house open and in silence. The dentist entered the living room to find the elderly woman lying on the floor in a pool of blood. A large knife protruded from one of the eight stab wounds in her chest. Later examinations proved that Ernestine had been bashed with her toaster repeatedly before being stabbed to death.

The note, with Allen's name and phone number, was found near Ernestine's body and on August 4, 1987, Allen was arrested for the woman's murder as well as an arson and burglary attack on June 2 and the assault of a woman on May 18.

After extensive questioning, Allen confessed to Ernestine's murder, saying he had returned to the home of Mrs Griffin on July 14 to ask further about the car. He had entered the home of Ernestine and hit her before stabbing her to death. He also ransacked the home stealing less than $20 in money and the woman's camera.

On June 11, 1988, Allen was found guilty of the charges of assault and robbery, as well as a charge of being a habitual criminal. The killer was then also found guilty of Ernestine's murder. On August 30, 1988, Allen was sentenced to 88 years in prison for the assault and burglary charges before being sentenced to death for the elderly woman's murder.

Currently Allen has not been charged officially with the murder of Laverne Hall, though the attack, murder and close proximity to the Allen household makes him the prime suspect in the case. He is also suspected of over eleven other robberies and assaults that had taken place during the same period.

Beverley Allitt

Born on October 4, 1968 in Corby Glen, England, Beverley Gail Allitt was the second child to parents Richard and Lillian. Her childhood years were as normal as one could expect, except that she would always seem to be suffering from some form of worry or illness, often appearing with bandages or plasters on her body.

At sixteen, Allitt expressed an interest in caring for sick children and so enrolled at a pre-nursing course in Grantham. After that course ended, she began her nursing training at Grantham and Kesteven Hospital in September 1988 as a trainee nurse.

At the end of the two-year course, Allitt successfully passed the examinations, but her attendance records show that she had missed a total of 126 days due to a variety of illnesses. One of the ward sisters at the hospital, concerned at the number of absent days, suggested that Allitt should be given psychiatric help - none was offered.

Allitt's first attempt to find work as a nurse was rejected on the basis of her attendance record, in addition to the interviewer's belief that she appeared to have a lack of basic knowledge.

Allitt was not yet registered as a nurse and was required to work an additional ten weeks to satisfy the requirements; the time would be spent on Ward Four, the Children's Ward. Having completed the additional ten weeks, Allitt was employed permanently on Ward Four on February 15 1991. Seven days later Liam Taylor died.

Liam Taylor

Liam was the second child of Chris and Joanne Taylor and at seven weeks old the baby had contracted a cold and both parents were understandably concerned. Due to his cold, the baby had hardly slept the previous two nights and therefore neither had his parents. On February 21, 1991, Joanne telephoned the family doctor for a third time in as many days as the baby's cold was getting worse. The doctor suggested the family take the baby to the Hospital. At 1.00pm, Liam was booked into Ward Four at Grantham Hospital and diagnosed as suffering from Bronchiolitis.

Liam was given an oxygen mask to help his breathing and instantly he began to look better. Chris and Joanne felt happier. A staff nurse met with Liam's parents and introduced them to Nurse Allitt who was about to feed him, the staff nurse suggested that both Chris and Joanne go home for a while and rest, they agreed.

Less than two hours later Chris and Joanne returned to Ward Four to see their baby. Once there they realised that things had taken a turn for the worse. Nurse Allitt described how Liam had suddenly violently vomited as she was feeding him. He also was producing yellow faeces. Liam was lying still in his cot, not moving and his parents began to panic. A consultant, Doctor Charith Nanayakkara, arrived with two nurses and told Chris and Joanne that Liam had pneumonia on his lungs and that the next twenty-four hours would be critical in Liam's short life.

The next twenty-four hours were indeed critical, Chris and Joanne stayed with their son constantly. Liam would appear to be improving, he would smile and giggle, but then the next moment his muscles would tighten and his face grimace in pain. The doctors were perplexed. Consultant, Dr Nanayakkara once again sat with the parents and informed them of Liam's condition, he believed that Liam was brain damaged but was unsure of the severity. Both Chris and Joanne requested that Liam be taken off the drugs and breathing apparatus and allowed to fight for himself, the doctors tried to discourage them from their request but reluctantly agreed. Liam was baptised by hospital chaplain Reverend Ian Chaplain, and then the medical equipment was turned off at 6.30am. In the middle of the afternoon on February 22 1991, Liam Taylor died in his parent's arms.

Doctor Nanayakkara completed the death certificate giving the cause of death as 'probable septicaemia'. The coroner, T J Pert, rejected this as he believed that the word 'probable' does not belong on a death certificate and therefore requested that a post mortem be carried out. Doctor Terry Marshall completed the autopsy on February 25 and concluded that Liam had suffered a heart attack. He further stated that tissue in the left ventricle was virtually destroyed, which for such a young child is considered rare, he compared Liam's heart to that of a middle-aged person who drinks and smokes. The death certificate was re-issued with cause of death modified to read natural causes.

Tim Hardwick

Tim Hardwick had suffered all his life, he had Cerebral Palsy from birth, was virtually blind, and had little control over his arms and legs, but he still knew how to be happy. Tim would giggle if he liked something, Tim giggled a lot actually. Since he was a child he had been cared for by Nottingham County Council and because of his mother's own disability, she thought it was for the best. Tim had spent the weekend at home with his mother and family around him. On March 5 1991, Tim suffered a fit while at Appleton Gate School, the teachers there cared for him during this time, but he suffered a further four fits in a three hour space. The decision was made to take the eleven-year-old to Newark Hospital where, after a treatment of Valium, managed to calm Tim's body down allowing him to sleep. Doctors agreed that Tim should stay in hospital for observation but were unable to do that at Newark. It was arranged to transfer Tim to Grantham Hospital. He reached Ward Four at 3.15pm. At 5.00pm, Nurse Allitt sought assistance from fellow nurse Mary Reet after Tim appeared to be uncomfortable. The pair turned the boy onto his side that seemed to improve the situation. Forty-five minutes later the alarm was raised again by Nurse Allitt, Tim had suddenly stopped breathing. His face had turned white and his lips were now blue. Mary checked his pulse – nothing, Tim's heart had stopped beating. The crash team were called; doctors and nurses immediately ran from their posts to be in position for the emergency. The crash team used the defibrillator in an attempt to save Tim's life, but it was too late. At 6.15pm, Tim Hardwick died from suspected heart failure.

UK law dictates that any patient that dies in a hospital within a stay of less than 24 hours is required to undergo a post mortem. Doctor Marshall completed his report with Status Epilepticus (continuous Epilepsy) stated as the cause of death. Despite the fact that Tim was not fitting at the time of his death, and despite the fact that Dr Marshall discovered 'tiny bleeds on the lungs' which is normally a sign of asphyxia.

Kayley Desmond

Kayley Desmond entered Ward Four at Grantham Hospital and at only fifteen weeks old, under nourished, dehydrated, and suffering from a chest infection, the prospects of long-term survival were not good. At 1am on March 10 1991, Nurse Allitt requested help from colleague Nurse Lynn Vowles to modify some medical equipment at Kayley's bedside. Careful not to wake Kayley's mother Maggie, who was sleeping in the same room, the nurses adjusted a drip monitor. Nurse Allitt noticed that Kayley did not look right, her colour was noticeably different. A closer look revealed that she was not breathing. Lynn instructed Allitt to call for the crash team while she administered mouth to mouth. Maggie stirred from her sleep, woken by the hive of activity surrounding her daughter and demanded to know what was going on. Lynn continued to work on Kayley's chest and breathing into her mouth, Kayley responded but was still very weak. The crash team initially believed that the chest infection was the cause; Nurse Allitt added that she heard the baby crying and went to investigate. Kayley underwent some tests to determine the cause, none could be found and Kayley appeared fine after the scare, everyone sighed in relief.

Kayley lay asleep in her crib with Maggie by her side; Nurse Allitt was given strict instructions to stay in the room to watch over the child. Maggie visited the hospital canteen. Dr Nanayakkara and the crash team burst into the ward responding to the emergency call at 4.00pm. Kayley's heart had stopped. An injection of Aminophylline was administered along with a heart massage and Kayley jumped back to life. Over the next few minutes and with some more treatment, her breathing and pulse returned to normal. Dr Nanayakkara decided to transfer the little patient to the Queens Medical Centre in nearby Nottingham, where she suffered no further attacks. The doctors at Queens could not believe that Kayley had stopped breathing; as the speed of her recovery surprised everyone, within two days Kayley was back to normal.

Paul Crampton

It had been weeks since the mysterious illness of Kayley Desmond and the ward was regaining a sense of normality. Children were continuing to be treated for their ailments and new patients were admitted. Paul Crampton was one such patient. At 6.00am on March 23, 1991, Nurse Kate Lock made a visit to the five-month-old in order to feed him. She asked Nurse Allitt to wake Paul from his sleep while she went to the kitchen to prepare his meal. She soon returned and the nurse began feeding young Paul.

A few minutes later Kate Lock noticed that the young boy was slow with his intake. A third nurse, Betty Asher, entered the cubicle and noticed that Paul was turning grey. Kate looked closely and agreed that something was wrong. Nurse Allitt suggested that Paul was suffering a hypoglycaemic attack, which was unusual because Paul was not diabetic, but the test was done anyway. The test highlighted a 3.7 blood sugar result, low but not dangerous. A few minutes later a second test was completed which would highlight a result of only 1.7, very low and very dangerous. Paul was indeed having a hypoglycaemic attack just as Nurse Allitt had said originally said. Doctor Nanayakkara was called; he set up a drip with 10% dextrose solution. It appeared to work, and Paul's colour returned to his cheeks. The attack was over.

Later in the evening, Paul's father David sat with him on his knee, bouncing him up and down. However, Paul was not responding, the greyness was returning, his arms went limp it appeared that the attack was happening again. David rushed with his son out into the corridor to seek assistance. Help arrived and Doctor Nanayakkara was able to bring the second attack under control. However, nobody was able to answer why the attacks happened. With Paul suffering a third attack the next day, the decision was made to transfer Paul Crampton to Queens Medical in Nottingham. Blood samples were taken to get to the root cause, but the sample, although requiring urgent results would not be tested for a further fifteen days because of an administrative error.

During this delay, five more children would be suffering from the mystery attacks, one of which would prove fatal. The blood test, once completed, would show an insulin level so great that it was off the scale. The amount of insulin present was over 30 times the normal level. In order to confirm that Paul's body had not introduced excessive amounts of insulin into his system, a second test on his pancreas was undertaken. C-Peptides are produced by the pancreas at the same rate as insulin; therefore, if his C-Peptides level was also high it could be ascertained that Paul's pancreas had caused Paul's death. However, the result was low. Somebody had injected insulin into Paul, but it may still have been by accident, there was no way to tell.

Brad Gibson

Brad Gibson was another child rushed into Grantham Hospital; the five-year-old had woken that morning, March 29 1991, wheezing heavily. The diagnosis at the ward was that Brad was suffering from pneumonia. Brad's parents, Steve and Judith, although concerned felt confident enough to return home, believing that their son was in safe hands. Judith made a final call to Ward Four at midnight and was reassured that Brad was fine.

Three hours later the phone rang at the Gibson home, Judith answered the call. It was Ward Four requesting that she and her husband hurry to the hospital as Brad's condition had suddenly taken a turn for the worse. Finally reaching the hospital, Night sister Jean Savill met with Steve and Judith and gave the pair more details as to the call. Brad's heart had stopped; the crash team were with the child now. Half an hour passed before Dr Nelson Porter met with Brad's parents giving them the latest news. Brad was now in a stable condition after the trauma, but he admitted that he was unable to determine why his heart had stopped. Later in the morning, Brad Gibson would be transferred to Queens Medical in Nottingham. Initially Dr Porter believed that it was Brad's pneumonia that had caused his heart to fail. But the x-rays would show that pneumonia was not the cause, the blood samples revealed high potassium content, but the doctors did not believe that to be of great concern.

Nurse Allitt was checking on Brad because he was complaining that his arm hurt. A shout came from the bed from Allitt calling for Nurse Catherine Morris for urgent assistance. As Nurse Morris checked Brad's pulse she found none and the crash team were called.

Henry Chan

Two days after the mystery of Brad Gibson's stopped heart, Nurse Allitt was again asking for Nurse Morris's help. Two-year-old Yik Hung Chan (known as Henry) was crying. He had been admitted to Ward Four with a fractured skull, after falling from a first floor window at his house. Because Henry was Chinese, Nurse Allitt believed that Nurse Morris, who could speak Chinese, should talk to him to try to calm him down. As Nurse Morris approached Henry's bed she could hear no crying. At the bedside she could see why, Henry was not breathing, his face was a deep blue colour. Once again the crash team burst into ward four and after a few minutes the two-year-old was breathing normally again. But approximately 30 minutes later Henry began fitting, his eyes rolled, his skin colour changed, turning almost black. Ten minutes would pass before the doctors could relax after being successful with their treatment.

Yik Hung's mother, Jenny, was called to the hospital to be informed of her son's illness and that the attack was probably caused by the skull fracture. Henry would be transferred to Queens Medical in Nottingham.

Becky and Katie Phillips

Twins Becky and Katie Phillips were born on January 31 1991, three months premature. They spent the first five weeks of their lives at Grantham Hospital. In March 1991, the proud parents, Peter and Sue, were able to take their children home for the first time and were told that if any problems arose to come back. In late March they did, both twins were not feeding well and vomiting their food. Both were examined and the doctors concluded that they were both well enough to return home, but Becky was to come back after the weekend for further tests. On Thursday April 4 1991, Peter and Sue Phillips returned to Grantham Hospital to collect their daughter Becky after her short stay. Dr Nanayakkara had checked the young girl that morning, declaring her fit to go back home.

Nurse Allitt claimed that Becky was not fit to go home; she stated that Becky felt cold and clammy to the touch, no-one agreed with her diagnosis and so the young girl went home with her parents. Late in the evening, Becky cried out in pain, Sue tried to calm her down but believed that she was fitting. Katie lying in the cot next to her was sleeping peacefully. Doctor Higgins arrived at 10.30pm and managed to calm Becky's crying claiming that it was probably Colic, the doctor left and the family returned to sleep.

But the rest did not last long, a couple of hours later Becky was again crying in pain. Sue turned on the lights and saw Becky's condition, it was not good. Her eyes were rolling up into her head, her face was twitching, and her skin felt cold. Again, Sue was able to soothe her daughter back to sleep. But again, it did not last long.

Sue woke with a start; her instincts told her that something was wrong. Sue moved towards the twins' cot, Becky was not breathing. The panic stricken mother quickly woke Peter up and told him to call for an ambulance. However, when the ambulance did not arrive quickly enough, Peter and Sue took their own car. Arriving at Grantham Hospital early in the pre-dawn hours of April 5 1991 with Becky's limp body in their arms, they found the door was locked. Peter banged on the doors until a nurse opened them; immediately taking Becky out of her mother's arms and into the casualty area. The crash team managed to start her body breathing again but it was no avail, soon after a doctor met with Sue and Peter and told them of their loss.

Dr Nanayakkara spoke to the grieving parents, he told them of his belief that Becky's death was due to an infection and would be required to undergo a post mortem. In addition, because he thought it was due to an infection, they should bring Katie in for tests. Sue immediately drove home, picked up the other twin and returned to the hospital. Katie was given a bed, and due to a lack of sleep Peter and Sue Phillips went home at approximately 3.00pm to rest.

Soon after Nurse Allitt raised the alarm, Katie had stopped breathing and was turning blue. Allitt together with fellow nurses Betty Asher and Mandy Poole carried the child to the treatment room and managed to get her breathing again, the panic was once again over. The parents were called, the hospital chaplain baptised young Katie, Sue and Peter would stay by Katie's side from now on.

For two days, Katie lay in her bed connected to various electronic devices that monitored her heartbeat, breathing, pulse etc. Nothing was going wrong. Doctor Nanayakkara was happy with his patient's condition and so removed the monitors. Sue and Peter were able to relax slightly and made a visit to the canteen, leaving Katie alone with Nurse Allitt. As they returned, things were not as peaceful as when they left. The crash team were working on the young girl and the monitors were back. The beep of the machines was becoming less and less constant, the doctors were working feverishly, then the beeps stopped, Katie was not responding.

The doctors and nurses had another child die and the room was silent, how could they tell the parents that Katie had died just like her sister. The silence was broken by an electronic beep, and then another, Katie had fought back from the dead.

At 4.30 pm, the following day Dr Nanayakkara confirmed with Queens Medical Hospital in Nottingham that Katie Phillips was being transferred. An accident in the ward left Nurse Allitt again looking after the baby on her own. A few minutes later and Katie was a dark blue colour and fitting. The ambulance arrived to take her away to Nottingham, the fitting was brought under control before the transfer, but she was still in danger.

The post mortem was carried out on Becky Phillips; the report concluded that Sudden Infant Death Syndrome (SIDS) was the cause of death. The report did note however, one odd point, Becky's heart appeared to have blistered, which the pathologist stated was unusual. Consultant Terence Stephenson from Nottingham City Hospital confirmed that no infection was present in Katie Phillips.

Michael Davidson

As Katie Phillips was being transferred away from the dangers of Ward Four at Grantham Hospital, another child was being admitted. Six-year-old Michael Davidson entered the hospital on Sunday April 7, 1991 having been accidentally shot by his uncle with an airgun pellet. Two days after his minor operation to remove the pellet, Michael was on his bed with junior doctor Karen Bradshaw looking after him.

As Karen went to inject some antibiotics into Michael's arm, he suddenly stopped breathing. His body went rigid as if in pain and his face turned a deep blue colour. The crash team were called. But before they reached the source of the emergency, the episode was over and Michael was breathing normally again. Dr Nanayakkara believed that Michael had suffered a Carpopedal spasm; however, the blood tests proved that this was not the case. Michael had suffered a cardiac arrest, but again the doctors could not see a reason why.

Chris Peasgood
On April 13 1991, the crash team once again burst into Ward Four. Eight-week-old Chris Peasgood was admitted into hospital with a chesty cough but now he was suffering from cardiac arrest. Only minutes before he was fine. His mother, Creswen, asked a nurse to feed him. Nurse Allitt happily accepted and suggested Creswen go to the canteen while Chris was fed. The crash team then responded to Allitt's call when Chris stopped breathing, his face blue.

The crash team were successful in their task, Chris's lungs were filling with air again, but he was struggling to breath on his own and nobody could understand why. Chris was transferred, like the other survivors, to Nottingham.

Chris King
Three days earlier Belinda King was in the ward next door to Chris Peasgood, when the crash team saved his life. Now it was her baby son, Chris, who needed emergency treatment. Chris was recovering from an operation on his stomach to solve a minor concern, but he was still struggling to hold down food.

On April 16 1991, Chris's condition suddenly took a turn for the worse, his heartbeat increased, his oxygen levels went down and he turned a grey colour. Belinda had taken Nurse Allitt's advice and gone to the canteen for a cup of tea, by her return the attack had begun. Doctors and nurses surrounded the five-week-old child.

X-rays and blood samples were taken in an effort to understand the cause. The baby began to make a recovery from the sudden attack, but the improvement did not last long. Less than fifteen minutes later, his heart once again began to slow and his lungs failed. Oxygen was forced into his lungs to keep Chris alive, while an ambulance was arranged to, yet again, transfer a patient to Queens Medical Hospital, Nottingham.

Patrick Elstone
On April 18 1991 at 4.00 pm, Nurse Allitt raised the alarm, seven-week-old Patrick Elstone's breathing was very shallow, and the colour had gone from his skin leaving him grey. After giving him oxygen, nurses Allitt and Mary Reet were able to bring his colour back. Nurse Reet connected an apnoea monitor to Patrick in order to alert the nurses if his breathing faltered again. A few minutes after Nurse Reet left the room, Patrick's breathing stopped, but the alarm never sounded – it had been switched off. Nurse Allitt again raised the alarm and the crash team came. Patrick's parents, Bob and Hazel were called and Patrick was given manual assistance during his transfer to Nottingham.

With three deaths and nine suspicious incidents in 2 months, Doctor Nelson Porter began to believe that something was wrong on Ward Four and requested security cameras to monitor people who went into the ward. Fellow consultant Dr Nanayakkara disagreed, there was no concern, but he would review the cases to look for anything suspicious. However, no additional security would be put in place. While the two doctors discussed, debated, and argued the need for additional checks in the ward, Claire Peck entered the ward.

Claire Peck
At fifteen months old, Claire Peck had been back and forth into the hospital due to breathing difficulties. In late April 1991, Claire Peck's doctor sent her again into Ward Four. The doctors there suggested that she would be well enough to return home the next day, April 22, after one final breathing monitoring session.

Claire's parents, David and Sue, sat with their daughter while the nurses attempted to help with her breathing. The nurses tried three different machines, but each failed to perform properly. Dr Porter was called, who ordered a chest x-ray and a tube to be put down Claire's throat allowing her to breathe more freely. The two nurses took Claire to the treatment room to prepare her for the procedures. Dr Porter left the treatment room to set up the requisite drugs for the young patient.

The second nurse returned to the cubicle to talk with Sue and David, leaving the remaining nurse to comfort Claire. In the few moments they were alone, Claire was turning blue, and she had stopped breathing. The second nurse ended her chat with the parents and returned to the treatment room. She immediately saw Claire's condition and that Nurse Allitt was just standing watching. The nurse quickly put an oxygen mask on the child and slapped her back to kick-start her breathing. Dr Porter returned and injected Claire with Aminophylline to improve her breathing. After twenty minutes, she was breathing normally.

X-rays were taken as well as a blood sample. Dr Porter went back to inform Sue and David of the incident. Minutes later Nurse Allitt burst into the ward, Claire's breathing had failed again, she was turning blue. Dr Porter rushed through but Claire was already dead, her lungs and heart had stopped but Dr Porter refused to accept it. The crash team were called, they burst in and shocked Claire's heart. A faint pulse could be heard but then it failed again. Adrenaline was injected directly into her heart, but it would not restart. Twice more Dr Porter tried to inject life into the 15 month old but he had to admit failure.

He could not believe that Claire Peck had died; he gathered the blood samples he had taken during the incident, and also gathered all the intravenous drips and requested urgent testing to be performed. He wanted some answers as to why Claire had died. Alan Willis, the science officer in the hospital laboratory tested the equipment and samples and indicated a high content of Potassium in the baby's blood; in fact, the level of Potassium was off the scale. Despite this, the pathologist, Dr Chen, after performing the autopsy, pronounced the cause of death to be asthma.

With the death of Claire Peck still vivid in his mind, along with the questions coming out of Queens Medical Hospital in Nottingham, Dr Porter once again pushed for an investigation into the suspicious incidents in the ward, the incidents that resulted in the deaths of 3 children – Liam Taylor, Tim Hardwick, and Claire Peck. On May 1, 1991, Lincolnshire police became involved. A meeting was arranged between Doctors Porter and Nanayakkara, Grantham Hospital manager Martin Gibson, Detective Superintendent Stuart Clifton from Lincolnshire Police. They were joined by Professor David Hull from Queens Medical Hospital in Nottingham as an independent medical advisor. At the end of the heated meeting, and after constant disagreements between the two doctors, Professor Hull would review the cases of all suspicious incidents.

The Investigation

Detective Clifton and his team investigated all attacks and deaths that Doctor Porter considered suspicious; he talked to parents, doctors, nurses and other patients in the ward. They investigated the post mortems of the children who died. Paul Crampton's blood samples were again checked; the high insulin levels were again confirmed.

Using Professor Hull's advice, Detective Clifton as able to deduce that the insulin had been injected into Paul's bloodstream between 9.30am and 1.30pm on March 28 1991. With this in mind, Clifton's team rechecked everyone's stories as to their locations within that timeframe, and then they crosschecked the alibis against available sources for confirmation.

The process left everyone exhausted; people were eliminated from the enquiry thus reducing the number of potential suspects. Additional testing was completed on Paul Crampton's blood sample taken on the day of the attacks. Detective Clifton and Professor Hull were able to shorten the time span to between 12.45 and 1.15pm. Officer John Griffiths finally completed his analysis of the movements of all those involved at the hospital. His prime suspects name appeared on his chart as being present in all instances where an attack took place; the name was Nurse Beverley Allitt. She was present at all of Paul Crampton's attacks and off work in the days between. Stuart Clifton decided to arrest her.

On May 21, 1991, a little after 7.00am, six police officers arrived to arrest Beverley Allitt at her home for the murder of Paul Crampton. Two officers escorted Allitt to Grantham Police Station while the remaining officers searched the house. They uncovered a syringe, various items that clearly belonged to the hospital and a book entitled 'Ward Allocation Book'.

The next day, after questioning, Allitt was released on police bail. The officers had no real evidence to confront Allitt with, and as she also denied knowledge of any attacks or murders, Stuart Clifton had no options.

Clifton, after the failure of Allitt's interview, was down but not completely out. Convinced that Allitt was the prime suspect, he set his team the task of finding evidence to prove the case. For each child, two detectives were tasked in finding the medical evidence as to why the children had died. This information was vital to the case.

Slowly the results of the medical searches began to filter through. A sample of Tim Hardwick's brain, blood from Becky Phillips and from Claire Peck, x-rays from Martin Gibson were re-examined. Each piece of evidence was sent for independent analysis. Professor Marks returned his report on the analysis of Paul Crampton's blood; it contained 43,167 milliunits of insulin per litre of blood. Because the c-peptide result was low, Professor Marks concluded that the high result of insulin did not naturally occur, thus Paul Crampton was injected. Doctor David Fagan, from Queens Medical Hospital in Nottingham, had checked the medical work on Liam Taylor. While he agreed that Liam had died because his heart had stopped, Dr Fagan was able to find the cause (where originally Dr Marshall could not). Liam had been either smothered or injected with insulin. Professor Marks gave insulin as the cause of the death of Becky Phillips; her blood contained 9660 milliunits of insulin per litre of blood. Stuart Clifton now believed he had evidence that four children had been murdered.

Despite their grief, while the Phillips family was at the hospital, they became friends with many of the nurses, and in particular Nurse Allitt. The Phillips' were so grateful for her help during their time at the hospital that they insisted that Allitt became Godmother to the remaining twin, Katie. She agreed.

During her time on police bail, Allitt herself was admitted to hospital. She was suffering from a urinary problem that required her to be fitted with a catheter. However, the catheter mysteriously broke which meant a longer stay in the hospital. The nurses on the ward noticed that although during the day Allitt offered no concerns, problems always arose during the night. She complained of feeling unwell, of her temperature rising and her breasts feeling painful. It was suspected that Allitt was injecting her own breasts with water, which would cause higher temperatures and painful breasts.

While the investigation into the murders on Ward Four was underway, Nurse Allitt was told to take time off. Allitt would spend this time with her new found friends and her Goddaughter Katie. Throughout June 1991, Allitt was a regular visitor at the Phillips' home.. Sue, Peter and Allitt would often take Katie and her elder brother James out for trips. At this time Allitt saw fit to tell Sue about the police blaming her for the attacks on Paul Crampton. Sue felt for her friend and offered help in any way she could. On June 15, 1991, Allitt once again visited the Phillips' house and asked Sue if she could take Katie out for a walk Sue happily agreed and off the pair went. Ten minutes later, they returned. Allitt complained that Katie was having convulsions, Katie's face was bright red and drenched with sweat. Sue immediately called the doctor. A few minutes later, the doctor arrived and suddenly Allitt made excuses to go. Despite Sue insisting she stay to help the doctor, Allitt left and Katie was taken to Grantham Hospital.

Two days later two detectives arrived at the Phillips' door. The purpose of the visit, the detectives explained, was to inform Sue and Peter that their children's illnesses at the hospital were deliberate and the person responsible was Allitt. Sue and Peter struggled to believe it. Sue mentioned to the detectives about the incident 2 days previously and confirmed that it was Allitt who had seen the symptoms. DCI Alan Smith was convinced that Allitt had also caused this latest attack and ordered the Phillips not to talk again to Allitt. All the medicines in the house were seized and a guard was placed at the door to Katie's bed at the hospital.

Further evidence of foul play became known during Stuart Clifton's regular briefing. Dr David Fagan had now completed his analysis of the tissues found by the team of detectives and concluded that in the cases of Claire Peck and Tim Hardwick, the original post mortem results were wrong. Tim had not died from epilepsy and Claire had not died from asthma. Both children had died from an unknown poison. In addition, Phillip Small from Queens Medical Hospital had determined that, via x-rays, Kayley Desmond had 'dark streaks' present in the flesh of her right armpit. Phillip Smith strongly believed that the streaks were air bubbles. These air bubbles were caused by either injecting Kayley's arm with air or she was injected with a poison. He also reported on Katie Phillips. Her x-rays revealed small fractures on her ribcage. He admitted however, that the fractures could very easily be missed due to their size, but he was under no doubt, someone had broken Katie's ribs.

Further investigations took place to determine what the unknown poison may have been. After several days and more tests on the available blood samples, it was determined that the unknown agent was Potassium Chloride. Potassium itself is produced by the body and increases after death when red blood cells leak the element into the bloodstream. This was the case with Claire Peck. Her blood contained 16 millimoles of potassium per litre, a very high result, but the result was taken before her death.

Despite all the medical evidence proving murder and attempted murder, Stuart Clifton and his team were still without evidence on a viable suspect. Allitt was still a suspect, because of strong circumstantial evidence that placed her in the vicinity of the children when all attacks took place.

After weeks of gathering evidence, Inspector Neil Jones drove to Peterborough on September 3, 1991, where Allitt was temporarily staying, to arrest her for the murder of Becky Phillips. Again, the interview did not go according to plan. Allitt again refused to answer any questions, so reluctantly they were forced to allow her to go free after an 8-hour stay.

The nursing agency that originally employed Allitt was now sending memos to all of its branches instructing them that Allitt was not to be hired. Stuart Clifton talked to psychiatrists; he wanted to understand the motives behind the attacks, having given them the information that a nurse was the main suspect. The experts gave the probable cause as Munchausen Syndrome by Proxy. An illness where the 'sufferer' inflicts injuries on others. The psychiatrists described that many sufferers would follow a career path with a hospital. Many would feign illness and then progress onto making others ill and then call a doctor.

The investigation into Allitt was beginning to end. During the case, Allitt was found to be acting suspiciously in many other cases where a patient had suddenly become ill. However, in each incident there was no reason to suspect any foul play.

At 7.00pm on November 20 1991, Stuart Clifton made a call to lawyer John Kendall, who was representing Allitt; the call was the instruction for Kendall to 'bring his client in'. An hour later and Allitt was seated next to John Kendall in the interview room at Grantham Police Station. Inspector Neil Jones sat opposite and read out the charges.

Allitt had been arrested for the murder of four children, the attempted murder of eight others and finally eight additional charges of grievous bodily harm, making twenty charges levied against Allitt. Her only words were 'thank you very much'. After a night in the cells Allitt was remanded in New Hall Women's Prison in Wakefield for trial. It was judged that Allitt would be safer in prison. During her time at Wakefield

Prison, doctors noted that Allitt had stopped eating and as a result was losing weight. Because of this Allitt was transferred out of Wakefield and into Rampton Prison, which had better hospital facilities.

Additional charges were bought against Allitt on February 11 1992. She was now also charged with attempted murder on Michael Davidson on April 9 1991, the attempted murder of Dot Lowe on April 27, 1991, at a nursing home in Waltham-on-the-Woods and the attempted murder of Jonathon Jobson on August 4, 1991 in Peterborough. Police also charged Allitt with grievous bodily harm in these three cases.

On February 15, 1993 the trial of Beverley Allitt began at Nottingham Crown Court under Mr Justice Latham. Prosecutor John Goldring QC opened his case based on circumstantial evidence against Allitt, backed up with the medical evidence found during the long searches at the hospital. Due to the lack of direct evidence against his client, defence counsel James Hunt QC presented his defence of reasonable doubt.

The trial itself consisted of serious debate about the effects of various medical practices and their effect on the human body. Munchausen Syndrome by Proxy was briefly mentioned, but not by name. Five weeks into the trial Allitt collapsed in her cell and was rushed to Bassetlaw Hospital in Worksop, where doctors diagnosed Anorexia Nervosa. The trial would resume on March 22 while Allitt was still in hospital. Eventually, on May 11, the arguments for and against ended and the case was passed to the jury.

The jury discussed the case behind closed doors for 2 days until they returned to the courtroom to announce their decisions. Beverley Allitt was found guilty of the murder of Becky Phillips and Claire Peck. The jury also returned guilty verdicts against Allitt for the charges of grievous bodily harm of Kayley Desmond, Henry Chan and Chris King. A not guilty verdict was given on the charge of attempted murder on Kayley Desmond. In the remaining charges, the jury was unable to reach a verdict and so were required to go back into discussion. At 3.45pm on May 17, the jury once again returned to the courtroom, this time with their final judgement. The final count against Allitt ended with verdicts of guilty of four murders- Claire Peck, Becky Phillips, Liam Taylor and Tim Hardwick, guilty of three attempted murders -Paul Crampton, Brad Gibson and Katie Phillips and finally guilty of six counts of grievous bodily harm- Kayley Desmond, Henry Chan, Michael Davidson, Chris Peasgood, Chris King and Patrick Elstone. All other counts were rejected. With that verdict Mr Justice Latham, sentenced Allitt to life imprisonment with a minimum of 30 years to be served.

Marcelo de Andrade

Brazilian Marcelo de Andrade, a devout Christian, was arrested at home in 1991 for the murder of six-year-old Ivan de Abreu. The man was arrested for the murder following Ivan's ten-year-old brother Altair told police about the attack and murder.

Altair went to the police, telling them how de Andrade approached the brothers at a bus station, promising to give them money if they helped him at the church. Eager for some cash, the brothers agreed and followed the man along several alleys and side streets. As the trio approached the church, de Andrade suddenly grabbed Ivan around the throat and strangled him until he died. As soon as he fell limp, de Andrade raped the dead body as his older brother stood watching in shock.

De Andrade walked over to the fearful Altair and hugged the boy, professing his love for him. Scared for his life, Altair agreed to spend the night with his brother's killer. As soon as de Andrade was asleep, Altair ran for his life straight to the police station.

In custody de Andrade confessed to the murder of the six-year-old Ivan, but his confession did not end there. Inspector Romeo José Vieira believed de Andrade was guilty of other unsolved crimes and continued to question his suspect. Two months of questioning ended with a detailed confession of a nine month killing spree. De Andrade had killed fourteen young boys, ranging from six to thirteen years of age. He would rape his victims before beheading them with a machete. De Andrade would revel in the blood squirting from his victims' necks before drinking it from a cup in the belief it would make him beautiful.

Richard Angelo

It is not unusual for patients of an intensive care ward to die without raising any suspicion. However, in September and October of 1987, six suspicious deaths were recorded at the Good Samaritan Hospital in West Islip, New York.

On October 11, 1987, Giralomo Cucich was resting in bed after a recent operation when a male nurse entered his room and politely told him that he had something to make him feel better and promptly injected a drug into Giralomo's IV drip. Giralomo began fighting for breath and his muscles steadily grew numb. He managed to press the help button for assistance. Medical staff performed emergency procedures and following his recovery, Giralomo was able to provide detectives with a description of the male nurse.

Twenty-five-year-old Richard Angelo, a nurse at the Good Samaritan Hospital was interviewed by police on October 22, 1987 as part of the routine investigation. However, he became the number one suspect as he matched exactly the description given by the patient.

The hospital laboratory confirmed that Giralomo had been injected with a drug named Pavulon, which paralyses muscles. Vials of the drug were found during a search of Angelo's hospital locker and additional vials were recovered from his apartment resulting in Angelo being arrested on November 15, 1987. During questioning, Angelo confessed to a string of attacks throughout September and October. He had hoped to save the patients and become a hero. Hospital records showed twenty-five patients had died during that period, with a further eight instances where the patient recovered from the unexplained condition.

Nineteen of the deceased were tested for Pavulon and in addition to the first-degree assault on Giralomo Cucich, Angelo was charged with the second-degree murder of Frederick Lagois on January 13, 1988. Milton Poulney was another patient proven to have been injected with the drug, and a further four charges were laid against Angelo as the evidence came through from the laboratory.

At his trial, Angelo was found guilty on one count of second degree manslaughter; one count of criminal negligence and six counts of assault. For his crimes, Angelo received a sentence of 50 years.

Ann Arbor Hospital Murders

In Ann Arbor Hospital during a period of six weeks in 1976, at least fifty-six people were murdered. The victims were poisoned with the drug Pavulon. As the numbers increased, the FBI was called in to try to find the culprit.

In June 1976, two nurses, thirty-year-old Filipina Narcissco and thirty-one-year-old Leonora Perez were arrested and charged with eight murders as well as the charge of conspiracy and attempt to poison.

At the trial, the jury was unable to find enough evidence to convict the two nurses, even though on one particular night eight patients died while the two women were working on the ward.

Therefore, the nurses were released.

After the nurses were exonerated, a hospital supervisor wrote a confession to the murders and committed suicide.

The case remains open.

Ramiro Artieda

Ramiro Artieda's own brother Luis was his first murder victim. The two men were about to inherit their family's fortune and Bolivian estates but Ramiro did not want to share the fortune and dispensed of his brother quickly. He also had proposed to a young woman who said she would marry him once he was wealthy. When he went to tell her that he was going to inherit everything as he had killed Luis, the woman was horrified and ended the relationship.

Artieda left Bolivia for America soon after and gained work as an actor for a few years before retuning to his homeland and a murderous campaign.

The first death of his new agenda was the strangulation of Margarita Rios in a deserted building in the city of Cochabamba.

The next victim was Rosalina Villavencio who was lured to an apartment in La Paz where she was told she would be able to audition for a film company executive. She was murdered as she walked in the door.

Artieda murdered eighteen-year-old Teresa Ardiales in Villa Montes on the Pilcamayo River. The next strangulation victim was Maria Perez in November 1937 after Artieda told her a convincing story about being a professor at her college in Cucre.

Next Mariana Aramayo fell victim to Artieda's role as a monk. He walked her to church where he strangled her at the altar and hid her in the vestibule.

Ramiro Artieda's next role was as a 'travelling salesman'. Answering a knock at her door in La Paz, Bolivia on December 8, 1938, Julia Caceres was strangled.

On May 9, 1939, the killer attempted to strangle another woman who escaped and ran away. This young woman was later able to identify Artieda as her attacker.

He confessed to the murders of seven women and the murder of his brother.

Artieda claimed he was killing woman who looked like the girlfriend who had jilted him.

Ramiro Artieda was found guilty on all counts of murder and was executed according to Bolivian practice by a firing squad in the courtyard of Cochabamba prison on 3 July 1939.

B
Bai Baoshan

Forty-one-year-old Bai Baoshan was executed on May 6, 1998 for the murders of 14 people; many of the victims were Beijing police officers.

Baoshan began his killing spree in 1966. A police officer was the target as Baoshan was determined to wreak havoc for revenge for the thirteen years he had previously spent in prison for a string of robberies and murder.

The killer used a semi-automatic rifle to ambush a police sentry. He killed one police officer and injured four others in the attack.

He went on to kill a shop owner during a robbery and several other police officers in the province of Hebei.

In Urumqi, Baoshan and an accomplice murdered 10 further victims, including police officers, security guards, and civilians, during a robbery, netting almost US$180,000. In his greed, Baoshan murdered his accomplice and fled with the money alone.

The killer was arrested on October 16, 1997 and found guilty of the string of murders and robberies as well as various drug trafficking crimes.

Marcel Barbeault

Marcel Barbeault murdered eight young women in seven years in the French province of Nogent-sur-Oise. Like Ted Bundy, Barbeault preferred a particular type of victim, all his victims had brown hair, and he stalked them at night killing them in the dark. The media dubbed the killer the "Shadow Killer" because of his preference for the nighttime assaults.

Barbeault was born on August 10, 1941 in Laincourt, France. His parents were normal working-class people who brought up a well-adjusted young boy.

Like many boys in France, with the Algerian War raging he enlisted in the army in 1960 and spent two years of the war as a stretcher runner after failing to become a parachutist due to giddiness.

When he returned from the war Barbeault married Josiane, the couple had two children and built themselves a home.

After a succession of deaths in Barbeault's family during the late 1960's and early 1970's the man became irrational and began a murderous campaign.

Barbeault's first victim survived an attack on the night of January 10, 1969. The young woman was shot at close range by Barbeault but was not killed; she was taken to the hospital but was unable to give police a description of her attacker.

The second victim was also lucky. Before dawn on January 14, 1969 a mere four days after the first attack Barbeault struck again, he shot his victim in the stomach. Although she suffered a large blood loss, she managed to get help. However, police were again unable to get a description of the shooter.

The third victim was not as lucky; she would become Barbeault's first murder victim. Forty-nine-year-old Therese Adam was entering her home on the evening of January 23, 1969 when Barbeault struck her from behind. He hit her on the back of the neck, causing her to fall to the ground. The killer then stood over her and shot her dead with one bullet fired into her throat.

Therese was not found until the next morning. By then the killer was long gone, and again he was able to elude capture.

Strangely, the next ten months passed without the killer attacking again. After attacking three women in three weeks, he was able to resume his normal life for almost a year before he decided to kill again.

Suzanne Merienne was watching the rain outside her window in Lecron, France on the evening of November 16, 1969 when Barbeault broke into her house. The killer, soaked from the wet weather, held a gun to the woman's face and demanded that she and her nineteen-year-old daughter Micheline head outside. In the rain, the killer marched the women to the nearby railway tracks. He shot forty-four-year-old Suzanne dead with a single shot fired at her temple. When Micheline saw her mother's body collapse to the ground, she ran. Micheline was able to escape from Barbeault eluding his attempts to catch her. The nineteen-year-old went to police and gave them a description of her mother's killer.

A composite drawing of the man was released and a country-wide search began, yet Barbeault had gone back to his domestic life with his wife and children. No-one suspected the gentle giant to be the killer that the police sought.

Barbeault did not kill again until 1973.

Twenty-nine-year-old Annick Delisle was shot dead by Barbeault on February 6, 1973. The killer had bashed the woman across the back of the head before firing the deadly shot into her throat, the calling card of the Shadow Killer. It appeared that Barbeault had also attempted to rape the woman, as she had been found with some of her clothing missing.

Again, Barbeault took a break from murder. He waited another three months before killing again. Yet this time the killings escalated. He no longer killed just women.

The next victims were a couple who had gone parking together. On May 28, 1973, twenty-five-year-old Eugene Stephens and his twenty-three-year-old girlfriend Mauricette Van Hyfte were sitting together in the car on the outskirts of Laingeville when Barbeault approached them.

Barbeault shot the male victim where he sat. Eugene never saw the man aiming his rifle at him.

Mauricette was not as lucky. After Barbeault shot Eugene dead, she tried to run from the car, as Barbeault chased her a few metres into the forest. Barbeault fired several shots at her before she fell to the ground; she died soon after from the gunshot wounds.

Josette Routier a twenty-nine-year-old bank teller was killed as she entered her home in Nogent-sur-Oise on January 8, 1974. Barbeault knocked his victim unconscious before shooting her dead, two shots fired at her temple. He sexually assaulted his victim, and left Josette without clothes. Yet the killer had also added a new element. To remove the woman's clothes he used a knife.

The violence during the murders was escalating, yet Barbeault was able to control his murderous lust and hid for almost two years.

The next victim was Julia Goncalves. The twenty-nine-year-old was attacked as she walked through a park in Nogent-sur-Oise on November 25, 1975. Barbeault had grabbed her from behind and bashed her over the head before shooting her in the throat. He stripped away most of her clothing, leaving her to be found two days later by a groundskeeper.

On January 6, 1976, twenty-one-year-old Francoise Jakubowska became Barbeault's last victim. The young woman was on her way to work on that dark cold morning when she was struck from behind by her killer.

Once she was on the ground the killer changed his MO. Barbeault knelt over his victim and stabbed her several times before shooting her. The killer then stripped off the woman's clothing, sexually assaulted her and fled the scene.

By December 1976, police had interviewed Barbeault several times, after being seen near some of the murder scenes. He would always claim that it was because he walked to work, usually early morning or late at night, yet police remained suspicious.

Then an anonymous caller rung police and told them to search the house of Marcel Barbeault., They claimed the man to be the killer and still had the gun in his cellar. On December 14, 1976, a search warrant was executed and the property of Barbeault was searched. As the anonymous caller had said, a rifle was found in the man's cellar. Ballistic tests matched it to the two final victims.

Barbeault was subsequently arrested as he arrived home, his arms full of Christmas presents. Police were surprised at how closely he resembled the composite picture released to the public years earlier.

Barbeault denied any involvement in the crimes, yet the evidence found at his home was damning. At trial, he pleaded not guilty, but was found guilty of five of the eight murders committed and sentenced to life in prison. He still maintains his innocence.

Donald Bashor

On October 11, 1957, Donald Bashor was executed for the murders of two women in Los Angeles during 1955 and 1956.

Karil Graham, aged 38, was found beaten to death in her home on February 15, 1955. Her house was ransacked and several items were believed to have been stolen, but her killer had left behind a considerable amount of palm prints.

The same prints were present following the May 27, 1995 attack on a woman who had survived being beaten and strangled in her home.

In January 1956, another woman was attacked in her home. The male intruder strangled his intended victim and attempted to rape her, but fled when her screams alerted the neighbours. Los Angeles officers were able to link another attack on February 8, to the previous incidents.

On May 24, 1956, Laura Davies was at home when a male intruder entered, beat her to death and left. This time however, a witness came forward, but the description did not give the police much to go on. Unfortunately, it described too many people in the Los Angeles area.

The authorities got the break they needed, when, during a stakeout, they spotted a man breaking into a nearby house. Donald Bashor tried to escape, but was quickly arrested after he was shot in the arm during the chase. Bashor's handprints matched those found at the murder scenes and the other attacks.

At his trial, Bashor admitted his guilt and was sentenced to death.

Elizabeth Bathory

Elizabeth Bathory has been accused of killing hundreds of young women and girls. The legend claims that she bathed in their warm blood to preserve her beauty.

Elizabeth was born Erzebet Bathory in 1560, and the Bathorys were a wealthy and prominent family in Hungary. She was the daughter of Baron George and Baroness Anna Bathory. Elizabeth enjoyed a cultured life, was educated, and spoke fluent Hungarian, German and Latin.

Kings, cardinals, bishops and judges, sheriffs and governors bore the Bathory name. The Prime Minister of Hungary, Gyorgy Thurzo was her cousin and Sigismund Bathory, Prince of Transylvania her kinsman. Sigmund, one of Hungary's greatest military leaders was known for his madness as well as his genius.

At the age of 11, she was betrothed to Ferenc Nadasdy, the "Black Hero of Hungary". Because the Nadasdy family was of a lesser social status, Elizabeth kept her name and that of her husband hyphenated. Elizabeth went to live with her future mother-in-law and while there, the young woman had a brief yet torrid affair with one of the peasant villagers. The liaison produced a daughter that was quickly given away to the man and his wife along with a substantial amount of money to keep the affair and offspring a secret.

In 1575, to Castle Csejthe in Nyitra, Hungary, was where the twenty-one-year-old Count Ferencz Nadasdy brought his beautiful young bride. The fifteen-year-old Countess Elisabeth Bathory. Her beauty was renown throughout the château. Her stark white skin, her long shimmering black hair, and plump red lips, which complimented her deep doe like eyes.

Had the young Count stayed at the Castle with his bride who knows how the story may have gone. However, because Count Nadasdy went off to battle destined to become a great warrior, his wife was left to her own devices. Her consuming interest in witchcraft, sorcery, and diabolism kept her occupied. And her family heritage kept her safe.

One of Elisabeth's aunts was the most distinguished women of the royal court and was known to be a witch and a lesbian and a notorious corrupter of young girls. An uncle was also a sorcerer, and a worshipper of the Devil. Even her brother was known for his depravities, no one was safe from his cravings.

As if this wasn't influence enough, Elizabeth was raised with the vicious teaching of her nurse Ilona Joo, a woman learned in witchcraft, magic and Satan worship.

Left alone by her husband in the Castle, Elisabeth surrounded herself with witches and sorcerers. Darvula, Joahannes Ujvary, Thorko, and Dorottya Szentes were among those the young Countess sought out for their powers.

However the young woman's lustful desires soon led to elopement with a young man, rumoured to be a vampire, but she soon returned to the castle. Her infidelities forgiven by her Count who understood the young woman's desires, while he was away in battle.

Elisabeth absorbed herself again in witchcraft and spent her nights with two of her personal maids, Barsovny and Otvos as lovers. However the whisperings in her ear from the witch Ilona Joo, hinting at pleasures that were more perverse.

After ten years of unsuccessfully siring an heir, the witches were called to assist in the conception. Soon after her twenty-sixth birthday, the Countess gave birth to her first legitimate child, followed by three more.

This interruption consumed the maternal Countess; she sent many messages to her Count away on crusades telling him of the news of their children's lives.

Until Count Nadasdy's death when she was 40, Elisabeth had resisted the urgings of Ilona Joo. However, once the Count had died, Elisabeth fell into the darkness of black magic and sorcery.

In the village, surrounding the Castle, rumours began. At night, the peasants locked their houses and listened in fear to the agonizing screams from the castle. Young women and girls were disappearing, both travellers and those from the village.

Maids and former lesbian lovers of the Countess found themselves as procurers for Elisabeth. If women could not be tempted with the promise of jobs in the Castle, they were drugged or beaten into submission. For the next eleven years, the peasants in the village lived in fear when the coach from the castle came to them.

The women were taken not for the sexual pleasure of the Countess, but for their blood.

It had happened one day shortly after the death of her husband, that the Countess hit one of her maidservants hard across the face. So hard in fact, that blood was drawn. Some of the maid's blood fell onto Elizabeth, who cleaned it away in disgust. However, Elizabeth noticed that the skin that had been touched by the blood seemed to be younger and more vibrant. It was the moment that changed the course of Elizabeth's life and brought about the murders of up to 600 women and girls.

Obtaining more blood, Elisabeth bathed her face in it. She had been right, the blood made her skin more youthful.

Soon she decided that to keep her entire body youthful she must bathe in blood. Therefore, her procurers would scour the countryside for young women for the Countess' sadistic ritual.

The other witches as well as Ilona Joo had always told their mistress that only human sacrifices would assist their spells. In alchemy, skulls and bones were needed for potions. Soon all those in the castle were deriving erotic pleasure from the sadistic orgies of torture and murder. The witches were therefore enthusiastic about the Countess' blood baths as it made it possible for their own rituals to succeed.

In the dungeons beneath the castle, girls and women were chained to the filthy walls and fed like cattle being fattened for the slaughter. The Countess assumed that the fatter they were the more blood in their veins.

When emerging from her blood baths the Countess refused to be dried by cloth, she had girls, chosen for their beauty and delicate touch, lick her clean. If a girl refused or became ill (noting that blood is an emetic) a horrible torturous death awaited her. When a girl reacted with pleasure, she would win the Countess' favour. This favour may have been a deferment of death - but that was rare, most of Elizabeth's maids ended up murdered. Frequently the Countess derived pleasure in inflicting the cruellest tortures upon those who had been her favourites.

Rumours of the goings on at the Castle were delivered to the King of Hungary years before any action was taken. Due to the Countess' family connections, it was difficult to do anything. Even her cousin, the Prime Minister was not willing to confirm the rumours. But reluctantly something had to be done. After talking with the village priest and several villagers who complained that the Castle was haunted by a vampire, a raid was planned for New Years Eve during a party held by Bathory

The raiders, including the Prime Minister, were able to ascend on Csejthe Castle unnoticed. They found the main door ajar and they walked into Hell.

The search party encountered the dying and dead bodies of over 600 young women in the Castle's basement.

On January 2, 1611, Countess Elizabeth Bathory was arrested and charged by her cousin Count Thurzo with the murders of 610 young women from the villages around her Hungarian Castle, Cséjthe.

At the trial, Ilona Joo and Thorko, along with others testified that hundreds of girls and women had been kept in the dungeons and milked of their blood. Incisions were made into their skin and blood taken as required. According to the witches, the Countess not only bathed in the blood but drank it as well.

Some of the girls were also human sacrifices for alchemy and witchcraft. Girls were bound by rope which was twisted until it cut into the skin. After this, the veins rising through the skin were cut with scissors and the blood spurted under the pressure, drenching the walls and the others in the dungeon. Girls were beaten with whips and their flesh slit with knives. Sometimes the girls were flayed and then frozen in baths of ice. Others were forced to hold heated metallic objects in their hands. Paper placed between victims' toes and set alight. There is also a rumour that some were bitten to death by the Countess.

The corpses, skeletons and other human remains found at the Castle where given into evidence, as well as the testimonies of the survivors.

All involved, including the Countess were charged to stand trial on eight counts of murder. However the real number was in the hundreds.

After a speedy trial that lasted five days the companions of Countess Elizabeth Bathory were sentenced to death for their part in the murders.

The sentences meted out were:
Bathory's mentor, Ilona Joo had her fingers torn off one by one, before being burned alive and her ashes strewn across unholy ground.
Maidservant Dorottya Szentes had her fingers also torn off and then burned alive.

The other guilty parties Johannes Ujvary, Thorko, Darvula Barsovny and Otvos were beheaded.

It was the strenuous efforts of the Prime Minister that saved Elisabeth from sharing the same fate as the others. Elisabeth was sentenced to spend the rest of her life in her room. Her windows were bricked in and only tiny slits were left in the door for food and ventilation. Elizabeth Bathory spent four years in her prison inside the Castle. She never uttered a sound.

Her death on August 21, 1614 was only detected when her food remained untouched. She was fifty-four.

Dieter Beck

In Rehme, Germany, Dieter Beck was a ladies man, handsome and charming, a modern Casanova. However, he also had a penchant for violent sex. This violence culminated in the 1961 rape and murder of Ingrid Kanike, and again in 1965 with Ursula Fritz and finally for a third time in 1968 with Anneliese Herschel.

During his trial in June 1969, several of Beck's girlfriends gave accounts of how Beck would attempt to strangle them during sex. Beck was found guilty on three murder counts and received a life sentence.

Mary Bell

Mary Bell, one of the world's youngest serial killers was born in Newcastle, England on May 26, 1957. She grew up in a rough neighbourhood where families lived among abandoned and boarded up houses.

This was the scene where on 25 May 1968, three boys – Walter Long, Freddie Myhill and John Southern – searching for scrap timber, discovered the body of four-year-old Martin Brown inside one of the abandoned buildings. Two workers, upon hearing the boys' tale, rushed to the scene but failed in their attempts to resuscitate the boy. Nearby, watching the scene unfold stood eleven-year-old Mary Bell with a second girl, thirteen-year-old Norma Bell (no relation). The girls walked towards Rita Finlay's house (Martin's aunt) and told her of the accident claiming there was blood all over him, which was not true.

An ambulance quickly arrived on the scene, but was unable to revive Martin. With no obvious signs of trauma, it was assumed that Martin had been poisoned, because several empty pill bottles were found at the scene, but a post mortem found that this was not the case and no obvious cause of death was found.

For the moment, Martin's death was put down as an accident.

When a three-year-old boy fell from the roof of a disused air raid shelter on May 11, it was also deemed an accident and suspiciously, both Bell girls were witnesses.

On May 27, 1957, the day after Martin's death teachers at the Woodlands Crescent Nursery School arrived to find that vandals had broken into the school. Amongst the damage, several notes were found:

'I murder SO THAT I may come back'
'Bas Fuch off, we murder, watch out Fanny and Faggot'
'You are mice Y Becurse we murdered Martain Go Brown you Bete Look out there are Murders about by Fanny and auld Faggot you Screws'

And finally

'We did murder Martain Brown Fuckof you Bastard.'

On June 1, 1968, another break-in at the school occurred, but this time a silent alarm was triggered. The police were waiting for the culprits upon their exit, and were shocked to find that the vandals were Mary Bell and Norma Bell. When questioned they denied responsibility for the previous break-in.

About 3.30 pm on 31 July 1968, three-year-old Brian Howe vanished from sight, he was last seen playing with Mary Bell and Norma Bell. Throughout the afternoon and evening concerned relatives and neighbours searched the local area searching for Brian. At 11.10pm, the search came to an abrupt end with the little boy's body found wedged between concrete slabs. Brian's body was covered with bruises and scratches on his throat; there was also blood and saliva on his lips.

At the post mortem, Dr Tomlinson concluded that Brian's death was caused by manual strangulation probably caused by a child due to small amount of force used. Questioned on the August 1, Mary Bell was vague in her answers to police concerning the death of Brian Howe. The next day when questioned further Bell suddenly recalled that she has seen an older boy 'attacking' Brian.

Norma Bell told a different story and as a result, on August 4, Mary broke down and confessed that she had taken Norma to the body of Brian and shown her how it was done by squeezing Norma's throat. In addition,

Norma Bell admitted that Bell had stabbed Brian with a pair of scissors (a fact missed during the original post mortem).

On August 7, both girls were arrested and charged with the murder of Brian Howe, Mary Bell's reply, "that's all right by me".

The trial began on December 5, 1968 at Newcastle Assizes with both pre-teen girls pleading not guilty. The trial lasted for twelve days with Mary Bell continually pinning the blame on her 'partner' and the "older boy" for Brian's murder.

In the end, it was three pieces of evidence that proved her guilt. Fibre evidence lifted from the bodies of both Martin and Brian was identical to clothes owned by Bell.

Secondly, a handwriting expert testified that the notes were written by Bell (with some words written by Norma Bell). The third piece of crucial evidence was the admission of the use of scissors to cut Brian after death.

On December 17, after three hours and twenty-five minutes of deliberation the jury returned a verdict of guilty of manslaughter on grounds of diminished responsibility for both Martin and Brian against Mary Bell, she was sentenced to detention for the rest of her life. Norma Bell was cleared of all charges.

In 1977, when aged twenty, Bell escaped from Moor Court Open Prison with another inmate but was captured three days later. She grabbed the tabloid headlines after her capture, giving the media the story of how she lost her virginity whilst on the run. After serving twelve years in custody Bell was released from Askham Grange Open Prison having been granted a new identity.

In 1984, she gave birth to a daughter, who became a ward of the court with 'Bell' listed as her carer.

The media challenged Bell's anonymity in May 2002 after the injunction preventing her name being released ended when her daughter reached 18. Journalists had tracked Bell to her house on the south coast on England after the publication of the biography *'Cries Unheard'* that Bell had collaborated with author Gitta Sereny.

However, in September 2002, a permanent injunction was ordered preventing "Bell's" new name and identity from ever being published.

Manuel Bermudez

Known as the Sugarcane Monster, Manuel Octavio Bermudez, a forty-two-year-old ice cream seller from Columbia, confessed to the murders of thirty-four male children. The victims, all raped, were found in the sugarcane fields of Valle de Cauca, the first being discovered in 1999.

The final victim, twelve-year-old Luis Carlos Galvis, was found dead during July 2003; Bermudez was the last person to be seen with Luis and was quickly arrested by police. A search of his home uncovered numerous pairs of boy's underpants and lengths of rope similar to those found with the victims. The case against Bermudez was sealed when he took authorities directly to the body of his latest victim.

Bermudez stated in his confession that he had to kill the boys, as they would recognise him and tell police of his sexual advances.

Kenneth Bianchi and Angelo Buono

Kenneth Bianchi was born in Rochester New York in 1952 and was raised by foster parents before moving to Los Angeles in 1977 at the age of twenty-five to live with his cousin Angelo Buono, who was seventeen years his senior.

Bianchi admired his older cousin immensely and was quickly seduced into Buono's life of sexual perversion.

Buono introduced Bianchi to the world of perverse sex, with an endless stream of prostitutes coming into the house. However, this was only the beginning. Within a few short months of Bianchi arrival in LA, the two cousins went on a killing rampage that had police baffled and ruined the lives of the families of ten young women who would become victim to the sexual predation of the two cousins - who the media had dubbed the Hillside Strangler[3].

Between October 6, 1977 and February 17, 1978, the bodies of naked girls were found dumped on hillsides around LA.

All of the young women had been brutally raped and police would discover that two types of semen would point to two killers working in tandem. However, this scary point was kept out of the press for quite some time - hence the singular name Hillside Strangler.

On October 6, 1977, twenty-one-year-old Elissa Kastin became the first victim of the killing cousins. She was lured to Buono's house where she was subjected to repeated acts of rape and sodomy; she was also beaten before being killed. Her body was dumped on Chevy Chase Drive, a street near Buono's house.

On October 18, the killers struck again, this time they chose a black prostitute, Yolanda Washington. The woman was working on Hollywood Boulevard when she was picked up by Bianchi and Buono. After being raped and beaten to death by the men, her dead and defiled naked body was found at the Forest Lawn Cemetery near Ventura Freeway. The piece of cloth that had been used to strangle her was still around her throat. There was, however, something artificial about how she was found, she had been posed grotesquely, displaying her genitals like a showpiece. The ritual was another part of the killers' calling card.

Next to die was fifteen-year-old Judy Miller on November 1, 1977. She was a runaway that had fallen into the hands of the killer pair. Her abused and naked body was found in La Crescenta, a suburb near Glendale. She had had been raped and sodomised before being strangled. Her feet and hands were also shackled.

Eighteen-year-old Jill Barcomb died on November 9 after been raped and beaten by the two men.

On November 20, 1977, the men performed a triple act. They first killed twelve-year-old schoolgirl Dolores Cepeda and fourteen-year-old Sonja Johnson and dumped the bodies in Elysian Park. The killers then continued on to kill twenty-year-old Kristina Weckler and dumped her naked body in Highland Park.

As more bodies began to turn up, police saw the pattern emerging. Most, though not all, of the girls had been part-time prostitutes, they had been bound and gagged during their ordeal that consisted of rape and sodomy. The victims' bodies were then cleaned after death to avoid detection and then dumped on roadside hills.

November 23 saw another victim of the Hillside Strangler dumped, this time Jane King, a twenty-eight-year-old Scientology student was found on the exit ramp of Golden State Freeway. She had been raped and murdered, and her stockings were still around her throat.

---

[3] At first it was assumed it was only one person

Police were getting frantic as the body count grew. Eighteen-year-old Lauren Wagner was the next young woman murdered. However, the killers had upped the stakes, this time burns on her hands suggested that Lauren had been tortured before being strangled.

A piece of vital evidence was given to police but its significance was not realised until later. A neighbour saw Lauren being abducted from outside her house. The neighbour could describe the two men she saw. But the next day she received a phone call from a man telling her to keep quiet or she would be dead too.

What police did not realise was that to get the witness' phone-number someone would need to have inside information from the telephone company. Had they checked, the police would have found the identity of one of the Hillside Stranglers. Angelo Buono had worked at the local telephone exchange and had heard that there was a witness to the abduction.

Seventeen-year-old part-time prostitute Kimberley Martin was raped and murdered by the men on December 15, 1977. Her body was found posed grotesquely on a vacant block near City Hall. She had gone to the Tamarind Apartments in Hollywood after being requested by Buono from the call-girl agency where she had worked.

Then everything went quiet. The escalation of the killings worried police, but the quiet period that followed worried them even more. Had the killers been caught somewhere else? Had they just decided to stop? Had they died? No one knew. The police followed up any information they received but nothing was of any value.

Another body was found two months later. Twenty-three-year-old Cindy Hudpseth was found naked in the trunk of a car on February 17, 1978. Again, the body and car had been immaculately cleaned leaving no clues for police.

Then again nothing. No more killings. After a few months the special taskforce set up to catch the killers was disbanded after no further information or leads came through.

Little did they know but Bianchi had grown weary of Buono and the filth he chose to live in. So he moved back to Washington State and began work as a security guard. However, the killings were always on his mind. And this time Washington would be in the killer's grip.

On January 12, 1979, in Bellingham the bodies of Karen Mandic and Diane Wilder were found in the boot of a car. The night before, Karen had told her boyfriend that she had been offered $100 by Ken Bianchi to housesit for him; it was a crucial mistake for Bianchi. He had given his victims his real name and now police had a prime suspect.

Bianchi was immediately arrested. Evidence found at his house proved that he had been the killer. A pubic hair found on the steps that led to the basement of the house matched Bianchi and he had menstrual bloodstains on his underwear that had come from Diane Wilder.

Police from LA quickly made their way to Bellingham to question Bianchi about the Hillside Strangler murders.

However, Bianchi was ready for them. He feigned a split personality, claiming his alter ego was responsible - meaning he could possible plead guilty by reason of insanity and therefore get a more lenient sentence. In addition, he was their only hope in charging Buono with the Hillside Strangler crimes in LA. Therefore, if Bianchi was declared insane, the case would fold.

Thankfully, experts quickly dispelled Bianchi's story. In October 1979, Bianchi was declared sane and able to stand trial. Therefore, Bianchi needed to try something else. Knowing he would go the electric chair if convicted in LA, he quickly pleaded guilty to the two murders in Bellingham, so he could begin his plea-bargaining.

However, it was not successful. After hundreds of witness and evidence exhibits both men were sentenced to life imprisonment. Bianchi's sentence was handed down on October 21, 1983; Angelo Buono received his sentence on January 9, 1984.

This, however, is not where the story ends.

While serving his sentence in prison Bianchi was contacted by a strange twenty-three-year-old Los Angeles screenwriter named Veronica Lynn Comton who was seeking information for a book about a female serial killer. Together they hatched a plan to free him where Veronica would take a sample of his sperm, kill a woman, and deposit the sperm sample in her. Though a good idea, it never worked. She tried to strangle a woman but the victim was too strong and overpowered Veronica. Instead, it landed Veronica in jail, where Bianchi refused to speak to her ever again.

On September 21, 2002, sixty-seven-year-old Angelo Buono was found dead in his cell at Calipatria State Prison, having suffered a heart attack during the night.

Bible John

The killer known only as Bible John murdered his first victim on February 23, 1968. Twenty-nine-year-old Patricia Docker was abducted from outside of Barrowland Dance Hall in Glasgow. She was strangled and had her handbag stolen, her body was found the next morning in a doorway near the nightclub.

The killer, Bible John picked up thirty-two-year-old Jemima McDonald on August 16, 1969 at the Barrowland Dance Hall in Glasgow. The woman was found the next day strangled with her own pantyhose. It was the killer's second murder.

Bible John killed for the third and last time on October 30, 1969 before again disappearing into the night. He had been on a date with twenty-nine-year-old Helen Puttock at the Glasgow Barrowland Ballroom. Friends had heard Helen's date "John" quoting the bible a lot during the evening and thought he seemed like a nice guy. Helen and her date caught a bus home together.

The next day Helen's strangled corpse was found near the bus stop.

The case perplexed police and a true suspect was never identified, though a few names were bandied around including that of John McInnes.

Thirty years after the murders, the body of John McInnes, who had killed himself in 1980, was exhumed in Lanarkshire in February 1996 to test DNA samples from McInnes against semen samples found on Helen Putlock's body. The tests were inconclusive and the case remains officially unsolved.

Andreas Bichel

Andreas Bichel, the Bavarian Ripper was a cannibal killer who, in the early 1800's enticed young single women to his house with a promise of knowing their futures. Bichel would tell young women a story of owning a magical mirror that when a spinster looked into it, staring back would be the man she would marry. A fantastical story by today's standards but the killer was able to lure many women to his home.

Once the killer closed the door of his house behind his unsuspecting client, he would pounce on them. The young women were hit over the head and knocked unconscious. When the victims regained consciousness, they would find their hands tied behind their backs.

Bichel then began the torturous and slow murders of these victims.

Many of the victims were raped before having parts from their bodies severed, as they lay helpless and screaming in agony in the home of Bichel. Others were stabbed to death, their clothes soaked with blood.

Bichel's victims were usually sliced open, a long brutal cut from their sternum to their pubic bone. The internal and sexual organs of his female victims fascinated Bichel. He would plough his hands into the abdominal cavities of his still alive victims who writhed in pain during their torture.

In the European summer of 1806, Bichel murdered Barbara Reisinger. She was lured into Bichel's house before being raped and slaughtered.

The killer used a variety of weapons in his attacks, only caring about the result; Catherine Seidel whom he murdered around 1808 was hacked open with a hammer and chisel. The woman was helpless against her killer. She had been tied down and could only attempt to struggle from her bindings as Bichel brought the hammer down into her chest repeatedly. With each strike, the killer's excitement grew. He explains at his trial, the feelings he had;

> "During the operation I was so eager, that I trembled all over, and I longed to rive off a piece and eat it"

Of the murder of another one of his victims, Bichel would later tell Bavarian authorities the immense pleasure he felt during the attack;
> "I opened her breast and with a knife cut through the fleshy parts of the body. Then I arranged the body as a butcher does beef, and hacked it with the axe into pieces... I may say that while opening the body, I was so greedy that I trembled and could have cut out a piece and eaten it"

In 1809 after finally being caught while attempting to sell the clothes of his victims, Andreas Bichel was executed.

Arthur Bishop

The case began with the mysterious disappearance of four-year-old Alonzo Daniels on the afternoon of October 14, 1979. Alonzo was playing alone in the sunshine outside his home in Salt Lake City. His mother sat watching him for some time before she returned inside the house for a few minutes before checking on her son outside once more. However, Alonzo was nowhere in sight. A search of the surrounding area by relatives, neighbours and the police failed to find the young boy or any evidence of what had happened.

Alonzo was still missing, on November 9, 1980, when eleven-year-old Kim Peterson vanished. He was last seen, by his parents, rushing out of the family home on his way to sell his roller skates to a man he had met the previous day. Kim never returned home. Witnesses came forward describing a man seen with Kim as tall, with short, dark hair and bushy eyebrows. But again, no arrests were made.

Almost a year had passed since Kim's disappearance when another young boy vanished. On October 20, 1981, four-year-old Danny Davis was on a shopping trip with his grandfather in Salt Lake City. Sometime during the trip, the pair became separated. Other shoppers assisted store employees in the search for the youngster, but he was nowhere to be seen. Witnesses believed they saw Danny talking to a man, but could provide no further information. Despite a reward of $20,000, Danny was gone.

Twenty months later, the list of missing children had increased to four. June 22, 1983 was a day of celebration for the Ward family. It was Troy Ward's sixth birthday and as a treat, his parents allowed him to play at the nearby Liberty Park. Just before 4pm, his arranged pick up time, Troy was seen walking off with an adult male. Witnesses in the park assumed that the man was the boy's father. Salt Lake police looked into potential links between the four cases but could find none.

Graeme Cunningham joined the list on July 14, 1983. Graeme was due to go on a camping break on July 16 with a school friend and an adult minder by the name of Roger Downs. Officers decided to visit Downs to see if he could add anything to the case.

It was a classic hunch that led to Detective Steven Smith and Sergeant Bruce White inviting Downs to the police headquarters for additional questioning after their initial meeting. The officers' hunch was right, under increasing pressure Downs confessed to the murder of the five missing children.

Following his confession, Downs took the officers to the burial sites of his young victims. Buried near some trees in Cedar Fort lay the bodies of Alonzo Daniels, Danny Davis, and Kim Peterson. The bodies of Troy Ward and Graeme Cunningham were uncovered using directions given by Downs in Big Cottonwood Creek. Downs confessed that he killed the boys so that they would not tell of the sexual assaults after their abductions.

Officers checked into Downs' background and discovered that his real name was actually Arthur Bishop. Born in Hinckley, Utah, Bishop was a dedicated Mormon who had spent time in the Philippines as a missionary. Bishop vanished in July 1978 after being arrested for forgery; this resulted in his excommunication from the church. He reappeared in October 1979 using his new name of Robert Downs. When Alonzo Daniels disappeared, investigators discovered that Bishop was living in the apartment opposite and in the other cases, Bishop resided within a block of the family homes. Additional checks on Bishop uncovered other aliases and numerous sexual attacks on young children, particularly young boys. In his home Bishop kept a folder containing hundreds of photographs of naked and semi naked boys.

At his trial, the jury found Bishop guilty of five counts of murder, 5 counts of kidnapping and one count of sexual abuse. During sentencing, the jury listened to sections of his taped confessions in which Bishop states that had he not been caught the sexual attacks and murders would have continued.

Bishop was duly sentenced to death. Under Utah law the choice of method of execution is left to the defendant. Bishop chose lethal injection over firing squad. By his own admission Bishop wanted to die, he waived all appeals by his lawyer and was executed by lethal injection on June 9, 1988.

Bernd Bopp

Bernd Bopp preyed upon women and young girls in Western Germany using a hammer to murder and rape to satisfy himself, killing nine and allowing four others to survive.

The first victim was assaulted on April 17, 1975. Twenty-eight-year-old Lillian Dresch stood at a bus stop in Mannheim-Neckarau, late in the evening. Bopp stopped his car, got out and walked purposely towards Lillian. Thrusting an arm around Lillian's chest to prevent her easy escape, Bopp pierced her throat with a knife he held in the other hand. Lillian screamed, kicked out, and broke free. Her screams alerted the neighbourhood, and so Bopp quickly returned to his car and sped off. Lillian was taken to the local hospital where she was treated for her throat wound.

Monika Sorn was not so fortunate. On June 9, 1975, Monika left her parents home in Hemsbach to go to school, but by the evening Monika had failed to return home. Knowing their daughter would not forget to tell them that she would be late, they notified the police. A search of the local area took place and Monika's body was found late that night, her head had been smashed by a rock that was found nearby soaked in her blood. Doctors determined that Monika had also been raped but were not able to tell whether it was before or after death.

Like Monika, Bopp's next victim suffered a similar fate. On September 13, 1975, eleven-year-old Liane Woessner left her home in Elmendingen to visit her aunt in Bruchsal, she never arrived. Frantic phone calls to the police resulted in a search of the area between the two towns. Liane was found dead on the roadside near Bruchsal. The autopsy revealed that she had been killed with a blunt force to the head probably a hammer. Liane had also been raped, but the killer had struggled to penetrate her and left his own blood on her body. Samples of the blood would confirm the presence of type AB that matched semen found at Monica's murder.

Another three months passed before Bopp's murderous actions returned. Susanne Bach was walking through the city park in Weinheim on December 22, 1975 when Bopp ran up behind her and struck her twice on the rear of the head with a hammer, knocking Susanne to the ground. Bopp stood over her unconscious body. However, something disturbed the man and he ran away. Susanne was found and taken to the local hospital for treatment. She had suffered a severe concussion, however the hammer had not penetrated her skull.

Ten months passed before another attack took place. Monika Pfeifer was reported missing to Mainz police on October 11, 1976 and a search of the area would fail to recover her dead or alive. It was not until January 6 the following year that her body was found. A fisherman angling in the waters of the Rhine near Mainz dragged to the shore the naked body of Monika. The autopsy revealed that she had died after her skull had been fractured multiple times, probably with a hammer.

The day after Monika Pfeifer was found dead, Bopp had another target in his sights. Twenty-two-year-old Barbara Kiel was walking home from the university in Mainz on January 7, 1977, when suddenly Bopp struck her from behind in his Volkswagen car. She was thrown her into a stonewall along the side of the road. The force of the car broke both of her legs on impact. Barbara, despite her injuries, had the presence of mind to lie on the ground close to the wall thus preventing Bopp from hitting her again, as he continued to drive against the wall over her body. Finally, Bopp gave up and drove away, leaving Barbara to be found by passers by. Barbara eventually recovered from ordeal. Bopp's next victim however would not.

Like Barbara, twenty-three-year-old Sylvia Lauterbach also studied at Mainz University. On March 29, 1977, Sylvia's body was found in a field between Mainz and Bretzenheim, having disappeared the previous day. She was found naked and her skull crushed, she had also been raped. The autopsy determined that the murder weapon was a four pound hammer. In fact, the force of the blows left an imprint of the hammer in the unfortunate girls' skull. It was Sylvia's murder that first brought Mainz police to the belief that they had a serial killer on their hands.

Like previous victims, twenty-one-year-old Marie-Theresa Majer had been walking along a lonely road near Schriesheim when she was murdered. Her slain body was found on April 29, 1977 on the roadside. She was naked and had the distinctive marks of hammer blows to her skull. Like the other victims, she had also been raped. Again, the semen blood grouping matched the other murder victims. Despite an intensive search of the area, no other clues were uncovered.

After Marie-Theresa's murder, the killer did not kill again for almost two years.

Just short of the second anniversary of Marie-Theresa Majer's death, another victim was killed, this time fifteen-year-old Gudrun Thome was the unfortunate victim. On April 21, 1979, Gudrun disappeared from her village of Rot and a search party was quickly assembled. The group of searchers found her body lying in a field less than a mile from the village. Gudrun had been raped, the bruises on her thighs indicated that she had been alive at the time; her head also showed the marks of two hammer blows to her head. Her fingernails had dug into her attacker, pieces of skin and hair remained behind, and the evidence was tested and matched samples taken from previous attacks.

Less than two weeks after Gudrun's death Bopp struck again. This time he murdered in the town of Saarbruecken. Ellen Abel had spent the night out with friends and when the sixteen-year-old did not return home, her parents called the local police to report her missing. She was found the next day, with the familiar hammer blows to the back of the head.

On June 4, 1980, twenty-year-old Marie-Elsa Scholte was found murdered near Ludwigshafen on the banks of the Rhine. Bopp had once again crushed the young woman's head with strikes of a hammer, leaving Marie-Elsa with multiple fractures. Having killed her, Bopp raped her dead body, before dumping it in a field. Ludwigshafen police had noted that the killer did not kill in the same town in consecutive attacks, and so was confident enough to say that the town was safe for the moment.

However, they were wrong.

Ludwigshafen citizen Gabriella Bohn, sixteen, was the next to die. Her body was found on February 23, 1981, her head shown the signs of one clear hammer blow that left a significant pool of blood on the ground where she fell. The killer had also raped Gabriella after death.

Returning to Mainz, Bopp drove around the deserted back roads of the town on May 15, 1981, until he found his next victim. Bopp saw ten-year-old Ulrike Hellmann walking home from school and decided she was to be his next victim. Bopp stopped his car in front of the girl and strode purposefully towards Ulrike, hammer in his hand.

Ulrike spotted Bopp and turned to run, but before she could get away, the hammer struck her fully on the back of the head and knocked her to the ground, but she was not unconscious. Bopp mounted the young girl and attempted to rape her.

Karl Lenk was cycling down the road when he saw the pair on the ground, as he got closer he noticed the female was a young girl who started to scream. Karl quickly dismounted from the bicycle and ran toward Ulrike shouting at the man to stop. Bopp leapt to his feet, got back into his car and sped from the scene. Karl reached Ulrike made sure she was safe and well, Ulrike said only one thing to Karl, the registration number of her attacker's car.

Later that day with the car registration number in their hands, Mainz police searched the area for the red Renault car driven by Bernd Bopp. Finding the car parked twenty miles away in Alzey, Bopp was lying in the sunshine near the car reading a book as police approached and arrested him. A search of the car revealed a hammer still stained with Ulrike's blood. In custody, Bopp - a teacher at a secondary school - confessed to other murders but admitted he could not recall how many or any great details about the crimes. During his trial, Bopp admitted that he could not help himself and would, upon release, continue what he was doing.

Bopp received a life sentence on October 8, 1981.

William Burke and William Hare
Burke
William Burke was born in Orrey, County Tyrone around 1792. The family, despite being poor, were proud, hard working members of the community. Burke, along with his brother Constantine, eventually left the family home to join the army. During this time, he met and married a young girl. The union produced two children, but in 1818, Burke departed for Scotland leaving his family behind him for good. He settled in Maddiston, finding work labouring on the Union Canal.

It was in Maddiston that he met Helen McDougal and eventually the pair moved in together. Despite never marrying, they assumed the role of husband and wife, which was frowned upon under Scottish law. After the Union Canal work ended, Burke was unemployed, so he and Helen travelled to Edinburgh, repairing and selling old clothes and shoes.

Hare
William Hare was born in Newry and, as with Burke, also emigrated to Scotland to search for work, which he found on the Union Canal. It is unknown as to whether he and Burke knew each other during their employment at the Canal. However, Burke and Hare would meet after it ended. Hare lodged in a filthy bed-sit in Tanner's Close, in the West Port area of Edinburgh and began an affair with the owner's wife, Margaret Logue. The owner recognised Hare's closeness to his wife and threw him out. Hare returned after hearing of Logue's death, taking Logue's wife as his own and also the ownership of the profitable bed-sit.

In autumn 1827, Burke and Helen McDougal moved in to Hare's lodgings, with Burke and Hare becoming such firm friends that Helen would liken them to brothers. At the house, a man named Donald was gravely ill and on November 27, 1827, he died. Hare was furious, as Donald owed him rent for the bed. It was Burke who suggested that if they pretend that the body had been taken from a grave, they could sell it to Professor Monro at the University for dissection.

At the time, the law stated that bodies used for dissection could only be those of executed criminals. This meant that there were not enough bodies to cover the requests. It became common for grave robbers to deliver bodies for such uses for a fee and no questions were asked. These people became known as Resurrectionists. Burke suggested using Donald's body to make some money; Hare saw the logic and agreed. After a mock funeral, so as not to raise suspicion, Burke and Hare took the body to Professor Monro, but after they were given incorrect directions, they ended up at the door of Dr Robert Knox.

Knox
Dr Robert Knox was born in 1793 to parents Robert and Mary. Robert Knox Snr taught Natural Philosophy and Mathematics at the George Heriot School. The young Knox would follow in his father's footsteps by taking a professional career, choosing medicine as his preferred expertise. His course at Edinburgh University was put on hold when he joined the army in 1815 serving for 5 years before returning to his studies in Edinburgh. After completing the course, he joined with his University lecturer, Dr Barclay, in 1825 to teach at the Anatomy School at No 10 Surgeon's Square, Edinburgh. Dr Knox would inherit the school following his mentor's death in 1826 and became the most successful medical lecturer in Edinburgh.

Dr Knox and his assistants examined the body, asked no probing questions and offered the men £7 10s. Burke and Hare had never seen so much money and readily agreed. As they went out into the night, a voice called out to them that should they have any more bodies, they would be glad to accommodate them.

However, the money from selling Donald's body soon ran out, meaning that Burke would have to return to gainful employment. It was about this time that another tenant, a man named Joseph, fell ill. Burke and Hare saw this as an opportunity to sell his body once the old man died, but he fought back against the illness. Frustrated that Joseph would not die, Burke and Hare furnished him with enough whiskey to drift off into unconsciousness. As soon as Joseph fell asleep, Burke placed a pillow over his face until he was dead. That night, forgoing the funeral, Joseph's body was placed in a sack and taken to No 10 Surgeon's Square, where Dr Knox's assistants paid a handsome £10. Once again, no questions were asked.

The money lasted for some time, but eventually ran out. It was then that the men had a sudden shift in thinking. Instead of waiting for somebody to die in the house, Burke and Hare decided to go out and hunt for a 'victim'.

On February 11, 1828, Burke and Hare met Abigail Simpson, an elderly woman, and invited her back to Tanner's Close, where she and her hosts drank through the night. All three got so drunk that the men forgot the reason for bringing Abigail home with them. The following day they gave Abigail more to drink, while being careful with their own consumption. Once she was unconscious, she was smothered until she was dead. That night Abigail lay on a slab at Dr Knox's halls with Burke and Hare £10 better off.

With their newfound wealth, Burke and Hare, along with their lovers, began to spend it on more lavish clothing and better food. It was not long before the locals noticed, but their questions were dismissed by explanations of a large inheritance. However, because of their increase in spending it meant that the money would run out more rapidly. Burke and Hare concluded that another body was required. A tenant at Tanner's Close became ill with what was suspected jaundice. This was considered bad for the house, and had to be eliminated. Hare put his weight down on the unfortunate man's body while Burke covered his mouth and nose with his hands. The victim suffocated within a few minutes, leaving Dr Knox with another body to dissect and money in the killers' pockets.

Soon Dr Knox had yet another body, that of an elderly woman who was invited to stay at Tanner's Close by Margaret Hare. She gave the old woman plenty of whiskey to drink and then suggested that she lie down. Hare took the opportunity and smothered the woman, as she lay asleep. Burke later helped his partner take the body to Surgeons' Square.

On April 8, 1828, teenager Mary Paterson and her close friend Janet Brown were arrested by Edinburgh police and held overnight in the cells. The next morning they were released and the pair headed straight to a bar to share a drink. Inside William Swanston's pub stood Burke, who watched the two young women for a while before joining them at their table. After some sweet-talking, Burke persuaded both Mary and Janet to come back to his house for some breakfast. Following something to eat, the three of them began to drink heavily. After a while, Mary fell asleep on the bed and Burke and Janet went out for a stroll. When they returned Mary was still unconscious. Burke tried to seduce Janet but was interrupted by Burke's wife. The resulting argument turned violent when Burke threw a glass, cutting Helen's forehead. Burke, leaving Mary behind, escorted Janet out of the house. It was not long before Burke and Hare returned to the house and murdered Mary Paterson. Janet returned to the house later that day to look for Mary, but she was not there. By that time, she was lying on the slab at No 10 Surgeon's Square, where Burke and Hare had been paid £8 for her body.

A woman named Old Effie was next for Dr Knox, Burke knew her well, and he offered Old Effie drink and lodgings, forgetting to mention death. The murders were steadily increasing in frequency.

In June 1828, Burke came across an elderly woman with her grandson who were lost in the backstreets of Edinburgh while searching for their friend's house. Burke claimed he knew the address and would take them there, but first he offered them lunch at his house. The pair were thankful to their new friend for the offer and gladly followed. The grandmother was offered drink after drink until she fell unconscious. Hare joined Burke in suffocating the woman to death while their wives looked after her twelve-year-old grandson. After some debate as to what to do with the child, he too was murdered and sold for dissection.

A woman named Mrs Oster vanished after visiting Tanner's Close and this was quickly followed by the murder of Burke's common law wife, Helen McDougal's cousin Ann McDougal who was sold for £10.

Elderly prostitute Mary Haldane was taken to Tanner's Close by Burke and Hare, plied with drink, and murdered that same night. However, Mary's daughter Peggy soon went looking for her mother and was told that Mary was seen entering Tanner's Close. Helen and Margaret denied knowing the woman at all when questioned by Peggy Haldane. Hare admitted that Peggy's mother had indeed been at the house, but had left earlier. Hare invited the young woman inside, offering her a drink. It would be her last. As with her mother, Peggy was smothered by Burke and Hare and sold for dissection.

Eighteen-year-old Jamie Wilson, known as "Daft Jamie", had lived on the streets of Edinburgh since leaving home after one of his mother's severe beatings. In October 1828, Jamie found himself at Tanner's Close being entertained by Hare. He tried to get Jamie to drink whiskey, but he refused. As time went by and night came, Jamie fell asleep on the bed. Burke and Hare took their chance and tried to smother Jamie, but the young man fought back. Despite Jamie's bravado, it was two against one and he was overpowered and smothered. His clothes were given to Burke's nephews, while Dr Knox's assistants paid £10 for the body.

On October 31, 1828, Burke stood in Rymer's shop in Edinburgh enjoying his regular early morning drink, when he met Mary Docherty. Burke recognised Mary's accent as being from the same region of Ireland as himself, and her surname matched his mother's maiden name. Burke invited his newfound friend back to his house, where she met and was warmly welcomed by Burke's wife. After a short stay, Mary decided it was time to leave, but her hosts persuaded Mary to stay for a Halloween celebration taking place that night. Burke left the house on the pretence of purchasing more whiskey, but his objective was more sinister, he had already decided that Mary was to be his next victim and he had left the house to search for Hare.

The party in the evening went well, but Burke and Hare wanted it over quickly so they could complete their murderous plan. Throughout the evening, Burke continually persuaded Mary to stay, while simultaneously making efforts in persuading the other party guests to leave. Just past midnight, a neighbour, Hugh Alston, heard a scuffle and then a cry of murder. Hugh went to investigate, but when the sounds quickly abated, he returned to bed believing that it was just an argument which was now over. However, Mary Docherty lay dead in the basement, murdered by the smothering hands of Burke and Hare.

The following morning the party guests began to ask questions as to the whereabouts of Mary Docherty. Helen McDougal responded by saying that she was thrown out of the house for attempting to seduce her husband, yet her body was actually still lying under some straw in the basement. One of the guests, Ann Gray, went looking around the house for some of her belongings, when Burke saw her near the pile of straw concealing the body, and rudely ushered her away. With Burke having to go out for an errand, he demanded that another guest, John Brogan, stand guard over the straw until he returned. Of course, this made Ann very suspicious and as soon as John moved away, Ann seized the opportunity and took a peek. Under the straw, she saw the naked body of Mary Docherty, the blood on her face made Ann Gray believe that Mary's death was murder and not from natural causes.

Ann Gray and her husband, James, immediately packed their bags to leave. At the door, they were met by Helen, who wanted to know where they were going in such a hurry. Referring to the body, Ann asked what was going on in the house. Helen instantly knew to what Ann was referring and offered cash in return for her silence. Ann refused the bribe and was equally steadfast when Margaret Hare joined in. As the Grays left the house, they made it clear they were going to inform the police of their discovery.

Helen and Margaret rushed off to tell their husbands and Burke and Hare immediately had Mary's body taken in a large chest to Surgeon's Square for dissection. James Gray reported the body to Sergeant-Major John Fisher who began an immediate search. Sergeant Fisher and patrolman John Findlay went to Tanner's Close to find evidence of the crime, but they could find no body. Blood was found on a pile of straw, which Helen argued came from a woman during childbirth.

A search was also made of 10 Surgeon's Square on November 2, 1820 and, in a corner of the surgery's basement, Patrolman Fisher opened a tea chest and found the body of Mary Docherty. She was identified by the guests at the Halloween party. William Burke, William Hare, Margaret Hare, and Helen McDougal were arrested for her murder.

William Newbigging completed the autopsy on November 3, his report indicated that Mary Docherty died due to smothering, but he was unable to determine whether this was due to an accident or murder. Burke and Helen McDougal were separately questioned; each gave differing accounts as to how Mary came to be at the house and the circumstances surrounding her death. Burke suggested that Hare was totally responsible for the body being at the house. A week later Burke changed his story. He now claimed that after a night of drinking, both Hare and himself found Mary Docherty dead and decided to sell the body to the doctors at Surgeon's Square.

The case of Mary Docherty made the evening newspapers and rumours spread quickly across the city of other disappearances and murders and the dead being sold. Janet Brown, a friend of Mary Paterson, went to the police to tell them her story of meeting Burke and Hare, and how they were the last people to see her friend alive. A search at Tanner's Close recovered numerous items of clothing some of which Janet claimed belonged to Mary. Other items found included those belonging to Mary Docherty and Jamie Wilson. Members of the public began to come forward describing close encounters with Burke and Hare at Tanner's Close.

Lord Advocate, Sir William Rae, felt that the case against the four was entirely circumstantial and the medical evidence on the one available body did not conclusively prove murder. Sir William believed that despite the lack of evidence, something had to be done. On December 1, 1828, William Hare was interviewed again, during which he was heavily pressured into turning evidence against Burke in exchange for his immunity. Hare readily agreed and told the tale of murder, implicating Burke in all cases. The following week William Burke and Helen McDougal were charged with the murder of Mary Docherty, Burke was also charged with the murders of Mary Paterson and Jamie Wilson. As agreed, Hare escaped all charges and his wife had no charges bought against her.

On Christmas Eve 1828, William Burke and Helen McDougal were transported from Calton Jail to Parliament House to stand trial for murder. At 10.15am, the trial came into session with Sir William Gull acting as lead prosecutor and Sir James Moncrieff heading the defence team. For the three charges levied against him, Burke pleaded not guilty, similarly McDougal also pleaded not guilty for the single murder charge against her.

On the evening of the first day, William Hare was called to the stand and questioned about the murder of Mary Docherty. He described in detail how Burke knelt over the woman, his hands over her throat and mouth thus preventing her from breathing. After Mary was dead, Burke alone stripped the body of all clothing and arranged her disposal. Margaret Hare was also called; she testified that it was Burke who was responsible for Mary's death. Asked why she never reported the death, Margaret claimed that if she did, she would have been murdered herself.

The trial continued through the night, at 3am on Christmas morning, all the evidence had been presented; the defence had offered no witnesses and so closing arguments could begin. Sir William Rae, arguing for the prosecution, appealed for a guilty verdict. Sir James Moncrieff argued for not guilty, whereas Henry Cockburn, defending McDougal, went a little further and asked for a verdict of not proven to be given. At 8.30am, the jurors rose and filed out to begin deliberations.

In just under an hour, the jury returned with their verdicts. Foreman John McFie, a merchant from Leith, announced to the court that the jury had found William Burke guilty of the murder of Mary Docherty; the charge against Helen McDougal was not proven. The judge donned his black cap and announced that Burke was to 'suffer death upon the gibbet…and thereafter be given for dissection'. The date of execution was set for January 28, 1829. The trial had lasted without any stoppages for a full twenty-four hours.

Helen McDougal was held in her cell until December 26, when the crowds began to disperse. She went back to her house in Tanner's Close hoping to continue as if nothing had happened. Despite being found not guilty in court, in the eyes of Edinburgh's public she was guilty. Shopkeepers refused to serve her, locals followed her everywhere, threatening their own justice until the police were forced to protect her from the mobs. Eventually Helen was forced to abandon her home and Edinburgh and headed south into England. What became of Helen after this is not known. It is however, believed that she immigrated to Australia, dying around 1868.

Despite having no charges bought against her, Margaret Hare had spent her time since her arrest in a prison cell. On January 19, 1829, she was released from Calton Jail. As with Helen McDougal, Margaret Hare also felt the wrath of the public. She was pelted with mud and snowballs as she tried to get home. Police officers escorted her home, where she immediately packed her bags and left for Glasgow and then Belfast where she was not heard from again.

At 4am on January 27, 1829, Burke was moved from his cell at Calton Jail to Liberton Wynd Police Station. From there it was a short walk to the gallows that were being erected in the street. Windows overlooking the gallows were being offered to let during the event and each was snapped up quickly. The gallows were completed at 2am on January 28, as it began raining heavily. Despite the rain, the crowds began to appear at 5am, numbering 25,000 by 8 am, taking all available vantage points.

Burke sat in his cell with Father Reid, the two recited prayers in readiness for Burke's execution. He was soon moved to another room at the police station so that he could dress in an ill fitting black suit, and some black boots. Burke drank a glass of wine, offering a toast to all those around him. The hangman, a man named Williams, prepared Burke for his execution, tying the condemned man's hands together. Burke thanked all those present for their kindness towards him. He was now ready.

At 8am, the procession entered the square, when a huge cheer went up as the 25,000 strong crowd saw Burke for the first time. The crowd hurled insults and chants of 'Hang Hare' and 'Hang Knox' were heard. On the gallows, the hangman gave Burke his instructions concerning the execution. He asked Burke to pray whilst on the gallows and offered him a handkerchief to hold in his hand. When Burke had finished his prayer, he was to speak the name of Jesus, drop the handkerchief, and die with the Lord's name in his mouth. Burke nodded his agreement and Williams covered Burke's eyes.

At 8.15am, Burke dropped the handkerchief, Williams pulled the switch, and the trapdoor opened. Burke fell and the crowd cheered. For 5 minutes Burke's body hung still, then gave the occasional twitch, each met with a loud cheer. After the third twitch, Burke's body was still. He was now dead.

Burke's body was cut down from the scaffold at 8.55 and taken directly to Edinburgh University where it would be held until his public dissection the following day. Dr Munro carried out the second part of the sentence in front of doctors and students of the University. For two days following the dissection, Burke's body was on view. An estimated 25,000 visitors walked through the lecture room. Burke's skeleton has since been preserved and is permanently held at the Anatomical Museum at the University of Edinburgh.

Despite the assurances that he was immune to prosecution, some members of the legal profession were unhappy that William Hare was a free man. Lord Gillies and Lord Alloway wanted Hare to be put on trial for his crimes. After questioning him, the Lords decided that there was no case to answer. On February 5, 1829, Hare, using the alias Mr Black, slipped unnoticed out of Calton Jail a free man. Jailer John Fisher accompanied him to a coach heading for Newington and onwards to England, where he was seen begging in Oxford Street, London.

Which left Dr Knox. He continued to ignore the abuse from the Edinburgh public that sat outside his lecture halls calling for his execution. On February 12, 1829, a committee hearing began which would determine the extent, if any, of Dr Knox's knowledge or guilt concerning the crimes. In March, the committee reported their findings. Neither Dr Knox, nor any of his assistants or students had any knowledge of the murders. Nor could the committee find any evidence to suggest any deliberate attempt to hide the identities of the bodies they received. The report did however blame Dr Knox for failing to determine the origins of the bodies sold to him. Despite being exonerated of all possible links to the murders, Dr Knox's career began to take a downturn. The number of students attending his lectures reduced over the subsequent years.

He tried for chairs at the University of Edinburgh but was twice rejected. He left 10 Surgeon's Square in order to take a lecture tour of Scotland, after which he moved to London, but was the subject of a forgery scandal resulting in the removal of his license to lecture. Dr Knox wrote several books on anatomy and fishing, each selling well. In 1856, he was appointed Pathological Anatomist at the Lancer Hospital in London, a position he held until his death on December 20, 1862.

In 1832, British law changed with regard to bodies used for dissection with the 1832 Anatomy Act. The law required that all bodies used in dissection could only come from those persons who had died in hospitals and only from bodies unclaimed after 72 hours.

Jerome Brudos

Jerome Henry Brudos was born on January 31, 1939 in Webster, South Dakota the second son of parents Eileen and Henry. The family, in search of employment, was always on the move during Jerome's youth. Jerome was five-years-old when his fascination with shoes first became known. After finding a pair of high-heeled shoes at the local dump, Jerry took them home and paraded around his room wearing them, until his mother caught him and threw them out. Jerry retrieved the shoes and hid them away continuing to wear them in the privacy of his room whenever he could.

In 1955, when he was 17, Brudos, wearing a mask, forced a young girl that he knew to strip naked holding a knife to her throat. While naked, the terrified girl was photographed then let go. The incident was not reported to police.

Several months later, after he assaulted a girl for refusing his sexual advances, Brudos was arrested for assault and battery. Pulk County refused to treat him as a juvenile delinquent and so he was committed to Oregon State Mental Hospital in Salem for assessment. After eight months at the hospital Brudos was released, the doctors not finding anything specifically wrong with him.

After leaving college, Brudos joined the United States Army and trained at Fort Gordon in Georgia, training for the Signal Corps. However, after seven months on October 15, 1973 he was discharged.

Brudos' discharge came as a result of an initial meeting between him and the chaplain who directed Brudos to meet with the staff psychiatrist. Captain Theodore Barry listened to Brudos' story that a Korean woman entered the barracks nightly to seduce him and each night he would react by beating her. Captain Barry recommended Brudos for discharge due to 'bizarre obsessions and not fit for duty'.

On leaving the army, Brudos met and married Darcie, which was followed soon after by the birth of their first child.

After Brudos' wife Darcie had refused him entry into the delivery room for the birth of their second child, he became very depressed and very angry. Friends and family noticed a subtle change in his personality.

In Portland, Oregon on May 18, 1967, Brudos followed Joyce Cassell because he lusted after the shoes she was wearing. He continued to follow Joyce in his car until she reached her home. Brudos waited outside the apartment until he saw the lights go out for the night and silently made his way in to her house to steal the shoes. However just as he knelt on the floor to pick the items up, Joyce awoke. As her eyes became used to the darkness she made out the shadowy figure of a man at the side of the bed. Brudos had been watching Joyce and before she was able to open her mouth to scream out, he clasped his hands powerfully around her throat and began to squeeze until Joyce fell unconscious. Brudos climbed on top of the unconscious woman and raped her before silently leaving the apartment carrying his prized shoes. Brudos would not be linked to the attack until his arrest in June 1969.

On January 16, 1968, nineteen-year-old Linda Slawson was out in the Oregon rain knocking on doors selling encyclopaedias. After a mix up with house numbers Linda knocked on the door of Jerome Brudos who invited the rain-drenched teenager in. Brudos suggested that they go down to the basement where they could talk undisturbed, Linda happily agreed. As Linda began to demonstrate the books, Brudos moved himself behind the unsuspecting woman, lifted a length of wood, and brought it crashing down onto Linda's head causing her to collapse unconscious onto the ground.

Brudos knelt down over his victim and felt her chest to see if she was dead. Certain that he could feel her still breathing, Brudos clasped his hands around Linda's neck and squeezed powerfully until she went limp.

Alone with his now dead victim, Brudos stripped Linda naked and then dressed her in clothing he had stolen over the years. When he finally finished dressing and undressing Linda's body, Brudos took a saw and cut off her left foot, dressed it with a black high-heeled shoe and put it in the freezer he kept in the basement workshop. Early the next morning, Brudos drove Linda's body to the St John Bridge that crossed the Williamette River. After tying the body to a car engine block, Brudos dropped the weight into the river below.

Twenty-three-year-old Jan Whitney had been visiting friends on November 26, 1968 and at the end of the evening she got in her car to drive the 2 hour journey from Eugene along the I-5 to her home in McMinnville, but she never made it.

Brudos had spotted Jan Whitney with two young men waiting by her car that had broken down by the side of the road near Albany. Brudos approached Jan and offered to fix it. Making the excuse that his tools were at his house he gave Jan and the two men a ride to Salem, where the two males got out and Brudos continued on to his house. Once there he told Jan to wait while he went to get his tools. In fact he was checking that his wife Darcie was not in. Returning to the car, he got in the back seat behind Jan and lied to her saying that he could not get in the house and that they will have to wait until his wife came home. As Jan sat in front, Brudos picked out a thin piece of leather from his pocket, wrapped it around his hands and quickly looped it around Jan's throat and pulled tightly. Within a few minutes, Jan Whitney was dead.

Her car was later found in a rest area north of Albany, Oregon with no evident damage and all doors locked. A full check of the car for blood and fingerprints would reveal a single print by persons unknown, on one of the hubcaps. It was not until Brudos' surprise confession in May 1969 to Jan's murder that authorities were able to close the investigation into her disappearance.

Brudos had sex with the dead body in his car before moving Jan's body to the workshop where he raped her again. He then hung the body from the hook attached to the roof of the workshop. Over the next few days, Brudos returned to his locked hideaway to dress and photograph his victim. Brudos also removed her breast in an attempt to make a paperweight, but he made a mess and threw it away with the rest of her body into the Williamette River.

Karen Sprinker was a nineteen-year-old student at Oregon State University who was studying to follow in her father's footsteps in medicine. Karen was visiting her parents in Salem during the mid-term break. On Thursday March 27, 1969, Karen made her way towards the Meier and Frank department store in Salem. She parked her car and headed for a noon lunch date with her mother. She never arrived.

Brudos watched the young woman cross the parking lot towards the staircase of the Meier and Frank department store. As Karen reached for the door to the main shopping area, Brudos grabbed her by the shoulder and pointed a gun at her chest. Karen stood frozen, terrified by the weapon being held by the stranger. Directing Karen into his car, Brudos drove to his house and forced the terrified teenager into the workshop where he raped her. Due to her fear of being shot, Karen complied with all of Brudos's requests. He made Karen strip and wear various panties he had set out, Brudos took numerous photographs during the session.

When the photo session was over Brudos tied Karen's hands behind her back with the pretence of making sure she wouldn't run off. He lied. Brudos tied a rope around her neck attached it to the hook in the ceiling and pulled it up lifting Karen off the ground. Brudos yanked the rope several times hanging the woman until she died. After her death, he raped the body several times, before cutting off both of her breasts. At approximately 2am Brudos dressed Karen's mutilated body and drove to the Long Tom River where he tied her body to a car engine and threw her into the cold river

Karen's mother became worried when her usually punctual daughter failed to arrive, so she called home to see if Karen had forgotten her lunch date and found no one home. Mrs Sprinker immediately drove home, and called her husband and Karen's friends in the hope that she was with one of them. Nobody had seen the young woman.

Mr Sprinker arrived home to find his wife in a state of panic and together they reported their daughter missing to Salem police. That night, officers went to the deserted parking lot of the department store and found Karen's car. It was locked with several of Karen's university books still on the passenger seat. A forensic check of the car would reveal no trace of blood and only Sprinker family fingerprints were present. In essence nothing indicated foul play. Detective Jim Stovall searched the distance between the parking lot and the shopping centre looking for clues, perhaps even droplets of blood, but, like the car, no clues could be found. It was two months before her weighted down body was recovered from the Williamette River.

Linda Salee from Portland had not heard of the disappearances of the three Oregon women but the twenty-two-year-old was soon to join the same list. On April 23, 1969, Linda planned to meet her boyfriend at 6.30 pm at the YMCA where he worked as a lifeguard. First, she drove her VW to the Lloyd shopping centre in order to buy her boyfriend a birthday present to give it to him later. She visited a jewellery and a clothing store, leaving the second store at 5.15pm and returned to her car.

Linda Salee was crossing the car park with her arms full of shopping, Brudos strode straight up to her and flashed a fake police badge and introduced himself as store security. Linda was required to come to the station under suspicion of shoplifting, Linda denied the accusation but was willing to go to the station to defend herself and got into Brudos' vehicle. Instead of driving to the police station, Brudos drove to his house in Salem where he led Linda into the workshop and tied her up. His wife Darcie, under strict orders never to go near the workshop, called on the intercom to say that dinner was ready. Brudos left his captive tied up and went to the main house.

When Brudos returned Linda was free of the ropes but sitting in the chair. He put a leather strap around Linda's neck and pulled it tight lifting the girl off her feet as she struggled to breathe. However, Brudos was too strong for Linda and she died with Brudos still pulling on the strap. He then tied Linda to the ceiling hook and stripped the body. He stuck two needles in her, one under each armpit, tied electrical cables to them, and turned the power on to see what would happen. Nothing happened except the current burned Linda in the needle site under both arms. Two days after she was reported missing Linda was thrown into the Long Tom River.

By 7.30pm, Linda's boyfriend had finished his shift and had waited for Linda to turn up for over an hour. He wasn't overly concerned, as she liked to surprise him. He went to her house, but found neither Linda nor her car. The next morning when Linda's workmates noticed she had not turned up and contacted her parents, they reported her missing that day. Her car was found locked in the Lloyd shopping centre parking lot. Three weeks later Linda's body was found.

A single angler was standing on the Bundy Bridge fishing on the Long Tom River in Oregon late in the day on May 10, 1969. He spotted a large object lying in the shallow waters. Grabbing a long pole, he pulled the mysterious object closer to the bank. As it neared he put the pole down and stepped into the waters to take a closer look at what had caught his attention. He recoiled in horror at the sight of a naked human body bloated by its stay in the water. Benton County Sheriff's department officers raced to the scene of the grizzly find. She had been weighted down by an engine transmission. Pathologist Dr William Brady performed the autopsy and identified the woman as Linda Salee. She had been strangled with an unknown ligature and two needle marks were found, one below each armpit, the reason unknown.

With the body of Linda Salee found in the Long Tom River two days earlier, a search of the river continued, searching for additional clues to the as yet unknown killer. Approximately 50 feet from where the fisherman first spotted Linda, a diver recovered a second female body. Unable to haul the unknown woman to the surface the diver called out for assistance, additional divers went down into the water to bring the weight to the bank. The body of Karen Sprinker had also been tied to part of a vehicle engine using electrical wiring. Dr William Brady performed the autopsy. His report indicated that her death was caused by 'traumatic asphyxiation', via a ligature of unknown origin. The red markings were still present on Karen's neck. Karen was fully clothed when found, wearing the same items that her mother had described on the day of her disappearance. But as Karen was stripped for the autopsy Dr Brady noted that Karen's bra was clearly too large for a woman of her figure. As the bra was removed, large quantities of sodden paper towels fell out. Karen's killer had removed both of her breasts after death.

Detectives Jerry Frazier and Gene Daughtrey had virtually no clues as to the killer's identity. The bodies found in the Long Tom River were both weighted down with sections of vehicle engines, suggesting a mechanic and both were tied to the components with electrical wiring, suggesting an electrician but that was not enough to work with. Therefore the detectives went back to basics, and travelled to Corvallis, Oregon where Karen Sprinker had lived during her time at the university. The detectives wanted to question other students to find out whether they had encountered any strange men recently.

One young woman came forward to tell of a man who claimed to be a Vietnam veteran and wanted some company, she had agreed. The pair chatted over a drink about general subjects, but when he got up to leave he made a comment about how it takes two people to carry a car engine and suggested she come to try. When she refused the man replied 'what do you think I'm gonna do, strangle you'. Detective Gene Daughtrey asked that if he should call again, that she should call the police.

On May 25, 1969, he called.

After a short conversation in which the admirer said he wanted to meet again, she managed to persuade him to meet in the lounge of the dorm block in an hour. As soon as the phone called ended she called the Corvallis police department, detectives B J Miller and Frenchie De Lamere went to the proposed meeting place in plain clothes and waited for this mysterious stranger. As the hour approached Jerry Brudos walked in and sat down. The detectives looked at Brudos and recognised him as fitting the description given by their informant and they got up to question him. Brudos quickly and calmly answered all queries regarding his purpose in the building; Brudos claimed he helped to tend the gardens. With no due cause to arrest him the detectives let Brudos leave, but he was added to the list of potential suspects and an investigation began into his activities.

Brudos sat and waited in the parking lot at the Portland State University on April 21, 1969 looking for his next victim. Twenty-four-year-old secretary Sharon Wood would be the unlucky choice. Sharon was feeling sick and her mind was on other things as she crossed the road heading towards her car completely unaware that she was being watched. Due to the thoughts in her head, Sharon reached where she thought her car was parked then realised that she was on the wrong level and spun around to head back to the stairs. A tap on the shoulder made her turn back around and stare straight into the eyes of Brudos. It was then that Sharon saw the gun pointed at her chest. Brudos barked out an order

'If you don't scream, I will not shoot you'.

Sharon refused, screaming at the top of her voice and began to back away. Brudos lunged at Sharon before she could get away and put his arm tightly around her neck. Despite the clear height and weight advantage that Brudos had, Sharon fought back. She grabbed at the gun, and twisted it in her attacker's hand. Brudos tried to stop Sharon screaming by placing his hand over her mouth. So Sharon bit deep onto her attacker's hand and would not let go, Brudos howled in pain as teeth gripped tightly down on his thumb. Using his strength to force Sharon to the ground, Brudos slammed her face into the ground several times. Sharon was tiring quickly. In her haze she made out the headlights of an approaching car, so she released her grip on Brudos and passed out. Brudos picked up his gun and fled from the scene. Sharon was able to describe her attacker to Portland police officers as having freckles, thinning hair and being a large man over six feet tall. Nobody linked the attack to the recent murders, until Brudos was arrested on May 30, 1969.

With Brudos a suspect in the April attack on Sharon Woods as well as a May attack on an unnamed woman, detectives had been tailing him for several days.

On May 30, 1969, Detectives Jim Stovall and Gene Daughtrey, armed with an arrest warrant, joined the unmarked car following Brudos travelling north on the I-5. At 7.28pm Detective Stovall turned on his vehicle's siren and signalled the Brudos vehicle to the side of the road. Darcie Brudos pulled over and waited for the officers to reach her door. Detective Daughtrey looked inside the car and found a concerned Darcie with her two children and in the backseat, hiding under a blanket, he found Brudos. Ordering Brudos out of the car, Detective Stovall read the Miranda rights and arrested his suspect. At the Salem police station Brudos was fingerprinted, photographed and given overalls to wear. As he changed, the detectives exchanged glances and smirks because Brudos revealed he was wearing women's panties as he stripped off his clothes.

Detective Jim Stovall sat opposite Jerry Brudos in the interview room. The initial chat centred on formal information – name, address etc. It ended with Brudos being led back to his cell. Several hours later Brudos and Detective Stovall sat at opposite sides of the table, but despite Stovall touching on the disappearances of the young women, Brudos continually refused to discuss the case but Stovall was a patient man and the interview ended for the time being.

Later Brudos made a phone call to his wife. He explained that he needed her to destroy some items from his workshop. Brudos had always refused Darcie access into his secret place, but now he needed her to go in and destroy a box of women's clothes and another box that contained photographs. Darcie replied saying that she would do so, but instead as soon as the phone call ended Darcie called attorney Dale Drake who told her not to touch them as she may be incriminated. So Darcie gathered a case, threw clothes in it and drove to her mother's house taking her two children with her.

Back at the Salem police station, Brudos asked to speak to Detective Stovall again, but this time it was Brudos who wanted to ask the questions, particularly about what the police knew. As Stovall discussed the clothing, Brudos jumped in and asked if any of the clothing on the bodies was out of place. Stovall believed that his suspect was talking about Karen Sprinker's bra being too large for her body, but for the moment he let it go. Brudos began to mention his love for shoes and how he would steal shoes from women. Stovall asked Brudos how he stole the shoes. The reply came as a confession. Brudos admitted to sneaking into a woman's apartment in Portland and raping her before taking her shoes. Stovall sat stoically in his seat as he didn't want Brudos to stop talking so soon after he had admitted to a rape.

Detective Stovall asked another question

> 'Did anything else happen in Portland?'

Brudos's reply came as another confession. Linda Slawson disappeared on January 26, 1968. Brudos began by describing exactly what she was wearing on the day she vanished after knocking on Brudos' door selling encyclopaedias. He went on to describe how he threw her dead body from a bridge into the Williamette River after tying Linda to a car engine. Brudos calmly added that prior to disposing of Linda's body, he took a hacksaw and cut off the left foot and kept it for a few days trying various shoes on the severed limb.

Stovall sat back taking the story in, but Brudos hadn't finished talking yet. He was now confessing to all his crimes. Brudos began telling how he picked up Jan Whitney in November 1968 and strangled her in his car with a thin strip of leather before taking the body home to his workshop. It was there that Jan was hung from the rafters, Brudos returning to the workshop occasionally to have sex with the body. Brudos continued to tell Stovall how he disposed of the body into the Williamette River, this time weighing it down with scrap iron. The subject of Karen Sprinker was next, Brudos described how he went up to Karen in the stairwell of the car park at the Meier and Frank department store and pointed a gun at her, forcing the young woman to get into his car. At his workshop Brudos raped Karen before putting a noose round her neck and hung her.

Finally Brudos ended his confession with the murder of Linda Salee, as with other victims he strangled the young woman using a thin leather strap before raping the body in his workshop. This time however, Brudos went one step further. He told Stovall that after hanging Linda from the rafters he performed electrical experiments on her before throwing the body it into the Long Tom River.

In total, Brudos was interviewed for two days, and ended with him being charged on June 2 for only one offence, the murder of Karen Sprinker. The following day officers entered the Brudos home in Center Street, Salem and in the attic officers found locked chests that contained a large quantity of women's shoes. In another, a significant amount of freshly laundered ladies underwear was found. In the workshop, hooks were found in the ceiling on a pulley. A locked toolbox was opened revealing large quantities of photographs, several photographs had a nude woman hanging from a hook, and it proved later to be Jan Whitney. Pictures of Karen Sprinker were also among the pile. One of the photographs did give officers something they did want to see, in the corner of one of the 'victim' pictures was Brudos himself caught in a mirror holding the camera.

With Brudos currently charged on only one count of murder, that of Karen Sprinker in March 1969, he and his defence team lead by George Rutin appeared in Judge Sopers courtroom for his arraignment on June 4, 1969. When asked 'how do you plead?' Brudos gave his reply as ' not guilty and not guilty by reason of insanity'. This same plea was followed on June 13 after Brudos was charged with two further murders, that of Jan Whitney and Linda Salee. Due to the insanity plea, Brudos was required to undergo psychiatric examination to determine his state of mind. Seven different examiners would independently interview Brudos. He talked candidly about his life, his marriage to Darcie and the murders. Brudos asked for help during the interviews so he could live a normal life. After the interviews were completed, the psychiatric report read that Brudos was 'an antisocial personality with sadistic tendencies', but in their opinion Brudos was of a sane mind.

The defence team, after hearing the results of the psychiatric analysis, spoke with Brudos about its implications. This discussion resulted in a return to the courtroom on June 27, 1969. Defence lawyer Dale Drake made the announcement that, in the three murder charges against his client, his plea of not guilty by reason of insanity was changed to a plea of guilty. After confirming that Brudos understood the implications of his decision, Judge Sopers found him guilty of three murders and sentenced him to a maximum sentence of life to be served at Oregon State Penitentiary.

For Darcie however the nightmare had not yet ended. On July 17, 1969, Detectives Jim Stovall and B J Miller arrived at Darcie's mother's house, where she had stayed since moving from the Brudos home. Authorities took the two children away to become wards of the court while an investigation of Darcie took place. The investigation centred on Darcie's role in the murders., This was because of a woman named Edna Beecham, the sister of a neighbour of the Brudos'. She had recently told police that during the afternoon of March 27 she witnessed both Darcie and Jerome Brudos guiding a woman from the workshop into their home from a window at her sister's house. The woman had a blanket over her head but she could see a gag in her mouth. The date suggested that the unknown woman was Karen Sprinker. Darcie would plead her innocence and despite her husband admitting that Darcie had no knowledge of his crimes, the case went to trial in September 1969. At the trial, the statements that Edna gave were proved not to be completely true. Darcie's defence lawyer, Charlie Burt, presented photographs taken from the window where Edna claimed she witnessed the scene. The photographs clearly proved that Edna could not have seen what she had claimed as the view was permanently blocked by large trees. The jury agreed and after deliberating for a little under four hours Darcie Brudos was acquitted of aiding and abetting in the murder of Karen Sprinker on October 2, 1969.

Darcie's marriage with her husband ended in divorce in August 1970.

Butcher of Kingsbury Run

The first indication of a killer at large occurred on September 5, 1934. Cleveland carpenter, Frank La Gossie, was making a morning stroll along Euclid Beach, Cleveland. Whilst watching the waters drift in and out, Frank spotted what he assumed to be driftwood stuck in the sand and went to get a closer look. Approaching the object, Frank recoiled in horror at the remains of a human body. The body was taken to Cuyahoga County morgue for an examination conducted by coroner Arthur J Pearse. The remains proved to be the lower torso of a female severed at the knees and the waist. The coroner concluded that the body had been in the water for at least three months and that the woman had been dead for at least six months.

The next day, after reading about the discovery of the remains, Joseph Hedjuk contacted Cleveland authorities to tell them of a discovery he had made two weeks earlier. He had found body parts which he buried assuming them to be animal remains. Joseph guided Cleveland police officers back to the 'burial site' where the upper half of a woman's torso, without head or arms, was uncovered. Coroner Pearse was able to determine that the two halves of the torso came from the same woman. A further search of the waters at Euclid Beach uncovered part of an upper arm, but no more body parts were recovered and the victim was not identified.

A little over a year later on September 23, 1935 two school friends, James Wagner and Peter Kostura were playing on an area of the Kingsbury Run known locally as Jackass Hill. Racing to the bottom of the hillside, James spotted an unusual object partially hidden in the weeds and decided to investigate. Clearing the weeds for a better view, James froze then shouted to Peter about the dead body he had found. The pair ran home, and the police were called. Sergeant Arthur Marsh and Officer Arthur Stitt arrived on the scene and quickly found the naked and headless body of a white male that had also been castrated. A brief search of the immediate vicinity revealed a second body found in a similar condition to the first. A continued search unearthed the heads and genitals of both victims.

Coroner Pearse performed the autopsy, his report indicating that the first body found, that of a young man, had only been dead for 2-3 days. The head had been cut off with a very sharp knife between the 3rd and 4th vertebrae. Coroner Pearse noted that decapitation was the cause of death. Fingerprints taken identified the victim as twenty-eight-year-old Edward Andrassy, who worked as an orderly at the City Hospital in Cleveland. Authorities learnt that Edward was last seen on September 19. The second body found at Jackass Hill was that of an older man, whom Coroner Pearse believed was also killed by decapitation and had been dead for two weeks, but in this case his identity could not be established. No clues to the killer(s) could be found and the investigation ran cold. In December 1935, Elliott Ness had arrived in Cleveland to take up the post of 'Director of Public Safety' with the task of cleaning up corruption within the city police force.

In January 1936 the unknown killer returned.

On Sunday January 26, 1936 at 11.00am a woman walked out onto the street to investigate the cause of a dog's continual barking. At 2315 East 26th Street she found a dog leashed to a lamppost trying to reach an unattended basket. Believing the basket contained some meat, the woman contacted the local butcher, Charles Paige. Worried that his shop had been burgled Charles raced to the scene, peered into the basket and found a human arm, wrapped in the previous days' newspapers. Fingerprints identified the arm as belonging to forty-one-year-old prostitute Florence Polillo. A police investigation would only conclude that her last known movements would end two days earlier on January 24. Further body parts of the unfortunate Florence were found in the rear yard of an abandoned house on February 7, the parts recovered would include the upper torso, the lower legs and the left arm. No further parts were found. Coroner Pearse wrote in his autopsy report that Florence had probably been killed by decapitation and that the body had been divided after rigormortis. Again no clues to the killer or killer's motive or identity were discovered.

On June 5, 1936, two black youths discovered a pair of trousers in a neat bundle beneath a bush less than a mile from Jackass Hill. Hoping that they might be lucky enough to find money in the pockets, one of the boys unravelled the trousers and uncovered a severed head. The boys ran home and told their mother of their discovery who in turn called the police. The next day railroad workers on the Kingsbury Run discovered a male headless body less than a quarter of a mile from where the two boys found the head. Coroner Pearse determined that the two parts belonged to the same person. Despite fingerprints being taken the victim remained nameless, although authorities believed that the victim was a vagrant. Coroner Pearse believed that the head had been removed while the victim was still alive and had occurred two days prior to being found.

By July, authorities had five victims and no clues to the identity of the killer and on July 22 that figure rose to six victims.

In a West Cleveland woodland, a female hiker through the woods when she came across the naked, decomposing body of a headless man. Police officers at the scene recovered the skull of the victim ten feet away. The victim, again believed to be a vagrant, was not identified. Coroner Pearse concluded that the victim had been killed during May 1936 at the location where the body was found.

Throughout The Depression, vagrants would regularly travel the country using the railroad to get from city to city looking for somewhere to stay. Jerry Harris was one such person. On September 10, 1936, Jerry was waiting alongside the Kingsbury Run for a train that would take him away from Cleveland. Moving towards the next boxcar that came his way, Jerry tripped over the upper torso of a human body minus its head and arms. Horrified by his discovery, Jerry ran from the torso and found Leo Fields, a railroad clerk, who called the police. A police search of the area resulted in the recovery of the lower half of the torso cut at the knees; officers believed that the two sections had come from the nearby sewer, which emptied into a pool. The pool and sewer were searched but no further body parts were found.

Coroner Pearse took on the task of identifying the victim and determined that it was the body of a young man in his 20's and had been dead for two days. The head had been cut cleanly from the body and there was little blood present in the heart that indicated that the decapitation was a likely cause of death. As with the previous male victims, he had been castrated. With seven similar victims, Cleveland police now believed they had a string of murders all committed by the same unknown person or persons.

Paranoia began to grip the citizens of Cleveland; suspicious characters were frequently reported to police. The railroad workers began patrolling in pairs, the number of hobos in and around Cleveland was noticeably smaller. Cleveland newspapers began referring to the unknown killer as 'The Mad Butcher'; 'Phantom of Kingsbury Run' as the murders appeared to end.

On February 23, 1937, near the scene of the first discovery at Euclid Beach, Robert Smith had been collecting driftwood when he came across what he thought was a dead animal, in fact it was the upper half of a female torso, again minus head and arms. Coroner Strauss, who had recently replaced Coroner Pearse, performed the autopsy. As with previous victims, the body had been cleanly severed with no hacking of limbs, although in this case, the cause of death could not be established. Coroner Strauss determined that the yet to be identified woman had been in the water for two days and had died up to forty-eight hours prior to that.

More than two months later on May 5, 1937 the lower torso surfaced in the waters of Lake Erie, but again no further clues to the victim or killer were found.

Russell Tower was making his way home along the Cuyahoga River on the afternoon of June 6, 1937. Amongst the rocks by the waters edge, Russell found a human skull and called the police. A police search of the area revealed a sack, near the skull, which contained parts of a skeleton without arm or leg bones. The victim appeared to have been left undiscovered for approximately one year, a newspaper dated June 5, 1936 also in the sack helped the estimated date, however it was misleading. A check and subsequent investigation on the teeth tentatively identified the victim as forty-one-year-old Rose Wallace who had vanished on August 21, 1936.

A month later on July 6, another victim was found, this time by a national guardsman on patrol on the West Third Street Bridge in Cleveland. At 5.30 am the guardsman spotted an object floating in the Cuyahoga River below. Looking at the object closely, he realised he was looking at the lower half of a male torso. As police officers arrived at the scene, more body parts began to float to the surface including the left leg, in halves, the upper section of the torso and the right thigh. Two hundred and fifty feet from the bridge police located the upper left arm.

The next morning, the search continued and police recovered both forearms including the hands. Further parts were found over the next week including the right upper arm, the lower right leg and foot. Although Elliott Ness and his "Untouchables" were continuing to bring crime levels down in Cleveland, The Butcher of Kingsbury Run continued to commit his crimes without leaving clues.

Ten months later on May 2, 1938, Albert Hahaffy, the West Third Street Bridge tender, spotted 2 canvas sacks floating in the river. He dragged the sacks to the shore and looked inside; Albert found the two halves of a female torso and a left foot. However, as with recent victims, the female victim would not be identified. By now Cleveland detectives were highly frustrated, Cleveland citizens were claiming a cover up and doctors were being questioned because of the apparent precision with which limbs were removed. Yet still police had no suspects and no clues.

In Cleveland's North Street, substantial building work was underway throughout the summer of 1938, with many buildings having a facelift. It was here on the afternoon of August 16, that twenty-one-year-old James Dawson and two friends discovered the bloody remains of a female torso. During the police search of the area, officers found the head wrapped in paper a few metres from the torso, further away a large cardboard box contained the arms and legs wrapped in a neat package.

As the evening wore on, spectators at the scene made a second discovery. Todd Bartholomew and his wife had been watching the police search the area for some time, when they noticed a stench emanating from a nearby pile of rubbish. Todd went to investigate the source. He moved some trash to one side and uncovered a pile of bones. Officers raced over to search the remainder of the pile, recovering over 40 bones including the skull.

The next day, Coroner Gerber began his examination of the latest victims. His report indicated that he believed the corpse was approximately six months old and had been dumped at the building site up to three weeks earlier. Fingerprint checks were done but again the identity would remain unknown. In addition, the incomplete second skeleton found at the same dumpsite also remained unknown.

Two days after the latest finds, Elliott Ness ordered numerous raids on the 'homes' of vagrants and hobos throughout Cleveland in the hope of finding the Mad Butcher or even catching him in the act, but the raids were unsuccessful. However, Elliott Ness could claim some success, as no more torsos were found. On December 26, 1938, a letter arrived at Central Station, allegedly from the killer. Postmarked Los Angeles and dated December 21, 1938, the letter claims that he had moved to California. Authorities dismissed the letter as a crank.

By spring of 1939 only one detective, Peter Merylo, remained on the case. He discovered that the sheriff's department frustrated with the lack of closure on the case had employed a private investigator, Lawrence

'Pat' Lyons, to look at the case on their behalf. After nine months of work, Pat Lyons had found a clue. He discovered that three of the victims, Edward Andrassy, Florence Polillo and Rose Wallace were all visitors at a tavern located at the corner of East Twentieth and Central.

Over several weeks, Pat became a regular at the tavern, talking to employees and their customers about the murders; several would tell of a man called Frank Dolezal who frequented the bar. Pat discovered that Dolezal had worked in a slaughterhouse, had a violent temper and more importantly had been seen with Florence Polillo. Soon Pat discovered where Frank Dolezal lived and managed to get inside the apartment. Pat noticed a dark stain on the floor, which, when analysed, was determined to be blood. However, more evidence was required before an arrest could be made.

Further investigations took place into the background of Frank Dolezal. His neighbours admitted that both Florence Polillo and Rose Wallace had been seen with Dolezal and also believed that Edward Andrassy was also a regular at Dolezal's home.

Deputy Sheriff John Gillespie arrested Dolezal on July 5, 1939. Two days later the sheriff's department announced that Dolezal had signed a confession admitting his guilt in the murder of Florence Polillo.

Dolezal's confession stated he had hit Florence with his fist, smacked her head into the porcelain bath, and then used a knife to cut off her arms and legs. With the arrest and subsequent confession in place, everyone in Cleveland was satisfied that the case was closed and Dolezal was officially charged with the murder of Florence Polillo on July 11.

However, despite the evidence that authorities collected in the remaining murders, Dolezal denied any involvement and refused to discuss them. Further questioning cast doubts on his confession. Dolezal's tale of where he dumped Florence's body was inconsistent with police reports and the timing of the murder was inconsistent with Coroner Pearse's report. In light of these discrepancies, the Sheriff's department announced that Dolezal had changed his confession. This made Detective Merylo suspicious of the methods employed to gain the confession, Merylo believed that the Sheriff's department fed Dolezal the facts of the case, as they understood them.

Dolezal was officially discounted as having any involvement with any other of the 'torso' murders. Coroner Gerber countered this by stating that the same person committed all the murders and that if the Sheriff's department did not believe that Dolezal committed any of the remaining murders then by default he was not responsible for the murder of Florence Polillo. On July 12, 1939 Dolezal was granted Fred Soukop as his defence counsel. Immediately after his first visit, Fred announced that his client had fully retracted his confession and complained about mistreatment during questioning. Fred Soukop requested that the 'blood stain' found in his clients property be re-examined. Pathologist Dr Enrique Ecker announced that the stain was not blood, a point that severely damaged the case against Frank Dolezal. The sole murder charge was reduced to manslaughter during a preliminary hearing on July 17.

On August 24, 1939, Sheriffs Hugh Crawford and Adolph Schuster were assigned to the supervision of Frank Dolezal. During visiting hours at the county jail, the two sheriffs would take turns in prisoner supervision and visitor escorting. After three minutes away from the prisoner, Sheriff Crawford returned to Dolezal's cell to find him hanging, using rags as a noose. Despite efforts to revive him, Frank Dolezal was dead.

Coroner Gerber reported that the death was suicide and hence no autopsy was required. The relatives of Frank Dolezal were not happy and insisted on an autopsy and an inquiry into his death. The principle question they wanted answered was how a man of 5'8" could hang himself from a hook 5'7" off the ground. After the autopsy Coroner Gerber stated that asphyxiation was the cause of death, however Gerber also stated that Dolezal must have been hanging for 12–15 minutes, clearly well above the three minutes claimed by Sheriff Hugh Crawford. In addition, Gerber wrote that Dolezal suffered six fractured ribs a month before his death, thereby backing up Frank's claims of brutality during questioning, a charge the sheriff again denied. The inquest into the death of Frank Dolezal solved nothing and the "Kingsbury Run Torso Murders" remain officially unsolved.

C

Ricardo Caputo

Ricardo Caputo was born in 1949 in Mendoza, Argentina, the second son of Alberto and Alicia, his mother left the family home when he was young. Caputo claimed his father beat him and that several men had raped him at a young age. At age seventeen Caputo voluntarily committed himself to Mendoza Psychiatric Hospital where he was diagnosed as psychopathic.

Yet he was released and allowed to roam free as a danger to himself and others.

Natalie Brown met Caputo during November 1970. She worked in a Manhattan bank as a cashier when Caputo struck up a conversation with her during a visit to make a deposit. After a few more 'chance' meetings in the bank, Natalie asked Caputo for a date, he agreed. Several months later, the couple went on vacation together to Puerto Rico, on their return to the USA, they decided not to live in New York but instead relocated to San Francisco. Soon Caputo asked Natalie to marry him (his temporary visa was running out) but it was around this time that Natalie began to have doubts about her fiancée and his deteriorating behaviour.

According to Caputo's confession, on July 30, 1971 the pair had retired to the bedroom with Caputo wanting to make love, but Natalie rejected his advances. Caputo continued to pressure Natalie, so she left the room and headed downstairs to the kitchen. Caputo was incensed. In the kitchen, Natalie continued to reject Caputo's advances, so he grabbed a long bladed kitchen knife and stabbed his fiancée again and again. Natalie dropped to the floor in a pool of blood. Dropping the knife, Caputo put his hands around Natalie's throat and squeezed until she was dead. Panicking, Caputo fled the house but he soon realised that he didn't know what to do. He walked into a gas station, went to the public phone and called 911. As soon as police arrived Caputo told them what he had done and was immediately arrested. At the trial Caputo was declared incompetent to stand trial and sent to a mental hospital.

In Autumn 1973, at the Matteawan Hospital for the Criminally Insane, twenty-five-year-old Judith Becker was assigned to the case. Under her guidance Caputo was transferred to the lower security Manhattan State Hospital, where Judith continued to work on his case.

Soon Judith was given permission to take Caputo outside the facility on day release, due to Caputo's perfect behaviour at the hospital. After a number of outings, the pair soon became lovers and the relationship continued until the Summer of 1974 when Judith decided to end it. She felt Caputo was becoming more unreliable and more unpredictable. He began turning up at her apartment unexpectedly or phoning her in the middle of the night for no reason. Judith also believed that Caputo was getting dangerous.

During October 1974, Judith and Caputo were quarrelling in their apartment when Caputo threw Judith on the bed, jumped on top of her and punch her repeatedly in the face and head, breaking her nose and cheekbones. Grabbing a stocking from a bedside table drawer, Caputo slipped it around Judith's neck twisted it and pulled until she was dead. Again, Caputo fled the scene of the crime taking Judith's money and car. The following day, Judith was found dead by her parents who had come to visit.

By Easter 1977, Barbara Taylor had thought she had gotten ex-boyfriend, Caputo out of her life, but he called her from San Francisco airport asking for a place to stay. She reluctantly agreed, picking him up from the airport and taking him home. That evening, Barbara once again rejected Caputo's advances and told him to get out of her life - he was gone that night. However, two days later Caputo returned to her house and beat and kicked Barbara to death. Her father found her body the next day during a visit.

In September 1977, twenty-three-year-old Laura Gomez was Caputo's next victim. Caputo picked Laura up from her family home to take her to Mexico City for a karate exhibition they had planned to see together. However, Caputo took Laura to his apartment where he viciously beat her. He burnt Laura's body with cigarettes before he finally ended Laura's life by crashing a steel bar into her skull no less than 10 times.

On January 21, 1994 Caputo visited lawyer Mario Luquez and confessed his crimes. Caputo requested that he be sent to a mental hospital in New York. At his arraignment Caputo's lawyer, Michael Kennedy, requested that his client be given 'psychiatric medication' in order to control his schizophrenia. The request was granted and Caputo was led away from the court in chains.

Caputo appeared on American television station ABC after his arraignment. The interviewer, Chris Wallace, questioned Caputo on his motives for murdering Natalie Brown and then confessing. Caputo talked candidly about killing Natalie saying he was not really aware of what he was doing.

The next day Caputo was again in court, this time to determine if he was competent enough to stand trial for murder. The court ordered a psychiatric examination of Caputo. The court-appointed psychiatrist examined Caputo and indicated that Caputo was feigning his illness and was competent to stand trial. Caputo changed his plea to guilty and Judge Dunne sentenced Caputo to serve up to twenty-five years in prison.

At his second trial for the murder of Judith Becker, Caputo was sentenced to a further twenty-five years in prison to run consecutively with the sentence received for the murder of Natalie Brown.

In October 1997, Caputo died of a heart attack in the prison yard, a mere two years into his jail term.

Douglas Clark and Carol Bundy
Carol

Carol Bundy, was born Carol Mary Peters on August 26, 1942, to Charles and Gladys Peters. Carol was an unattractive and awkward child, unable to live up to her mother's expectations. At the age of eight, for some reason unknown to Carol, Gladys cut her off completely. Carol came home from school one day to find herself locked out of the house. Despite her tears and pleas to be allowed in, Gladys told her to go away because she wasn't her little girl anymore. It was only the intervention of her father that changed Gladys's mind. Carol was allowed to come home, but from that day onwards Carol's mother treated her as if she didn't exist.

Carol learnt at an early age to ignore the beatings inflicted on her by her mother. Once she sat and read a book while Gladys beat her severely around the face and body with a belt. By refusing to acknowledge the pain, she was able to remain in control of the situation. Carol had already discovered the superior position of being the victim who forgave the weaknesses of her abuser, a position in which she would learn to thrive.

Though she preferred to paint a glowing picture of her father, the truth was far from her ideals. When her mother died suddenly, her father told Carol and her sister, that they had to take their mother's place in the matrimonial bed. During the years that the abuse continued, Carol took to running naked through the streets and used her sexual promiscuity to her own advantage, to feel the affection she craved, if only for a brief period of time.

The beatings from her father grew worse over time and he even attempted to kill the entire family, including his new wife, but Carol got the gun away from him after he had killed the family cat. The girls were shipped off to foster homes and grandparents before Charles went and got his daughters back.

To escape her father's clutches, at the age of seventeen, Carol married a fifty-four-year-old man, Leonard, but soon left him because he was a drunkard and had wanted her to prostitute herself.

Soon after she had left Leonard she met Richard Geis, a thirty-two-year-old writer of pornography and science fiction. He had found her to be a convenient companion, with a pathetic eagerness to please. Believing her to be an intelligent and witty woman, Geis encouraged her to pursue her writing talents. She wrote a short story, which was published, that gave her the confidence to write a novel but stopped after writing only twelve pages.

In 1962, Carol's father Charles hung himself. Carol believed she was to blame for his death and the abuse she and her sister had endured. This victim role saw Carol abuse herself in sexual relationships. She moved between both female and male lovers, but soon returned to security with Richard.

However, when he found out she was sleeping with men for money, he was furious but decided to help her by sending her to nursing school. She graduated as valedictorian and began nursing in 1968. Life looked liked it was beginning to settle down for Carol.

But it was short lived.

She soon met Grant Bundy, a fellow nurse, and together they had two children, which did nothing to help the relationship. Grant was just like her father and beat and belittled her constantly until Carol took the kids and escaped to a shelter for women. Grant had become unbearable. Carol's poor eyesight deteriorated until he had to look after the children. In January 1979, she fled again with her two boys to a home for battered women.

After a short period she moved with her sons to Valerio Gardens apartment house in Van Nuys, a suburb in the San Fernando Valley. There she made friends with the managers of the complex, Jeanette and John "Jack" Murray. Jack was a known "lad", his wife was well aware of his philandering, but saw no threat in the thirty-eight-year-old dumpy woman with extremely thick glasses. She in fact was more than keen for her husband to help the single mother who was down on her luck. She felt no problems with Jack being called to Carol's apartment often to fix things, or when he drove her to appointments or the Social Security Office.

Jack however, found Carol to be a captive audience for his stories. She enjoyed hearing about his time in Vietnam and his old home in Australia. Carol also let Jack know how the men in her life had treated her and he was sympathetic. She fell in love with the suave man and made sure she always had his favourite beer stocked in the fridge. Soon the two became lovers. Carol was always calling Jack to her apartment to do odd jobs because her eyesight was failing. Sometimes Jack would call her to one of the vacant apartments for sex, or they would have sex in his van on the way to her appointments., However, sex consisted mainly of oral sex rather than intercourse.

Jack helped her to find out more about benefits and entitlements to which she had access and also suggested she seek a second opinion on her failing eyesight. Carol found out her blindness could be reversed through surgery. She confused his help and sex with love, and imagined a life with Jack, but he told her it would be years before he could leave Jeanette.

After the eye operation, Carol could see again but her self-image was different to the fat and ugly woman she saw staring back at her from the mirror Carol knew that Jack felt something for her and any woman would be envious. She also received $25,000 from the sale of the home she had shared with her ex-husband. She spent some of it on furniture and other things for her and the children, but she also bought Jack a new VCR and desk for the office. To try and keep Jack for herself, she opened a joint account with him and deposited $13,000.

Jack told Carol he couldn't leave Jeanette as she had been diagnosed with cancer so Carol gladly handed over $10,000 to Jack to help. When this didn't make his commitment any stronger, she attempted to make him jealous by having an affair with Jeanette's younger brother Warren.

When that failed to enhance Jack's commitment to her, she planned a romantic trip for the two of them to Las Vegas. But there he left her alone and only came back when it was time to return home. Carol had deliberately left her bag in Jack's car, to try and split the married couple up which caused an uproar between Jeanette and Carol on their return home. Later when Carol brought up the subject of Jeanette's cancer, she was shocked to hear that she had never had cancer. The money had been used to pay off Jack's van.

Carol offered Jeanette $1500 to leave Jack, but the plan backfired when Jeanette told her husband and Jack told Carol to get out of his life.

She didn't want to believe this was happening to her and went to the Little Nashville Club, in the hope that Jack would be there. He was, looking adoringly into the eyes of his wife. Carol knew it was over.

But it was only the beginning for her new life.

Standing in the corner of the same club, smiling at her was Doug Clark. The handsome blond man came over to Carol they spent the evening dancing. Carol had never met such a gentleman before. Doug promised to call her again and she looked forward to their next meeting.

Doug

Doug Clark was born on May 10, 1948 in Pennsylvania where his father Franklyn was stationed in the Navy. He was the third son of five children. The family moved often with the Navy. Including a time in India, living like royalty with servants and maids.

Later, Doug and his brother Walter were sent to Ecolat, the International School in Geneva attended by the children of UN Diplomats, international celebrities and European and Middle-Eastern royalty. Unlike his brother Walt, who was popular and outgoing, Doug was considered sullen and arrogant and made few friends. He did not do well with his studies as he couldn't be bothered doing the work or completing assignments. Doug Clark claimed that he had developed his preference for kinky sex while living in Geneva.

Despite the fact that Doug's parents had been called to the school on a number of occasions because of his bad behaviour, they claimed that Doug had never shown any signs of behavioural problems as a child. After his expulsion, sixteen-year-old Doug was sent to Culver Military Academy in Indiana. Although rather intelligent, Doug was happy to scrape through his schooling with minimal effort.

Whether people wanted to hear it or not, Doug would often brag of outrageous sexual exploits with the town girls to anyone within earshot.

Like most teenage boys, Doug and his classmates were obsessed with teenage girls and the fantasy of sex, but for Doug it was much more than fantasy. He would often bring a girl to his room where he would record their moans and groans as he had sex with them. He would then replay the tapes to his classmates, revelling in their obvious jealousy.

In 1967, at the age of nineteen, Clark graduated from Culver and went to live with his parents who were now retired and living in Yosemite. When he was drafted, he enlisted in the Air Force in radio intelligence to ensure that he would not end up in the front line in the Vietnam War.

After an honourable discharge from the Air Force, Doug decided to move to Mexico. With $5,000 in his pocket, he headed south but stopped when he got to Van Nuys. In Van Nuys he moved in with his sister Carol Ann, and her abusive husband.

At twenty-four he met twenty-seven-year-old Beverley in a North Hollywood bar. Beverley, blonde and heavy, saw herself as fat and ugly but found that Doug, with his big dreams and ambitions, would always try to boost her confidence. In 1972 the couple married.

However their plans were not to succeed. Anytime they got a little ahead with money, Doug would blow their savings, so their marriage began to waiver. As Beverly gained more and more weight during their marriage, Doug spent less and less time at home, preferring to go to bars.

In 1976, four years after they were married, Doug and Beverly separated and later divorced, although they remained close friends.

Doug began working at the Jergen's factory in 1979. His duties as stationary engineer required him to tend to the large boiler. He was lucky to get the job after the poor reference he had received from his previous job.

In 1980 he set fire to his car outside the Jergen's factory, while he was working night shift, in order to claim the insurance.

When he met Carol he had found he had a talent for making unattractive and fat women feel good about themselves. This he used to his own advantage, getting free rent, food and sex.

So when Doug invited himself to Carol's for dinner a few nights after their first meeting. Carol was a little apprehensive but glad he had called.

That evening, after the children were in bed, the two of them made love. Carol recalls it was the most tender and beautiful feelings she had ever experienced; Doug had whispered to her how attractive she was and seem to enjoy the entire experience.

It was time for Doug to begin his rouse. Carol woke to find Doug staring at her, perplexed. He asked her if could he stay for a while as he was having problems with his landlady. She happily obliged, though she was still in love with Jack Murray.

When She moved to a two bedroom apartment a few miles away, Jack helped her to move her things, then came around for sex up to three times a week. While Carol accepted this as genuine friendship, he used this as an opportunity to get her to buy him things he had needed.

But Carol also had plans of her own, Jack and Doug hated each other immediately and Carol played them against each other. Doug won out, when he proved to treat her better than Jack ever did. But Doug was also self-centred and spent a lot of time talking about himself. But Carol did not seem to mind;, their lovemaking made up for any other inadequacies Doug may have had.

After a while the couple began to discuss, in lurid detail, their sexual fantasies, Doug would describe how he wanted to get a girl and keep her bound as his sex slave, and Carol would encourage his fantasies with her own about bondage and torture. Soon the fantasies went further and the couple would describe killing a woman, Doug reinforced his psychological grip on Carol by making her say that she would kill to prove her love for him.

But Doug also liked his freedom and often would leave and come back as he pleased. After a time, Carol grew a little bored with his behaviour and answered an advertisement from a man looking for marriage. The man, Art Pollinger, was the antithesis of Jack and Doug; he was unattractive and overweight, but he was kind to Carol and soon she told him of the abuse she suffered from Jack and Doug. She also told Art about the cash deposit box she shared with Jack. Art got her to immediately go and close the account, only to find that Jack had already taken over $6000 from it.

The relationship with Art failed to succeed, Carol was a woman who was used to the emotional abuse and torment of the relationships she had had. The care and love she received from Art did not satisfy her. She was soon back with Doug. Doug convinced Carol to buy a big station wagon when she got her licence and he also convinced her to buy a gun for protection. The two of them went together and purchased two .25 calibre Raven automatics. Doug said they needed to use her name as he had been jailed for robbery years earlier. It was a lie, but to Carol it made him more exciting.

The Murders
Carol was completely under Doug's spell and the man used it to his advantage. Even when Doug told her he no longer wanted to have sex with her, she did not mind. Doug had recently suffered erectile problems anyway. She would often sit in the car, while Doug had prostitutes attempt to stimulate him with oral sex, mostly without success.

Doug still came and went as he pleased, moving in with other girlfriends for a time, before coming back to Carol, who graciously took him back each time. In 1980 Carol gave custody of her children over to their father and began looking for a new apartment closer to where Doug worked in the hope of winning him back permanently.

Soon the couple were cemented together in a frenzy of sex and murder.

On Wednesday June 11 1980, Clark was cruising through the sunset strip in Los Angeles in his Blue Buick. A gun that was registered to Carole was tucked down the side of the driver's seat. Doug spotted sixteen-year-old Cindy Chandler and her fifteen-year-old stepsister Gina Marano sitting on a bench by the roadside. The Buick pulled up to the kerbside next to them and after chatting to the girls briefly, Doug enticed them into his car. The two girls got in; Cindy in the front and Gina in the back.

Clark drove the car to a secluded parking lot and persuaded Cindy to perform oral sex on him. Unimpressed with her efforts, Clark pulled out his gun, pointed it at Gina in the back and fired. The bullet stuck her in the head above her left ear. Cindy, hearing the gunshot looked up and was also shot in the head. However the two girls were not yet dead, so Clark fired again hitting Gina in the heart and Cindy again in the head, killing them both. Clark drove the car back home with the girls inside and parked the Buick in the garage where he raped the girls' dead bodies.

Later that night, Clark took pictures of the girls before driving to the Ventura Freeway Forest Lawn exit ramp where he dumped the bodies of Cindy and Gina down the embankment.

The next day, a highway worker found the bodies of Cindy and Gina. The scene was a short distance from where the body of Yolanda Washington was found on October 18, 1977 after being murdered by the Hillside Stranglers

Clark could not stop talking about the murders with Carol Bundy and spent the next week trying to persuade her to join him in his next murder hunt.

On June 20, Clark's plan was underway. A prostitute by the name of Cathy was standing near Hughes Market on Highland Avenue in Hollywood, when Clark called her over to his car. He craved oral sex and so Cathy got into the front seat next to Clark. Bundy sat in the back with the gun hidden. The trio drove to a secluded area and after a few minutes, Bundy got the gun ready, but couldn't shoot. Clark grabbed the gun and as Cathy looked up she was shot in the head. She was thrown into the backseat and Clark drove away. When they reached a country lane by the Magic Mountain Amusement Park, they dumped Cathy's naked body.

On June 24, 1980, Clark was again circling the Sunset Strip looking for prostitutes, when he soon spotted two women on a corner. He paused and waited until the two drifted apart before deciding which one to take. Exxie Wilson was a twenty-four-year-old prostitute who had arrived in Los Angeles earlier that week. Clark asked for oral sex, and Exxie got into the car. Clark drove off to a secluded road and as Exxie began to fellate Clark, he pulled out his gun and fired it into the back of her head. Clark proceeded to drag her body out of the car to the waste ground nearby. He then returned to the car and picked up the 'kill bag' that he and Bundy had prepared earlier that day. The 'kill bag' contained items that Clark and Bundy felt they might need including knives, paper towels, cleaning fluid and rubber gloves. With the dead Exxie now out of the car, Clark took his Buck knife and hacked off her head, placed it in a plastic bag and put it in the boot of the car.

Clark became concerned that the second prostitute, originally standing with Exxie on the corner, might remember him, so he went looking for her. Circling around the block, he found the twenty-four-year-old Karen Jones, a close friend of Exxie. The pair had travelled together from Little Rock to Los Angeles. As soon as she got into Clark's car he shot her in the back of the head and threw the body on the roadside near the Burbank studios where she was found at 3.08am.

Two days later on June 26, 1980 Clark and Bundy left their home to dispose of Exxie's head. Bundy had cleaned the head and placed it in a wooden box. After about half an hour of driving, Clark finally decided on the location; an alley near Hoffman Street. The next morning Jonathon Caravello found the wooden box, looked inside and discovered Exxie's head looking back at him.

Clark revealed to Bundy his other murder fantasies; he wanted to use a sniper rifle to shoot drivers on the freeway and he also wanted to raid a Mexican restaurant and kill everyone inside. Thankfully, the fantasies never came to fruition.

By July 1980, the pair argued constantly and Bundy blamed herself. On July 29, she attempted suicide by injecting herself with 1250 units of insulin and 200 milligrams of Librium. She then telephoned her place of employment at Valley Medical Centre to tell them that she would not be in to work because she was committing suicide. Bundy then attempted to go for a drive but parked the car after only two blocks and fell unconscious. She woke the next day in St Josephs Hospital, having been found by Clark.

On August 1 she was released.

On August 3, 1980 Bundy went to see her ex-lover Jack Murray at the club where he worked. When the pair were alone Bundy told Jack about the murders that she and Clark had committed. However Jack wasn't convinced the story was true, so Bundy left the club.

An hour later Jack left the club and found Bundy waiting for him outside. She asked him for a ride home and Jack agreed. On the way home Bundy retold the story of her and Clark's involvement in the Sunset Strip attacks but again Jack was uninterested in what she had to say; he was more interested in having sex with his ex-lover.

Parking his van Jack got in the windowless rear of his van and talked Bundy into having sex. He stripped off his trousers and motioned for Bundy to join him. Bundy moved to the rear of the van, pulled out a gun and shot the man in the back of the head. Bundy knelt down to check he was dead, but instead felt a strong pulse, so Bundy held the gun to the side of Jack's head and fired again.

Retrieving a knife from her purse Bundy stabbed Jack in the back six times and once in the anus. She also slashed his buttocks to make it look like a sex attack. Concerned that the police would be able to trace the bullets that were still in Jack's head, Bundy coldly picked up the knife and proceeded to hack off her ex-lover's head. Bundy phoned Clark and told him what she had done. Clark insisted that she get home immediately. So Bundy returned to the club carrying Jack's head in a bag, got into her own car and drove back to Clark. Early the next morning, the head of Jack Murray was thrown into one of the garbage bins near Griffith Park.

On August 11, 1980, Bundy took the last of her pills in one handful and went to work. An hour after arriving she was overheard by a work colleague, Leanne Lane, telling one of the elderly patients about her lovers' involvement in the killings, Leanne ignored it assuming that Bundy had made up the story.

A few minutes later, Bundy told the story to Leanne directly. She told her how Clark had shot two prostitutes while she was present and how she had killed Jack Murray. At the end of the story Bundy told Leanne that she was going home to surrender herself to authorities and left to get changed. Leanne, shocked by what she had heard, rushed to the administrator's office and dialled 911. Police officers reached the hospital quickly but Bundy had already left.

At home Bundy tried to call various police departments, without much success. Eventually she reached Detective Kilgore at Northeast PD and gave enough details of the murders to convince the detective of her own involvement but Bundy refused to name Clark as the killer.

Detective Kilgore told the woman to stay where she was. He drove to the woman's house to escort her to the police station for further questioning. Before Bundy left the house with the police officer she deliberately led Detective Kilgore around her home, and presented him with evidence that connected Clark with the murders. She then confessed to the murder of Jack Murray, saying it was all her own work.

At 11.30am, as Clark left work to go on a lunch break, Detective Pida stepped forward to arrest him. Detective Pida and Detective Leroy Orozco interviewed Clark, but he refused to admit to any murder charges. However, he did admit to having unlawful sexual relations with a twelve-year-old girl named Theresa, an admission that lead to three counts of child molestation.

Detectives were now fully immersed in the hunt for evidence against Clark, with Bundy assisting where she could. The Buick was impounded and investigated in which bullet holes were found in the front seats; accompanying bullets would also be found. Bloodstains were found on the rear seat and blood found on the front and rear mats matched blood typing from both Karen Jones and Gina Morano. On August 26, and again on August 28, detectives recovered two more bodies. Both were linked to the Sunset Strip murders. Bundy told detectives that Clark acted on his own in killing those victims. He had previously confessed them to her, but at the time Bundy wasn't sure whether to believe him or not.

Clark was charged with the multiple murders and pleaded not guilty, Bundy was charged with the murder of Jack Murray but pleaded not guilty by reason of insanity.

After two years of evidence gathering, the trial of Doug Clark facing six counts of murder began on October 8, 1982, in the court of Judge Ricardo Torres. Within five days Clark sacked his legal team and represented himself.

The prosecution's case against Clark ended after almost two months and 231 items of evidence. Then it was the defence's turn. Judge Torres was unimpressed with Clark's continual abuse of his privileges and revoked his right to defend himself and therefore Maxwell Keith was bought in to defend Clark. His first witness was Carol Bundy. After her testimony the trial broke for the Christmas break and returned with Clark taking the stand. Clark told the court that he was guilty and that the deceased Jack Murray along with Bundy were the real killers.

The jury left the courtroom to begin their deliberations on January 23, 1981. After five days of discussion they returned to the courtroom where they found Clark guilty on all six counts of first-degree murder.

After Clark's guilty verdict, the sentencing took place. Clark took the opportunity to plead for his life to the jury. The jury left the courtroom for their deliberations on February 10, 1983 and five days later they returned to give their verdict. On the six counts of murder Clark received a sentence of death, Judge Torres confirmed the sentence on March 16, adding that the sentence will be carried out at San Quentin at a date to be confirmed. Clark demanded that he be put to death within 10 days.

However. at the time of writing, Clark still sits on Death Row.

On May 2 1983, Bundy changed her plea from not guilty by reason of insanity to one of guilty. Seven years later Bundy was found guilty and sentenced to two consecutive twenty-five year sentences by Judge Torres.

After months of heart and respiratory problems and complications with her diabetes, Bundy was admitted to hospital on December 3, 2003, where she died of heart failure at 11.20am

Liao Chang-Shin

Between April and July 1945 in the small town of Changshow, China, people disappeared with an alarming regularity. The Chinese police were able to trace the last movements of some of the missing people, which lead them to a small inn ran by Liao Chang-Shin. When confronted by police, Liao Chang-Shin confessed that he and accomplice, Hsui Chang-Shan murdered and robbed a total of seventy-nine people, many had stayed at the inn.

For their crimes, both men were executed in late 1945.

George Chapman a.k.a. Severin Klosowski

George Chapman was born Severin Antoniovich Klosowski on December 14, 1865 in Nargornak, Poland. After several years at school, his father, Antonio, sent him to become an apprentice to Dr Moshko Rappaport, a Senior Surgeon in a hospital in Zvolen. Klosowski showed promise as a surgeon and by 1880 began studying medicine and surgery. Klosowski completed his studies by October 19, 1880 and began working at Praga Hospital in Warsaw. It was during this time that Klosowski married his first wife.

His natural skills in surgery allowed him to become an assistant surgeon in 1886 but after failing to progress any further in his studies, he moved to England by mid 1887, leaving his wife behind in Poland.

As was common for surgeons in Victorian England, Klosowski became a barber's assistant soon after his arrival. His surgery skills were put to use with the old-fashioned medical remedies of the time. He worked in the store of Abraham Radin at 70 West India Dock Road, London.

The position with Radin did not last long and soon Klosowski bought his own barbershop at 126 Cable Street, St George's-in-the-East. He lived there until early 1890 when he began working in a Whitechapel barber shop at the corner of Whitechapel High Street and George Yard.

While working in Whitechapel, Klosowski also used the name Ludwig Schloski. The reason for this is unclear; it may have purely been an attempted bastardisation of Klosowski. By the time Klosowski became the manager of the barber store in Whitechapel, he had met Lucy Baderski, at the St John's Square Polish club in Clerkenwell. After five weeks of courtship the pair were "married" in October 1889.

Little did Klosowski's new wife know, but the man had never divorced his first wife in Poland and she soon arrived in England to reclaim her husband. The three of them, Klosowski and his two wives shared a home for a short period of time. However, the first wife soon got tired of her husband and his womanising, and as she was unable to woo Klosowski back from the now pregnant Lucy, she left, returning to Poland.

Klosowski and his new wife Lucy had a baby boy, Wladyslaw, in September, 1890 after which they moved residences several times. They lived briefly in Cable Street, then Commercial Street and Greenfield Street, Whitechapel before they were forced to make a major relocation after the tragic death of the baby from pneumonia. .

The couple emigrated to New Jersey, USA around 1891 and Klosowski quickly found work as a barber in Jersey City. By 1903 the couple's life together was nearing it's end.

Klosowski had continued to seek company of females whenever he could and this enraged his wife. The pair got into violent arguments over his behaviour and the fighting culminated in Klosowski attacking the pregnant Lucy for a final time. He pinned her to the bed and stifled her cries by covering her mouth with his own.

When Klosowski heard a customer enter the shop in the front of their house he got off Lucy and served the man. Lucy found a knife secreted under the pillows, and on his return to the room, Klosowski confirmed that had he customer not come to the shop he was going to cut off her head.

In February 1892 Lucy, fearing for her life and that of her unborn child returned to England to live with her sister in Whitechapel. She gave birth to a daughter in May, and Klosowski, hearing the news of the baby's birth also returned to England. The couple attempted to reconcile but failed. They parted ways permanently.

Klosowski remained in Whitechapel working in a barbershop in South Tottenham and once again sought the company of various women.. His first affair in England was with a woman called Annie Chapman (no relation to the Ripper victim of the same name). The pair moved in together for 12 months before Annie returned home one day at the end of 1894 to find Klosowski had replaced her with another.

In February 1895, Annie told Klosowski that she had given birth to their baby, yet he denied any responsibility for the child and refused to see Annie or her baby again. Klosowski did take something else from the woman however. After Annie Chapman and Severin Klosowski officially parted ways, Klosowski adopted the name of George Chapman. A name he used until death.

Klosowski, as Chapman, soon moved in with another woman, Mary Spink in Hastings. They "married", and Mary gave Chapman a dowry of £500. A handsome sum in 1895. The pair opened their own store, where Chapman worked as a barber as Mary entertained the waiting clients by playing the piano. The store became famous and the couple were soon wealthy.

Yet as the store grew in success, the relationship of Chapman and Mary lost it's spark. The pair had violent arguments and more often than not, Mary ended up covered in bruises from the beatings. The relationship was facing a gruesome end.

Chapman bought an ounce of tartar emetic from a local chemist and began the systematic poisoning of Mary. As Mary became sicker, the musical barbershop also began to falter and soon the store closed. Chapman then took a job managing the popular Prince of Wales Pub.

By December Mary was bed-ridden, the poison slowly killing her. On December 25, 1897 Mary died, her body had been entirely ravaged by the antimony in the tartar emetic. The doctor who attended Mary throughout her illness suspected her death was from consumption.

The doctor later commented on Chapman's behaviour at the news of his wife's passing. He cried momentarily before continuing with his work, opening the pub as usual.

The marital bed was also not vacant for long. After Mary's death Chapman hired a new manageress for the pub, Bessie Taylor. The pair became lovers and soon married.

However Chapman returned to his old ways of beating his wife, and openly pursued other women.

The fights between Chapman and Bessie were violent. During one such incident, it was reported that Chapman had pointed a gun at Bessie. The relationship was doomed, and Chapman resorted to antimony once again to dissolve the marriage.

Bessie became ill, and prone to attacks of diarrhoea and vomiting. The episodes were severe and the woman became weak. On February 14, 1901, Bessie finally succumbed to the "illness" that ravaged her body. The doctor documented that her death was due to 'exhaustion from vomiting and diarrhoea'.

During Bessie's waning health, Chapman leased a new pub, the Monument Tavern. However the pub was not as successful at the couple's previous tenure and in desperation Chapman attempted to burn the place down.

In August 1901, barely six months after Bessie died, Chapman found his next wife. Maud Marsh, a barmaid in Chapman's pub soon married her boss, but the union was short-lived. When the man met Florence Rayner, he began beating his wife viciously and soon Maud was being slowly poisoned.

When Maud's mother question the man over his wife's illness, it scared him into acting irrationally. Chapman gave Maud a large dose of arsenic and antimony that killed her within 24 hours, her ravaged body expired on October 22, 1902.

The doctor, who had been called to examine Maud, refused to issue a death certificate without a post-mortem examination.

When the autopsy was performed, 7.24 grains of antimony were found in the woman's body, as well as trace evidence of arsenic.

George Chapman was arrested on October 25, 1902 by Inspector Godley, (one of the senior officers in the Jack the Ripper investigation), for the murder of his wife. It was then discovered the true history of George Chapman and Severin Klosowski.

The bodies of Bessie Chapman – nee Taylor and Mary Chapman – nee Spink were both exhumed on suspicion that they too had met with death at the hands of their "husband".

Bessie's body was still quite fresh, though covered in mould, tests were conducted and, as suspected, large amounts of antimony were found in her body. Mary's body, although having been interred for almost 5 years, looked remarkably well-preserved, a property of antimony that sealed Chapman's doom.

Chapman was charged with all three murders and faced trial in March 1903. By the end of the trial on March 20, the jury took eleven minutes to find Chapman guilty of the murder of Maud Marsh. They believed there was insufficient evidence for a guilty verdict in the other two charges.

He was sentenced to death for Maud's murder.

While awaiting his sentence, several newspaper articles appeared in the Pall Mall Gazette, asking the question "Was Chapman 'Jack the Ripper'?". The articles quote Chief Detective Inspector F Abbeline, formerly of Scotland Yard saying;

> "I have been so struck with the remarkable coincidences in the two series of murders that I have not been able to think of anything else for several days past... there are a score of things which make one believe that Chapman is the man"

Klosowski a.k.a. Chapman maintained his innocence and never confessed to murdering his wives or any responsibility for the Ripper murders. He was hanged in Wandsworth prison on April 7, 1903 and still remains one of the principle "Ripper" suspects.

Richard Chase

Richard Trenton Chase was born on May 23, 1950. He grew up in an unhappy, strict and angry household and was beaten often. As he grew older he enjoyed harming, mutilating and killing small animals. He was also an incessant fire starter.

Richard Chase had been institutionalised prior to his four day killing spree, in January of 1978. While in the mental institution, Chase had complained that his head kept changing shape and that someone had stolen his pulmonary artery. The staff at the hospital had actually started calling him, "Dracula." But by 1978 they felt that his medication had finally begun to help him and that his paranoid schizophrenia was under control, so he was released. Upon his release he naturally stopped taking his medication so his delusions of grandeur and blood lust returned.

He now thought his blood was turning to powder and that his mother was being paid to poison him by the Nazis. He was also hearing voices telling him that the way to treat his "powdery blood" illness was to drink the blood of others.

After robbing and ransacking several homes in Sacramento on January 23, 1978, Richard Chase arrived at the home of twenty-two-year-old Theresa Wallin who was twelve weeks pregnant. He broke into the house and was met in the hallway by Theresa. Chase raised the gun and pointed it at the woman's face. She put up her hands in front of her as Chase fired the pistol into the woman's hand. The bullet exited Theresa's elbow and cut into the side of her neck.

A second shot entered the woman's skull and she dropped to the floor. Chase leant over Theresa's dying body and aimed the gun at her temple and fired for a final time.

Chase then moved Theresa's dying body into the bedroom. He then grabbed a knife from the kitchen and mutilated the pregnant woman's body. Her clothes were cut open to expose her entire torso. Chase cut open the woman's stomach and removed her intestines, pancreas, kidneys and spleen.

He sliced off one of her nipples and stabbed her repeatedly in the chest. He also stabbed the knife into the woman's removed internal organs. He threw Theresa's mutilated kidney back into her abdominal cavity.

By now Chase was covered in the woman's blood. He attempted to drink some of Theresa's blood that he collected in an empty yoghurt carton. With lines of red running from the sides of his mouth Chase went to the bathroom to watch himself lick the blood from his fingers and rub it over his face.

Yet Chase had not finished. He went out to the yard and collected a piece of dog faeces and returned to Theresa's body. He opened her mouth a put the excrement inside as a final indignity to the young pregnant woman.

Later that evening Theresa's husband came home to find his wife's mutilated body.

Four days after he murdered pregnant Theresa Wallin, Richard Chase killed again.

On January 27, 1978 Evelyn Miroth and her six-year-old son Jason were minding her baby nephew, David Ferreira at home. Evelyn had invited her friend Daniel Meredith over for company. Soon the newborn baby dozed off. After a while Evelyn decided to go and take a bath.

The house was quiet when Chase arrived and knocked on the front door.

Daniel opened the door to Chase and was shot immediately in the face at point blank range. The man fell dead to the ground.

Evelyn had been in the bath when Chase burst into the bathroom. He immediately shot her dead and then carried her naked dead body to the bedroom. He raped and sodomised Evelyn's dead body before stabbing and mutilating her corpse including sodomising her with the knife. The knife drove through her anus and into her cervix.

Then as he had done to Theresa, Chase cut up Evelyn's stomach and removed several of her organs and intestines. Evelyn had also suffered several cuts to her throat and Chase had attempted to remove her eye without success.

Six-year-old Jason came to see what was happening, when he heard the gunfire and Chase shot the young boy in the head twice. He was found in the bedroom with his mother's mutilated corpse.

Chase then turned his attentions to the baby, David. He shot him in the head in his cot, before taking him into the bathroom to be mutilated. He opened the soft skull of the baby and attempted to drink the blood.

A neighbour, who had heard gunfire went to Evelyn's house but found it in silence. He knocked on the door several times, and though he could see shadows moving inside, he could not get anyone to answer the door. Little did he know but Daniel was lying behind the door, dead from the gunshot wound fired into his skull.

The next morning, after a worrisome night, the neighbour broke into the house, to find the carnage that Chase had left behind. The police were called to investigate the three murders and the disappearance of baby David.

The only clue that police had to go on initially was a footprint in the blood that matched one left at the scene of Theresa's murder. They knew they were hunting a maniacal serial killer.

The next day, police were inundated with calls about a suspicious man that had been hanging around, some even knew his name, Richard "Rick" Chase. Police investigated the man's background and found he had a history of mental illness and a criminal record for weapons charges. At the same time as police pounded the pavement looking for clues; the FBI's Robert Ressler drew up a profile. With witnesses' reports and the profile pointing to Chase, officers decided to pay the man a visit.

They tricked him into coming out of his apartment, after he refused them entry and found he was carrying Daniel Meredith's wallet. Chase was arrested and taken to the police station for questioning. Throughout the interviews, Chase maintained his innocence.

Criminalists searched his apartment looking for baby David. They found several body parts and brain matter in the fridge and on the bench. Chase's entire apartment was covered in bloodstains.

With disbelief, police also found a calendar with dates for murder detailed on it. The two days that he had killed four people were on it, so were another 44 days scheduled for future murders.

Three months later on March 24, 1978 the body of baby David Ferreira was found in a churchyard.

The trial opened on January 2, 1979. Chase entered not guilty pleas to all six murders due to insanity. The trial lasted four months and saw many theories of blood mania being brought in for the defence. However, on May 8, 1979, after only five hours of deliberating, the jury came back with guilty of murder for all six murders.

Chase was sentenced to death and sent to San Quentin. However the executioner would never need to fulfil his duty with Chase as he killed himself by taking an overdose of anti-depressant drugs on December 26, 1980.

The Chicago Rippers

The men dubbed "the Chicago Rippers" by the media, mutilated and murdered at least seven[4] women during a blood thirsty-rampage in Chicago during a seventeen-month period. The killers, twenty-one-year-old Edward Spreitzer, the Kokoraleis brothers, nineteen-year-old Andrew and eighteen-year-old Thomas were led by their older leader and mentor, thirty-year-old Robin Gecht. Gecht, along with the others practiced satanic rituals and devil worshipping. Gecht convinced his gang that they required blood and human sacrifices to please Satan.

Twenty-eight-year-old Linda Sutton was abducted on May 23, 1981, from Elmhurst, Chicago by the men. She was pack-raped and sodomised; she then had her left breast removed with a sliver of wire before being stabbed to death. The killers used Linda's severed breast for sexual acts before being eaten as part of their Satanic worship ritual.

Her mutilated body was found on June 2, 1981 in Villa Park, near the hotel where the men were staying.

Almost a year later on May 15, 1982, twenty-one-year-old Lorraine Borowski became the killers' second victim. She was abducted as she arrived for work, spilling her handbag in the struggle. She was taken to the hotel where the men were staying and repeatedly raped before having wire wrapped around her breast until it was severed. She was murdered by Gecht with a hatchet. Her body was found five months later on October 10, in a cemetery south of Villa Park. Like Linda before her, Lorraine had had her breast removed for the men's sexual gratification.

Two weeks after the murder of Lorraine the men abducted Shui Mak, on May 29, 1982 from Hanover Park. Her mutilated body was found buried at Barrington on September 30, her body mutilated beyond recognition. Like the other two victims, the killers had removed her breast and had sex with the open wound. The breast was taken home by the men and the flesh scooped out and eaten.

On June 13, 1982 the gang picked up prostitute Angel York. Once inside the gang's van Angel was handcuffed and her breast slashed open. The killers, assuming their victim was dead dumped her from the back of the van. Angel however survived the brutal attack and went to police.

On August 28, 1982 the body of teenage prostitute Sandra Delaware was found stabbed and strangled to death on the bank of the Chicago River, her amputated left breast was the hallmark of the gang.

The four men next abducted and murdered thirty-year-old Rose Davis on September 8, 1982. Police found her in a deserted alley. Like the other six victims, she had had her breast sliced off and her skull had been smashed in. There was also evidence to prove the woman had been gang-raped and sodomised before her death.

On September 12, 1982 forty-two-year-old Carole Pappas, vanished from a department store in nearby Wheaton, Illinois. She was a victim of the Chicago Rippers, though her body has never been found.

On October 6, 1982 twenty-year-old prostitute Beverly Washington was picked up by the Chicago Rippers. She was pulled into the van after rejecting their offer and stripped naked. She was pack-raped and sodomised; her left breast sliced from her body. The men attempted to also sever her right breast without success. Beverley was dumped on the side of the road, however even with the massive bleeding from her

---

[4] The estimate is that the men killed at least nineteen women.

severed left breast and partially severed right one, she survived the attack and was taken to the hospital, where police interviewed her.

Beverly was able to give the police a good description of her attackers and the van they drove, the police closed in on the Chicago Rippers and they were arrested on October 20, 1952 and charged.

After several attempts at an insanity plea, Robin Gecht, the ringleader, was found mentally competent to stand trial.

The trial opened on September 20, 1983 when Gecht took the stand and confessed to the attack on Beverly Washington but claimed he was innocent of the other charges of attempted murder, rape, and aggravated battery.

Brought into evidence was the trophy box found by police and owned by Gecht that housed fifteen breasts. Also presented was how the women were held captive. They had been tortured with needles, knives and ice picks, gang-raped, and finally sacrificed to Satan by members of the tiny cult. The men severed one or both breasts with wire, usually while the victim was alive and each of the men took communion by eating a piece of the breast before it was put into Gecht's trophy box.

By the end of the trial the killer was found guilty on all counts and received a sentence of 120 years in prison.

On April 2, 1984, Edward Spreitzer pleaded guilty to four counts of murder including of Rose Davis, Sandra Delaware, Shui Mak and drug-dealer Rafael Torado. Spreitzer was sentenced to life on each count of murder and extra time for charges of rape, deviant sexual assault, and attempted murder.

For his role in the murders of several women, Andrew Kokoraleis was given the death penalty. He was executed on March 17, 1999.

On May 18, 1984, Andrew's brother, Tommy was convicted of Lorraine Borowski's murder and was sentenced to life in prison.

An interesting sidebar is that Robin Gecht had once worked for serial killer John Gacy, the man who had murdered at least 33 young men and boys in Chicago during 1972-1978.

Hadden Clark

Hadden Irving Clark Jnr was born in October 1951 in Troy, Connecticut, to mother Flava Scranton and father Hadden. Family and friends remembered Clark's childhood as awkward and undisciplined. He was often the cause of neighbourhood trouble and accidents and was regularly taunted by the local children. As his revenge he would often kill their pets.

At four-years-old, a doctor at Yale University studied Clark and concluded that he suffered from brain damage, which had resulted from his difficult birth. Prior to beginning his elementary school years, Clark was forced by his parents to wear girl's clothes; frilly underwear and pink dresses were the norm.

His childhood set the scene for a serial killer in the making.

Carl Dorr and his wife Dorothy had their problems, they constantly bickered, and their six-year-old daughter Michelle was often in the middle of it. Eventually the pair separated, and the couple shared joint custody of Michelle.

Carl moved out and found a place to stay two doors from his close friend Geoff, the younger brother of Hadden Clark.

On May 31, 1986, Michelle was staying at her father's house. Carl had set up a paddling pool in the garden for her while he was busy inside the house. After completing a few chores around the house, Carl returned to the garden to check on his daughter, but she was nowhere to be found. Carl assumed that she had gone to play with Eliza Clark, Geoff's daughter, and returned to the house to watch some television. It wasn't until much later in the day that Carl decided that it was time for Michelle to come back home, so he walked the short distance to Geoff's house. Geoff and Eliza were there, but there was no sign of Michelle and neither Geoff nor Eliza had seen her that day as they had been out. Obviously Geoff was very concerned for his daughter's welfare and searched the neighbourhood both on foot and by car without success. Eventually Carl drove to the Siller Spring Police Department to report her missing.

Hadden Clark lived with his younger brother, Geoff, until his erratic behaviour caused arguments in the household, and Geoff told him to leave. On May 31, they day of Michelle's disappearance, he returned to the house to gather more of his belongings. At the time Geoff was out. Michelle Dorr knocked on the door and asked Clark if Eliza was in. Clark replied that she should check in the bedroom, so the unsuspecting Michelle entered the house. Clark closed the door and locked it behind her. Michelle walked up the stairs heading for the bedroom with Clark following. Behind his back he was carrying a large 12inch knife he'd taken from the kitchen.

Clark threw Michelle to the floor as soon as they entered the bedroom; he used the knife to slash her across the chest, quickly followed by a second wound. He then stabbed the terrified girl in the throat. Michelle was dead; she never stood a chance. Clark then put Michelle's body in a large bag and washed the blood from the walls and the floors of the bedroom. He put the bag containing Michelle's body in the boot of his car and drove to work. After finishing his shift at the Country Club, Clark drove to Paint Branch Park near Columbia to bury Michelle's body. Clark carried the body and a shovel into the woods and proceeded to dig a grave. Before he put Michelle into the grave, he tasted Michelle's blood. Finally, he finished the burial by covering the shallow grave with leaves.

As with many cases where children are reported as missing, the finger of suspicion points towards the relatives of the missing child. When Carl reported his daughter missing, he became the number one suspect. Carl passed two polygraph tests yet police still considered him the most likely suspect. A thorough search was conducted of his house but no evidence was found. The fact that no evidence was found anywhere, further indicated that Carl was involved with Michelle's disappearance.

Detective Mike Garvey led the police during a door to door questioning. One of the neighbours remembered seeing a man outside Geoff Clark's house, and also a girl matching Michelle's description. The man seen by the neighbour was Hadden Clark. Detectives decided to bring Clark in for questioning.

At 9.30am on June 8, 1986, Clark turned up at the police station for his interview with Detective Mike Garvey. After a few short 'getting to know you' questions Mike Garvey went straight in and asked Clark if he had killed Michelle. The interview took a dramatic turn with Clark mumbling what sounded like a confession to himself. Before he was ready to talk he asked to use the toilet. In the toilet he vomited, but detectives stood over him and continued with the questioning. Clark was clearly agitated but did not confess to the officers. Instead he stated that he was at work on the day Michelle disappeared and could prove it, he then asked for a telephone to call his doctor, which was granted.

Clark called a psychiatrist, who formally requested that the interview be ended. The detectives reluctantly agreed. After the interview, Detective Mike Garvey drove to the Chevy Chase Country Club to check on Clark's employment record, which showed that he had attended work on that particular day. Hadden Clark was no longer considered a suspect in Michelle's murder.

And the case remained unsolved.

Over the next few years, Clark's mental problems increased along with his need for revenge on anyone whom he considered had wronged him.On one occasion Clark was renting a room in the home of Paul Mahany. Paul would eventually need to ask Clark to leave, as he believed his lodger to be 'evil and crazy'. Clark warned Paul that he would have his revenge. Days later, the Mahany family found their pet cats dead on the doormat; one of them had been skinned. Clark also left dead fish in various places around the house, sprayed black dye on the carpets and stole numerous items. When Paul Mahany pressed charges against Clark, the resulting court case gave Clark a one year suspended sentence for destruction of property and was also ordered to seek psychiatric treatment.

In July 1989, Clark visited a Veterans Hospital in Maryland for help, but as soon as he booked in, he wanted out. He quickly became highly agitated, and as a result, was put in restraints and given the antipsychotic drug Haldol. Over the next few days Clark calmed down. A psychiatric examination listed Clark as suffering from 'psychosis with questionable etiology'. Clark told doctors that animals talked to him, that he had been depressed for many years and was paranoid. After five days at the hospital, Clark was released.

Clark was now unemployed and homeless and was living in the woods in a tent. He regularly volunteered for work at the church. In 1992, Clark volunteered for a gardening job at the home of Penny Houghteling in Bethesda. Penny trusted Clark enough to allow him use of the kitchen whenever he pleased and to come and go as he pleased. On October 17, 1992, Penny left for a weeklong break in North Carolina, leaving her twenty-three-year-old daughter Laura, who was home from working in Philadelphia, in charge of the house.

The next day, Sunday October 18, Laura was in bed asleep after a late night out with fiends when a gun barrel prodded her awake. Clark was holding the gun but his appearance was more surprising then the weapon. Clark was dressed in a woman's wig and a blouse he had stolen from Penny's drawers. Clark covered Laura's mouth and nose with some duct tape, that caused her to suffocate. Clark attempted to cut the tape off with a knife as the scared woman struggled, but missed and stabbed Laura in the throat. Clark later claimed that Laura's death was an accident. Laura slowly suffocated and bled to death in her bed. Once she was dead Clark wrapped Laura's body in sheets and carried it outside to his Datsun under the cover of darkness. Before leaving the property, Clark stole jewellery, trophies and other valuables. He cleaned up the blood soaked bed and drove away, leaving no immediate clue as to the events of the day.

Diana Holfman was concerned as to why Laura had not turned up for work on Monday morning. Knowing Laura was never late for work, Diana contacted her daughter Hilary, who was friends with Laura, to check in on her. Reaching the house, Hilary saw Laura's car outside. She went to the front door but got no response. She tried the door, but found it was locked. Not giving up, Hilary went to the rear of the house and found the rear glass door unlocked and she walked in. Although nothing appeared to be out of place, Hilary felt uneasy, as if something was not quite right. She called Warren, Laura's brother, to visit the house. That evening, he called around and checked the house, but could find nothing unusual. He decided to check the neighbourhood on foot. After about a ten minute walk he saw Penny's gardener, Hadden Clark, and flagged him down. Clark pulled over, but as soon as Warren got close to the car, Clark drove off at high speed. Laura's body was in the back of his truck.

After the close call with Warren, Clark immediately drove to the woods near the I-270 and buried Laura's body in a shallow grave.

Warren went to Bethesda Police Station to report his sister missing. Clark drove to Warwick, Rhode Island and deposited the bloody sheets taken from Laura's bed into a storage locker; he kept the pillowcase for a further day before discarding it in the woods behind the Houghteling home.

Montgomery County Detective Edward Golian was in charge of the investigation into Laura Houghteling's disappearance and recognised the gardener as a suspect in the disappearance of Michelle Dorr, three years earlier. Clark was again the prime suspect and was asked to come in to be interviewed at the police station on the day of Penny's murder. When asked about speeding away from Warren, Clark claimed he thought it was a carjacker. Without any solid evidence to hold him, Clark was released.

On October 24, officers turned up at Penny Houghteling's house with sniffer dogs for a search of the grounds. The dogs lead officers into the woods, where the bloodied pillowcase and an extensive collection of women's clothing, particularly lingerie, which belonged to Penny was located. A chemical test on Laura's bed proved that large quantities of blood had been present; hair from a wig was also found, along with other, as yet, unidentified hair samples. Police were sure that would match Clark and needed samples from him.

Detectives Richard Fallin and Ed Tarney stopped Clark in his truck in Bethesda and took him to the station for further questioning. Yet Clark would not answer any questions, so the detectives were forced to release him again.

However, while Clark was in the police station a search warrant was issued on his truck, which ensured that it was impounded for twenty-four hours. The search resulted in numerous hair samples being found in addition to a hand drawn map, which at the time officers believed may indicate where Laura was buried. A set of keys was also in the truck for a storage locker in Kensington, Maryland.

Inside the locker detectives found a small collection of women's clothing that belonged to Penny Houghteling.

A forensic check on the pillowcase, found in the woods, produced a single useful fingerprint.

On November 6, the forensic report was completed and indicated that the fingerprint belonged to Hadden Clark. At 10.17 that night officers located Clark's truck parked in the car park of the First Baptist Church in Bethesda, Clark was asleep inside. A loud knock on the window woke him and he was arrested for the murder of Laura Houghteling. Clark's only reply was 'ok'. At this time, his Miranda rights were not read to him and when Clark was questioned, officers ignored his requests to see a lawyer. For three hours Clark sat in the interview room with three officers who continually badgered, cajoled and tried to trick Clark into confessing. His only words were to request his lawyer. At 2.52am Detective Mike Garvey came into the interview room to talk about Michelle Dorr. Clark had still not been read his rights nor been granted access to his lawyer. At 6.10am the questioning ended and Clark was booked on a charge of murder.

In court on December 17, Clark was indicted for the murder of Laura Houghteling. His lawyer, Benjamin Vaughan successfully argued that the police interview was inadmissible in the trial.

The trial date was set for June 1993.

Just prior to the trial, authorities privately admitted that the only evidence linking Clark with Laura Houghteling was the bloody fingerprint found on the pillowcase. They believed that it was possible that this evidence could, in court, be argued away. Kathleen Toolan offered the defence a deal, if Clark would plead guilty to second-degree murder. Clark agreed, but his defence counsel added the condition that the sentence is carried out at the Patuxent Institution at Maryland, the reason being that the Institute was also a psychiatric hospital.

During the trial on June 14, 1993, Judge Irma Raker accepted the plea but could not guarantee admission to the hospital. Clark stood up and made a statement admitting to the murder of Laura Houghteling and burying the body. Clark was found guilty and he immediately gave authorities the details as to where Laura's body could be found. Two weeks later on June 25, Clark was sentenced to the maximum 30 years to be served at the Eastern Correctional Institution at Delmarva with a six-month evaluation period at Patuxent Institution

Clark's time at the Institute was not to his advantage. He was caught on tape talking to a fellow inmate about how he had murdered Michelle Dorr at his brother's house. Detective Ed Tarney heard the tape and immediately visited Clark's brother's house with forensic experts. In the bedroom, officers found many samples of blood, but due to the age and probable contamination, they could not definitively state whether or not the blood was Michelle Dorr's. Despite that, Clark was charged with the murder of Michelle, twelve years after her death.

In late 1999, the trial of Hadden Clark for the murder of Michelle Dorr began, despite the fact that no body had been found, nor that the blood could positively identified as Michelle's. The jury spent four days in deliberation before finding Clark guilty of second-degree murder. Judge Mason sentenced Clark to thirty years on October 20th 1999.

In January 2000, after being given directions by Hadden Clark, Detective Ed Tarney and other county officers recovered the decomposing body of Michelle Dorr and gave her a formal burial on January 15, 2000.

Since his incarceration, Clark has confessed to many more murders, however at the time of writing, police have been unable to substantiate any of his claims.

Rory Conde

The Tamiami trail is the nickname given to the final section of Highway 41 from Tampa through to Miami. It was also the dumping ground of Rory Conde, the Tamiami Strangler, where six victims were slain.

The first victim was cross-dressing male prostitute, Lazaro Comesana. The man's body was found on September 16, 1994. He had been strangled to death and dumped at the roadside.

Elisa Martinez was identified as victim number two after she was found strangled to death on October 8, 1994.

Victim number 3 was Charity Nava, who was found dead just off the Tamiami trail on November 20, 1994. Like the other victims, Charity had been strangled. This time, though, the killer left evidence, taunting police at the scene. Conde wrote several phrases including 'Third' and 'if you can catch me' on the woman's back.

Wanda Crawford was added to the list of victims after being recovered on November 26, 1994.

The fifth victim was identified as Necole Schneider, followed by the sixth, Rhonda Dunn. The women were found strangled on December 17, 1994 and January 12, 1995 respectively. After the discovery of Rhonda's body, Miami police connected the six victims to one unknown suspect via DNA samples left at most of the scenes.

The case took a dramatic turn when on June 19, 1995, frantic banging could be heard from a house belonging to Rory Conde. Neighbours called police who arrived promptly on the scene. Inside the house officers found Gloria Maestre, gagged and bound. Police issued a warrant for the arrest of Rory Conde for the abduction of Gloria and was also suspected of being the Tamiami Strangler.

Conde was arrested on June 24, 1995 at his grandmother's house in Hialeah and taken to the local police station for questioning.

During the questioning, Conde confessed to the six murders and blamed his split from his wife Carla as the catalyst for the killings. He explained that he killed Lazaro after discovering, during sexual intercourse, that the prostitute was a man. In each of the six murders, Conde took the victim home where they were strangled. Conde then sodomised the victims' dead bodies before dumping them along the Tamiami Trail.

On July 12, 1995, after confessing, Conde was officially charged with six counts of first-degree murder.

Conde faced separate trials for each murder, the first being the murder of Rhonda Dunn. In October 1999, the jury heard Conde's confession and found him guilty. Judge Jerald Bagley concurred with the jury's recommendation and sentenced Conde to death.

In April 2001, as part of a plea bargain, Conde pleaded guilty to the remaining five murders. In return he was sentenced to 5 consecutive life sentences.

Conde returned to court on September 4, 2003 to find that he had failed to get his death sentence for the murder of Rhonda Dunn, overturned.

Dean Corll

Dean Arnold Corll was born in Waynesdale, Indiana on Christmas Day December 25, 1939 to over-affectionate mother Mary and Arnold, a father who did not like children. Early family life was not happy for Dean and his brother Stanley with their parents constantly arguing.

Arnold Corll was a strict disciplinarian and the boys were always being punished. Arnold and Mary eventually divorced in 1946 and soon after, Arnold joined the army. Mary found life without Arnold lonely so she bought a horse-trailer and moved to Tennessee to be closer to the base where Arnold was posted. Dean and Stanley were left with an elderly couple most of the time while Mary went looking for work.

The arguments between the Corll's continued and again they separated.

The two Corll boys were at different ends on the personality scale. Stanley was friendly and outgoing, always playing with other children from the neighbourhood or school. Whereas Dean was always a loner, preferring to stay inside and way from the other children.

By 1950, Mary and Arnold tried again to reconcile, but failing again they eventually gave up on the relationship and in 1950 Mary, with the two boys, left Tennessee for Houston.

Around the same time Dean was diagnosed with a congenital heart aliment after a bout of Rheumatic fever and was told that he should avoid sports wherever possible. Dean, not being a sporting type, found this good news.

In 1953 Mary remarried; her new husband was travelling clock salesman Jake West. Soon after the marriage the couple had a daughter. With both his parents working long hours, Dean was extremely protective of his younger siblings and always watched out for them and tried to keep them out of trouble.

Dean found enjoyment in scuba diving but had to give it up after fainting one day while diving, a symptom of his heart defect. At school, he enjoyed music and was a keen trombone player. Teachers remembered him as a quiet and polite student.

After a suggestion from a candy sales representative Mary set herself up with a little candy shop to help support the family. Dean was a runner for the candy shop that had its humble beginnings in the garage of the family home. Dean often found himself exhausted from running orders to people in town, but never complained.

After high school graduation, Dean moved back to Indiana to help look after his stepfather Jake's elderly mother while the rest of the family moved to Houston.

When Dean moved back to the family home he decided to get a job with the Houston Lighting and Power Company during the day and still help make candies with the family at night. His drive to succeed impressed many of the town's young women but Dean failed to notice.

In 1964, Dean was drafted into the US Army. Life in the army caused a change in the young man. Dean found himself desiring after fellow officers he shared his quarters with and Dean finally realised he was gay. Until then Dean had known something about life was wrong but until his realisation about his homosexuality, he had been unsure what had been missing.

Returning home after an eleven-month assignment in the Army, Dean found his parents arguing and fighting. The Wests' had begun to argue over the business. Jake saw Mary as a rival and soon threw her out.

Mary took the children and began her own lolly shop.

Dean found himself an apartment near his mother and started hanging out with teenage boys from the neighbourhood. It was easy to get them to come to his apartment. Dean always had piles of candy around and most of the kids couldn't resist.

Once again Dean's mother decided to marry. This time her husband was a seaman, andMary soon found flaws in his character. She found him dull company and quite stupid. Yet the marriage survived two divorces until finally on the advice of a psychic, Mary left the marriage and Houston and went to Dallas.

Corll decided to stay in Houston. He liked it there and found the freedom away from his protective mother to do as he pleased, satisfying.

Dean's first attraction to the younger boys was to play the part of an older protective brother. At first he would never say anything or do anything overtly sexual. He just preferred the company of the teen boys who hung around his apartment. But lurking beneath the kind exterior was a sex maniac waiting to surface; it was just a matter of time.

One day in 1969, Dean had learned that some of the boys would allow oral sex in exchange for money. This is how Corll first met fourteen-year-old David Brooks.

Brooks enjoyed the older man's company and looked up to him as a big brother- someone to ask for guidance and for help through the tough and tumultuous teenage years. Soon David became completely emotionally dependent on Dean and spent most of his time with him rather than at home. Brooks actually moved in with Corll for a while.

Dean hired a storage shed to keep his few possessions in that were not needed in his tiny apartment.

On Christmas Day 1969, Dean Corll turned 30. It was a turning point in his life. He became morose and depressed. He lost his thrill for life and became further introverted. But David Brooks was often around and tried to cheer Corll up. Often it would end with Corll paying Brooks $5 for oral sex.

University of Texas student, Jeffrey Konen, left the campus and began to hitchhike home to Houston. Twenty-one-year-old Jeffrey was last seen on September 25, 1970 trying to get another lift. He was picked up by Corll who took him to his apartment at 3300 Yorktown. There the young man was bound by his hands and feet and gagged. Corll sodomised the student before murdering him and dumping his body.

Being a renowned area for down and out teens, Corll had his pick of victims. He found that a lot of them were willing to come over for a party. The parties usually included glue and paint sniffing, pot smoking and pill popping.

Some of the boys would allow Corll to perform oral sex on them for $5. Many of the boys Corll chose were usually in trouble or runaways. When they went missing no one really noticed, at first.

However Corll was no longer happy with only oral sex, he wanted penetration, he wanted to perform sodomy on his victims, and when they refused they often wound up dead.

> *"He killed them because he wanted sex and they (the boys) didn't want to"*, Brooks told police later.

Brooks would later tell a fantastical story to police about the various victims who would live or die at Corll's whim. In one case, Brooks arrived at Corll's place unannounced in 1970 and let himself in. He found Corll wondering around the house naked and when the killer saw Brooks he was furious, demanding to know why he had arrived without telling him. Brooks thought this was unusual until he noticed two younger boys strapped to a homemade torture rack in Corll's bedroom.

Brooks left the apartment confused and dejected. Corll later tried to make it up to his friend by giving him a new Corvette. No doubt it was to buy Brook's silence about what he had seen. Corll told Brooks that he had killed both of the teens and dumped their bodies.

But the Corvette was another part of Corll's plans. He saw it as an opportunity to have Brooks with him while they went driving around looking for victims.

One potential victim who went on to become a police officer said

> "I was one of the boys that Corll and Brooks tried to abduct. I felt something was wrong and told them to get lost"

Yet others were not so intuitive.

One unnamed victim accepted the offer of a pot-smoking session back at Corll's apartment. When the trio arrived at the unit, Corll tied the boy to his torture rack in his bedroom and sodomised him. Corll then strangled the boy, while Brooks watched. No doubt Brooks would have then helped Corll to get rid of the body near Lake Sam Rayburn.

Just before Corll's 31st birthday, he decided to have a party. It was December 15, 1970 at his new apartment on Columbia Street Houston where the guests were Brooks, fifteen-year-old Danny Yates and fourteen-year-old James Glass. The two boys were friends from a church social group. Glass had also been to Corll's apartment previously and found Dean to be a happy and pleasant man to be around.

However this time he would not find Corll so obliging. Both boys were quickly tied to Corll's bed torture rack and sodomised. Danny and James were then strangled. This time Corll decided not to dump the bodies but hide them at the boat shed he hired on Silver Bell Street.

On January 27, 1971 Dean Corll decided he needed another double murder to satiate his appetite. He had another new apartment at 3200 Magnum Road, Houston and wanted to christen it with murder.

David Brooks went with Corll for a drive and with the promise of food and alcohol, the men were able to entice brothers, thirteen-year-old Jerry and fourteen-year-old Donald Waldrop, back to the apartment.

Once the young boys were inside Corll's apartment they were raped and strangled before joining Danny Yates and James Glass' bodies in the Silver Bell Street Boat Shed. Brooks blandly admitted later to being there when the bodies were buried.

> "I believe I was present when they were buried".

There was another short gap between killings. This time Corll waited four months before murdering two more boys. On May 29, 1971 the victims were thirteen-year-old David Hilligiest and sixteen-year-old George Winkle. The boys had been on his way to the local swimming pool when they accepted a lift from Corll. They were last seen climbing into Corll's white van. Later that evening George called his mother to say he had gone to Freeport with some friends and they would be back home soon. But he was never seen alive again.

At Corll's apartment the two boys were tied to the bed before being sodomised, tortured and strangled. They were then buried with the others at the boat shed.

George and David's parents were worried when the boys did not return. They had posters made up to hand out and stuck some to poles, hoping someone may have seen the two teens. A psychic was even brought in to see if he could help in the search. But he only had bad news for the parents. The psychic told them that their sons were dead.

One of David's best friends tried to comfort the family. Elmer Wayne Henley told the Hilligiests that he was sure that David had just run away and would return soon.

It was not long before another boy disappeared. Seventeen-year-old Ruben Watson was last seen on his way to the cinema on August 17, 1971.

Brooks and Corll picked him up along the way and took him back to Corll's apartment where he was brutalised for hours until Corll grew bored of his victim and killed him.

The next victim that Brooks bought to the house for Corll was Elmer "Wayne" Henley.

The first time Corll had met Henley, he was meant as a victim, but Corll saw him as a better procurer than Brooks had been. He therefore arranged a test for the new young man. Henley was made to knock Brooks unconscious which he did without hesitating.

Even though Brooks was so emotionally dependent on Corll, he always refused Corll's offers of anal sex. But on one occasion he found himself a victim of Corll's, luckily living to tell the story.

When Brooks woke, he found himself tied to Corll's bed and was bleeding from his anus. Corll had sodomised him while he was unconscious. Yet Brooks did not tell anyone about the incident until after Corll's death. He also remained a true and loyal friend.

However now there was another person in the equation, Brooks felt a little jealous of Henley; it appears that Corll was beginning to fall in love with the younger man and Corll liked Henley's independence. He was tiring of Brook's complete emotional reliance.

Also Henley could be bought. He was willing to do almost anything for money, including selling his friends to Corll as sex slaves. Though Henley would later deny it, it is rumoured he was paid $200 per male he brought to Corll. Corll would try and rationalise his behaviour to Brooks and Henley, telling them that the boys were no loss to society, most of them were delinquents and a burden; they were no great loss.

Another victim was abducted on February 24, 1972. Frank Aguirre was a little older than most of Corll's victims being nineteen when he disappeared. He had a girlfriend at the time, fourteen-year-old Rhonda Williams, who would later be a witness to Corll's own murder.

On May 21, 1972 Dean and his cohorts grabbed another two victims. Sixteen-year-old Johnny Delome and seventeen-year-old Billy Baulch were taken to the apartment where they were tortured and raped for hours. Johnny was then shot dead by Henley. Henley later claimed he had fired the gun up the teen's nostrils. The two boys were taken to Corll's original dumping ground on High Island and buried.

On October 3, 1972 Corll again chose a double murder. The victims were thirteen-year-old Richard Hembree and fourteen-year-old Wally Simoneux. The teens were taken back to Corll's apartment on the premise of a party. The boys sniffed paint fumes and other substances that rendered them unconscious. Once the boys were unconscious, Corll took them to his room and strapped them to his torture rack. The victims were repeatedly anally raped.

According to Brooks, the boys, like others, were kept alive for days of torture. The boys were always procured in the same way. Brooks or Henley would lure victims to Dean's house with the promise of an 'alcohol party'. The victims would then be allowed to drink themselves unconscious. Dean would then tie them up, molest them, and then kill them.

Once Corll was done with his victims they were strangled and dumped. Wally and Richard were buried at the Boat Shed with many of the other victims.

During November 1972, fifteen-year-old Michael Baulch, the younger brother of previous victim Billy Baulch, became the next victim.

The boy was subjected to days of torture including having his pubic hairs pulled out one-by-one, Corll anally raped the boy with foreign objects, and glass rods were shoved into his penis.

On June 11, 1973, fifteen-year-old Billy Lawrence was taken to Corll's apartment for a party. The boy did not leave alive. He was brutally raped and murdered by Corll.

Fifteen-year-old Homer Garcia joined the list of sexually tortured and murdered victims of Corll on July 7, 1973.

On July 27, less than three weeks after Homer's murder, seventeen-year-old Charles Cobble and eighteen-year-old Marty Jones are murdered after being tortured by Corll.

And the list of victims continued.

A nine-year-old boy disappeared around the last day of July, followed by the murder of thirteen-year-old James Dreymala during the first week of August 1973.

The killings were getting more frequent and more brutal.

But the end was near.

On the afternoon of August 8, 1973 Henley had arrived at Corll's apartment at 2020 Lamar Street with two victims. He had brought sixteen-year-old Timothy Kerley for Corll and Rhonda Williams – the girlfriend of one of Corll's previous victims for himself.

Rhonda had decided to run away and confided in Henley. Henley asked her to come with him to a party at Corll's home. Henley had thought it would be okay if he brought a girl, but it wasn't. When Corll saw Rhonda with Henley he was furious, but kept his temper under control. He would punish Henley later.

After a glue sniffing session, Henley, Timothy and Rhonda all passed out. Corll seized the opportunity to teach Henley a lesson for bringing a girl.

Corll tied all three of them up. When Henley woke and saw his predicament he begged Corll to let him live. He pleaded to Corll, saying he would rape and kill Rhonda while Corll did the same to Timothy.

Corll took Timothy to the bedroom and stripped him of his clothes, gagged him and tied him to the torture board. Corll then demanded that Henley do the same to Rhonda.

Henley grabbed Rhonda and took her clothes off as Corll looked on. However, Henley was unable to get an erection, which Corll found funny. The killer began calling Henley names.

Henley was furious. He picked up Corll's .22 calibre pistol and aimed it at the killer. Corll laughed and egged on the young man, daring him to shoot him. He mocked him

> "Go on Wayne, kill me. Why don't you?"

As Corll came towards Henley he fired six bullets into Corll's chest killing him instantly.

Corll collapsed in a bundle to the floor. Henley felt free, but knew he had a long way to go. He untied his friends and called the police. He told them he had shot Corll in self-defence.

Police swarmed over the house, unaware of what was about to unfold. They were not to know the amazing story Henley would reveal.

Henley told police that Corll's house contained a torture room that contained a wooden board with handcuffs fitted at each top corner and rope knots at each bottom corner. He told them then about the victims. The young man's monotone story continued with details of Corll's parties. Where the killer would give teens drugs or glue to sniff to render them unconscious. He would tie the victims up and sodomize them on his torture board before murdering them.

To prove his tale was true the police asked for the names of the victims. The first three that Henley was able to recall were three that police had on their missing persons list. Then Henley told the officers where they would probably find all the victims. He took them to the Silver Bell Street boat-shed rented by Corll in Houston.

At the boat shed, police scientific officers began the dig. In no time, lime and the telltale smell of decay were uncovered.

The first body was found. The naked body of the thirteen-year-old boy was in a plastic bag and the excavation continued. As each body was brought out Henley cried more, he said at one point.

> "It was all my fault"

When asked why he replied

> "Because I introduced him to them boys".

When police finished their search they found the bodies of seventeen boys under the floor of the boat shed, and ten others were found at various other sites.

David Brooks watched the news reports as the body count grew and decided it was time to talk to police.

When he arrived at the police station, the officers interviewing Henley told him that Brooks had just turned up. Henley looked relieved and said:

> *"That's good, now I can tell you the whole story".*

Henley admitted to murdering some of the victims himself as Brooks claimed his involvement had been far less. He said he had helped with several murders but it was not until Henley joined the group that Corll lost complete control of the situation and the murders escalated.

> *"Most of the killings that occurred after Wayne came into the picture involved all three of us ... Wayne seemed to enjoy causing pain."*

Both boys were charged with a variety of murders and sent to trial.

Brooks was tried and sentenced for life for his involvement in at least six murders.

Henley was tried for murder in July 1974. He was found guilty of the murders and sentenced to six 99-year terms of imprisonment. His killing of Dean Corll was judged to be a justifiable homicide.

In December 1978, Henley's conviction was overturned on the grounds that the trial had suffered from pre-trial publicity. He was convicted a second time in June 1979.

Juan Corona

Outside Yuba City, California on May 19, 1971, as farmer Goro Kagehiro took a morning walk around his orchard inspecting his latest produce, he came across a large hole of approximately 7 feet long and 3 ½ feet deep. The farmer was puzzled by the trench but did not give it another thought until hours later.

Later that evening, Mr Kagehiro returned to the orchard to find the hole filled in. As no-one had permission to dig on his land he became suspicious and called the police. Sutter County officers arrived the next morning and began the dig that surprised everyone.

Amongst the rubbish in the hole, County Deputy Steve Sizelove recovered a body. He recognised the old man as Kenneth Whitacre, a man he had spoken to three days earlier in Yuba City. Follow up interviews around the city revealed that Kenneth was last spotted on May 19; the day the hole appeared and been subsequently filled in. The autopsy on Kenneth's body revealed multiple stab wounds in the chest and back, probably with a knife; the majority of which were post mortem. A large wound to the rear of the head had killed the man and the coroner surmised the weapon had been a machete.

Sheriff Whiteaker spoke further with farmer Goro Kagehiro and learned that the man employed Juan Corona as his labour -contractor, a person who hires and fires the farm hands.

The police also learnt that Corona had been the chief suspect in the vicious 1970 attack on José Romero Raya in Marysville. What intrigued the Sheriff was that the wounds on José's body were very similar to those found on Kenneth's body.

On May 24, 1971, Sullivan Ranch foreman Ray Duron, was called by one of his workers to view an area of land which, given the news from the Kagehiro orchard, looked suspicious. Their suspicions were confirmed when a police dig unearthed a body. With the find, the officers decided to search the remainder of the ranch.

Near a peach orchard, officers discovered another grave. Disturbingly, it had only recently been created. Within the grave officers recovered the body of Melford Sample. Further searches around the orchard produced three more graves, including that of John Jackson.

On May 25, the body of Pete Bierman was added to those unearthed. Pete's last sighting was in Marysville with Juan Corona; the police now knew they had their killer.

At 4am on May 26, 1971, Corona was arrested at his house in Yuba City. A search of his home uncovered a number of items, including a gun, that detectives later proved was used to fire bullets found in at least one victim. A large knife, boots and clothing all stained with blood were also taken away as evidence.

The police excavation continued, and William Kamp's body was unearthed at the Sullivan Ranch on May 27. He had been shot once and stabbed multiple times including several times in the head. Jonah Smallwood was next to be recovered. The diggers then moved to a northern corner of the ranch where further bodies were found.

Sixty-year-old Paul Allen was the first recovered. Paul was well known to officers; he was a drifter who had been arrested 45 times in his life, mainly for drunkenness. On May 12, 1971 Paul was last seen by a witness getting into a truck along with Elbert Riley and Jonah Smallwood. Twenty-seven-year-old Juan Corona drove the truck. The bodies of Elbert and Jonah were also found buried on the ranch. On June 4, 1971, the twenty-fifth and final body, that of Joseph Maczak was found. Within the grave, officers found important clues, two meat receipts were found, each signed by Juan Corona, which further cemented the man's guilt and he was charged with the murders of the twenty-five victims.

The trial of Juan Vallejo Corona took place in Fairfield, California in the Solano County Courthouse. Judge Richard E Patton resided over the courtroom as testimony began on October 3, 1972.

Corona's defence lawyer, Richard Hawk, questioned everything he could and objecting to whatever prosecution evidence was presented. He did, however, gain points during examination when police officers admitted that fingerprints were not taken from any items recovered from the grave, including the meat receipts.

Hawk also suggested that it was not Corona but Ray Duron, the farm foreman, who was the killer.

The prosecution, led by Dave Teja, presented their case in which they linked Corona to the murders. Blood stains on the back of his pickup were from three different blood groups, also a saliva sample from a cigarette butt found in one of the graves matched Corona's blood group. The most important evidence was found in the search of Corona's house, a ledger, written by Corona, listing the names of the victims.

During final arguments Richard Hawk presented an argument of reasonable doubt, citing that the prosecution had failed to prove beyond doubt that Corona was guilty. The jury of ten men and two women left to deliberate on Corona's guilt or innocence, on January 10, 1973.

While the jury deliberated, Corona was rushed from jail to hospital having suffered what doctors described as a 'prelude to a heart attack'.

On January 18, the jury finished their deliberations. For the first count, the murder of Kenneth Whitacre, the jury found Corona guilty of first-degree murder, Hawk was angry. He demanded the jury be polled; each jury member confirmed his or her personal judgement.

For count two, the murder of Curtis Fleming, Corona was found guilty of first degree murder, once again Hawk requested the jury be polled and once again their verdict was confirmed by all 12 jury members. Richard Hawk sat still as Judge Patton read out the further twenty-three counts of guilty. For the twenty-five murders, Judge Patton sentenced Corona to twenty-five consecutive life sentences.

The court ordered an appeal after his defence lawyers were ruled to have been incompetent to defend Corona. In 1982, Corona's new defence lawyers presented evidence that the killer was in fact Corona's brother Natividad. The jury rejected the claims and Corona was once again found guilty of 25 murders.

Antone Costa

Antone Costa began seeing a new girlfriend, Susan Perry in September 1968. The romance only lasted a week however, after which Costa stabbed the eighteen-year-old to death. He cut her body into small pieces and buried her on the Cape Cod National Seashore on September 10, 1968. Her mutilated body was found in Feb 1969 with three others.

Within six weeks of Susan's murder, Patricia Walsh and Mary Ann Wysocki, both twenty-three, were listed as the third and fourth victims of Provincetown resident Antone "Tony" Costa.

State police investigators found their bodies, along with those of Eastham woman Sydney Lee Monzon, 19. All the victims had been mutilated and chopped into pieces and placed into shallow graves near a spot inside the Cape Cod National Seashore that Costa referred to as his marijuana garden.

The killer went to trial for the murders and found guilty, though suffering schizophrenia. He was sent to prison, where on May 12, 1974 he was found dead, having hanged himself.

Mary Ann Cotton

Mary Ann Robson was born in Durham October 1832, (exact date unknown). Her father was seventeen-year-old Michael Robson, a coal miner; her mother was nineteen-year-old Margaret.

Mary Ann would go on to be Mary Ann Cotton, one of the most prolific poisoners in Britain.

When she was nineteen, Mary Ann fell pregnant and swiftly married twenty-six-year-old William Mowbray in Newcastle, England on July 18, 1852.

The couple eventually had six daughters in six years, all of them died from gastric upsets and fever. A son, John was born to the family but also died before his first birthday. The children's deaths were only the beginning.

Mary Ann's husband William Mowbray, died with gastric upset and fever on or about January 19, 1865 (exact date not known). The man had injured his foot at work and could no longer support Mary Ann.

After taking out an agreeable insurance policy on her husband, Mary Ann killed him with arsenic.

With her husband dead only seven months, Mary Ann married her second husband, George Ward on August 28, 1865. The pair had met while Mary Ann was working in the House of Recovery in Sunderland. George had been a patient.

The marriage lasted a little over a year, ending with George's death. He died of severe gastric upset on October 21, 1866. His wife had poisoned him with arsenic.

In November 1866, Mary Ann took on the job of housekeeper to widower James Robinson and his five children in Sunderland. After marrying her employer, Mary Anne began dispensing of her new husband's children.

For a while, Mary Ann had to go and look after her ill mother, Margaret Robson. After a volatile argument Mary Ann bought arsenic and her mother died a few days later on March 15, 1867 with severe gastric symptoms.

Mary Ann's stepson, six-year-old James Robinson, died of gastric upset on April 21, 1867 after being given several doses of arsenic.

On April 26, 1867, just five days after six-year-old James Robinson died of poisoning, his sister, eight-year-old Elizabeth died of similar gastric upset - brought on by arsenic poison administered by her step-mother Mary Ann.

On May 2, 1867 Mary Ann killed her daughter Isabella. She had killed her two stepchildren over the past fortnight and decided that her own daughter also had to go. The young girl was given arsenic in her food until she finally died in agony.

Mary Ann gave birth to a baby daughter, Mary Isabella Robinson on February 18, 1868, but the little infant died on March 1, 1868. The symptoms were the same as the rest of the family - severe gastro intestinal pains and fever - brought on by arsenic poisoning, administered by Mary Ann.

Soon after the baby's death, Mary Ann's husband James Snr found out that she had taken the money from all of his accounts and still not paid the home loan, he told her to leave. When he came home one day Mary Ann had left and taken their surviving daughter with her.

The serial poisoner found life as a single mother hard, and so left Robinson's daughter with a friend and never returned. James was quickly reunited with his daughter.

Soon after, Mary Ann met Frederick Cotton though her friend, Margaret Cotton. The man had two children and was struggling to look after them alone after his wife and two other children had died. Mary Ann found the situation perfect and was soon living with him.

On March 25, 1870 Mary Ann Cotton dispatched of Frederick Cotton's sister Margaret in the same manner that she had every other person. She poisoned the woman with arsenic.

Mary became pregnant with Frederick's child and yet still continued her search for the next victim. She gained employment as a housekeeper for a doctor. When the doctor did not accept Mary Ann's sexual advances she tried to poison him. The man survived and sacked her.

Mary Ann married Frederick Cotton on September 17, 1870. However, she was still legally married to James Robinson Snr.

Mary Ann gave birth to a son, Robert Robson Cotton, in January 1871 and soon after Mary Ann rekindled her affair with an ex-lover Joseph Natrass.

On September 19, 1871 Mary Ann Cotton's husband Frederick went off to work feeling fine, by the time he arrived he was in incredible pain, doubled over with excruciating stomach pains. He was sent home where he died soon after. His death was later believed to have been caused by arsenic, like her other victims, but when it came to exhume the body it could not be found.

Three months after the death of Frederick, Joseph Natrass moved in with Mary Ann. However Mary Ann tired of Natrass again and though he remained part of the family, becoming a father to the three sons of Frederick, Mary Ann found better company in John Quick-Manning.

On March 10, 1872 ten-year-old Frederick Cotton Jnr died of gastric upsets - brought on by arsenic being administered by his stepmother Mary Ann Cotton.

The next to die was baby Robert. His death was put down to problematic teething but in fact his mother had murdered him.

On April 1, 1872 Mary Ann Cotton murdered Joseph Natrass by giving him arsenic laced food. It had taken the man longer to die than any other victim as she had tried to kill him over such an extended amount of time that he grew almost immune to the poison.

After the death of Natrass, Mary Ann found she was pregnant with John Quick-Manning's child. However John would not marry her as she still was looking after Frederick Cotton's son, Charlie.

To mary the problem could be solved quickly.

Seven-year-old Charlie Cotton died on July 12, 1872, his stepmother Mary Ann Cotton had poisoned him with arsenic. The little boy had been the killer's eighth known victim.

An inquest was held into Charlie's death and afterwards a second chemical test was done on the boy's stomach contents and was found to contain arsenic.

Mary Ann Cotton was arrested for the murder of the boy. Soon after the bodies of Joseph Natrass, Frederick Cotton Jnr and Robert Cotton were exhumed; all were found to contain arsenic. The body of Frederick Cotton Snr could not be located.

While awaiting trial Mary Ann Cotton gave birth to a baby girl, Margaret.

On February 21, 1873 Mary Ann faced the magistrate and was charged and sent to face a trial after she refused to speak. At trial she was found guilty of murder and sentenced to death.

March 24, 1873 saw the date of execution for Mary Ann Cotton arrive. She did not have a last meal but only accepted a cup of tea at 5.30 am. She was lead to the gallows in Durham Gaol crying hysterically. At 7.50 am the hood was placed over her face and the noose put around her neck. The executioner pulled the trap door and Mary Ann fell through. She did not die instantly with a broken neck, but slowly strangled at the end of the hangman's rope. It took her three minutes to die.

Dr Thomas Cream

Four years after London prostitutes were falling victim to the murderous hands of the mysterious Jack the Ripper. London women were again falling to another serial killer. This time however, poison was the method and the killer captured and executed.

Dr Thomas Neill Cream was born in Glasgow, Scotland on May 27, 1850 to parents William and Mary. The family immigrated to Canada in 1854 when Cream was four-years-old.

When Cream reached twenty-two-years-old, he embarked on a career in medicine, enrolling in the McGill College in Montreal where, four years later, he received his medical degree. Cream, in 1876, met and quickly became engaged to Flora Brooks. The couple were forced to marry after Flora's father Lyman Brooks, discovered that she had aborted a child fathered by Cream.

Cream left for London to continue his medical studies, leaving his new wife in Canada. He arrived in the autumn of 1876 and attended St Thomas' Hospital for two years whilst working as an obstetrics clerk. During 1877, Cream failed in the entrance examinations at the Royal College of Surgeons but succeeded in being admitted to the Royal College of Physicians and Surgeons in Edinburgh, Scotland. Cream eventually qualified for a midwifery license.

Meanwhile back in Canada, Cream's wife Flora died of bronchitis in August 1877 (many years later Flora's death would be considered suspicious with Flora's relatives claiming she died as a result of the pills Cream regularly sent to her).

In May 1878, Cream returned to Canada and set up his own practice in Ontario, advertising himself as Dr Cream: Physician and Surgeon. On May 3, 1879, the dead body of Kate Gardener was found in the store situated below Cream's medical practice. An investigation into her death identified that an overdose of chloroform was the cause. Kate's friend, Sarah Long, told the inquest that Kate had visited Cream in order to get an abortion and offered Cream $100 to perform the operation. Cream admitted that Kate had approached him but turned down the money and the request. Sarah Long also accused Cream of suggesting blackmailing a male guest at the hotel where Kate worked, whom she claimed was the father of her unborn child. The jury at the inquest concluded that Kate's death was murder by persons unknown.

Cream quickly packed his bags and left Canada for Chicago and in August 1879 set up a new practice.

On August 20 1880, George Green noticed a stench in the building where he lived and called police. Lieutenant Steele from the local police station entered the second floor flat at 1056 West Madison Avenue and discovered the decomposing remains of the building's owner Mary Faulkener. The post mortem doctor could not identify the cause of death, but was able to determine that Mary had recently had an abortion. George Green gave police a description of the doctor who had repeatedly visited Mary's apartment. The description led police directly to Cream's drugstore nearby.

There, police arrested Cream and discovered a letter written by his coloured assistant Miss Hattie Mack stating that Mary Faulkener had died during an abortion. Hattie, once arrested, told police the story of Cream and Mary Faulkener.

Mary had visited Cream in order to have an abortion, because she needed to work and couldn't if she was carrying a child. Although not present in the room during the operation, Hattie became aware that it had failed. Cream decided to cover his tracks and began 'damaging' Mary's body in an attempt to prevent her identification.

Cream, arrested for murder, went to trial on November 16 1880. Cream's attorney Alfred Trude declared that the poor work performed on the unfortunate Mary Faulkener could not have been done by an experienced doctor, nor should the jury believe a coloured woman over the word of a white man. After fifteen minutes of deliberation the jury returned a verdict of not guilty.

Despite the close call of the murder trial, Cream continued his suspicious activities and in December 1880 Ellen Stack died after taking pills that Cream had prescribed for her. No investigation took place into her death.

Julia Stott, under request from her husband, Daniel, regularly visited Cream to pick up her husband's prescription pills for epilepsy; pills that Cream had been advertising as a cure all. After four months of taking the pills, sixty-one-year-old Daniel Stott died on June 12, 1881. Known to suffer from fits, doctors put his death down to his illness.

Though Cream was above suspicion he would not keep quiet. Cream contacted the county coroner in Chicago and stated the chemist at Buck and Rayner had put too much strychnine in the medicine that Daniel Stott had taken and would sue the company for damages. The Coroner tested Daniel Stott's pills on a stray dog, within fifteen minutes the dog was dead. Daniel's body was exhumed and examined by Professor Walter Haines. The report indicated that Daniel's body contained enough Strychnine poison to kill him 3 times over. But it was Cream who was charged with murder and not the chemist Cream had blamed.

Cream did not restrict himself to murder. He also attempted to blackmail upstanding Chicago citizens by writing scandalous notes on the back of postcards. Cream was arrested for the blackmail attempts on June 18, 1881 and given bail at $1200 that was paid by Mary McClellan, the mother of his new fiancé. Once on bail Cream fled back to Ontario, Canada, where, on July 27 he was arrested. He was extradited back to Chicago to stand trial for the murder of Daniel Stott. The trial opened on September 20, 1881.

Julia Stott told the court that Cream had plotted to kill her husband; a claim backed by evidence presented by Mary McClellan. Mary had overheard Cream plotting to murder Daniel Stott, using poison. Cream tried to claim that Julia Stott was the poisoner, but the jury was unimpressed and found Cream guilty of murder on September 23 1881. Cream was sentenced to life imprisonment to be served at Illinois State Penitentiary at Joilet.

Cream's brother Daniel, persuaded Governor Joseph Fifer to grant Thomas Cream clemency which resulted in the sentence reduced to seventeen years with additional time off for good behaviour. This meant that Cream was released from prison on July 31, 1891 having served less than 10 years of the original life sentence.

On his release Cream's appearance had changed dramatically and he was dependant on opiate drugs.

Cream decided to leave for England, arriving in London on October 6, 1891. On October 12, Cream purchased Nux Vomica (a mixture of Strychnine and Brucine) from a chemist in Parliament Street and signed the poisons register as Thomas Neil MD of 103 Lambeth Palace Road.

On the evening of October 13, 1891, nineteen-year-old prostitute Ellen Dunworth was seen struggling as she walked along Morpeth Place. Suddenly, Ellen fell to the floor face first. James Styles rushed over to help the young lady to her feet and helped her home to Duke Street where she began to convulse violently. A doctor was called who recognised the convulsions as an effect from Strychnine poisoning. Ellen gave the doctor a description of Cream. They had spent the last few hours together, and Cream had given her drinks from a white bottle. She described Cream as

"A tall gentleman with crossed eyes and bushy whiskers".

The convulsions worsened and Ellen was rushed to St Thomas's Hospital at 9.00pm but died before arriving. The post mortem performed by Thomas Herbert revealed large amounts of Strychnine present in her stomach.

On October 20, 1891, twenty-seven-year-old part-time prostitute and known heavy drinker Matilda Clover returned to her home on Lambeth Road after an evening encounter with a man named "Fred". At 3.00am Matilda's landlady was woken by loud screams emanating from Matilda's room; she was in agony and complaining that "Fred" had poisoned her with some pills.

The landlady, Mrs Vowles, called for a doctor but none arrived until 7 o'clock that morning. When Dr Frances Coppin arrived, he put the convulsions down to alcoholic poisoning and left, leaving some medicine behind. Matilda took the medicine but the convulsions were worse than before, again Dr Frances Coppin was called to the house but Matilda died shortly after 9.00am. No autopsy took place as alcoholic poisoning was suspected as the cause of death.

In April 1892, Cream, using the name Fred once more, befriended two women twenty-one-year-old Alice Marsh and eighteen-year-old Emma Shrivell. Early on the morning of April 12, landlady Charlotte Vogt was woken by the sound of both Alice and Emma screaming in agony. Rushing to the second floor of the house at 118 Stamford Street, Charlotte found Alice in the hallway foaming at the mouth and Emma convulsing on the bed. The police were sent for after Emma claimed that "Fred" had poisoned them with white pills he had insisted they swallow.

The two women were immediately taken to St Thomas's Hospital, but Alice died before arriving and Emma six hours later. The post mortem performed by Dr Thomas Stevenson on April 16, determined that both women had died of strychnine poisoning with Alice's stomach containing 6.79 grains of the poison and Emma's 3.26 grains. One grain of strychnine is considered a fatal dose.

At the same time, Dr Joseph Harper of Barnstaple received letters from a man calling himself W.H. Murray, claiming to hold evidence that Dr Harpers' son, Walter (an intern at St Thomas's Hospital) had poisoned both Alice and Emma. The letter said that in exchange for £1500 the evidence would be destroyed. The deputy Coroner, George Wyatt, received a similar letter but when he investigated the return address, it was found to be fabricated.

After the death of Ellen Dunworth, George Wyatt had received a letter from A. O'Brien, a police detective who claimed that Ellen had been poisoned with strychnine. The letter also stated that he knew the poisoner of Ellen and if George would pay £300,000 then the culprit would be named. A second letter from H. Bayne named an elected member of parliament as the killer of Ellen Dunworth. The police were notified and they attempted to contact H. Bayne, but without success.

Police decided to investigate the sales of strychnine at local chemists. The investigation placed several people under suspicion, one of whom was Cream. On May 12, 1892 officers began to tail Cream and took notes on his activities after Cream's close friend John Haynes, an ex-police detective, became suspicious of his extreme interest in the case.

Cream once, inadvertently mentioned to the ex-police officer that Matilda Clover had been poisoned. John forwarded his suspicions about Cream to the authorities. They were very interested. Given that Matilda Clover's death was officially put down as alcohol poisoning and not murder, London police decided to reinvestigate the cause of Matilda's death, and her body was exhumed from a pauper's grave in Tooting

Cemetery. On May 6, 1892 Dr Thomas Stevenson conducted the autopsy and was in no doubt that Matilda's death was caused by strychnine poisoning and not alcoholism as originally thought and an inquest followed.

On July 13, the inquiry into the death of Matilda Clover ended with the conclusion that Cream was responsible for administering the strychnine that killed Matilda and he was subsequently charged with her murder on July 18, 1892.

On October 17, 1892, the trial of Dr Thomas Neil Cream opened at the Old Bailey under Justice Henry 'Hanging' Hawkins. Prosecutor Sir Charles Russell, QC had an impressive list of witnesses. Each testified that they had seen Cream with the deceased woman. Dr Thomas Stevenson testified that when Cream was arrested he carried numerous bottles of pills; each pill containing lethal doses of strychnine. Walter De Grey Birch, a handwriting expert, stated that the letters claiming knowledge of the poisons were also penned by Cream. Defence counsel Gerald Geoghegan offered no defence witnesses, but presented his case based on the fact that no evidence directly linked his client with the murders.

The jury took ten minutes to reach their verdict – Guilty

Judge Hawkins sentenced Cream to death by hanging to be carried out after the traditional three Sundays had passed. After the sentence was set, Cream's lawyers claimed insanity, but on November 11, the appeal was denied.

Doctor Thomas Neill Cream was led to the scaffold that was erected in the yard of Newgate gaol on November 15 1892. Public executions in England had ended in 1868, but 5000 people turned up outside the gates in the rain to witness hangman Billington execute the prisoner. Cream's alleged last words before the trapdoor was opened was 'I am Jack the R......'

Almost one hundred and twenty years after the Jack the Ripper murders, Cream is still considered a suspect in the case. The fact that Cream was in prison in Illinois, USA from 1881-1891 – the murders having occurred in 1888 makes it impossible for him to be in London during the Ripper murders. Yet he's name is still high on the list of suspects.

D
Andonis Daglis

Twenty-three-year-old Andonis Daglis was caught after he let Englishwoman Ann Hamson escape. The Greek man who had mistaken her for a prostitute abducted Ann. However, the woman was able to convince Daglis that she, in fact, was not a prostitute and was spared.

Ann Hamson told police of her abduction and Daglis was quickly arrested for the abduction and the suspicion of three other sexual murders and six attempted murders between 1993 and 1996.

In an Athens court on January 23, 1997 Daglis was found guilty of three sex murders as well as the attempted murder of six other women. In court, Daglis was on the stand for weeks discussing how he had abducted three prostitutes, repeatedly raped them before cutting them up with a chainsaw in his house. The bodies were then discarded along the highway.

Daglis was sentenced to thirteen life sentences.

Jerome Dennis

Early in April 1992, the bodies of Elizabeth Clenor and Stephanie Alston were found dead. Both women had been abducted and raped by Jerome Dennis before being murdered.

On April 8, the body of Denise Gaskins was found, in an abandoned building, and more bodies continued to be uncovered. Fourteen-year-old Shakia Hedgespeth was also found dead on April 8. Like the other victims, her killer had raped her before death.

Sixteen-year-old Jamillah Jones vanished sometime during her walk home after a night out with friends in East Orange, Newark. At 2.49am on April 10, 1992, barely hours after she was last seen, Jamillah's body was found stabbed and raped. The location of Jamillah's body was just a short walk from where the bodies of Elizabeth Clenor and Stephanie Alston were recovered.

Two separate witnesses came forward and described to police incidents in which a black male approached them from behind and attacked them with a knife. In both cases the women were able to escape and gave police a description of the man that had attacked them. The descriptions that both women gave clearly indicated that it was the same man.

Jerome Dennis matched the description and had been released on parole during November 1991 having served time for two rapes. On April 12, 1992, Dennis was re-arrested, questioned by police and then confessed to four murders, those of Jamillah Jones; Elizabeth Clenor; Stephanie Alston and Shakia Hedgespeth. He denied any involvement in any other murders, including that of Denise Gaskins.

However Dennis did confess to a fifth murder that of Robyn Carter, who was found dead in December 1991.

At the trial on February 26, 1993, Dennis pleaded guilty to all charges and received a sentence of life in prison, with a minimum of 60 years to be served without parole.

Martin and Marie Dumollard

Martin and Marie Dumollard owned a small cottage in the woods near the French town of Lyon. It was here that the couple, posing as owners of a large chateau, lured at least 10 young women from Lyon to their deaths. The victims were either buried in the grounds surrounding their cottage, with one victim reportedly buried alive, or thrown into the River Rhone.

The case broke when the Dumollards attempted to murder Marie Pichon. Marie was hired as a servant by Martin Dumollard when she met him in Lyon. As the pair walked to the 'chateau' Marie felt that something was wrong and insisted that they return to Lyon.

Martin Dumollard would not let his victim go and produced a rope with which to strangle Marie. Marie was a strong woman and was able to elude her attacker. She ran to a nearby house, where the frightened girl had the owners raise the alarm. Police officers arrived at the scene and Marie told them her story.

Police went to the Dumollard's home, where a search uncovered clothing stolen from their victims. Marie Dumollard was quick to turn on her husband and told police of the murders, she also pointed out the graves of several of the victims.

The trial took place at the Bourg in January 1862. After being found guilty of murder, Martin Dumollard was sentenced to death and beheaded on March 8 1862. Marie received a life sentence to be served on the galleys.

Theodore Durrant

Eighteen-year-old Blanche Lamont had recently moved from Montana to San Francisco, staying at her aunt's house while she studied at the Powell Street Normal school. During her time in San Francisco she met and fell in love with a handsome student by the name of Theodore Durrant. Durrant himself was studying to be a doctor at the Cooper Medical College and in his spare time he was the assistant superintendent of Sunday School at the Emanuel Baptist Church on Bartlett Street.

On April 3, 1895, Blanche met her lover outside the gates of her school and together they walked towards the church. A neighbour of the church saw the pair enter at a little after four in the afternoon, it was the last time Blanche was seen alive.

Blanche's aunt, Mrs Noble, reported her niece missing that evening after she failed to return home. Durrant, having been the last person to see Blanche before she vanished, was questioned, but claimed to know nothing of her disappearance. He even suggested white slavery as a possibility.

Nine days later, on April 12, twenty-one-year-old Minnie Williams left her rented flat for a meeting of the Young People's Society being held at the home of Dr Vogel, who was the group leader. On the way to the house, she passed the Emanuel Baptist Church where she met Durrant. Durrant persuaded the young woman to join him inside, she would not leave alive.

Durrant, as a member of the Signal Corps, headed for an outing the next day at Mount Diablo (50 miles from San Francisco). While Durrant was away, the church was being cleaned and decorated for the Easter weekend, by a few volunteers. After completing their tasks in the main sections of the church, the women moved into the library. Immediately upon opening the door they were greeted with the mutilated corpse of Minnie Williams. Minnie had been gagged, with strips of her underwear forced down her throat with a stick that had pierced her tongue. Minnie's wrists were severely cut, her breasts had been stabbed once each and a piece of the broken knife still lay in a third stab wound on her chest. A post mortem revealed that Minnie had also been raped after death.

Durrant immediately came under suspicion. These suspicions were heightened when, after a search of his room, police uncovered Minnie's purse. It was considered possible that Blanche may also have been secreted in the church grounds and a further search was made. The bloated body of Blanche Lamont was found on the floor of the church's belfry. Clear marks of strangulation were still visible on her throat. The autopsy once again revealed that her body had been raped after death. Officers were despatched to Mount Diablo where Durrant was arrested for the murders of Minnie Williams and Blanche Lamont.

The trial lasted for three weeks during September 1895 and despite the defence trying to pin the blame on the church pastor, the jury took five minutes to find Durrant guilty as charged, for which he was duly sentenced to death. It took a further three years before the sentence could be administered. On January 7, 1898, Durrant was hanged. His last words proclaimed his innocence. Such was the anger aimed at Durrant, the San Francisco authorities refused to allow his body to be buried in the city, his parents instead transported it to Los Angeles for burial.

E

Marti Enriquetta

Marti Enriquetta was arrested in her native Spain in March 1912 for the murder of six children. A seventh attempted victim, Angelita, a young girl was found inside the woman's lair. She later told police her tale of watching other children murdered and that she had been forced to eat the flesh from their bodies by the "witch".

At trial it was claimed that Enriquetta abducted children from the streets of Barcelona, murdered them and boil the bodies down for use inside 'love potions', which she then sold. She was subsequently found guilty and executed later in 1912.

The case of Enriquetta was used as the basis of the fairytale "Hansel and Gretel".

Ellen Etheridge

In Spring 1982, Texan widower J D Etheridge married his second wife, Ellen, who took over as mother for his eight children. The marriage began well but Etheridge soon became increasingly jealous of her husband's devotion to his children. She decided that her only choice was to eliminate the children. In June 1913, Etheridge, using arsenic, poisoned two of the children. The killer successfully argued that the children died of natural causes.

Her husband's grieving equated to an understandable increased devotion to the remaining children. Etheridge was incensed. On October 2, 1913, her jealousy led to the deaths of two more children. Again she argued for death by natural causes but the authorities were suspicious and ordered autopsies. Their suspicions were confirmed when arsenic was found in all four bodies during the post-mortem. Etheridge confessed to the poisonings during police questioning and she received a life sentence for her crimes.

F

Albert Fish

How Many Victims?

It is a hotly debated subject. How many victims did actually fall prey to Albert Fish? It is speculated that Fish may have indeed murdered at least fifteen children and assaulted hundreds of children over the years. Many of the children that may have been murdered were just put onto the missing children's list in police files and never heard from again. Often the young children were from poor families who had little time to pursue the disappearance of one of their large brood.

There were some victims, however that were pursued and it was proven later that Fish was responsible. Fish brutally murdered eight-year-old Francis McDonnell, four-year-old Billy Gaffney and ten-year-old Grace Budd. This final case brought Albert Fish to justice.

It is very possible that Fish may have indeed gotten away with all of the murders had he not been compelled to write to Grace's mother many years after the girl's disappearance and describe the murder and subsequent delight he felt whilst eating parts of the little girl.

Only once he was on trial for Grace Budd's murder did people truly begin to understand how far the *deranged*[5] man had gone. His sexual practices included *every known sexual perversion and some perversions never heard of before*[6].

A Lucky Escape

On July 11, 1924, fifty-four-year-old Albert Fish decided, after years of sexually abusing victims, that it was time to murder and found the perfect victim. Playing alone on her parent's Staten Island farm, eight-year-old Beatrice Kiel had no idea that she was being watched, until the man approached her. Fish wandered up to the girl in the front yard and offered her money if she would come and help him look for rhubarb in the neighbouring fields. The offer seemed good to the innocent girl and took the old man's hand. She was about to leave the sanctity of the yard when her mother appeared and shooed the unkempt-looking man away.

Fish quickly left the scene but inexplicably returned later in the evening where he tried to sneak into the barn to sleep for the night. Beatrice's father, Hans Kiel discovered the dishevelled looking man and told him to leave immediately.

It was years later when Fish was finally arrested for murder, that the Kiels knew how lucky they had been on that fateful day.

The murder of eight-year-old Francis McDonnell

Three days after the altercation at the Kiel's homestead, Fish tried again and this time he succeeded in finding a victim.

On July 14, 1924, eight-year-old Francis McDonnell played on the front porch of his home on Staten Island. His mother sat nearby, nursing her infant daughter when she saw a gaunt elderly man with grey hair and moustache in the middle of the street. She stared as the strange shabby old man, who constantly clenched and unclenched his fists, mumbled to himself and stared at her son. When he noticed the boy's mother he tipped his musty, old hat to her and disappeared down the street.

---

[5] Deranged: Harold Schechter, Pocket Books, 1990
[6] Deranged: Harold Schechter, Pocket Books, 1990, p 299

Mrs McDonnell was glad to see him leave; however she took a mental note of the man's appearance, just in case. Mrs McDonnell would never forget the man's face. He spooked her for no apparent reason, but somehow Mrs McDonnell knew the man would be back.

Later that same warm and sunny afternoon, the old man was seen again watching Francis and four other boys play ball. The old man called Francis over to him. The other boys continued to play ball taking little notice of the older man. When the group of children looked up again to see if Francis was going to rejoin the game, both he and the old man had simply disappeared.

The disappearance of Francis was not noticed until he did not come inside for dinner. Mrs McDonnell quickly called her police officer husband, who organised a search for his missing son. It was not long before the little boy's body was located. The eight-year-old's sexually brutalised and mutilated body was found in the woods haphazardly concealed under some wooded brush, near the Kiel's farm.

Francis' body showed the marks of an attack by a madman. His clothes had been torn from his body leaving burn marks; his trouser suspenders were wound tightly around the little boy's neck forcing the boy's tiny face to bloat with the pressure.

The assault on Francis had been inflicted with such ferocity that the police first thought the frail old man seen hanging around the boys had neither the strength nor the stamina to wreak such an attack. But nonetheless Mrs McDonnell knew the old grey-haired man was responsible and he became the prime suspect.

The "Grey Man" as he was called, was being hunted for the ferocious and sadistic murder of Francis McDonnell, however the man had simply vanished as quickly as he had arrived. However, it was not the last that was heard from the man. He was to become the prime suspect in the murder of children though a link was later established.

Where's Billy?

A killer with the deviant lust that Fish had was unlikely to leave a four-year gap between killings. So when he had failed to abduct Beatrice Kiel, he tried again only three days later. So it can be assumed that in the years between Francis's murder and the next one that there may indeed be many more children who were attacked and murdered by Fish.

Their stories remain untold and unknown.

Like most days, February 11, 1927 had begun as any other. Four-year-old Billy Gaffney played in the hallway outside his apartment with his three-year-old neighbour Billy Beaton, the younger Billy's older brother was watching the two boys play but left them for a moment to return to his family's apartment. It was such a brief moment but enough for Fish to spirit the two toddlers away from the apartment passageway.

After looking up and down the corridor and into the stairwell the older boy raised the alarm and a search party was formed to look for the two missing boys. After a search, the younger Billy was found. His father asked him,

> *"Where's Billy Gaffney?"*

> *"The boogey man took him,"* the little boy replied.

The police initially ignored what Billy had said as simply a child's imaginary story.

However, after some careful prompting the three-year-old witness gave police a better description of the "boogey man." He was a slender old man with grey hair and a grey moustache. It had been several years since the Francis McDonnell case with a similar suspect, however, police did not link the two and it would be almost a decade before the cases were eventually linked.

Billy was never seen alive again. With the old man, he had just disappeared. Over the next few months the Gaffney's were dragged all over the country to sightings of their little boy, they were often told to prepare for the worse when corpses of little boys were found – all, though promising, turned out to be false leads. Billy was never found.

According to Colin Wilson[7], Albert Fish may also be responsible for the death of eleven-year-old Yetta Abramowitz in 1927. The little girl was strangled and tortured in the Bronx area shortly after the murder of Billy Gafney.

The Budd Family

Eighteen-year-old Edward Budd was eager to work, coming from a poor family where money was always scant. He was prepared to go out and make his own money to help the family. He yearned to travel and thought finding a job in the country would be a good way to experience life.

The keen young man placed a classified advertisement in the Sunday Edition of the New York World on May 27, 1928. It read:

> "Young man, 18, wishes position in country. Edward Budd, 406 West 15th Street."

He was an eager young fellow who waited patiently for responses to his advertisement. Little did he know but he had just written his sister's death warrant. It was Albert Fish who answered the advertisement.

On Monday, May 28, Edward's mother Delia answered the door to a friendly-looking elderly man. He introduced himself as Frank Howard, a farmer from Farmingdale, Long Island, who had seen Edward's classified and wanted to interview him about a job on his property.

Delia told her five-year-old daughter Beatrice to get her brother who had gone to a friend's apartment. The old man gave little Beatrice a nickel for her trouble as she skipped out of the door.

Mr Howard told Mrs Budd how he had raised his now grown children after their mother had left them many years before. Once the children had moved on, he retired from his city job as an interior decorator to a prosperous farm in Farmingdale, Long Island.

He went on to tell Delia that one of the farmhands was leaving and Frank Howard had to replace him. Edward's advertisement had come at the perfect time.

Edward and his friend Willie came bounding through the door eager to meet Edwards' prospective employer. Edward assured the old man he was a hard worker and quite strong. Howard was pleased with what he saw and offered Edward fifteen dollars a week as a farmhand on his farm. Howard also offered Edward's friend Willie the same deal. Both of the young men gladly accepted the more than generous offer.

---

[7] Colin Wilson and Donald Seaman, The Serial Killers, 1992 True Crime p 173

Mr. Howard looked at his watched and apologised that he had to leave for another appointment. He promised to come back on Saturday to pick them up.

Gracie Budd

Saturday, June 2, 1928 was the supposed to be the big day; the two young men sat in the living room of the Budd family's apartment with their worldly belongings packed in small suitcases. They waited eagerly for Mr Howard to arrive; however he did not show up. Later the same afternoon, as the two young men began to give up hope, a hand-written note from Mr Howard arrived, saying that he had been delayed and would call in the morning.

On the Sunday June 3, 1928 Mr Howard called on the Budds' as promised to collect Edward and his friend Willie. He showered the family with expensive gifts of pot cheese and fresh strawberries, which he told them had come from his farm. Delia Budd was delighted by the elderly man's gentle, soft-spoken nature, and invited him to stay for Sunday lunch with the family.

As the family and their guest sat down to lunch, Frank Howard saw ten-year-old Grace Budd for the first time. The family had been to church that morning and all of them remained in their Sunday best in preparation of Mr Howard's return. Grace wore her white confirmation dress with stockings and pearls. It was a sight that proved irresistible to the old man. The killer knew it was no longer Edward he wanted but little ten-year-old Grace.

After lunch Mr Howard again apologised saying he had to leave to go to his niece's birthday party. He promised he would return later for the boys. As Mr Howard was about to leave he asked Mr and Mrs Budd if Gracie could accompany him to the party, he said it would be fun for the little girl to play with a group of children her own age. Attempting to stall the invitation while she came up with a good excuse to stop Gracie from going she asked the man where the party was, he replied that it was at an apartment block at Columbus and 137th Street.

Mrs Budd's motherly instincts told her it was not a good idea, but her husband intervened and said

> "Let the poor kid go. She don't see much good times."

Gracie quickly took the old man's hand and was led away with the promise of a birthday party. As she waved to her family from the front stoop, little did the Budds know but it was the last time they saw Gracie alive.

The old man with Gracie in tow caught a train to Worthington in Westchester. Fish, with his tools for the murder under his arm in a package, only bought a one-way ticket for Grace. The mismatched pair walked along a remote road until they reached an abandoned two-story building called Wisteria Cottage in the midst of a wooded area. While Grace entertained herself outside picking wildflowers, Fish went up to the second floor bedroom, opened up his bundle of tools, and took off his clothes.

He then called Gracie upstairs. When she saw the old man naked, she screamed for her mother and tried to escape. But Fish grabbed the small girl by her throat and choked her to death. He was sexually aroused by the act of strangling her.

He had then propped up her head over a paint tin and decapitated her, catching most of the blood from her still warm body in the can. He attempted to drink the blood but found it made him nauseous. Afterwards he threw the bucket of blood out into the yard. He undressed the headless child, cut the body in two with the butcher knife and cleaver he had brought with him.

Fish wrapped up parts of Grace's body like meat from a butcher in paper. The rest he left there until he returned several days later, when he threw the remaining pieces near a stonewall at the back of the deserted house. He disposed of his tools in the same fashion.

After a frantic night of waiting for Grace's return, the Budds sent Edward to the police station the next morning to report his sister's disappearance. He gave police all the details of her abductor. His name, his farm address and the party at the apartment block address all proved to be false. The Budds knew their worse fears were coming true.

No mug shots they were shown matched the man who called himself Frank Howard. Once again the grey-hair man had disappeared.

The only lead police had was the hand-written letter to Edward and Willie. Police kept that piece of handwriting to compare to the killer when they found him.

Time Goes On
In June 1930, a man by the name of Albert Corthell was arrested as a suspect in the Budd case. He used the name as alias, his real name being Charles Howard; he had been arrested after a marriage-swindling plan had gone awry. The jilted bride had also made the suggestion that Corthell/Howard could indeed be the man the police were after for Grace Budd's murder.

At a line-up Mrs Budd was unable to identify the man and an alibi check for the time of Grace's disappearance proved the man was not the person they sought and he was subsequently released.

Fish was arrested and incarcerated in a psychiatric ward for two weeks for the incessant writing of lewd and pornographic letters to women who had advertised in newspaper classifieds. He was released on January 16, 1931.

When the police arrested Fish they had also confiscated many implements of sadomasochistic sex, including a cat 'o' nine tails and a large wooden paddle.

In November 1934, six years after the little girl's abduction, the case remained open with only one man, Detective William F. King, continuing to pursue the case. To keep the case active, he would let reporters know of phoney and false leads he had, just to keep pressure on the kidnapper and the public interested in the case. This type of ruse is still used today, in long term unsolved cases.

Letters and eyewitnesses came and went any gave the Budd family hope, only to be dashed.

In 1934, one woman saw a photo of a young woman in the arms of a sailor visiting the city. She quickly cut out the photo and sent it to the Budd family; they in turn took the photo to the police in the hope of having the young woman in the photo identified. It turned out to be unrelated woman who had an uncanny likeness to an older Grace Budd, nothing more.

The Letter
After another newspaper article fabricated by Det. King was published claiming they had a witness to the murder and would solve the case within the month, it was enough to force the killer to act out. On November 12, 1934 Delia Budd received a letter. Mrs Budd was completely illiterate but could read her own name on the front. Luckily that is all she had read. She gave the letter to Edward to read to her. Edward read it and ran straight to Detective King. The letter was abhorrent in its detail.

My dear Mrs. Budd,

In 1894 a friend of mine shipped as a deck hand on the Steamer Tacoma, Capt. John Davis. They sailed from San Francisco for Hong Kong China. On arriving there he and two others went ashore and got drunk. When they returned the boat was gone.

At that time there was famine in China. Meat of any kind was from 1 to 3 Dollars a pound. So great was the suffering among the very poor that all children under 12 were sold for food in order to keep others from starving. A boy or girl under 14 was not safe in the street. You could go in any shop and ask for steak -- chops -- or stew meat. Part of the naked body of a boy or girl would be brought out and just what you wanted cut from it. A boy or girls behind which is the sweetest part of the body and sold as veal cutlet brought the highest price.

John staid there so long he acquired a taste for human flesh. On his return to N.Y. he stole two boys one 7 one 11. Took them to his home stripped them naked tied them in a closet. Then burned everything they had on. Several times every day and night he spanked them -- tortured them -- to make their meat good and tender.

First he killed the 11-year-old boy, because he had the fattest ass and of course the most meat on it. Every part of his body was Cooked and eaten except the head -- bones and guts. He was Roasted in the oven (all of his ass), boiled, broiled, fried and stewed. The little boy was next, went the same way. At that time, I was living at 409 E 100 st., near -- right side. He told me so often how good Human flesh was I made up my mind to taste it.

On Sunday June the 3 --1928 I called on you at 406 W 15 St. Brought you pot cheese -- strawberries. We had lunch. Grace sat in my lap and kissed me. I made up my mind to eat her.

On the pretence of taking her to a party. You said Yes she could go. I took her to an empty house in Westchester I had already picked out. When we got there, I told her to remain outside. She picked wildflowers. I went upstairs and stripped all my clothes off. I knew if I did not I would get her blood on them.

When all was ready I went to the window and Called her. Then I hid in a closet until she was in the room. When she saw me all naked she began to cry and tried to run down the stairs. I grabbed her and she said she would tell her mamma.

First I stripped her naked. How she did kick -- bite and scratch. I choked her to death, then cut her in small pieces so I could take my meat to my rooms. Cook and eat it. How sweet and tender her little ass was roasted in the oven. It took me 9 days to eat her entire body. I did not fuck her tho I could of had I wished. She died a virgin

The letter was perverse. Everybody who saw it hoped it was just another crank. But, Detective King knew it contained things that only the kidnapper would have known. Also, the handwriting on this horrible letter was identical to the letter the elderly kidnapper had written to Edward and Willie six years earlier.

The stationery used for the letter and the envelope gave the detective the break he had waited nearly seven years for. The envelope used had a business address printed on it, which the author had poorly attempted to scribble out. The etchings were magnified and the printed address was easily read. The address was traced to a New York City address of the NY Private Chauffeur's Benevolent Association. No man by the name of Frank Howard was employed there. A meeting was called by Det. King of all the employees of the company to ask if they had any way to help with the case regarding the stationery. After the meeting, a man admitted to having taken some home and had left it in a boarding house where he used to reside.

Police descended on the boarding house and enquiries discovered that the next tenant in the room matched the description of the elusive Frank Howard.

The old man had checked out of the room only a couple of days before the police arrived.

The former tenant had called himself Albert H. Fish. The landlady mentioned that Fish had told her to hold a letter that he was expecting from his son who worked for the Civilian Conservation Corps in North Carolina. The son regularly sent money to his elderly father. Nearly a month after the letter arrived at the Budd household, Albert Fish resurfaced. On December 13, 1934, the landlady called Detective King. Albert Fish had returned looking for his letter.

As the police officer entered the rooming house, Fish knew the time had come. However Fish was not going to go easy, he reached into his pocket for a razor but King grabbed him.

"I've got you now," he said to the old man he had spent the past six and half years pursuing relentlessly.

At the police station Fish confessed. Fish told him that in the summer of 1928 he had been overcome by what he called his "blood thirst" -- his need to kill. When he answered Edward Budd's ad for employment, it was the young man, not his sister Gracie he had planned to murder. He had the plot all worked out, he intended to lure Edward to a remote location where he would tie him up, sever his penis and watch as the young man bled to death.

It was only after seeing Gracie that Fish changed his mind and his plans. It was she he desperately wanted to kill and eat.

After his confession, Detective King had a final question. What caused him to do this horrible thing?

"You know," Fish answered. "I never could account for it."

The next day, the police went to Wisteria Cottage and recovered the remains of Gracie Budd

That night, the capture of Albert Fish was leaked to the newspapers and reporters descended on the Budd apartment with the news. Shortly afterwards, Detective King drove Mr. Budd and his son Edward to the police station to identify Fish.

Edward did more than identify Fish. He threw himself at the old man.

"You old bastard! Dirty son of a bitch!" Edward screamed.

Looking into his background Albert Fish was no stranger to police. His record stretched back to 1903 when he had been jailed for grand larceny. Since then, he had been arrested six times for various petty crimes, such as sending obscene letters and petty theft. He had been in mental institutions more than once

Who was Albert Fish?
He was born Hamilton Fish on May 19, 1870, in Washington, D.C. His father was seventy-five when Albert was born and died when he was 5. Fish, along with his eleven siblings, was placed in St. John's Orphanage in Washington by his mother soon after his father's death. He blames his years at the orphanage

for his later problems. "We were unmercifully whipped. I saw boys doing many things they should not have done."

Fish was never adopted from the orphanage and only left when he reached maturity where he got an apartment and lived with his mother.

Fish continues his life story;
> "We lived at 76 West 101st Street, and that's where I met my wife. After our six children were born, she left me. She took all the furniture and didn't even leave a mattress for the children to sleep on."

> "I'm still worried about my children," he sniffled.

In 1934 his six children ranged from age 21 to 35.

> "You'd think they'd come to visit their old dad in jail, but they haven't." he complained.

When Fish's son found out his father had been arrested for the murder of a young girl, he asked an officer the name of the child. When told Grace Budd, the young man cupped his hands over his mouth and exclaimed:

> "My God. That's the name he used to scream out in his sleep."

Apparently the murder of little Gracie plagued Fish. He had nightmares of the child rising from the cottage gardens and attacking him, the killing had scared the man significantly.

Albert Fish was facing indictments in Manhattan and Westchester County. First Westchester County indicted him on a charge of first-degree murder, while Manhattan was preparing an indictment for kidnapping.

The media went into frenzy over the long-time coming arrest of Fish for Grace Budd's murder. He was given many nicknames in the press.

"Vampire Man", "Werewolf of Wisteria", "Ogre of Murder Lodge"

These names did not come close to describing the maniac the police had arrested.

Billy Gaffney Finally at Peace
The press brought forward many new leads about other children and accounts of Albert Fish being seen with children, one lead proved extremely fruitful. The trolley-driver on the Brooklyn tram line saw a picture of Fish in the newspaper and came forward to identify Fish as the nervous old man that he saw February 11, 1927, seven years earlier. The man was trying to quiet the little boy sitting with him on the trolley. Joseph Meehan, the retired motorman, watched the two carefully. The little boy, who didn't have a jacket or coat, was crying for his mother continuously and had to be dragged by the old man on and off the trolley. The little boy, as it turned out, was the kidnapped Billy Gaffney.

Ultimately, Fish confessed the unspeakable things he did to Billy Gaffney:

> "I brought him to the Riker Ave. dumps. There is a house that stands alone, not far from where I took him...I stripped him naked and tied his hands and feet and gagged him with a piece of dirty

> *rag I picked out of the dump. Then I burned his clothes. Threw his shoes in the dump. Then I walked back and took the trolley to 59 St. at 2 A.M. and walked from there home."*

Fish left the boy unfed, and tied up for another twelve hours before returning to finish the torture and subsequent death of the four-year-old.

> *"Next day about 2 P.M., I took tools, a good heavy cat-of-nine tails. Home made. Short handle. Cut one of my belts in half, slit these halves in six strips about 8 inches long. I whipped his bare behind till the blood ran from his legs. I cut off his ears -- nose --slit his mouth from ear to ear. Gouged out his eyes. He was dead then. I stuck the knife in his belly and held my mouth to his body and drank his blood. "*

> *"I picked up four old potato sacks and gathered a pile of stones. Then I cut him up. I had a grip with me. I put his nose, ears and a few slices of his belly in the grip. Then I cut him through the middle of his body. Just below the belly button. Then through his legs about 2 inches below his behind. I put this in my grip with a lot of paper. I cut off the head -- feet -- arms-- hands and the legs below the knee. This I put in sacks weighed with stones, tied the ends and threw them into the pools of slimy water you will see all along the road going to North Beach."*

> *"I came home with my meat. I had the front of his body I liked best. His monkey and pee wees and a nice little fat behind to roast in the oven and eat. I made a stew out of his ears -- nose -- pieces of his face and belly. I put onions, carrots, turnips, celery, salt and pepper. It was good. "*

> *"Then I split the cheeks of his behind open, cut off his monkey and pee wees and washed them first. I put strips of bacon on each cheek of his behind and put them in the oven. Then I picked 4 onions and when the meat had roasted about 1/4 hour, I poured about a pint of water over it for gravy and put in the onions. At frequent intervals I basted his behind with a wooden spoon. So the meat would be nice and juicy."*

> *"In about 2 hours, it was nice and brown, cooked through. I never ate any roast turkey that tasted half as good as his sweet fat little behind did. I ate every bit of the meat in about four days. His little monkey was a sweet as a nut, but his pee-wees I could not chew. Threw them in the toilet."*

More cases came to light that Fish was tied to, including the 1932 murder of a fifteen-year-old girl named Mary O'Connor in Far Rockaway. The girl's mauled body was found in some woods close to a house that Fish had been painting.

With all of those indictments in different counties, there was very little chance that Albert Fish was going to be acquitted. His only opportunity to beat the death penalty was to be declared insane.

Fish was ready for the doctors.
Fish's attitude towards his situation was one of complete detachment.

> *"I have no particular desire to live. I have no particular desire to be killed. It is a matter of indifference to me. I do not think I am altogether right."*

Fish's family had a history of psychosis.

> *"One paternal uncle suffered from a religious psychosis and died in a state hospital. A half brother also died in a state hospital. A younger brother was feeble-minded and died of*

> *hydrocephalus. His mother was held to be 'very queer' and was said to hear and see things. A paternal aunt was considered 'completely crazy.' A brother suffered from chronic alcoholism. A sister had some sort of 'mental affliction."*

He claimed that his real name was Hamilton Fish, named after a distant relative. Tired of being called "Ham and Fish" he took the name of Albert instead.

When he was twenty-six, he married a young woman of nineteen and had six children in quick succession. When the youngest was three, his wife ran off with another man, leaving Fish to raise the children. He "married" again three more times, however the subsequent marriages where bigamous as he had not divorced his first wife.

Dr. Wertham considered Fish's unparalleled perversity unique in the annals of psychiatric and criminal literature. "Sado-masochism directed against children, particularly boys, took the lead in his sexually regressive development."

Fish told him:
> "I always had a desire to inflict pain on others and to have others inflict pain on me. I always seemed to enjoy everything that hurt."

Wertham, enthralled by his subject's sexual habits wrote down explicitly what the man had done,

> *"experiences with excreta of every imaginable kind were practiced by him, actively and passively. He took bits of cotton, saturated them with alcohol, inserted them into his rectum, and set fire to them. He also did that with his child victims."*

Fish confided in Dr. Wertham a long history of preying on children -- "at least a hundred." Fish would bribe them with money or candy. He usually chose African-American children because he believed that the police did not pay much attention when they were hurt or missing.

He never went back to the same neighbourhood twice. He said that he had lived in at least 23 states and he had killed at least one child in each state.

He had also had a compulsion to write obscene letters and did so frequently. According to Dr. Wertham, "they were not the typical obscene letters based on fantasies and daydreams to supply a vicarious thrill. They were offers to practice his inclinations with the people he wrote his graphic suggestions to."

Initially, Dr. Wertham had some concerns about whether Fish was lying to him, especially when he told the psychiatrist that he had been sticking needles into his body for years in the area between the rectum and the scrotum: "He told of doing it to other people too, especially children. At first, he said, he had only stuck these needles in and pulled them out again. Then he had stuck others in so far that he was unable to get them out, and they stayed there." The doctor had him X-rayed and sure enough, there were at least twenty-nine needles in his pelvic region. Some had begun to decay proving they had been there for an extended period of time.

About the age of fifty-five, Fish started to experience hallucinations and delusions. "He had visions of Christ and His angels...he began to be engrossed in religious speculations about purging himself of iniquities and sins, atonement by physical suffering and self-torture, human sacrifices....He would go on endlessly with quotations from the Bible all mixed up with his own sentences, such as 'Happy is he that taketh Thy little ones and dasheth their heads against the stones.'"

Fish believed that God had ordered him to torment and castrate little boys. He had actually done so a number of times.

Wertham was amazed as Fish described the horrible cannibalism of Billy Gaffney's body. "His state of mind while he described these things in minute detail was a peculiar mixture. He spoke in a matter-of-fact way, like a housewife describing her favourite methods of cooking...But at times his voice and facial expression indicated a kind of satisfaction and ecstatic thrill. I said to myself: However you define the medical and legal borders of sanity, this certainly is beyond that border."

Fish told the doctor:

> "What I did must have been right or an angel would have stopped me, just as an angel stopped Abraham in the Bible [from sacrificing his son]."

Fish's children had seen him "hitting himself on his nude body with a nail-studded paddle until he was covered with blood. They also saw him stand alone on a hill with his hands raised, shouting: 'I am Christ.'"

Dr. Wertham, believed that Fish was legally insane: "I characterized his personality as introverted and extremely infantilistic...I outlined his abnormal mental make-up, and his mental disease, which I diagnosed as paranoid psychosis...Because Fish suffered from delusions and particularly was so mixed up about the questions of punishment, sin, atonement, religion, torture, self-punishment, he had a perverted, a distorted -- if you want, an insane -- knowledge of right and wrong. His test was that if it had been wrong he would have been stopped, as Abraham was stopped, by an angel."

Wertham believed that Fish had actually killed fifteen children and mutilated about a hundred others. "That figure was verified many times to me by police officials in later years." He said.

Two other defence psychiatrists testified later at the trial that Fish was insane. The prosecution psychiatrists testified that Fish was sane. One doctor for the prosecution was the head of the psychiatric hospital where Fish had been detailed for observation a couple of years after the Budd and other murders and where he had been judged "both harmless and sane."

The trial of Albert Fish for the premeditated murder of Grace Budd began on Monday, March 11, 1935. Dempsey, the defence attorney planned to attack the competence of the Bellevue Hospital doctors who had observed Fish in 1930 and declared him sane. He also planned to establish that Fish was suffering from "lead colic," a dementia often suffered by house painters.

Gallagher's key strategy was summarized early in the trial: "Now in this case, there is a presumption of sanity. The proof, briefly, will be that this defendant is legally sane and that he knows the difference between right and wrong and the nature and quality of his acts, that he is not defective mentally, that he had a wonderful memory for a man of his age, that he has complete orientation as to his immediate surroundings, that there is no mental deterioration, but that he is sexually abnormal, that he is known medically as a sex pervert or a sex psychopath, that his acts were abnormal, but that when he took this girl from her home on the third day of June, 1928, and in doing that act and in procuring the tools with which he killed her, bringing her up here to Westchester County, and taking her into this empty house surrounded by woods in the back of it, he knew it was wrong to do that, and that he is legally sane and should answer for his acts."

Defence attorney Dempsey focused on Fish's strange life and the self-flagellation with nail-studded paddles and needles. Then he brought up Fish's competence as a father and his love for his children: "In spite of all these brutal, criminal and vicious proclivities, there is another side to this defendant. He has been a very fine father. He never once in his life laid a hand on one of his children. He says grace at every meal in his house. In 1917, when the youngest one of his six children was three, his wife left him. And from that time down until shortly before the Grace Budd murder in 1928 he was a mother and father to those children." He closed his remarks by reminding the jury that it was up to the prosecution to prove that a man who killed and ate children was sane.

Grace's parents and brother testified. Dempsey seemed determined to make the point that both Mr and Mrs Budd gave their consent to Grace going to a birthday party with Fish. When it came time for Grace's father to testify, he was overcome with emotion and began to weep loudly.

On the third day of the trial, over the strenuous objections of the defence attorney, a box of Grace Budd's remains was brought into the courtroom as evidence and as Detective King recreated from Fish's confession how the girl was killed, he put the skeleton together, producing high drama in the court-room.

Dempsey focused on the cannibalism issue as a central part of the insanity defence. It was clear that he was trying to establish that Fish had eaten parts of the girl's body -- something that no sane person would do. But he was unsuccessful in establishing and proving that Fish actually did what he said he did with her body.

Fish appeared to be completely indifferent throughout the trial. Although, at one point, he expressed to his attorney that he had a desire to live because "God still has work for me to do."

Dempsey put several of Fish's children on the stand to testify to his bizarre behaviour -- self-flagellation and sticking needles in his body, as well as his religious delusions. They also testified that he was a good father who always provided for them and never physically abused them.

To further demonstrate Fish's strange behaviour, Dempsey called to the stand a woman who had received several obscene letters from Albert Fish. The courtroom was cleared of women as Dempsey read the obscene correspondence.

Another defence witness was Mary Nicholas, Fish's seventeen-year-old stepdaughter. She described how Fish taught her and her brothers and sisters a game. "He went into his room and he had a little pair of trunks. He would put those on and came out into the front room, and he got down on his hands and knees, and he had a paint stick that he stirred paint with."

"He would give the stick to one of us, and then he would get down on his hands and knees and we would sit on his back, one at a time, with our back facing him, and then we would put up so many fingers, and he was to tell how many fingers we had up, and if he guessed right, which he never did, why, we weren't supposed to hit him. Sometimes, he would even say more fingers than we really had. And if he never guessed right, why, we would hit him as many fingers as we would have up."

Sometimes a hairbrush was used instead of the paint stick. He also stuck pins under his fingernails in front of the children.

Eventually, Dempsey had a chance to attack the prosecution doctors. Dr. Charles Lambert, after a three-hour interview with Fish," pronounced him a "psychopathic personality without a psychosis."

Dempsey asked Lambert, "Assume that this man not only killed this girl but took her flesh to eat it. Will you state that that man could for nine days eat that flesh and still not have a psychosis?"

Lambert answered, "Well, there is no accounting for taste, Mr. Dempsey."

Fish is Found Guilty

The trial lasted ten days and the jury took less than an hour to reach its verdict.

"We find the defendant guilty as charged," the foreman said.

Fish was not happy with the verdict, but the prospect of being electrocuted had its appeal to him. A Daily News reporter wrote, "his watery eyes gleamed at the thought of being burned by a heat more intense than the flames with which he often seared his flesh to gratify his lust."

Fish thanked the judge for his sentence of death by electrocution. January 16, 1936 was the date his execution was set. His final meals were T-bone steak for lunch and roast chicken for dinner – both had the bones removed.

Fish was seated in the electric chair at Sing Sing Prison and after the electricity had coursed through his body the world's most vile killer was pronounced dead at 11.09pm.

The media made up stories about the needles in his body short-circuiting the electric chair.

Kendall Francois

Kendall Francois was born in Poughkeepsie on July 26, 1971and was remembered by the neighbours as a large boy who was taunted by the local children about his size. During his time at Arlington High School he was an average student who kept to himself. By the time he was fourteen, Francois had reached 6'4" and weighed 250 pounds. Due to his size he had successfully joined the wrestling and the football (gridiron) sports teams.

After graduating from Arlington High in 1989, Francois enrolled in the army and was based at Fort Sill in Oklahoma before transferring to Honolulu.

In 1994, Francois was discharged from the army and returned to Poughkeepsie, moving back into the family home. He gained employment as a substitute custodial worker for the Arlington School District until April 1996 when he was promoted to hall and detention monitor for Arlington Middle School.

While working at the school Francois began to receive complaints about his appearance and his body odour. Some of the children called him 'stinky' behind his back; the same comments made later by the working girls in the Poughkeepsie red light district.

On October 24, 1996, thirty-year-old prostitute Wendy Meyers was standing on the corner of Jewitt Avenue and Main Street waiting for clients, when Francois, in his red 1984 Subaru, pulled over. They haggled over a price that resulted in Wendy getting in the car. She was driven to his house and the two entered his second floor bedroom where Wendy insisted on being paid first. During Francois' later confession to the police, he recalled the incident. She insisted that the sex was over after a short period of time together and demanded that he take her back to the street corner. Instead Francois strangled the young woman to death. After calming down, Francois carried Wendy's limp body into the bathroom where he washed it, and placed her into a black plastic bag. He carried the bag into the attic where it remained until September 1998. Two days after her murder, on October 26, Wendy's boyfriend reported her missing.

A similar murder to the first occurred on November 11, 1996. The second victim was Gina Barone. Twenty-eight-year-old Gina was only working the streets that night because of a heated argument with her boyfriend, Byron Kenilworth, when she was picked up Francois and was driven to a secluded spot.

After having sex in his car, Francois got angry and claimed he was ripped off. His hands gripped tightly around Gina's throat and he did not release until she was dead. Forcing the dead girl's body down under the seats of his car, Francois drove back to the safety of his garage, where he left Gina's body until the next morning. The following day he placed it in a black bag and positioned the bag next to Diane's in the attic.

Two days after killing Gina Barone, Kendall Francois killed thirty-one-year-old prostitute Cathy Marsh. Once again Francois became angry after sex and squeezed Cathy's throat until she went limp. After carrying the body from his bedroom, he washed the corpse in the bathroom and placed it in the attic with the previous two victims. Cathy Marsh was not reported missing until March 7, 1997.

Prostitute Kathleen Hurley disappeared on January 15, 1997 and was reported missing the same day.

Her body was recovered from the house of Kendall Francois along with another seven bodies in September 1998.

Kathleen Hurley had not been seen for three days when she was reported missing on January 15, 1997. Mary Giaccone disappeared in February 1997, but was not reported missing until November 13, 1997, her body was one of those recovered decomposing in the attic of the Francois residence.

In September 1997, Michelle Eason disappeared, her body was never recovered.

The *Poughkeepsie Journal* highlighted the disappearance of the women during December 1997 and asked *'Is There A Serial Killer Loose'*. The article put pressure on police who asked the local working girls for help in solving the mystery.

A name that came up several times in the conversations was that of Kendall Francois. The women complained that he would squeeze their necks a little too hard during sex.

On January 18, 1998 the police followed Francois to the red light district of Main Street where they arrested him for questioning. A polygraph was done with respect to the missing women. Francois passed the test.

Francois again cruised the streets of Poughkeepsie on January 23, 1998, when he spotted Lora Gallagher. Francois persuaded the prostitute to join him back at his house for sex.

It was during sex in his bedroom that Francois' hands grasped the neck of his captive; he squeezed hard until Lora fell unconscious. Yet the woman quickly regained consciousness and fought back. She managed to get out from under her attacker's massive weight and demanded to be taken back to Main Street immediately.

The killer calmed down and reluctantly agreed to return her to where he picked her up.

After being dropped off Lora told of her experience to one of her fellow workers, who in turn relayed the incident to a member of the vice squad.

Lora was bought in for questioning later that day and gave a statement about the attack. But she would not sign the deposition until a month later on February 26. When Lora finally signed her statement, Francois was arrested immediately and charged.

Francois' trial began on May 18, 1998, but after pleading guilty to third-degree assault he was sentenced to 15 days in jail. After a week he was released, four weeks later he claimed another victim.

Fifty-one-year-old soon-to-be grandmother Sandra French became Kendall Francois' latest victim on June 12, 1998. As with the other victims Sandra was manually strangled during sex. She was taken to the bathroom where she was bathed, dried and carried up to the attic.

However, by now the attic was getting overcrowded, so the next day, Francois carried Sandra's body down into the basement, placing her on the floor whilst he dug a shallow grave into the crawlspace earth and interred her.

Audrey Pugliese would join her buried in the crawlspace on August 12.

Audrey was a prostitute working Noxon Street when Francois pulled up. Audrey recognised him as one of her regulars, quickly negotiated a price and got into the car. Francois drove his companion to his family house and headed down to the basement. Unfortunately for Audrey, Francois once again 'flipped out' during sex and began punching Audrey in the face. She managed to struggle free from under her attacker's weight and made for the basement door and freedom, she never made it. Francois pulled her back and carried on punching her around the head and face. Audrey fell to the floor but the attack did not stop. Francois used his foot to crash down hard on her face, on her ribs and again on her stomach. Audrey tried to rise off the floor but Francois' hands clamped around her neck to prevent her. The killer's hands did not release their grip until she was dead. Her body was dumped on top of Sandra French's in the crawl space.

Thirteen days later on August 25, 1998, Kendall Francois committed his final murder. Twenty-five-year-old Catina Newmaster, another regular of Francois', was picked up by the killer. Once the price was negotiated she got into his car. Later the woman was lying on the floor of the garage, dead. The next day she was buried in the crawl space.

On September 2, 1998 prostitute Diane Franco negotiated her latest trick with Kendall Francois in Poughkeepsie, New York and drove off to conclude the agreement at his house.

After sex, Diane requested the money, however, Francois got angry and manually strangled the woman, crushing her throat with his massive hands. Somehow, Diane managed to escape from her attackers grip and tried to persuade him to forget the incident and leave.

After a brief stand off Francois agreed to drive the frightened woman back to her pick up point on Main Street. Once there, Diane raced out of the car not looking back, little did Francois know but he was already under surveillance.

Detective Skip Mannian pulled his vehicle into the gas station where Francois had just dropped Diane off. Hearing a man yelling for help, Mannian headed into the store finding attendant Jim Meadows shouting. Displaying his badge, Mannian asked the attendant what the problem was. Jim Meadows explained that a woman had just come in, claiming she had been raped. Diane was walking slowly down the road when the detective caught up with her and convinced her to go to the station with him to report the incident.

During the interview Diane admitted she knew the man who attacked her, as he was a regular, giving the officers the name of Kendall Francois. By mid-afternoon two officers, detective sergeants Daniel Lundgren and Jon Wagner, arrived at the home of Francois in Fulton Avenue and asked him to accompany them to the police station.

At 4pm the interview began with the reading of the Miranda rights to which Francois said he was willing to talk without the presence of an attorney. The questioning centred around the alleged assault of Diane Franco with Kendall Francois admitting that during sex he had choked her, calmed down, continued having sex then finally drove her back to Main Street. This admission fitted in with the story told by Diane, who was by now willing to press charges.

Normal procedure for statements is to have both a written and then a recorded version of events. Just after 4.30 pm the tape recorder was set up allowing a recorded statement to be made.

Once the interview was completed the suspect was left alone in the interview room. After a short time he called out requesting to talk to a prosecutor and also to see photos of missing prostitutes since 1993. The police had already been investigating the disappearance of prostitutes in Poughkeepsie since 1996, but Francois wanted to talk about cases heralding back to 1993. The photos were given to Francois who began to look through them. On one pile he placed the photos of four missing women saying, "I killed them". Another pile of three photos "I'm not sure about those".

By 1am the next morning, a group of police investigators assembled outside the home of Kendall Francois. The suspected killer's father McKinley Francois opened the door to be greeted by detectives informing him of a warrant to search the premises.

McKinley, his wife Paulette and their daughter Kierstyn were requested to leave the house as the search began.

Having been given directions by Kendall Francois, the forensic specialists headed down into the basement crawl space. Shining their torches into the darkness a black plastic bag was clearly visible, a knee joint could be seen with the skin and tendons not yet fully decomposed, peering from the top of the bag. A second bag could also be made out in the darkness; this one appeared to contain a collection of bones.

Having made their initial notes on the findings, the investigators headed out of the basement and went to the second area of interest given to then by Kendall Francois. In the corner of the attic, in plain view, was a clear plastic bag containing the skeleton of at least one person. During the next three days a further eight bodies were removed from the crawl space and attic of the house Kendall Francois shared with his parents and sister. The forensic team closed their investigation at the home of Kendall Francois after almost four weeks of searching.

On October 13, 1998 a grand jury handed down an indictment containing eight counts of second-degree murder and one count of second degree attempted assault on Diane Franco. The next day Kendall Francois was formally arraigned. With Rudolf Treece as his attorney and in front of the relatives of his victims he pleaded not guilty on all counts of murder. Thus ended his brief appearance. As he left the courtroom he smiled to himself.

Knowing that his client was guilty, based on the overwhelming evidence, Rudolf Treece attempted to cut a deal with the District Attorney. He requested a deal involving a life sentence for Francois in exchange for pleading guilty. DA Bill Grady rejected the plea. At 2.00pm on Christmas Eve 1998, Bill Grady announced that the death penalty would be sought in the case of Kendall Francois.

Dressed in the standard prison orange and with his ankles shackled Francois made another appearance in Judge Dolan's courtroom on June 22, 2000. This time Kendall Francois pleaded guilty to all eight murder cases and again guilty in the assault of Diane Franco. Francois also stated that no other person helped him in committing the crimes. His attorney also told the court that Francois was HIV positive.

Under a plea-bargaining, on August 8, 2000, Francois received twenty-five years to life for each murder charge to be served consecutively, resulting in a total sentence of 200 years. In addition, he received between one and a half and three years for the assault of Diane Franco. No appeal was allowed due to the plea-bargaining. His sentence was to be served at Attica prison, New York.

G

John Gacy

Growing Up Gacy

John Gacy is one of the few serial killers that most people know, along with Jeffery Dahmer, Ted Bundy and "Son of Sam" David Berkowitz. John Gacy gained his notoriety from burying 29 of his 33 victims in the soft earth beneath his house.

John Wayne Gacy Jnr was born to John and Marion Gacy on March 17, 1942. He was the middle child of three siblings, having two sisters, one younger and one older. John Gacy Jnr was adored by his mother but was picked on by his father, who was not endeared to his effeminate son.

Gacy was no good at sports, which infuriated his macho sports-crazy father even more and became a source of resentment between the two.

At school, Gacy was an unexceptional child, doing the bare minimum to scrape through. He fell off a set of swings when he was eleven-years-old hitting his head quite hard. After the incident he complained of headaches often and later had several blackout episodes that he blamed on the swing incident.

At the age of sixteen, after a severe fainting episode he was diagnosed with a blood clot and also told people he suffered from a heart-condition. He would avoid strenuous activities most of the time and spent most of his spare time stealing from local stores or homes.

He was a compulsive liar and boaster, telling people interesting stories to gain their sympathy or to get something he was after. He left school without graduating and went to a local business college where he found his boasting skills made him a successful sales and businessman.

He left home after finishing his college certificate and headed to Las Vegas. He was hired as a funeral home assistant for six months but failed to gain any significant work or schooling. Gacy returned to the Gacy family home in Chicago.

By the time he was a young adult he was exploring his sexuality. Refusing to believe he was homosexual he dated a string of young women before marrying in 1964.

Gacy met Marilyn Myer while working at a men's clothing store and once married, the couple moved to Iowa where Marilyn's father offered Gacy the position of manager at one of the Kentucky Fried Chicken franchises he owned. Gacy was not an ideal worker, abusing the authority he was given by his father-in-law.

However, as a member of the local community, he was well known and liked. He joined the local chapter of the Jaycees and was a supporter of local events and charity drives.

Gacy harboured a dark secret, a penchant for young men. For years he had been able to keep his sexual activities hidden, he would often take young men home to his house for anal sex when his wife, with their two daughters, were away visiting relatives.

While at work at the restaurant early in 1967, Gacy chained up one of his younger male employees, Edward Lynch and strangled him into unconsciousness before raping the boy. Edward was fired soon after the attack and went to police to tell them about Gacy.

When police interviewed Gacy he told them that Edward had been making up the story out of revenge for being fired. The police believed Gacy's story and the matter forgotten.

In August 1967, Gacy again attacked one of his employees. Fifteen-year-old Donald Vorhees was forced to perform fellatio on his boss after work one evening and to silence his victim, Gacy paid the young boy substantially. Gacy forced the boy to fellate him on a number of occasions after working at the chicken outlet.

Gacy's face appeared around Waterloo during the Christmas of 1967 as he ran for state chaplain of the Jay Cees and was heralded as their Man of the Year. Donald became very depressed and morose. Most people thought Gacy was a good man and yet the young boy knew otherwise.

By March 1968, Donald could no longer hide the sexual abuse he was suffering at the hands of Gacy and told his father about the attacks, who went to police.

Gacy was quickly arrested by Iowa police for the sexual assault of the teenager. He was charged on May 10, 1968 with sodomy[8]. The man was concerned about the affect the charges would have on his reputation as President of the Jaycees and paid one of his employees, seventeen-year-old Russell Schroeder to beat up Donald.

On August 30, 1968 Russell Schroeder coerced Donald to a wooded area where he sprayed the fifteen-year-old with mace. Russell then proceeded to beat the boy to prevent him from testifying against Gacy at the trial for the sexual assault charges.

The attack incapacitated the young boy for a while and Gacy hoped that the attack would see the charges dropped. Instead it had the opposite affect.

Donald made a second visit to the police station, to tell them about the attack by Russell. Schroeder was arrested and quickly told police that Gacy had arranged the attack, further charges were then added to the list that Gacy faced at trial.

Gacy pleaded guilty to performing sodomy on his victim and on November 7, 1968 he was sentenced to ten years in prison. While in prison Gacy's wife, Marilyn divorced him and the couple never spoke again.

Like many cases, Gacy did not serve his full sentence. He was exceptional model prisoner, working as a chef and he also opened a prison chapter of the Jaycees. The man was paroled on October 18, 1970, against the recommendations of the prison psychiatrist who said that Gacy was a predator and a possible future risk. He served a little under a year and a half in the men's reformatory in Anamosa, Iowa.

With his mother ill, Gacy returned once again to Chicago. He purchased his home at 8213 Summerdale Ave and began his own construction company PDM. His mother moved in with him; his father had died while Gacy was serving his prison term.

However, the short amount of time that Gacy spent in prison had not been a deterrent from seeking out young men to sexually conquer.

Again Gacy was arrested after interfering with a young boy on February 12, 1971. He was charged with disorderly conduct, however the charges were dropped. Had police looked closer into the background of Gacy, they would have discovered that he had been recently released from prison and the case would have

---

[8] An interesting fact is that a charge of sodomy in Iowa includes oral sex.

been pursued.

Gacy had been lucky on that occasion but decided that any future victims would not be able to tell anyone.

The Greyhound Boy
On January 1, 1972 John Gacy killed for the first time. According to Gacy the murder was in self-defence.

Gacy wanted to take his mother home around 12.30am on New Year's Day after a rowdy party. When Mrs Gacy refused her son left alone.

Feeling dejected by his mother Gacy went prowling the streets for anyone in the need of company. Gacy picked up a young man from the Greyhound Bus Station at Chicago's Civic Centre. In his confession to his attorneys on February 2, 1979 Gacy explains what happened next.

"If you want, I'm just cruising around, if you want a ride".

The boy accepts a lift from Gacy. Once inside the car, Gacy propositions the boy. He says:

> *"Have you ever been blown by a guy?, He didn't seem to think there was anything wrong with that. He came out to my house, we both got into oral copulation. After it was over, I think I just fell off to sleep and I woke up and I seen him coming in the room with a knife. Well when I flew out of bed I knocked him off balance. While I was wrestling with him was when I got stabbed, 'cause that's what made me mad, 'cause I took the knife. I think I stabbed him in the chest for or five times. I think after the first or second stabbing all you could hear was the gargling of blood in his lungs or something, I don't know..."*

Once the young man was dead, Gacy decided what to do. He put the body down into the space under his house. A few days later he buried it under there before covering the area with lime.

The boy, known only as the "Greyhound" boy was the first victim of John Gacy. Over the years Gacy would kill another 32 times. Yet between the murder of the Greyhound boy and the next victim would be another three and a half years before he killed again.

To maintain his act of normality, Gacy began seeing Carol Lofgren. The pair married in July 1972, the reception was at Gacy's home. A few people noticed a strange smell lingering through the house. The guests were unaware that the odour was in fact the smell of decay from the body of the unnamed boy in the crawlspace below Gacy's home.

On June 22, 1972 Gacy was arrested by police on charges relating to sexual misconduct. Again Gacy was lucky and the case was not pursued. Eventually these charges were dropped and Gacy continued his sexual conquests.

Little John
The second victim of Gacy was sixteen-year-old John Butkovich. John told his father Marco, that he had been underpaid by two weeks by Gacy and was rather bitter with his employer. John's father told him to go and see Gacy and remind him that if he did not correct the pay that he would tell the taxation department about Gacy not paying the correct taxes.

So on July 31, 1975 "Little John" as he was called by Gacy's wife Carol went to see Gacy. He took two friends with him to confront him. Gacy later claimed that the three teenage boys had threatened him, so Gacy told them to come into the house while he got the paperwork to prove that he had not underpaid the young man.

Gacy came out of the office with a book. He told John Butkovich that he still owed him $300 for the interior decorating that Gacy had arranged for Little John's father's apartment. The two friends who had come with John calmed down; it was clearly just a misunderstanding. Gacy appeared to be a nice guy to Little John's friends and all three of them stayed a while to smoke marijuana and have a few drinks. To Little John's friends, Gacy appeared to be a nice boss. Little did they know that Gacy was seething under his friendly persona. He knew once he had Little John alone, he would torture and kill him.

Later that evening Gacy was out cruising the streets for a victim, he spotted Little John getting out of his car at the corner of Sheridan and Lawrence Streets in Chicago. Gacy called the young man over to his car to make sure that they were still okay and that the afternoon's unpleasantness was behind them. Gacy kept talking, it was obvious to the sixteen-year-old that the man was very drunk; he had obviously continued drinking after Little John and his mates had left.

Nevertheless, John got into Gacy's car and returned home with him, leaving his car behind. Back at Gacy's house the pair drank more alcohol and shared a joint. The sixteen-year-old was not in charge of his faculties. The combination of alcohol and marijuana had left him relaxed and he soon brought up the argument again about his pay.

Gacy ignored the young man's insults and decided instead to use a little trick he had used from his time as a clown. Gacy grabs a pair of handcuffs from behind the bar and asks John if he'd like to see a trick. The odd question threw the young man off his argument and he agreed.

Gacy turned around and held his hands out behind him, encouraging the young man to put the handcuffs on him, making sure they were nice and tight. Gacy then turns back to face the young man who was eager to see how long it took Gacy to release himself from the shackles. Gacy danced around the room, pretending it was taking him a bit longer to get the handcuffs off. Gacy had done the routine before for a lot of sick children, and knew how much they enjoyed it.

Little John smiled as Gacy held the handcuffs out in front of him, both locks were open. The young man was impressed by the trick and Gacy seized the moment to shackle him. Gacy got John to turn around; Gacy put the handcuffs on the young man and told him to try. John assumed there was a release on them and tried to find a button to open them without success.

Gacy's demeanour had changed. He felt like a boy poking a stick at a trapped wounded animal. Little John was trapped in the handcuffs. Gacy laughed at him and held up a tiny key. He mocked the boy;

"The secret to the trick is that you need the key" he hissed.

The young man was terrified; he struggled against the handcuffs, demanding that Gacy take them off him. Gacy continued to enjoy the trick and began yelling at the boy. He told him that the handcuffs were going to stay on his wrists until he sobered up and stopped abusing Gacy about underpaying him.

Little John promised Gacy that he would never mention it again; he made promises of working harder, anything that would make Gacy remove the handcuffs. The young boy was sobering up quickly. The terror was beating through his heart, the sweat was beading on his face and neck, as he felt the steel of the handcuffs against his wrists has he attempted to try anything to get the cuffs off. .

Gacy just laughed as the young man struggled. By 3am the fun was over, Gacy had sodomised John and had sat on him, forcing Little John to fellate him. Then Gacy strangled his victim, using a rope to garrotte the young man, as he sat on him. Gacy later told police how disgusted he was when John urinated as he fought for his last few breaths.

Once John was dead, Gacy uncuffed him. He checked to make sure the sixteen-year-old was dead and then went to the garage for a tarpaulin. He brought one back to the house and wrapped the dead man's body in it. Before morning Gacy dragged the body to the garage. He went back inside the house and slept for the remaining few hours of darkness.

The next day Gacy spent his time digging a ditch in the garage. There had been a drainage problem in there and he knew it was something that needed to be done. However, by now Gacy had other plans for the ditch in the garage. Once he had dug quite a large hole he dragged the rigid body of John Butkovich into it. The young man's body did not fit, it was larger than the killer had expected and so he jumped up and down on the body until it was squashed into the drainage pit.

The next day Gacy filled the hole with concrete. There, John Butkovich's body remained until after Gacy's arrest in December 1978.

April-May 1976

By March 1976, Gacy and his wife Carol no longer lived together. Carol was suspicious of Gacy's intent with the young men who hung around the house, and her husband's abusive behaviour. She moved out of the house leaving Gacy to murder without fear of being caught by his wife.

On April 6, 1976, Gacy murdered his third victim, Darrell Sampson. The young man had accompanied Gacy back to his home, possibly with the lure of a job and a bit of a party. Darrell, was raped and abused before being strangled by Gacy. He was the second corpse buried in the crawlspace under the killer's house.

After successfully murdering three victims without anyone asking Gacy about the boys' whereabouts, he became confident and the next two victims were killed on the same day.

On May 14, 1976 a little over five weeks after the murder of Darrell Sampson, Randall Reffett and Samuel Stapleton both disappeared.

Randall was the first teen to disappear. Gacy picked the boy up in broad daylight and took him to his West Summerdale Avenue Home, where he was subjected to acts of sexual abuse and violence.

Gacy's lust was still boiling when later that same evening he went prowling again.

Fourteen-year-old Sam Stapleton was walking home from his sister's house at 11pm that night when he was also picked up. The boy had been only a block from his own house when Gacy pulled up beside him and offered him a lift.

Gacy took the boy instead to his house where Sam was strangled and raped. Both Randall and Sam were interred in the same grave under Gacy's house.

Mike Rossi

Luckily, Gacy's next victim survived being attacked by the killer. Sixteen-year-old Mike Rossi met John Gacy on May 22, 1976. The pair instantly hit it off. Mike liked the older man's candour and spent the night at Gacy's home, drinking and smoking drugs.

The next day Mike's new friend was not so kind.

Gacy was showing off in front of Mike when he decided to use the handcuff trick. Talking about his tricks as a clown, Gacy got the young man to put the handcuffs around his thick wrists; he then turned around and pretended to struggle to Mike's amusement. Within no time Gacy had the handcuffs off and dangled them in front of the impressed young man. The killer then encouraged Mike to do the same thing. With reluctance, the boy put his hands behind him and Gacy clicked the handcuffs shut on Mike's wrists.

The boy struggled without success. He was unable to get the handcuffs off. Gacy then produced the key. He cursed the boy for being so stupid but was pleased to have the boy captive. Gacy threw Mike to the ground, sat on the boy's chest and forced his penis into the young man's mouth, demanding that Mike perform fellatio on his captor.

Mike never reported the attack to the police and actually continued to visit Gacy at his home. He was given a job by the killer and threatened with the sack if he ever told anyone about the attack. Mike never told anyone about the rape and soon not only worked on Gacy's various building jobs but also performed as "Patches" a clown sidekick to Gacy's Pogo.

Later Mike moved in with Gacy and, after the killer's arrest, became a suspect in some of the killings. No evidence to link him to the crimes was ever found even though he had lived in the home with the stench of rotting bodies.

Mike was one of the lucky ones who lived through the experience of abuse by Gacy. Others were not so lucky. Michael Bonin was the next victim of Gacy, and like many others, his body was found in the crawlspace of Gacy's home.

June – December 1976
Seventeen-year-old Michael Bonin told his mother he was going to help a friend with a painting job on June 3, 1976. The painting job was for Gacy, and after the young man had finished work for the day he went home with Gacy for a few drinks. He was never seen alive again. Later, after the killer's arrest, several of Michael's personal items were found in Gacy's possession.

On June 10, 1976, teenage William "Billy" Carroll Jnr was working part-time as a prostitute when he was picked up by Gacy and taken to the killer's home. Once alone in the house, Gacy raped and tortured Billy before strangling him to death. Billy was then pushed down into the crawlspace under Gacy's house, where he joined the other six bodies in various stages of decomposition.

The eighth murder victim of John Gacy was eighteen-year-old Rick Johnson on August 6, 1976. His mother dropped him off at concert on the other side of Chicago that evening. He told her that he would find his own way home. Several of his friends were going to be at the concert and he would catch a lift home with them. As Mrs Johnson waved to her son as she pulled away in the car, she was unaware that she would never seem him alive again.

The young man vanished. His friends had decided not to go to the concert and after Rick's fruitless effort to find them he decided to hitchhike home. On foot, Rick headed home. Gacy knew about the rock concert and decided to head over there. He had hoped to pick up a young man to take home to fulfil his lust.

The killer saw Rick heading away from the concert alone and decided to offer him a ride.

Gacy took the boy home where he tied him up, raped him and killed him. Rick was buried away from the others. He was buried in the floor under the laundry where he would be uncovered on December 29, 1978.

Nineteen-year-old David Cram was luckier than most. He was able to escape from Gacy. The young man moved into Gacy's house in August 1976 after starting work at PDM the previous month.

On August 11, 1976 after spending the day celebrating his birthday, David returned to Gacy's house. Gacy was drunk and dressed as Pogo the Clown. He grabbed the handcuffs and decided to perform the trick on David. As David discovered the secret of the trick he knew he had to fight.

Gacy did not expect the young man to be strong, yet even with his arms cuffed behind his back David was able to overpower Gacy. David had done a stint in the army and knew about fighting the enemy. As Gacy, still dressed as a clown pushed David around, the young man head-butted his attacked, knocking the drunk Gacy off-balance.

Greg then shoulder-charged the killer. David then grabbed the keys from the man and struggled out of the handcuffs. David went and locked himself in his room.

On Saturday December 11, 1976 seventeen-year-old Gregory Godzik had been on a date with his girlfriend Judy. After dropping Judy home, Greg decided to visit his boss, John Gacy, at home. Gacy opened his front door and happily invited Greg inside.

Greg had helped out around the Gacy home several times in the past. Once he had been part of a group of boys that dug a long trench in the crawlspace of Gacy's home. Gacy told the boys that the trench was so he could lay some extra pipes and tiles because of a broken sewer pipe. The killer was adamant that the boys dig in only a certain spot and that they were not to deviate from the string lines he had placed around the crawlspace. It was so the boys would not discover any of the buried dead bodies.

The boy would never leave Gacy's house alive.

Gacy plied the young man with alcohol before deciding to show Greg the rope trick he used in his clown act at various hospitals. Gacy tied Greg's hands behind his back. As the seventeen-year-old struggled against his bindings Gacy began to laugh. He slapped his employee, calling him a stupid kid before explaining that he will not be able to get out of the rope.

Greg panicked and attempted to push and pull against the rope as it tightened further.

Gacy grabbed Greg around the throat and squeezed. He watched the boy pass out – helpless against the maniacal Gacy and the ropes around his wrists.

The killer sexually abused Greg for hours, strangling him and reviving him over and over again before finally killing him.

Greg's body was pushed down into the darkened crawlspace where he was buried near the other bodies.

To cover his tracks further, Gacy drove the young man's 1965 burgundy coloured Pontiac Cataline to a pet store in a neighbouring suburb. He left the car unlocked and hitched a ride home.

When Greg's mother reported her son missing, the case, like that of many of the other boys who had fallen prey to Gacy, was dismissed as a runaway. A friend found Greg's car soon after his disappearance and his family came to claim it. The car had been the pride of the young man and he would never have left it unlocked. His family knew something bad had happened, yet it would take another two years and over two dozen more deaths before Gacy would be finally caught.

1977

Gacy murdered nineteen-year-old John Szyc on January 20, 1977. Gacy picked up the young man at Bughouse Square. It was raining and Gacy knew he had a better chance of picking up a victim. John Szyc was relieved of the offer of a lift.

The pair returned to Gacy's house and engaged in sex. Once the act was over John Szyc asked Gacy for $20. Gacy laughed at the young man and refused to pay. The two men got into an argument before Gacy decided it was time for his rope trick.

He calmed the young man down and told him about the trick he did as Pogo the Clown. He got John to stand in front of him, with his hands behind his back.

Soon the young man was struggling for breath against the rope, as Gacy had tied it around John's wrists and then looped around his throat. As John struggled, the rope tightened.

Later during a psychiatric evaluation, Gacy told a very different story. According to his version, Gacy blamed Mike Rossi for the murder. In the interview, he was asked to write down words that came to him as he tried to remember the murder of John Szyc; one word he wrote was "Rossi". Gacy tried to suggest that in fact Mike Rossi was perhaps responsible for some of the murders, or at least involved. According to Joseph Koszenzak - the detective in charge of the case - there was indeed a second person involved, though they have never been charged. According to Koszenzak, the accomplice was a young man who worked for Gacy and had a close relationship with him.

Gacy then tried to tell police that John Szyc had been trying to sell his car and went to see Gacy – he was supposedly in a hurry to leave town, an excuse Gacy would use repeatedly with success.

Regardless, John Szyc became the ninth young man to be buried in the crawlspace under Gacy's house.

The morning after John's murder, Gacy took Mike Rossi with him to collect the victim's car - a 1971 Plymouth Satellite. Gacy had coerced the details about the car out of the young man the previous night. Gacy stole the television from the back seat of the car before selling the Satellite to Mike Rossi for $300.

The television was still in Gacy's possession when he was arrested.

Victim number eleven was twenty-year-old Jon Prestige. It was less than two months after the murder of John Szyc before Gacy murdered again. Jon Prestige had been feeling bored on the evening of March 15, 1977 and told his flatmate that he was going to head to the Bughouse, a place he had heard about from friends. Also the place from where John Szyc disappeared.

Jon was enjoying himself at the club when he accepted a better offer from Gacy for a party at his house. Gacy offered the young man drugs and free alcohol if he was to come with him. Jon gladly agreed and like many of the young men before him, Jon never left Gacy's home alive.

Jon's body would be the first exhumed after Gacy's arrest during Christmas 1978.

In April 1977, Mike Rossi moved out of Gacy's home, leaving Gacy undisturbed to kill over and over again.

The twelfth victim of John Gacy was nineteen-year-old Matthew Bowman. The young man had been dropped off by his mother at a Chicago railway station on July 5, 1977. Moments later, Gacy arrived and offered the young man a lift. Matthew got into Gacy's car and driven back to Gacy's home.

Once inside the house, Matthew was drugged, raped and sexually abused before being strangled to death and buried under the house with the others.

Robert Gilroy met Gacy a little over two months after the murder of Matthew Bowman. The eighteen-year-old had set off on September 15, 1977 to meet with friends for a horse-riding trip. Robert, the son of a Chicago police officer, hoped to catch a bus to the riding ranch when John Gacy offered him a lift a mere four blocks from the boy's home.

He soon found himself in Hell, in the home of Gacy. The young man died like many of the others, after hours of sexual torture.

On September 25, 1977 nineteen-year-old John Mowery became the fourteenth known victim of John Gacy's murderous lust. On the day of his murder John had gone to visit his mother, a visit he made regularly. However, on that day, as he left her house, it began to rain, and Mrs Mowery gave her son one of her umbrellas for his short walk home.

The rain not only sent most people inside, it brought Gacy out to prowl. The killer saw John huddled against the handle of the umbrella, trying to avoid getting wet, as the rain continued to pour. Most people hope for a friend to drive by and offer a lift. For John Mowery, the friend turned out to be a foe. Gacy pulled up beside the man and offered him a ride home. Most people in the area knew Gacy, and he was seen around the city's various construction jobs and was an active member on many committees. John smiled at his killer and closed the umbrella. He assumed he'd be home and warm in no time.

How wrong the young man was.

Instead of driving John home, Gacy drove the nineteen-year-old to his own house. He tied the young man up and raped him before strangling him to death and putting the remains with the others in his crawlspace.

The next victim was twenty-one-year-old Russell Nelson on October 17, 1977. The man had been out at a disco on the night of his murder when Gacy offered him a lift home. Once at the Gacy home he was murdered and buried in the crawlspace under the killer's home.

The young man's fiancé and family reported him missing the next day, and fliers soon appeared beside those of the other missing boys. As always, police assumed the man had taken off, which was uncharacteristic of the victim, according to his family. His file was added to the growing number of missing boys in the area.

Robert Winch was one of the only victims who was not a Chicago resident. The sixteen-year-old had run away from home in Kalamazoo, Michigan after feeling stifled by his hometown. It was a usual feeling for most adolescent males. During the time when they change from a boy into a man is always confusing and they react in many different ways. Robert's way was to head to the highway and see where it lead him.

It lead him to the crawlspace of John Gacy's home in Des Plaines, Chicago.

Robert was picked up by Gacy on November 11, 1977 and taken back to the killer's house. Like the other young victims Robert was systematically raped and strangled until he died. He was interred with the other bodies in the rapidly filling crawlspace of Gacy's home where he remained for thirteen months. He would be the eleventh body pulled from the ground.

The killings were escalating and the next victim was murdered on November 18, 1977 only a week after Robert Winch. The seventeenth known victim of Gacy was twenty-year-old Tommy Baling. After a few drinks after work, Tommy rung his wife at home to say he was on his way, that he had been watching a movie playing over the bar and as soon as it was finished he'd leave.

When the film finished Tommy headed out into the cool November air, he felt okay, not having had too much to drink, but still thought it better to walk the short distance home. However, Gacy followed the young man for a few minutes before pulling up beside him and offering him a ride. Tommy accepted the lift and ended up at Gacy's home. Tommy was subjected to various sex acts before being shown Gacy's rope trick, where he was strangled to death as he struggled against the loops around his wrists and throat.

Like the others, Tommy was buried in the graveyard under Gacy's house.

The next to die was nineteen-year-old marine David Talsma. Like Rick Johnson sixteen months earlier, David was on his way to a rock concert when he met John Gacy on December 9, 1977.

Gacy made the man an offer of returning to his West Summerdale Avenue home to have a few drinks after the concert. After the concert, the two men returned to Gacy's home and once behind closed doors, according to Gacy, he became "Bad Jack", the name he gave to the killer within. Within hours of entering the house Gacy had sat on the young man and forced him to perform fellatio among other acts. When Gacy had finished with the boy, he strangled him and buried him under the house with the others.

Gacy later claimed he did not recognise any of the victims murdered during 1977. Yet he could not dispute the fact that all of them were found murdered and buried in the dark, damp, decaying dirt in the crawlspace. In addition, by the end of 1977, as the victim tally continued to grow, Gacy was diagnosed with syphilis.

Around December 30, 1977 another victim escaped with his life. Nineteen-year-old Robert Donnell was picked by Gacy on Montrose Avenue, Chicago. According to Gacy, he propositioned the young man offering Robert money to accompany him home. Robert agreed and Gacy drove to his house on West Summerdale.

Until morning, Gacy raped and sodomised Robert using dildos to penetrate his victim when he was unable to achieve an erection. Gacy also tied up Robert and whipped him with chains. Gacy pushed the man's head into the water-filled bath and held his head under. Robert stopped fighting and lost consciousness; Gacy then revived the victim and started the torture process again. He urinated on his victim, and also held a gun to Robert's head and spun the barrel, firing when it stopped, playing the sick game of Russian roulette. The torture continued for eight hours.

For some unknown reason however, Gacy decided not to kill the nineteen-year-old. He drove to the street where he had picked up his victim and dumped the man, bruised and battered on the side of the road.

Yet Robert still had his wits about him, even after the eight-hour attack, and as Gacy drove off the man memorised the number plate and stumbled to the police station to report the attack.

1978
A week later, on January 6, 1978 Gacy was arrested for the brutal attack on Robert, yet after interviewing the killer the officers believed Gacy's side of the story and the case was not investigated further and Gacy was released.

It was a close call for Gacy and yet he continued to kill some of victims and let others go.

The nineteenth known victim, Billy Kindred was not as lucky as Robert. He was last seen on February 16, 1978 by his fiancé. He had spent the day with the woman he was to marry. They had been planning their wedding, which would never eventuate. Instead Billy found himself that evening in Gacy's torture house, handcuffed and begging for his life as he was beaten and raped by Gacy.

Like the other victims, Billy's body was interred in the crawlspace the next morning, when Gacy had finished with him.

On March 21, 1978 bi-sexual Jeff Rignall stormed out of the apartment he shared with his girlfriend and headed towards a gay bay. On the way, Gacy pulled up beside the twenty-six-year-old and offered him a ride.

Once Gacy had Jeff inside the car, he lit up a marijuana joint and the two men shared it. As Jeff relaxed Gacy pounced. He grabbed the man around the head and shoved a chloroform soaked cloth over Jeff's nose and mouth. Instantly, Jeff began to panic and tried to fight against Gacy, but without success, he lapsed into unconsciousness quickly.

Jeffrey woke up inside Gacy's home. His head was heavy and buzzing, the chloroform giving the man a feeling of being hung-over. He questioned Gacy's motives, was he going to kill him, rob him, rape him? Gacy responded by putting a gun in the man's mouth. The man attempted to flinch away from the killer but could not move far. He was naked and locked in a homemade contraption modelled on medieval stocks. The man's head and hands were in one board, his feets locked into another. Gacy masturbated with his penis close to his victim's face before forcing Jeff to fellate his captor.

Gacy then took a dildo and anally raped Jeff, then used a larger one to again sodomise his victim, before finally forcing his penis into the man's anus.

When Jeff protested and begged for his life, Gacy pushed the rag with chloroform over the man's face again to render him unconscious. This he repeated several times. While the attack continued, Jeff attempted to remember everything he saw. He even believed he had heard an accomplice in the room as he was being sodomised; however as he was in a form of pillory device he was unable to confirm his suspicions.

The man, though battered and disoriented made his way home, after waking up the next morning near the street where Gacy had picked him up, before being taken to the Hospital and the police station.

The police believed the man's story; his battered and swollen face proved testament to the story he had told them, however he was unable to give a clear description of his attacker or the location of the assault. Police were helpless to do anything.

Jeff decided to take the matter into his own hands. He sat on the side of the road where Gacy had picked him up and waited in the hope that Gacy would again drive by. Though unsure of the number plate, Jeff did remember that it was a vanity plate with only three letters on it. It would only be a matter of time before the car came by.

Finally Gacy did drive past Jeff, the man knew it was his attacker and wrote down the number plate- PDM- and took it to the police. He was certain his attacker would see justice. Yet as time went on Jeff was not called to provide further testimony or evidence so, he knew that nothing had been done. Like the other boys who had told police about Gacy his report was noted but not followed up nor investigated.

Gacy believed he was untouchable. He relished in success and strove to achieve further fame from various city events. He was photographed shaking hands with the then first lady Rosalyn Carter on May 6, 1978 after hosting the Polish Constitution Parade. He even boasted of the Secret Service clearance pin he'd been given after supposedly having a background check performed, like the others that were to come in contact with the President's wife. Had the background check been done correctly, Gacy's criminal record would have been discovered and he would not have been allowed anywhere near Mrs Carter.

More boys had disappeared over time. In total the tally rose to thirty-three victims. Many were homeless boys picked up by Gacy for fun; others remained nameless even after their discovery.

One of the final victims was Tim O'Rourke, he remained nameless for quite sometime after his body was discovered. It was only through a tattoo Gacy remembered the boy having that he was finally given a name and able to rest in peace.

Tim met Gacy around June 14, 1978 and was never seen alive again. The young man had left his apartment to buy cigarettes when Gacy made him a better offer of marijuana at his home. The boy with the "Tim Lee" tattoo gladly accepted the killer's offer and returned with Gacy to his home.

Like the others, Tim was raped and abused before being strangled to death. Yet this time he was not buried in the cemetery underneath Gacy's home. The crawlspace was now full, the smell in the confined space was unimaginable, the smell of decaying bodies emanated through the floorboards of Gacy's house. There were up to 30 bodies now in the earth and the room was full. So now Gacy had to decide what to do with the bodies.

Tim's body was wrapped in a tarp and thrown into the Des Plaines River from one of the bridges along the I55.

The next victim was also thrown into the Des Plaines River. Nineteen-year-old Frank Landingin, a part-time prostitute had had an argument with his girlfriend on the night of November 3, 1978. The argument continued into the early hours of the next morning and by 2am on November 4, 1978 Frank stormed out of the house and headed into the night and into the clutches of John Gacy.

He was taken back to the house of horrors and raped and tortured for several hours before finally being strangled by Gacy. The body was thrown into the river as time began to run out for Gacy.

The penultimate victim of John Gacy was twenty-year-old James Mazzara at the end of November 1978. The young man had been out looking for a new place to rent when he found himself on the doorstep of Gacy. He was ushered inside the house and shown around. Gacy seemed like a nice guy to James and soon relaxed and enjoyed a drink or two with the killer. Soon the scene turned ugly and James found himself bound and gagged by Gacy. The killer raped the young man several times during which James choked to death, on his own underpants shoved down his throat.

Gacy, though disappointed that the boy expired before he had finished with him, took the body to the bridge over the Des Plaines River and tossed the body over under the cover of darkness. His body would be found near the banks of the river on December 28, 1978 as the other bodies were being pulled from Gacy's crawlspace.

In all, Gacy had so far murdered thirty-two victims. His final victim brought about his undoing.

Robert Piest

Robert Piest was the final victim of John Gacy and the one that most people know about. Robert was a handsome young man, with the longer hair-style of the day. The evening he disappeared was Monday December 11, 1978. Robert was working at the Nisson Pharmacy in Des Plaines with Kim Byers. It was cold that evening and Robert had given Kim his jacket to wear. He was always doing such things for his friends and family.

That evening he spoke to his employer at the pharmacy about a raise but was rejected. His boss would have liked to give him more money, however at that time it was just not possible. Rob was disappointed, he discussed with Kim that he wanted to earn more money. As the pair chatted about their wages, John Gacy walked into the store. He had come as arranged to discuss with the owner a refitting of the pharmacy. He listened to the young pair chat about their wages and gave Rob a wink. Rob took it as perhaps a chance to talk to the construction company owner about some work.

Kim wandered off to serve a customer with a photo order. When she had finished the order, she filled in an order for her own film processing. She filled in the stub and inadvertently put it into the pocket of Rob's jacket that she was still wearing. The film stub would later convict Gacy.

Just before Rob finished his shift, his mother came into the store. It was her birthday that day and the family was waiting for Rob to come home so they could have dinner together and celebrate. Rob told his mother he would be out in a minute. He wanted to see a man about a job.

Mrs Piest returned to her car to wait for Rob. Rob followed Gacy out of the pharmacy to his car to discuss a job. Gacy smiled at the handsome young man and told him to get into the passenger seat. It was cold and they could talk better in the car. Rob gladly got in as he believed he was about to get a higher paying job than the one at the pharmacy. Gacy leaned over towards the young man and clamped a cloth with chloroform on it over Rob's mouth, the boy struggled a moment before lapsing into unconsciousness.

Gacy drove home, as Mrs Piest sat outside the pharmacy not knowing that she would never see her son alive again.

The Discovery
David Genty had the job of looking in the crawlspace of Gacy's home. At that point, they were only looking for Robert Piest. The Des Plaines Police Department were sure that Gacy had something to do with the young man's murder and were determined to find out what had happened.

Officer Genty jumped down into the crawlspace through the trapdoor in the living room closet. The ground was damp and the smell of death lingered. Genty has smelled the scent before, that of rotting flesh. It was impossible that it was Piest. It had been cold leading up to Christmas and it would have preserved the body better. Therefore, what was the smell Genty asked himself? Was there another body? Genty had no idea what he was about to find.

The crawlspace was only two and a half feet hight, so Genty had to crawl on his stomach, a shovel in one hand and a torch in the other. He let the torch beam dance across the floor. The ground was uneven, there were piles of dirt and a wash of lime covered most of the ground. The piles of dirt looked like graves, and Genty crawled to the first one. He dug with his hands and the earth quickly gave up its secrets.

A decomposed foot protruded from the dirt that Genty moved. It was obviously not Robert Piest. Genty called from the trapdoor that he had found a body and he believed there were more. A team of technicians were assembled to continue the excavation; it was now a serial murder investigation.

The officers in charged quickly returned to Gacy's holding cell and charged Gacy with murder. However, Gacy was ready for them with an insanity defence. He began talking about "Bad Jack" who hated homosexuals as well as other personas.

On December 22, 1978, Gacy was furious when he learnt that the officers were pulling apart his immaculate house to get to the crawlspace. He asked for a pen and paper and drew them a map of where the bodies where buried, so they would not destroy his home. The map was accurate, and though it did not prevent the officers from completely removing the floor from Gacy's house, it did give the prosecution a map to overlay the exact locations of the bodies recovered, that then cemented Gacy's guilt at trial.

He also conceded that they would find around twenty-five to thirty victims in the crawlspace. Gacy was one of the world's most prolific serial killers. Gacy also told the officers that they would not find Robert's body in the crawlspace. He had in fact run out of room and so he had dumped the boy's body from the bridge on I55 that overlooked the Des Plaines River.

In total twenty-eight bodies were removed from the crawlspace of Gacy's home. The body of John Butkovich was dug up from under the garage concrete floor and Rick Johnson's body was discovered under the laundry room. Three others, Tim O'Rourke, James Mazarra and Robert Piest were eventually found in the waters of the Des Plaines River.

The trial

The trial of John Gacy opened in the Cook County Court on February 6, 1980 amid a frenzy of publicity. He was, until only recently, the most prolific serial killer in America. The prosecution's case was based on a wall of memories, the faces of the thirty-three boys that stared out from a poster kept in view at all times. Some of the victims had names, several, sadly, were buried without ever being identified. Yet all of them had met their demise at the hands of the killer who now stood trial for his own life.

By March 12, 1980 the trial had come to its conclusion and the jury left to deliberate its verdict. After two hours the seven men and five women of the jury filed back into the courtroom and handed their decision to the judge.

Gacy was found guilty of all thirty-three murders and the following day he was sentence to death by lethal injection.

As the years went on Gacy became more famous. His paintings grace the houses of the rich and famous as well as the serious "murderabilia" aficionado. Yet inside the prison walls his notoriety earned him several attacks. On February 15, 1983 Henry Brisbon attacked John Gacy and another inmate. Gacy, though injured, was not seriously hurt and was put into protective custody.

Eleven years later Gacy's life came to an end. At midnight on May 11, 1994 Gacy became the 100th person to be executed in Illinois. As over 2000 people arrived outside Joilet Prison for the killer's death, Gacy was being strapped to the gurney. He was asked for his final words and hissed at the gathered audience,

> "Kiss my Ass!"

The needle was put into the killer's veins and the toxins began to flow, yet before the execution had commenced the tubes became blocked and had to be replaced. As Gacy lay on the table the technicians fixed the liquid flow and after ten minutes the execution continued. At 12.58am he was pronounced dead.

In November 1998, a search of the area where Gacy had once lived, in the hopes of finding more bodies was carried out. The search proved fruitless. Nothing else has been found.

Luis Gavarito

Luis Gavarito is one of the world's most prolific serial killers. It is estimated that he brutally murdered approximately 140 children. The killer confirmed the count from a notebook he carried with him during his murderous campaign.

Most of the male victims, aged between seven and sixteen years of age, had been tortured and raped before being decapitated. Gavarito was working as a street vendor when, in 1992, he committed his first murder. He murdered the street urchins who hung around his market stall after giving them money and food.

Yet the Columbian authorities were unaware of a serial killer operating in the country until the bodies of thirty-six boys were discovered in the city of Pereira in 1997.

Gavarito was arrested in October 1999 after being caught attempting to rape a small boy. A chronic alcoholic from a violent and brutal home, he readily produced his notepad and confessed to 140 murders.

Relying on the killer's confession, the police in Columbia searched through almost 60 villages and found the remains of a further 114 victims.

Ed Gein

Ed Gein is probably one of the most famous serial killers, even though his victims only numbered two. Yet it is his extra activities that launched several movies and many books.

Gein was born in Plainfield in 1906 to a heavy-drinking father and a domineering God-fearing mother. A shy, lonely boy, Gein grew to be a reclusive man. When Ed was in his late twenties, his father died so Ed and his brother Henry took over the work on the farm. Both boys remained bachelors their entire lives due to their mother's incessant rantings about women never being able to return their love and only their mother ever truly loving them.

The farm was not at all profitable and it was a hard life for Ed Gein. Things began to slip even further when his brother Henry died fighting a barn fire and Gein's mother endured an incapacitating stroke in 1944, leaving Gein to nurse her for a year when a second attack took her life in December 1945.

Ed Gein was alone for the first time, at the age of 39. In his solitude, Gein began to withdraw from society and reality. His life became more and more bizarre as he left reality behind. The Government gave him a pension that was enough for him to stop working on the farm. He did, however, do odd jobs for townsfolk of Plainfield. While many residents of Plainfield thought he was a little odd, they thought he was just a lonely eccentric who wanted company. Little did they know his solitude had changed the loner into a maniac.

Soon, Gein had sealed off every room in the farmhouse with the exception of his bedroom and the kitchen.

His loneliness that had been compounded by his mother's domineering personality meant that he had not coped with her death well. As in true "Psycho" tradition he had attempted to raise her from the dead. When this failed he skinned her body and tanned the hide, preserving her female physique. He confessed that he often dressed up in it then wore his mother's clothes.

This fetish soon turned into an obsession. Gein became fascinated with the female form and poured over medical and anatomy texts. The first serious signal of Gein's impending madness came when he began grave-robbing fresh graves at night. In 1947, he robbed his first grave. He took parts of the corpses home, where he preserved them. The activity went undetected for years.

Ed's lack of knowledge about sexual relations meant he was confused about his love for the female form, whether he wanted to be female or just liked the feel of female genitals. Gein had actually entertained the thought of castrating himself, but then decided that wearing female genitalia over his own would suffice. To become a woman he would carve out the genitalia of female cadavers and wear them over his own.

His leather skills improved with time and soon he had a belt made out of nipples, a skin vest that he wore on special occasions, he hung mobiles made out of noses, had skulls on his bedposts, bowls made of skulls and drums made out of skin.

But then his fetish for human skin went further, and new graves were not always available. It was then that Gein apparently killed for the first time

His first known murder victim was fifty-four-year-old Mary Hogan, who disappeared from the tavern she ran in December 1954.

Gein then began watching Bernice Worden at the local hardware store. When Gein learned that her son, the local deputy sheriff would be away hunting on Saturday, November 16, 1957, he decided he would visit Bernice.

When Deputy Frank Worden returned from his trip late in the evening, he was alarmed to find the store's doors locked but the lights still on inside. After looking around he became concerned by his mother, Bernice's absence. He could also see a large bloodstain on the counter where the cash register should have been. Deputy Worden broke into his mother's store and discovered a receipt for anti-freeze, made out to Gein in Bernice's handwriting. Worden immediately informed the Sheriff and together they headed to the Gein farmhouse.

Police were not sure what they would find at the Gein farm, but what they found was beyond anything that they had expected. The evidence retrieved from Gein's farmhouse would be enough to spawn hundreds of horror movies in the years to come.

When police arrived at Gein's farm, the smell of decay was overwhelming. The officers spread out over the property to see what they could find. In the woodshed of the farm was the naked, headless body of Bernice Worden, hanging upside down from a meat hook and slit open down the front, dressed like a hunter would a deer. Her head and intestines were discovered in a box, and her heart on a plate in the dining room

Further searches found the remains of at least fifteen women at the house. The skins from ten human heads were found preserved, and another skin taken from the upper torso of a woman was rolled up on the floor.

Gein confessed to killing the two women, who, he said, resembled his mother. Despite the evidence, he insisted he had not committed necrophilia or cannibalism, but merely decorated himself and his house with female body parts.

Although police could only link him to the murders of the two women, he was suspected of having killed five other people, including his brother and two other men who had worked on the farm. A few 'fresh' vaginas were also found in the kitchen and police suspected he had recently killed again - as no cemetery records could be linked to the genitals – however they were unable to prove any further charges of murder.

Gein was found insane, and committed to Central State Hospital at Waupon, before being moved to the Mendota Mental Health Institute where he died in the geriatric ward in 1984, aged seventy-seven from respiratory and heart failure. It is said he was always a model prisoner.

Guy George

Guy George was born Guy Rampillon on October 15, 1962 in Vitry-the-François, to American soldier George Cartwright and Parisian Helene Rampillon. Cartwright was a cook in the army based in Paris, when he seduced the young woman. The single mother, already with a daughter Stephanie, found herself pregnant again with Guy. Cartwright had his own wife and children and soon left France for home, leaving Helene to look after the child alone. Helene's parents also rejected the baby when they found out his father was black.

Helene was unable to keep the child and gave him up as a state ward when he was still a baby. In 1968, the boy's surname was changed to George, the first name of his birth father, and his place of birth changed to Angers for the child's privacy in views of French adoptions.

The Morin Family who had five children already then adopted him.

By the age of ten George was an avid hunter, spending most of his time alone catching and chasing animals with a knife.

In March 1978, after attempting to strangle two of his adopted sisters, George was returned to the State where he remained until he was released when he reached the age of majority.

Guy George attacked an eighteen-year-old student in the 14th district of Paris on November 16, 1981. Nathalie L (surname not disclosed) was in the basement of her apartment building when George broke in and threatened her with a knife. He stabbed the woman in the chest and throat before stabbing her in the stomach. The woman was caught unaware by the attack and fell back onto the basement ground.

George leaned over Nathalie and cut the clothing from her bleeding body. He raped her before stabbing her once more in the throat. The attacker escaped assuming the young woman died from her brutal wounds. She survived the attack however and was able to identify George in a line up. He was sentenced to five months imprisonment for the attack.

Being in prison for five months for the deadly assault on the young woman did not deter Guy George. Soon after he was released he attacked another victim.

Violette K (surname not disclosed) was walking up the stairs of her front verandah on June 7, 1982 when George attacked her. George pushed the young woman down the stairs and under the high verandah. Hidden from sight, George threatened the woman with a knife and made her perform oral sex on him. When Violette struggled against her attacker, George stabbed her twice violently in the neck. The woman, in spite of her injuries continued to fight against George. He tried to strangle the woman but she kicked him hard and ran off screaming. A police officer and his dog heard the woman's screams and the officer let the dog free in attempt to find the attacker. George had run away but was caught by the dog. The dog grabbed the man's bag and tore it from his back, as George escaped.

He was caught three weeks later and sentenced to eighteen months in prison for the attack.

After being incarcerated for a second time, this time for almost eighteen months, Guy George was still undeterred about attacking young woman.

On the evening of February 27, 1984 George stalked another victim. Twenty-two-year-old student Pascale N (surname not disclosed) got into her car in an underground car park and was soon captured by George. He grabbed the woman as she was about to start her car and threatened her with a knife. He stabbed her once in the throat and told her to get into the back seat of the car. With blood pouring from her neck Pascale waited for the precise moment to try and escape her captor.

As George attempted to open the back door of the woman's car she broke free of his grasp and fled, raising the alarm by screaming. A car entered the car park and George was scared off. Pascale was easily able to identify her attacker and he was again arrested and sent to prison, this time the sentence was for ten years.

George was given day release from prison in January 1991 and soon began his murderous campaign during his time away from prison.

On January 24, 1991 nineteen-year-old student Pascale Escarfail was walking along the street late in the evening when she was attacked from behind by George as she entered her apartment building. The young woman's attacker forced Pascale onto her bed and tied her hands together with tape, he cut her clothes from her body and raped her before stabbing her twice in the chest and once in the side of her throat. Pascale slowly bled to death on the bed, as George washed the blood from his hands and stole a beer from the woman's refrigerator as well a few items of value.

Three months after Guy George murdered his first victim he went in search of new prey.

On April 22, 1992 Eleonore P (surname not disclosed) said good-bye to a friend around midnight as she entered her apartment building along Malsherbes Boulevarde, Paris.

As the door closed behind her, George pushed it open, and pounced on the unsuspecting young woman. He threatened her with a knife, before forcing the woman to perform fellatio. Eleonore screamed loudly and other residents of the building came to the woman's rescue.

George attempted to flee but was arrested by police who arrived swiftly.

The murderer and rapist was sentenced to five years for the attack and released in November 1993.

Twenty-seven-year-old Catherine Rocher became Guy George's second murder victim on January 7, 1994. The victim was climbing into her car in a car park in Paris when George grabbed her from behind.

He threatened the young woman with a knife, telling her that if she screamed he would stab her. George then made the woman get into the back seat of her car where he cut the clothing from her body. After raping her he rifled through her bag and stole her credit card, and forced the woman to tell him the code to access the funds. George then stabbed Catherine several times, leaving her to die on the ground beside her car.

Catherine's body was found the next day.

As Annie L (surname not disclosed) entered her building in Paris on January 13, 1994 Guy George pushed in behind her. He threw the young woman to the ground and threatened her with a knife. Like other victims, Annie screamed for help and people from the apartment building came to her aid. George fled the building and made his escape.

On November 8, 1994 Guy George murdered his third victim. Twenty-two-year-old Elsa Benady had been walking to her car in the car park at Auguste-Blangui in Paris when George accosted her.

He grabbed the woman and forced her into the back seat of her own car. He cut the woman's clothes from her body, slicing down the front as he had done with other victims. He raped the woman and stole money from her purse before stabbing her to death.

When Elsa's body was found police no longer were in doubt that they are searching for a serial killer. The identical murders of Elsa Benady and Catherine Rocher on January 7, 1994 were startling. Both women had had their clothes cut from their body and had been raped before being stabbed. However before the authorities would catch the killer, he was able to murder further victims.

Guy George's fourth murder victim was thirty-three-year-old Agnes Nikkamp. Agnes had been entering her apartment in Saint-Antoine, Bastille when George ambushed her on December 9, 1994.

George pushed a knife against the woman's throat and forced her on to the bed where he cut her clothes from her body.

He stabbed her in the throat after raping the woman. Her boyfriend found her soon after.

Six months later, Guy George attempted to kill another victim, without success. George pounced on twenty-three-year-old Elisabeth O (surname not disclosed) as she entered her Iveme apartment on June 16, 1995. He grabbed the woman and showed her his knife, threatening to kill her if she did not do as he said.

He told the woman he wanted to talk to someone; he was on the run and needed somewhere to hide. Elisabeth, terrified of the man, waited for him to turn off a light in her ground-floor apartment then jumped out of the window and called for help.

George fled the woman's apartment and was able to slip into the night before police arrived. Elisabeth attempted to give the police a description of the man, but did not do well, her details made police look for a dark middle-eastern looking man, whereas George was a fairer skinned, having a black father and a white mother.

The fifth murder victim was Helene Frinking, who was murdered at 4am on July 8, 1995.

Helene was seen sitting on her front verandah early in the morning talking to George. The two spoke for quite a while sharing a few cigarettes before Helene invited him inside her apartment.

Once inside the killer ambushed the young woman. He drew his knife and threatened her. He tied her hands together and made her lie down on the bed. He sliced her clothes from her body and raped her.

He stabbed Helene ferociously, before stealing a few items of value and leaving. Little did George know but he left a bloody footprint behind in the bedroom. Along with his sperm – which linked him to all five murders so far -- the footprint was later used in evidence.

Twenty-year-old Melanie B (surname not disclosed) was the next victim who was able to defend herself against serial killer Guy George. On August 25, 1995 George forced his way into Melanie's Marsh apartment and terrorised the woman with a knife, he threatened her and attempted to rape her without success. Hearing another person enter the room George fled, leaving his wallet behind in the room. Melanie took the wallet to police and reported the attack.

On September 9, 1995 Guy George reported his wallet missing to police. He had dropped it during the attempted rape and assault of Melanie. When police questioned him about the attack he claimed his wallet had gone missing before that time. However in a line-up he was instantly identified by Melanie and arrested.

A sample of his blood was taken for DNA and a print taken of his foot. When the footprint did not match, police decided not to have the expensive DNA test done.

George was sentenced to prison for the attack on Melanie and by June 1997 he was released to attack and murder again.

Twenty-four-year-old Estelle F (surname not disclosed) was attacked by Guy George on July 2, 1997 in a cinema complex in Paris. The woman was thrown up against a wall by her attacker and threatened with a knife. He attempted to cut her clothes from her body but as she began screaming for help, people came to assist the woman and George escaped the scene.

Yet again Guy George broke into another building to wreak havoc, murdering his sixth victim. On September 23, 1997 nineteen-year-old Magali Sirotti was home in her Paris apartment when George broke in. He forced the young woman onto the bed and tied her up with shoelaces. He shoved a piece of material into the woman's mouth and covered her head with a pillowcase. He threatened her with a knife like the other victims and told her to not make a sound or he would kill her.

He sliced the woman's clothes from her body and raped her as she lay bound on the bed. Once he had finished raping her he stabbed her several times in the throat. He then left after stealing items from her apartment.

Magali's fiancé later came home to find her dead. although police were unable to identify the killer through his DNA left at the scene, the way that Magali's body was placed and the MO, it was clear this was the hallmark of the killer and the murder was quickly linked to the other victims.

A little over a month after the last murder Guy George attacked another woman. On October 28, 1997 twenty-five-year-old Valerie L (surname not disclosed) was attacked in the staircase of her apartment building. George had broken into the building and laid in wait for a victim to enter the stairs.

When Valerie entered the stairwell leading to her apartment George grabbed her and threatened her with a knife, telling her not to scream or he will kill her. Valerie screamed regardless and called for help that came in the aid of residents of the apartment block. George fled when people went to see what was happening.

On November 15, 1997 twenty-five-year-old Estelle Magd became Guy George's seventh murder victim. The young woman was asleep in her Paris apartment when George broke in. He tied the woman up and gagged her. He cut the clothes from her body before raping her.

Once the killer has finished with the assault, he stabbed Estelle to death before stealing her handbag and leaving the apartment building. Two days later her parents found her dead body.

During the attack George had cut himself and blood found at the scene linked Estelle's murder to the other six.

A man was arrested in England on February 17, 1998, answering to the identikit image of Guy George. The man's DNA was tested and proved that he was not the killer.

As police clutched at straws trying to find the Parisian killer, a judge allowed DNA testing laboratories to test the DNA that they had on file from past criminals against that of the unknown killer.

On March 23, 1998 a Nantes lab found a match. A DNA sample taken from Guy George while in prison for one of the assaults he had committed matched that of the murders.

Guy George's days of freedom were numbered. On March 24, 1998, after several sightings, the man was arrested at 1pm as he left the Blanche subway station. George, armed with a large knife did not resist arrest.

George was formally charged with the murders of the seven victims, the killer admitted his guilt in the murders of Pascale Escarfail on January 24, 1991 and Magali Sirotti on September 23, 1997, but denied any involvement in the other five. He later recanted his confessions.

On May 29, 1998 after weeks of legal wrangling Guy George admitted to the murders of Helene Frinking on July 8, 1994, Agnes Nijkamp on December 9, 1994 and Estelle Magd on November 15, 1997. However, once again he recanted all confessions at a later date.

On March 14, 1999 after several confessions and recants, Guy George was formally charged with the murders of all seven murders and sentenced to stand trial.

While in a holding cell awaiting trial for the murders of seven women, Guy George attempted to escape prison with two other inmates on December 26, 2000. During a cell check, prison guards had found that all three men had sawn through the bars of their cells. The escape attempt was thwarted.

George, the ringleader of the escape attempt was placed in isolation.

The trial of Guy George finally began on March 19, 2001, three years after his arrest. During the trial the killer denied any knowledge of the seven murders or numerous attacks, yet the mounting evidence against him proved otherwise.

By the second week of the trial George again changed his mind and confessed to all of the murders and attacks.

He was asked in court:
> *Did you kill Pascale Escarfail on January 24, 1991?*
> *Did you kill Cathy Rocher on January 7, 1994?*
> *Did you kill Elsa Benady on November 8, 1994?*
> *Did you kill Agnes Nijkamp on December 9, 1994?*
> *Did you kill Helene Frinking on July 8, 1995?*
> *Did you kill Magali Sirotti on September 23, 1997?*
> *Did you kill Estelle Magd on November 15, 1997?*

George answered yes to each murder. He was found guilty of all seven murders. On April 5, 2001 Guy George was sentenced to life in prison for the murders. The minimum sentence was twenty-two years before being eligible for parole.

After the sentencing the killer asked if he could address the court. The court allowed the man to speak; he thanked the jury and alluded to his thoughts of suicide.

> *"You can rest assured, I know that I will never leave prison. But I can assure you that I will never serve my sentence. The sentence that you are going to impose me is nothing, I will inflict a sentence upon myself".*

Guy George currently is still alive and serving sentence.

John Glover

It began as a small article on page 7, entitled *"Woman, 82, dies - a victim of violence."*[9] As each victim was found the articles continued until they surfaced on the front page with "It was Lady Ashton's last walk"[10]

By that time the public in Mosman, indeed all of Sydney, was in a panic as each elderly lady was found battered and posed in lewd positions.

The "Granny Killer" Case was the first modern serial killer to stalk Sydney, Australia and though police indeed caught their man, one woman lost her life as police stood outside her door in wait.

Gwendolin Mitchelhill

Camelia Gardens is an apartment block on Military Road, the main arterial road through Mosman. However the front of the building is hidden from the road. A novice of the area would have difficulty spotting the entrance; the building appears to shy from the noise of the street. The portico of Camelia Gardens faces to the left rather than the front of Military Road and offers privacy for the comings and goings of residents, mainly the elderly, though there were families and singles that resided within. The killer used the privacy for murder.

On March 1, 1989 at 3.40pm Glover killed for the first time. When the elevator doors opened on the ground floor of the Camelia Gardens Apartments, two boys stepped out and saw a sight that remain with them still. Eighty-two-year-old Gwendolin Mitchelhill was attempting to crawl to the glass security doors at the entrance of the building. Blood dripped from the savage wounds across her head. Her stockings had been torn from her legs, her walking stick was tossed to the side and her handbag, found nearby, had been rifled through, it's contents neatly set out around it.

The boys quickly sort help; on such a busy road people were quick to come to the elderly woman's aid. It was assumed that Mrs Mitchelhill had fallen and hit her head. The neat arrangement of her personal items from her handbag was not seen as significant. The blood on the path was washed away.

The elderly woman was quickly rushed to the emergency ward by ambulance. One of the medics found the whole scene to be a little too unusual for a fall. He then had a thought about the woman's bag, how it had been rifled but was placed neatly with her other items. His suspicions nagged at him, so he reported the incident to Mosman police.

Over the next few hours doctors worked quickly to prevent further blood building up in Mrs Mitchelhill's brain from the severe knock she had taken. On further examination of the wound it was obvious to doctors that Mrs Mitchelhill had not simply fallen, her wounds were more consistent with a strike from a blunt instrument. Adding to her injuries were two black eyes and several broken ribs. The doctors decided to contact Mosman police as well.

Mrs Mitchelhill lost her battle for life later that same evening. Mosman police sent the Physical Evidence crew and homicide detectives to investigate what was possibly a murder. A check of her handbag found that it did not contain her purse that she had with her during a shopping excursion earlier in the day.

The post mortem examination conducted the next day revealed that Mrs Mitchelhill had suffered severe bruising to the right eye consistent with a fist, severe bruising to the right shoulder consistent with a blunt

---

[9] Sydney Morning Herald - 04 Mar 1989 p.7
[10] Sydney Morning Herald - 11 May 1989 p.1

object, two wounds to back of the skull consistent with a blunt object and seven broken ribs consistent with a fist.

The cause of death was attributed to her head and chest injuries which were consistent with a vicious attack. There was no evidence to suggest that Mrs Mitchelhill had been sexually interfered with.

With help from the Homicide Squad from Chatswood, the Mosman detectives began investigating the murder. Someone had attacked and murdered a defenceless old woman, and police wanted to find out quickly who it was.

Little did police know, but this murder would not remain an isolated incident. Two months later another elderly woman was murdered.

Lady Winfreda Ashton

On May 9, 1989, eighty-four-year-old Lady Winfreda Ashton had had a busy day. She had an appointment at the Sydney Eye Hospital, and then popped over to the Mosman RSL, leaving at around 2.30. She withdrew her shopping and spending money at her local bank, and then busied herself at the local supermarket, stopping to talk to some friends on the way. She then started her walk home; she stopped at her mailbox and then headed towards the front entrance foyer of the units where she lived.

In the foyer Lady Ashton met her killer.

Lady Ashton was found dead later that evening when another resident came down to the rubbish room. She was face down on the floor. Her shoes and walking stick, like Mrs Mitchelhill were placed near by. Her handbag had been opened and her purse was missing.

Her injuries echoed the attack on Mrs Mitchelhill. Her autopsy report read: Large bruise to the head, caused by a blow, bruise to the rear of her head consistent with her head being forced to the ground. Five left ribs were also fractured. However, this time her death was not due to her injuries, this time the killer made sure he had finished the job before leaving. She had been strangled with her pantyhose. The stockings had cut so deep into her skin that it left fibres imbedded in her skin. Again no sexual assault was evident.

Police knew that the similarities in the two attacks were alarming. Both women had suffered massive bodily injuries consistent with punching. The two crime scenes were in close proximity (only about 1km apart). Both women had their purse stolen. And the attacks happened at the entrance to the victim's residence. Police decided that the two murders were linked. Now the search was on before the killer struck again.

The worse problem was that robbery did not seem to be the motive; both women had little money with them. The violent attack appeared to be the reason that the killer struck. So investigators sought help in trying to provide a profile of the killer.

Police consultant Dr Rod Milton, a psychiatrist, was asked to assist police in constructing a profile of the offender they sought. The information was not released to the public, but pointed to a younger killer, a loner who was unstable. Little did police know but this profile was way from the mark. This killer was in a group on his own and did not fit into the usual serial killer profiles.

On July 9, 1989, two months to the day since her murder, Lady Ashton's purse was found, ironically, in Ashton Park. The woman who found the purse, not realising the significance of it, popped it into the mailbox of Lady Ashton after checking inside for identification, where police later recovered it.

Doris Cox

On October 18, 1989, eighty-six-year-old Mrs Doris Cox was found in the front garden of Garrison Retirement Village where she lived. She was sitting down, calling for help, her face covered in blood; she had several large grazes on her face and had lost a few of her teeth. Again people who had come to the elderly woman's aid thought she had fallen and not wanting to alarm other residents, the scene was washed down. The next day administrators mentioned the incident to police not thinking that it could have been an attempted murder. Police quickly asked the Medical Examiner who had examined the two deceased women's bodies to check Mrs Cox's injuries. The ME came to the conclusion that Mrs Cox's were consistent with being attacked, possibly by the killer. Doris Cox's grazes on her face were from having her face rammed into the brick wall after being hit on the head from behind. Though she survived the brutal attack, Mrs Cox was unable to help police in identifying her attacker.

Margaret Pahud

The next murder happened within a month. This time, however, the killer moved to new hunting ground in near-by Lane Cove. It did not take police long to link it to the Mosman murders and attacks.

On Thursday November 2, 1989, a nine-year-old girl found eighty-five-year-old Mrs Margaret Pahud along a pathway short cut. Mrs Pahud had been out shopping during the day and had been returning home when she was attacked. The young girl alerted her mother and another neighbour who rushed to the scene. Mrs Pahud was lying face down with her head surrounded by a huge pool of blood.

Someone alerted a nearby doctor. Mrs Pahud was unconscious and breathing faintly. By the time the ambulance arrived Mrs Pahud had died.

Before police could investigate, the scene was again washed down and all traces of evidence gone. Her bag in its entirety was missing.

The post mortem revealed striking similarities to the others. Mrs Pahud had suffered heavy blows to the rear of her head causing a fractured skull consistent with being struck with a blunt object and lacerations to face and head.

Mrs Pahud's bag did turn up later and was handed in to police. Only money was missing.

Olive Cleveland

A taskforce was implemented to investigate the alarming number of murders and to find the perpetrator. Leading the team was Mike Hagan and 'Miles' O'Toole. While police stepped up their investigation, the killer also raised the stakes.

Within 24 hours of the attack on Mrs Pahud, the killer struck again. On November 3, eighty-one-year-old Miss Olive Cleveland was attacked from behind as she entered the Westley Gardens Retirement Village where she lived. She was found lying face down across the pathway. This time however, the killer added to his signature. He pulled up the woman's dress to expose her legs. Her pantyhose had been removed and were tied tightly around the elderly victim's throat. Again, like the other victims, her head was surrounded by a halo of blood. Her personal items, her bag, shoes and glasses were near her feet. A nasty calling card of the killer. Again in a hindrance to police the blood was washed away so as not to worry the other patients of the nursing home.

The post mortem again resounded the others. Miss Cleveland suffered bruising and lacerations around her head and body. Her skull was fractured. Miss Cleveland's death was due to the pantyhose tied around the neck three times.

Muriel Falconer
Police were beginning to piece together even more clues about their killer. So far he always struck around 3.00 in the afternoon, and there were never any witnesses, though Mrs Pahud was out of the vicinity of the other murders they were all still in a relative close proximity.

As each day passed the police felt a sigh of relief that the killer did not strike, yet that feeling was short-lived and the worst had yet to come.

Mrs Muriel Falconer was still quite spritely for her ninety-three years of age. She was often seen doing errands around Mosman, going on walks and spending time shopping along the main promenade.

On November 24, 1989 Meals on Wheels called at the home of Mrs Falconer at 11.30am to deliver her food. When there was no answer a note was left, stating that they would call again at 1.00pm. When she did not answer the door a second time, concerns were made for her safety. A neighbour decided to go and check to make sure she was all right after not seeing her since the previous afternoon.

After knocking a few times, she used the spare key to let herself in. The sight that met her sent her running for police. Mrs Falconer was lying face down in the hallway. She had been stripped of her clothes from the waist down, and her dress and petticoat had been pulled up over her head doing nothing to conceal the large pool of blood stemming from the wounds she had suffered.

Her shoes and shopping from the day before were at her feet and her purse was open.

The post-mortem revealed the same afflictions as the others in the string of murders the media dubbed the "Granny Killings". Mrs Falconer had been beaten, her head sustained severe injuries, including fractures in three places. Her face also contained several broken bones. Her pantyhose and belt from her dress were wrapped tightly around her tiny throat.

This time, the killer had murdered inside a victim's home. Therefore the scene was perfectly preserved albeit from the neighbour and a doctor checking for any sign of life of the woman.

Pieces Slot Into Place – Margaret Todhunter and Euphemia Carnie
The police finally had a break-through on the case. In the hallway the killer had stepped in the victim's blood on his exit and had left some bloody footprints. These would later be checked against Glover and found to be a match helping to cement the case against Glover in court.

Now the case was front-page news all over Sydney.
- *Woman, 85, dies in fourth North Shore bashing (where two Mosman women have died this year).* [11]
- *2 in 2 days: another grannie slain. Madge (Pahud) murdered on her daily walk (at Lane Cove).* [12]
- *Reward doubled to 200,000 dollars to catch granny killer.* [13]
- *Rush of (North Sydney) `Granny killer' sightings.* [14]

The police began to receive hundreds of calls from the public, and along with Dr Milton's profile, one young man became a suspect, a known psychotic he was seen in the vicinity of several of the murders and

---
[11] Sydney Morning Herald - 03 Nov 1989 p.1
[12] Sydney Morning Herald - 04 Nov 1989 p.1
[13] Sydney Morning Herald - 08 Nov 1989 p.3
[14] Sydney Morning Herald - 11 Nov 1989 p.5

was also picked out by witnessed in photo line-ups. The suspect was in fact never eliminated from police enquiries.

The task force responsible for the case, decided to change tact. They requested from all near-by police stations records of any elderly women being attacked. Several were forwarded to the detectives and a common description of the unknown assailant appeared. The suspect in all recent assaults had been a white male, aged about 50 years with grey hair, not the young loner on which they had been trying to pin the murders. .

Two reports also stuck out from the rest.

The first was the attack on eighty-five-year-old Mrs Margaret Todhunter. On January 11, 1989, six weeks before the first murder, Mrs Todhunter was walking home when a man walked past her then turned behind her and struck her on the back of the head, as she fell to the ground the "grey haired man" grabbed her bag and fled the scene. Mrs Todhunter received a large gash to the back of her head requiring eight stitches.

Her description of the man was quite thorough. She said he was male, 50 years, 5'7", grey hair, well kept, broad shoulders, thick chest, large stomach, and wore a white business shirt and cream trousers.

The description fitted Glover perfectly; it was his first attempt at an attack.

The second report that drew interest was the attack of eighty-two-year-old Mrs Euphemia Carnie on August 25, 1989. When returning to her residence at North Haven Retirement Village, Mrs Carnie was punched in the chest and knocked to the ground. Her attacker took her handbag and drove away in a blue car. She suffered severe bruising to her ribs, chest and back of the head. Her description of her assailant matched the account given by Mrs Todhunter.

These two attacks were added to the five murders and one attempted murder attributed to the 'Granny Killer'. However the numbers were to increase still.

Daisy Roberts
On January 11, 1990 Mrs Daisy Roberts, an elderly patient at Greenwich Hospital was assaulted. Mrs Roberts said that a grey-haired male entered her room and placed his hands under her nightdress and held her breasts, he explained he was checking her body heat. He then walked away. Mrs Roberts raised the alarm and hospital authorities quickly informed police of the incident. One nurse told police she had earlier spoken to the *Four-and-Twenty* pie salesman. She had asked him why he was in an area of the hospital he shouldn't have been.

The salesman was quickly found on hospital grounds and when challenged about the assault on Mrs Roberts, he denied the allegation and quickly left. The man was John Glover.

No More Grannies
Police asked Glover to attend Chatswood Detectives office at 5pm pm January 13, 1990, to answer a few more questions. After waiting an hour for him to arrive, police decided to call at Glover's house. His wife answered and told them that her husband had attempted suicide and was now in Royal North Shore Hospital. The suicide note Glover had written included references to "no more grannies" and "Essie started it". Little did Mrs Glover know the significance of the note's contents.

Due to his mental state, the officers were not able to interview Glover that evening. When they returned they next day he refused to make any admissions on legal advice. He did, however, admit to being at the

Greenwich Hospital on January 11. Glover also allowed the detectives to take a Polaroid photo of him. The photo was shown to Mrs Carnie, Mrs Roberts and Mrs Todhunter who all identified him as their attacker.

From that point on, Glover was the main suspect in the Granny Killings. The police decided to not question Glover anymore, in fear it may scare him off. They kept a vigil at all times, as they furthered their enquiries into his background and history.

Who is John Wayne Glover

John Wayne Glover was born John WALTER Glover on November 26, 1932 to Walter and Freda in Wolverhampton, England. His mother failed dismally at being maternal. John felt unloved by Freda from a very young age. In 1935 John's brother Barry was born.

By 1941 Freda and Walter had gone their separate ways, both had been unfaithful during their marriage. Freda gained custody of the two boys.

Soon after her divorce came through, Freda remarried and had two more children, Patricia and Clifford. Freda's new husband did not father Clifford. The family moved constantly. Sometimes the boys were returned to their natural father and the interruption of changing schools made John uncomfortable. He never settled into a schooling routine and subsequently achieved poor grades.

In 1945 at the age of 13 John witnessed a friend's fall from a tree. The boy died from his injuries. This incident stayed with Glover forever.

In 1946 John left school and went into full-time employment. His first job was as an apprentice electrician, however the 15-year-old was still unsettled by his family life and he soon left the position due to a lack of concentration.

However, Glover soon found work as an off-sider for an odd-jobs man and enjoyed the work. It allowed Glover to move away from home and into a share-house with friends. It was during this time that he discovered sex. He would date as many young girls as he could and he would boast to friends about his sexual prowess.

By this time Glover also had begun pilfering. He would steal anything he wanted. Often resulting in appearances in front of the magistrate. By the time he was twenty-two-years-old, he had several robbery charges against him, these being:
>March, 1947: Break and Enter in Wolverhampton – fined 35/-
>October 1947: Theft of tools and stamps from employer
>May, 1952: Theft of clothing from Lincoln City Club – fined £4 and made to pay £1 in compensation to the club.
>December 1952: Stole a coat from a van before deciding to steal the entire van. He was fined £5 and disqualified from driving for 12 months.
>1954: Glove stole a handbag and with regards to his extensive record was placed on two years probation.

Glover also served in the English army, as national service. Even after the compulsory six weeks service, Glover remained with the army, serving for a total of two years. After his service, he was employed as a bus conductor from 1954 to 1957.

It was while working as a conductor that he noticed an advertisement for qualified tram drivers and conductors in Melbourne, Australia. Glover applied and was accepted as a conductor.

John arrived in Melbourne by ship in 1957 as a twenty-four-year-old. He had decided to leave the old John Glover behind; he changed his middle name to reflect his new start in life. Life settled down for a while for the young man.

But it was not long before the old Glover overtook the new Glover.

On September 11, 1962 Glover attacked seventy-three-year-old Myrtle Ince as she walked along Berrick Street, Camberwell, Victoria. The elderly woman was attacked from behind, and knocked unconscious; her dress was pushed up, though no sexual assault took place.

A month later on October 4, twenty-year-old Valerie Bird was attacked from behind at 10.30pm as she walked home in Camberwell. She screamed and a man came to her aid. The young woman's aid was able to identify Valerie's attacker as Glover. Glover was charged with indecent assault causing actual bodily harm. He also admitted to the earlier attack. Glover was given four years probation for the two assaults.

Beginning in 1967, John Glover began seeing Miss Jacqueline Gail Rolls – known as Gay to her friends. She was from a wealthy family. On June 1, 1968 the happy couple married, much to the disapproval of Gay's mother, Veronica – known as Essie.

After the marriage Glover began a job in liquor sales but was sacked for being lazy. However Glover enjoyed working in sales and found a similar job soon after, in Sydney.

The couple moved into a property in the well-to-do North Sydney suburb of Mosman and settled down to married life. Glover's in-laws Essie and John moved in with the couple, building a third story onto John and Gay's property. The relationship between Glover and Essie was strained but for the sake of Gay the pair were civil.

In 1971, John and Gay were blessed with a daughter – Kellie. Another daughter, Marney was born in 1973, completing the Glover family.

In 1981, Glover began his final job as a *Four 'n' Twenty* Pie Salesman in Alexandria. He was known by fellow workers as "smutty, … a bludger and a thief." [15] He was a well-known face around the Mosman RSL and was a participating member of various community groups around the area. Glover was extremely house and city proud.

Then Freda, his mother, immigrated to Sydney from England. Glover had such a hatred for his mother. Once when cleaning out one of the houses during a move, he found a photo of his mother, wearing nearly nothing and seductively posed. He had detested her for her loose morals, but this had cemented his hatred of her.

He refused to allow her to stay at his Mosman home, which already housed his over-bearing mother-in-law. Glover shipped her off to a near-by hotel where he would begrudgingly take his daughters to see their Grandmother, but would leave as soon as he could.

Then in 1988, life changed for John Glover forever, a change that would send him down a path of murder and violence.

---

[15] Garden of Evil, p 41

It was established that Glover had breast cancer, a rare but not unheard of diagnosis for a male. Glover saw this as a female only disease and took the news quite badly. After thirteen years, his mother-in-law Essie finally left the Glover house, and moved into a nursing home.

Freda, then aged 79-years-old became ill and was also hospitalised. Glover was the last person to see her alive on October 7, 1988. The attacks on the elderly women of Mosman began only three months later.

Ten days after the attack on Mrs Todhunter, Essie Rolls died at the nursing home. The weight of these deaths seemed to have been a catalyst for the Granny murders. It appeared that Glover hated his mother for leaving his father and re-marrying three times, and he also had a deep-seeded hatred for his mother-in-law.

The "Essie did it" quote in Glover's suicide note was blaming his mother-in-law for his murderous rampage.

The Trap is Set

Police needed hard evidence against Glover. Surveillance was set-up and police watched him, as he stopped time and time again. Glover was unaware of the surveillance, often stopping his car, getting out and wandering along the streets of Mosman looking for victims.

Police decided to use a new tracking device that was currently being trialled. With permission from *Four-and-Twenty* they had the Quiktrack tracking device fitted to Glover's vehicle. That way, with Glover's roving work and extra activities they never lost sight of him.

When police returned to Royal North Shore Hospital to ask further questions about the assault on Mrs Roberts, it came as a break and a failure at the same time. One receptionist interviewed admitted that she was, in fact, John Glover's wife and he had denied all the allegations. She also said she would tell her husband that police were questioning people about him. Detectives knew then that they needed to move a little quicker now; they feared that he might quieten down.

But this was not the case.

Joan Sinclair

On March 19, 1990, four days after their talk with Mrs Glover, police tracked Glover all over Mosman and Balmoral; it was obvious he was on the hunt. At 10.30am he stopped his car, fixed his hair, put on a tie, gabbed a briefcase and entered a dwelling. Police first assumed that he was meeting with his solicitor, so they sat outside and waited.

Later in the afternoon, two boys attempted to also enter the property. When they found the front gate locked, they went and got a neighbour to help them to no avail. A dog inside the premises was barking continuously. Something was wrong.

Using the dog as a reason to investigate, police went to the door to question the occupant about the dog's noise. The door was locked, so they went to the rear of the property and through a glass door could see a hammer and what looked to be blood on the carpet of the front landing.

Police forced their way through the front entry to investigate. The body of Joan Sinclair was found just inside the door. Near the body was a bloodstained claw hammer. Mrs Sinclair's head was wrapped in a towel and her lower clothes had been removed. Again her pantyhose were tied around her neck.

Detectives knew they needed to be careful; Glover must still be in the house. He was found in the bathroom. He was semi-conscious and naked in the bath. Glover was vomiting and moaning and his face was partially submerged in the water. Paramedics were called, who declared Mrs Sinclair dead and then treated Glover for alcohol and drug overdose.

Confession and Sentence.

Glover was moved to Royal North Shore Hospital and placed under police guard. Mrs Sinclair's post-mortem report stated she had suffered multiple head wounds from a blunt object - the claw hammer found at the scene.

Though there were many dissimilarities between the Sinclair murder and the granny murders, there was enough evidence to suggest they were all linked.

In hospital on March 20, 1990, Glover was briefly interviewed about the murders of the six women and the attempted murder of Mrs Cox. Glover admitted to committing each murder and the attempted murder. Later that day Glover was formally charged with the murder of Mrs Sinclair and the police officers made arrangements for further interviews on his discharge from hospital.

On March 28, 1990, Glover appeared at the Glebe Coroners Court where he was formally charged with fourteen offences: six counts of first degree murder, one count of attempted murder, one count of robbery with wounding, one count of robbery, one count of indecent assault and one count of assaulting a female.

During his trial Glover claimed that 'I felt detached, as though I was witnessing ... not doing it'.

On Friday November 29, 1990 Glover was found guilty on all accounts and sentenced to prison for the term of his natural life with the recommendation that he is never released. Glover showed little emotion as Justice Woods passed sentence.

Anatoly Golovkin

A television special on the case warned that program was to show the cruel murders committed by the killer and was not for children or those with a weak stomach. It is indeed one of the worst cases in the annals of serial crime.

Anatoly Golovkin was a pederast and serial killer. His victims were little boys aged ten to twelve. Golovkin terrorised Moscow for 16 years killing eleven known victims and many more unknown victims. The case closed with Golovkin's death sentence in 1994.

Golovkin would rape and sodomise the boys while he mutilated them, cutting their genitals, torso and throats.

Klaus Gossman

Klaus Gossman was dubbed the Mid-day Murderer for his penchant for killing his victims in the middle of the day, as the clocks of Nurumber sounded the hour.

In 1960 as a nineteen-year-old theology student, Gossman murdered for the first time. At midday as he left the campus' library he spotted a couple and shot them both dead, using the clock's hourly chimes to cover the sounds of the gunshots.

The killer felt fulfilled by the murders and returned to his studies after the killings. No one had any idea that the would-be priest had just murdered two fellow students.

Later he wrote an in-depth diary entry describing his emotions and feelings and the enjoyment of the killings.

In 1962, two years after the shooting murder of the young couple, Gossman struck again, this time the killer chose a bank in Ochenbruch. At midday the killer entered the back armed with a gun. He robbed the bank, shooting the manager in cold blood as he left.

Soon after, Gossman killed his fourth victim, a bank teller. Having success with the previous bank robbery and murder Gossman again entered a bank, robbed the place before shooting dead a bank employee chosen at random.

On March 29, 1963 the killer decided he needed more guns. Gossman walked into a German gun store and shot dead the owner and the owner's adult son, taking as many weapons as he could carry as he left.

The final murder occurred in April 1965. Gossman, having fled the army after joining in December 1963 attempted to steal the handbag of a woman in a shop. When the woman attempted to fight back, Gossman shot her dead. The killer was quickly subdued by other shoppers and held until police arrived.

Gossman was sentenced to life imprisonment for the seven murders he had committed. The diaries that the killer had maintained detailing all of the murders were used as evidence against him. The diaries also contained information about a plan to kidnap and murder popular German actress Elke Sommer. Her name was also engraved into the side of the killer's gun.

Gossman, at his trial, tried to blame his murderous campaign on his upbringing, saying he had witnessed the shooting murder of his father by US troops that had occupied Germany at the end of WWII.

Harrison Graham

It was Philadelphia, August 1987 and the neighbours of twenty-eight-year-old mentally retarded, drug addict Harrison Graham could not take any more. The stench from his third floor apartment at 1631 North 13th Street was terrible. After complaining to the landlord, Graham was evicted. However before he left, Graham boarded up the flat saying it contained personal items that he would return for in a few days. The stench continued to get worse and still there was no sign of Graham returning. Eventually the police were called on August 9, to open the door. As soon as they opened the door, the smell became unbearable. In the apartment's living room, officers were able to identify the decomposing remains of five bodies. A search of the rest of the flat recovered a sixth in a similar state of decomposition in a cupboard. On August 14, a seventh body was found three doors down from Graham's apartment.

It was only during the autopsies that all seven victims were identified as women. In only two of the cases were the causes of death identifiable, manual strangulation.

On August 16, a week after the bodies were discovered, Graham surrendered to police. He initially argued during a police interview that the bodies were already in the flat when he moved in. He then saw the ridiculousness of the story and confessed to the seven murders, one of which he admitted was his girlfriend, thirty-year-old Robin De Shazor. In all seven cases, Graham admitted to strangling them to death during intercourse. Graham was arrested and charged with seven counts of murder and seven counts of abuse of a corpse.

At his trial in April 1988, Graham waived his right to trial by jury and pleaded not guilty by reason of insanity before Judge Robert A Latrone. This plea was rejected and Graham was found guilty on all charges on April 27, 1988. For his crimes he received six death sentences and one life sentence in addition to fourteen years for abuse of a corpse. However the judge ordered that the prison sentences were to be served before any death sentences.

After the US Supreme Court ruled that the execution of mentally retarded prisoners is illegal, the lawyers of Graham returned to court during July 2003 to appeal against his six death sentences. His lawyers argued that IQ tests performed on Graham throughout his life indicate a score of between 60 and 70. The minimum IQ score to be judged mentally retarded was recognised as being 70. Psychiatrist John O'Brien testifying for the prosecution stated that Graham has the ability to function at a higher level than his IQ score signifies and as such cannot be categorised as abnormal. Judge William J Manfredi ruled on December 16, 2003, that Graham met the requirements of mental retardation and as such the death sentences ruled during April 1988 was to be changed to consecutive life sentences.

Dana Gray

At 9.15am on February 16, 1994, Alice Williams knocked on the front door of her neighbour Norma Davis, Norma an early riser, hadn't been seen for a couple of days. The knock made the unlocked door swing open and Alice made her way in. Calling Norma's name bought no response and a quick look around the downstairs rooms offered no clue to Norma's whereabouts, and so Alice slowly went upstairs.

At the top of the stairs Alice found Norma slumped in one of the chairs appearing to be asleep. It was only when she approached did Alice notice the two knives, one in Norma's chest, the other in her neck. Both knives were driven in with such force that only the hilts were showing. The autopsy would in fact reveal a total of 11 stab wounds in addition to manual strangulation. Alice gathered her composure and dialled 911.

Twelve days after the discovery of Norma Davis, a second body was found. Sixty-six-year-old June Roberts was last seen alive on the morning of February 28, 1994. By that evening, June's murder was reported to police by her friends, who had become worried by her failure to answer the door.

June had been strangled with a twice-looped telephone cord and hit on the head with a wine bottle. Over the next two days June Brown's credit card was used in multiple stores in Temecula, prompting a fraud check by the credit card company. The details of the check were passed onto investigating detective Joseph Greco. Detective Greco visited the stores where June Brown's credit card was used, looking for a description of the user. Several would recall the woman as approximately 5'2" with blond hair. She would also have a young boy with her, about five-years-old with blond hair whom she would call Jason.

Fifty-seven-year-old Dorinda Hawkins owned an antique store on Main Street, Lake Elsinore. In the afternoon on March 10, 1994, Dana Sue Gray entered the shop feigning interest in some picture frames that Dorinda turned around to fetch. Gray looped a nylon rope around her neck and pulled tightly, Dorinda fell to her knees trying to fight off her attacker. During the struggle Gray tried to manoeuvre Dorinda to the floor to finish her off but Dorinda fought back despite being choked by the rope taut around her throat. Dorinda attempted to use a nearby broom to fend the woman off. Unfortunately, she failed and lapsed into unconsciousness. Gray ended the attack, opened the cash register, stole $25 and left the store, with no witnesses. However Dorinda was not dead, and was able to give a description of the 5'2" blond haired woman to police.

Jeri Armbrust was Norma Davis's ex-daughter-in-law and up until the time of Norma's death continued to visit, looking after her when she could. On March 16, 1994 at 9.30. Detective Greco received an anxious phone call from Jeri. She claimed that the murder suspect might be her daughter-in-law Dana Sue Gray, as she seemed to fit the police description given by survivor Dorinda Hawkins.

Detective Greco checked Jeri's description of Gray – it matched. Greco asked about children, remembering the boy that was seen with 'June Brown'. Jeri's reply confirmed that she had a stepson of five-years-old – Jason Wilkins. Greco believed he had the killer and went ahead to get a warrant signed for the arrest of Dana Sue Gray.

At 11.10am Dora Beebe, 87, finished her appointment at the optician and headed to her home in Sun City. As soon as she was home there was a knock at the door. Dora opened it to find a woman 5'2" with newly dyed red hair asking for directions. At 12.00 a check for $110.05 was signed by Dora Beebe at a stationery store. The cashier would later describe the woman as about 5'2" with red hair.

Detective Chris Antoniadas investigated the Dora Beebe crime scene and would note the distinctive marks of ligature strangulation around Dora's neck, the obvious signs of a struggle in the master bedroom and into the bathroom where Dora was found dead her arm frozen by rigormortis out stretched in a defensive pose.

Detective Antoniadas determined from the blood spots on the walls the pattern of the attack. Dora had been bending or crouching when the first blow struck her on the back of the head. The second blow struck when Dora was on the floor. Officers found the object that was used; a heavily dented iron with bloodstains still present lay in the sink in the bathroom. A large stain of blood on the floor indicated that Dora was either crawling or was dragged along the hallway to the bathroom, where the beating continued until Dora died from the trauma to her head. The autopsy on Dora counted a total of 5 blows from the iron to the head.

At 5.45pm Detective Greco knocked on the door at 32524 Mission Trail, Lake Elinsore and handed the search warrant to Dana Sue Gray for the murder of June Brown. During the police interview Gray continued to deny her involvement in June's murder. The line of questioning focused on the use of June's credit cards in various stores on the day of her death.

However late in the evening, to Detective Greco's surprise, Gray began to mention a second name, that of Dora Beebe. Gray admitted using Dora's bankbook to take $2000 in cash from the account. Gray claimed that she had found the book by the side of the road; Detective Greco left the interview to do some quick checks on the whereabouts of Dora Beebe and discovered that she had been found dead at her home that day. Gray's partner Jim, who had also been bought in for questioning, denied knowing anything about the crimes but when asked if in his opinion Gray was innocent, Jim couldn't answer.

On March 21, 1994, at 3pm Gray was led shackled by the ankles to her arraignment. Cameras flashed getting a glimpse of Gray as she sat with her court appointed lawyer Stuart Sachs. Her plea was not guilty. Prosecutor Rich Bentley announced that he was seeking the death penalty.

On March 10 1995, Gray officially changed her plea from not guilty to not guilty by reason of insanity, thereby requiring a psychiatric examination. The interviews took place during the second quarter of 1995. Doctor Rogers examined Gray and came to the conclusion that she was fully aware of her actions in murdering June Brown and had shown the patterns of a serial killer in committing her crimes.

At 10.30am on September 9 1998, Gray made her final appearance in court; this time changing her plea once again, from not guilty by reason of insanity to a plea of guilty. Part of the plea-bargaining was to accept a life sentence as opposed to the death sentence that the prosecution was seeking. Judge Dennis Myers read out the charge of the murder of June Brown. Gray, in a virtual whisper, replied guilty and was duly sentenced to life without parole, a sentence to be served at the California Women's prison in Chowchilla.

Cleo Green

Cleo Green, a twenty-six-year-old black male from Louisville, Kentucky, gained the moniker of the Red Demon, because he believed that such a creature possessed him. He also believed that the only escape from its domination was to murder.

Four women were murdered because of Green's delusions during the summer of 1984. Each was stabbed multiple times through the neck. His first victim however was by far the worst of the attacks. Ida Mae York was stabbed by Green over 200 times and was decapitated before he was finally sated.

At his trial in 1984, Green was judged insane and was duly placed in a mental asylum.

Samuel Green

Samuel Green was probably America's first serial killer, who reined terror across New England from 1817 to 1822.

Born in the hamlet of Meredith New Hampshire, Green's poor hardworking parents thought the child was possessed at an early age. When he continually played truant from school they resorted to thrashing the child with switches to control him.

As a teenage apprentice blacksmith, Green was caught stealing, and was whipped again by his employer. On his return home his father whipped him again. In revenge, he threw the family dog down the well. The dead animal contaminated the water, and the well had to be cleaned. For the act, Green was whipped again.

In rage, Green stabbed the family pig, for which he was again whipped.

The family gave up and sent Green to Newhampton to live with a man called Dunne. For a short period of time Green settled down and went to school. But soon he began to truant again for which he was beaten. Samuel stole a Jew's harp from a local store and was flogged when apprehended. He fled from Dunne and went home to his parents who flogged him into unconsciousness when they had heard the news and sent him back to Dunne. Dunne flayed Samuel's back until a layer of flesh had peeled away.

Green decided to kill Dunne for this last beating. Green had arranged for an axe to accidentally fall on his master's head. If that failed a pitchfork was placed above the barn door. Dunne was lucky and escaped both incidents with only minor injury. For his deeds Green was tied to the barn door and whipped until his back was a welted bloody mass of flesh.

Again Green retaliated and destroyed a hogshead of cider. He was, of course, whipped for the destruction. Green then tried to burn down Dunn's barn unsuccessfully, and was beaten senseless with whips and Dunne's fists.

Eventually, Dunne gave up the fight and Green left to embark on a career of passing counterfeit notes with another youth named Ash in Newhampton.

As they passed a schoolhouse, Green decided to seek vengeance on those who represented the pain of his childhood and threw a large piece of timber under a speeding sleigh loaded with children, almost killing them.

The schoolmaster caught the two youths and beat them severely.

As revenge the two battered youths lay in wait for the schoolmaster in a remote spot. They knocked him unconscious with rocks, stripped him naked, tied him up and left him to freeze to death. (He was found hours later and narrowly survived).

Green and Ash moved through Guildford, and Burlington, Vermont where Green enlisted in the army. He quickly went AWOL and was flogged at the guardhouse after his capture. He fled again and went home to New Hampshire. He was quite wealthy with thousands of dollars worth of counterfeit notes. He purchased a cow for his mother (the only sign of love he ever showed) and spent the rest on himself with fancy clothes, a horse, expensive jewellery and meals.

When the money ran out, Green went to Boston and hired himself out as a servant to wealthy men. During the day he was a loyal servant, at night he robbed his masters and fled.

Outside Bath, New Hampshire, Green again teamed with Ash. They encountered a jewellery sales man who allowed the two to inspect his wares. Later the two men waited to ambush the peddler. When he strode past them, they knocked him from his mule and took his money. Ash suggested they should kill the man. Green hesitated a moment then brought his club down upon the unconscious man, crushing his head and killing him on the spot.

Green's wild adventures became less secretive as he ranged though New England, robbing and murdering at will. He was jailed several times on suspicion, but evidence was lacking in most cases. Ash also helped Green to escape on several occasions. Once in Montreal, Green fought his way through an entire posse of men when he was looting a jewellery store, shooting several of the men in the process.

He was finally caught and tried, convicted and sentenced to hang. As was expected, Ash broke Green out of jail and they returned to New Hampshire. After a quiet period of hiding out, Green went on another crime spree burglarising stores in Albany, New York and in New York City. He then went to Vermont, where he robbed and shot to death a wealthy French traveller. Nothing was beyond the ambitions of Samuel Green. He left a trail of rape, horse stealing, burglary, counterfeiting and murder, from Montpelier, Vermont to Schenectady, New York; from Saco, Maine to Barre, Vermont. He became America's first Enemy Number One. Half the country was looking for him.

Green's end was near when he was arrested in Danvers, Mass. for stealing $30 worth of goods from a store when he was blind drunk. He was convicted and sent to Boston State Prison for a four-year sentence. He attempted escape several times and was fitted with special shackles with weighted clogs to slow his movements; several more years were added to his sentence.

Green learned a Negro prisoner named Billy Williams had informed on him about his last escape attempt. Once release from solitary confinement, Green vowed revenge. He put poison into William's food, but the wary convict did not eat it.

Finally, Green cornered Williams alone in a shop on November 8, 1821. Wielding an iron bar, he pounced on the informer. He brought the weapon down on William's head giving him a fractured skull. While the man lay unconscious at his feet, Green kept hammering at him with the bar, breaking all of William's ribs and his arms and legs. William died a week later from his injuries.

It was the end for Samuel Green. On April 25, 1822 following a long trial, a rope was put around his neck.

Richard Grissom

On June 6, 1989 Terri Maness knocked on each door of her Wichita apartment complex to get signatures for her petition against the rising rates for the garbage collection. After getting quite a few she returned home to her apartment. A police officer friend watched her go inside. Little did the woman know but Richard Grissom was already inside her apartment burglarising it. When Terri entered, he grabbed her and took her to apartment's recreation room. There Grissom stabbed Terri savagely before strangling her to death.

The killer left a note on the girl's defiled body that read, amongst the profanity, "The Judge is next..."

Twenty-three-year-old Joan Butler returned home to her Overland Park apartment at 4.00am on June 18, 1989 after attending a party with friends. At the same time Richard Grissom was just leaving the apartment complex, having just robbed another residence. The lure was too great and Grissom followed Joan to her flat.

Joan's body was never found.

Twenty-two-year-old Christine Rusch and nineteen-year-old Theresa Brown were roommates. They had had a party a few days before their death, where Richard Grissom arrived to case the apartment.

Grissom abducted the girls and kept them alive for several days during which they were seen withdrawing money from their accounts. On June 24, 1989 the girls disappeared completely, never to be found.

On July 7, 1989 Richard Grissom made arrangements to meet with his girlfriend at a Dallas Airport - little did Grissom know but there were two airports and his girlfriend and a SWAT team were waiting at one while Grissom arrived at Fort Worth Airport. FBI Agent Mike Napier happened to be at the right airport and recognised Grissom instantly.

Grissom was arrested for the suspected murders of four women. In his luggage police found an air rifle, a blood stained claw hammer, two large hunting knives, duct tape, leather gloves and nylon rope.

The trial for the murders of Joan Butler, Theresa Brown and Christine Rusch opened on October 19, 1990.

The trial lasted two weeks after which Richard Grissom was found guilty of the murders of Joan Butler, Theresa Brown and Christine Rusch after a 36-hour deliberation by the jury.

Richard Grissom was sentenced to four life sentences plus 361 years for the murders of Joan Butler, Theresa Brown and Christine Rusch on November 23, 1990.

Edson Guimaraes

Another angel of death was Edson Isidora Guimaraes. Working as a nursing assistant in Salgado Filho Hospital in Rio, Guimaraes believed he was ending the pain and suffering of comatose or critical patients by removing their oxygen masks or administering drug overdoses.

He claimed it was easier on the families if the patients died. Guimaraes worked in the intensive care ward of the hospital, when the death rate in the ward began to increase alarmingly. After an investigation, it became apparent that Guimaraes was on duty each time a suspicious death occurred. A hospital porter also came forward to say she had seen Guimaraes filling a syringe from a bottle of potassium chloride in a drug office. Guimaraes should not have had access to this area.

Moments after the cleaner had seen the nurses-aide fill the syringe, she saw him inject the liquid into the drip of a comatose patient, who quickly died.

Guimaraes was moved to another ward, and the death rate in Intensive Care returned to its relatively low number. On May 4, 1999 he was allowed to return to the Intensive Care Unit where he quickly dispensed of four patients.

The nurses-aide was quickly arrested and confessed to the murders of five patients. He also confessed to calling the local funeral home, as soon as the murder had occurred, to claim the $60 'finders fee' that the funeral parlour offered.

It was claimed that between January 1, and May 4, 1999 the killer might have been responsible for the murders of up to 131 patients.

At his trial the killer was asked by the press if he had taken the oxygen masks off some of this patients, the man replied in the positive:

> *"The oxygen mask was taken away, yes. There were five patients that this happened to... I chose the patients I saw suffering, generally patients with AIDS, patients who were almost terminal. I am calm because the patients were in a coma and had no way of recovering."*

On February 21, 2000 Guimaraes was found guilty and sentenced to 76 years in prison.

H

William Heirens

On November 15, 1928 William George Heirens was born to Margaret and George Heirens in Rogers Park, Chicago. He was the eldest son of the couple and was born after a very traumatic pregnancy and delivery. The pregnancy almost terminated after 10 weeks, however Margaret Heirens carried the baby to term. He was delivered by forceps after a long 62-hour labour.

The boy was a normal young boy growing up during the Depression, the family struggling but they got by.

The moment everything changed was on June 13, 1942, when Heirens, aged just thirteen held up a local store with a gun.

The boy was arrested and soon confessed to a dozen burglaries. He was sent to a Catholic reformatory for boys, in Gibault, Terre Haute, Indiana. He escaped and soon found himself back in front of a judge for break and enter charges.

He was sent to a different Catholic school and thrived. He remained there until January 1945. After that time, he applied and was accepted as an under-aged student at the University of Chicago.

Being an on campus student he had the ability to slip out at night breaking into homes and stealing what he wanted. He had no one to answer to, only seeing his family on the weekends.

Sixteen-year-old William Heirens had a history of breaking into apartment building basements, looking for laundry washing lines, looking for lingerie. He liked to steal ladies underwear and put it on.

Sometimes just breaking into a home would produce an orgasm.

On June 5, 1945 while on his way to his summer job, Heirens decided he 'needed' to break into a house. After failing twice to gain entry to homes, at 10.30am Heirens third attempt was successful. He walked straight into an apartment building lobby in Kenmore Avenue, Chicago and took the lift to the top floor and tried every door on every floor until he found an open door on the fifth floor.

Little did the boy know but the owner, forty-three-year-old Josephine Ross, was sleeping in her bed, a bull terrier on the floor beside the bed.

When Heirens entered the bedroom the dog began to bark and startled the sleeping woman, who screamed as Heirens pounced on her.

He retrieved the knife from his pocket and stabbed her in the throat and chest as she attempted to fight off the sixteen-year-old. He bashed the woman and finally strangled her with her own stockings.

Once Josephine was dead, Heirens carried her body to the bathroom and cleaned off the drying blood, before returning the woman's dead body to the bed.

Heirens, cleaned the apartment for fingerprints and kicked and bashed the dog, which had tried to protect its owner, before leaving the scene. He took with him several rings and a fur coat.

At lunchtime, Josephine's daughter returned and found her mother dead on the bed, the dog injured and cowering in a corner. Police were called and assumed that the woman had disturbed a burglar in her house.

On the night of October 1, 1945 William Heirens broke into the home of Veronica Hudzinski. The nineteen-year-old woman was at home in her North Winthrop Ave, Chicago apartment when she was startled by Heirens breaking in through a window.

Heirens grabbed the gun from his pocket and aimed it at the woman who recoiled in fear. The seventeen-year-old fired two shots at Veronica. She fell to the ground, both bullets entering her shoulder. She survived the attack.

The boy dropped the gun at the scene and ran home to his dormitory room at the Chicago University.

After the shock of the shooting attack of Veronica Hudzinski only four days earlier, William Heirens again decided to break into another home. Late in the night of October 5, 1945 he broke into the Chicago apartment of Evelyn Peterson. The woman was alone, asleep in her bed when the attacker bashed her over the head with a metal bar. The woman was knocked unconscious and tied up, never seeing Heirens. The sight of the woman bound aroused Heirens and he soon ejaculated over Evelyn's body before escaping with money from her purse.

The woman regained consciousness after the attack, escaped from her binds and headed to the phone, intent on calling the police, but instead answered a knock at her door. Standing there was Heirens, he told her he had heard something and would go down to the foyer and call for help.

Heirens had the building manager call a doctor for Evelyn. He then disappeared into the night once again.

It was a little over six months after Heirens had killed Josephine Ross when he decided to murder again.

On December 10, 1945 Heirens broke into the apartment of thirty-year-old Frances Brown in Pine Crest, Chicago. As he climbed through the window the woman screamed and Heirens attempted to silence her by pistol-whipping her with his gun. The woman continued to fight her attacker until he fired the gun at her. He shot her twice and she fell to the ground in a pool of blood. The killer grabbed his knife, and to ensure that Frances was dead, he stabbed his knife into the left side of her neck. It was such a brutal wound, that the knife pierced through to the other side of her neck.

Once dead, the killer stripped the pyjamas from the woman and dragged the body of Frances to the bath. He attempted to wash the blood from her face and head, but tired of trying to hold the woman, so he left her kneeling beside the bath, her head immersed in the bathwater and her pyjamas wrapped around her throat concealing the knife.

Before leaving the apartment, Heirens took a lipstick from the woman's handbag and wrote on the wall:

> For heAvens
> SAke cAtch me
> BeFore I kill more
> I cAnnot control myselF

After getting drunk William Heirens decided he did not want to go back to his dorm room at the University of Chicago but decided instead to go and break into someone's home. The seventeen-year-old was quite drunk and less in control of his faculties.

The young man caught a train and fell asleep as it travelled through the night. The killer woke up just after midnight on January 6, 1946 as the train pulled into Thorndale. Heirens decided to try his hand at breaking into one of the wealthy homes; his fetish for ladies satin underwear driving his lust.

Heirens stole a ladder he found leaning on the side of one of the mansions, as he knew in his drunken state he would not be able to climb into the high windows of the larger houses.

At 5943 Kenmore Avenue, Thorndale the young killer spotted a window slightly ajar. He pushed the ladder up the windowsill and clambered up the ladder.

Inside the darkened bedroom, he saw the silhouette of a young girl. Six-year-old Suzanne Degnan was asleep in her bed when seventeen-year-old Heirens climbed through her window.

He shone his torch around the room, when suddenly Suzanne sat up in bed and started talking in her sleep. The noise startled Heirens and he pounced on the young girl, strangling her until she stopped breathing.

Once the girl was dead, the teenage shoved his handkerchief deep into her throat to make sure she would not revive.

By now Heirens had sobered and the act of breaking into the house and strangled the young girl had produced an orgasm in the teenage killer. Now he decided to finish the job.

He dumped Suzanne's body in an alleyway and went looking for an open basement window. He found one in a nearby street and returned to get the girl's body. Once inside the basement, Heirens placed the girl's body into one of the laundry tubs. With the water running over the corpse, he took his knife and proceeded to dissect the girl's little body.

He cut the body in half, before removing the head, arms and legs. Once the body was in smaller pieces he wrapped it up with rope and pieces of cloth that he found in the basement. He then took each piece and secreted it into manholes in nearby streets hoping the sewers would take the pieces away.

His last task was to clean the basement; to eradicate any evidence that would incriminate him. As he was about to leave the basement, he felt a rumpled piece of paper in his pocket and decided that he should write a ransom note for the young girl.

It read:

> GeT $20,000
> Reddy and
> WaiTe
> FoR word
> Do NoT NoTiFy
> FBI oR
> Police
> Bills iN 5s and10s

On the reverse side it read:

> BuRn This FoR heR SAFTy

He took the note back to the girl's home and threw it into the window of her bedroom. He then threw the knife away, and burnt his coat after finding blood on the sleeve.

The next morning as Heirens made his way to lectures, James Degnan discovered his youngest daughter missing. The police were called immediately and a search of Suzanne's room produced the ransom letter. The Degnans began recording messages to be played on the radio begging for the safe return of their youngest daughter.

By that evening, the first pieces of Suzanne's body were found in a manhole. A search was made of all the surrounding manholes and except for her arms, most of the young girl's body was found.

Coal soot in her the girl's hair directed the police search to nearby basements where coal is delivered for apartment building furnaces. The crime scene was found, despite Heirens attempts to clean it up. Suspicion instantly fell on the building's janitor, but he was released later.

On June 26, 1946 Heirens decided to break into another home, his compulsion and sexual energy from the burglaries was a driving force and his undoing.

He broke into the Pera's apartment in Wayne Manor Building in Chicago in the middle of the afternoon. Mrs Pera was home and bumped into the burglar as he made his way silently around the house, secreting items into a bag as he went. Mrs Pera screamed and Heirens ran from the building. He was chased by several of the tenants of the building but the young man was too fast and able to get away from them. Still with the stolen loot, Heirens climbed onto the balcony of the Willetts' home and bashed loudly on the door. Frances Willetts, a police wife, opened it.

The panting young man told the woman a story about being chased by hooligans and asked if he could have a drink while hiding out on her balcony. The woman was suspicious of the boy's story and so while inside, she called the police, who ask her to keep the boy there as long as she could.

They had received calls about the burglary in Mrs Pera's apartment and it appeared that Mrs Willetts had found the thief.

Two police officers arrived shortly afterwards and Heirens decided to shoot at them. Luckily for the officers, his gun misfired twice and they were able to return fire. The boy jumped from the balcony knocking over the officers, but they are still able to grab him. One of them struggles to keep hold as a third officer, hearing the gunshots, comes to their aid. He grabbed a concrete flowerpot and struck the boy over the head. He was knocked unconscious.

Heirens was taken to hospital, while police searched his dorm room looking for evidence of any further burglaries; they find enough to charge him with twenty-two counts of burglary.

The seventeen-year-old's fingerprints were also recorded while he was in hospital. They were compared to fingerprints from other open cases and a match was found. A palm print and fingerprint lifted from the ransom letter for six-year-old Suzanne Degnan matched Heirens.

They had found the little girl's brutal murderer.

While he remained in hospital, Heirens tried to convince police he was still severely injured, pretending to be in a stupefied state, refusing to answer their questions.

One doctor suggested the use of Truth Serum, sodium pentothal. It did not work, instead Heirens used the guise to blame an imaginary other person called "George" for the murders. Psychiatrists were called to examine the boy to see if he was suffering from schizophrenia. He was found mentally sane.

On July 9, 1946 after spending almost three weeks in hospital feigning injuries at the hands of police, seventeen-year-old William Heirens was charged with three counts of murder, four counts of attempted murder and twenty-two counts of burglary.

On July 26, 1946 William Heirens formally confessed to three murders. He confessed to the June 5, 1945 stabbing murder of forty-three-year-old Josephine Ross, the shooting murder of thirty-year-old Frances Brown on December 10, 1945 and the brutal slaying and dismemberment of six-year-old Suzanne Degnan on January 6, 1946.

To supplement his confession police had fingerprint identification from the ransom letter he wrote for Suzanne's murder. Also his handwriting and spelling matched that of the lipstick message and ransom letter.

Days later at a plea-bargain; Heirens recanted his confession, saying it was coerced from him.

After confessing and recanting his confession again at the end of July, William Heirens once again confessed on August 6, 1946 to the murders of three people. This time he offered to take police to the crime scenes to show them how he murdered each victim.

At trial William Heirens was sentences to three consecutive life terms, and one extra life term for the four attempted murders and 22 counts of robbery.

Johann Hoch

Johann Hoch was born Johann Scmidt in Horweiler, Germany in 1860. From an early age Hoch was a regular churchgoer. As his father and brothers were already active members of the local church, so Hoch's career path was destined for the same.

Hoch, however, had different ideas. In 1883 he fled Germany and sailed to America leaving his wife, Caroline Ramb and three children behind. Hoch settled down in Wheeling, West Virginia, bigamously marrying a widow named Caroline. After the wedding, Hoch was seen by Reverend Hermann Haas giving his new wife some white powder. Hours later Caroline died in agony. Hoch again fled, but not before collecting the money from selling the house and a $2500 claim for life insurance on his wife. During 1887, Hoch married two further women, Martha Steinbucher and Mary Rankin. Martha, like Caroline died in agony, whereas Mary only suffered the indignity of a run away husband and stolen money.

It is believed that between the years of 1887 and 1904 Hoch married a further ten women, some he murdered, others he just abandoned.

On December 5, 1904, Hoch met Marie Walcker, he quickly proposed and they pair soon married. After the marriage Marie offered Hoch her life savings, also mentioning that her sister, Julia Fischer, has $800 in a savings account. Marie was soon seriously ill, dying on January 12, 1905. On the day of his wife's death, Hoch proposed to Julia, they married three days later on January 15, moving in together in a flat in Chicago.

The marriage did not last long, Hoch once again ran off having stolen $750 from his bride. Julia notified the police about the theft. Inspector George Shippy was put in charge of the case, having already had dealings with Hoch, arresting him in the past for theft. Reverend Hermann Haas, who discussed his suspicions in the death of Caroline Hoch, contacted Inspector Shippy. In order to find the truth Caroline's body was exhumed, but her vital organs were missing.

Inspector Shippy checked on Hoch's movements that led to Marie Walcker. A post mortem of her body confirmed that she had died of arsenic poisoning. Hoch was now a wanted man, his picture appearing nationwide. In New York, Catherine Kimmerle's new tenant, who had proposed within twenty minutes of meeting her, matched the photograph of the fugitive so she called police. Hoch was quickly arrested and delivered back to Chicago and searched. A fountain pen found in his possession contained arsenic, Hoch claimed that it was for his own suicide. By now Inspector Shippy had identified five women whom he believed were murdered by Hoch.

Hoch was tried for the murder of Marie Walcker in May 1905, found guilty and sentenced to death, to which Hoch replied 'It serves me right'. An appeal was rejected, leaving Hoch to be executed on the gallows on February 23, 1906, his last words before the trap door opened were:

> *"I am done with this world, I am done with everybody."*

The answer to other potential victims was partially answered when, in 1955, the wall of a cottage once owned by Hoch was found to conceal the bones of an unknown person.

Dr Herman Holmes
Mudgett
Herman Webster Mudgett was born in New Hampshire on May 16, 1860. In his prison memoirs he wrote:
> *"I was born with the devil in me... I was born with the Evil One standing as my sponsor beside the bed where I was ushered into this world. He has been with me ever since".*

This is how the man, the world would know as Dr H H Holmes began life. And life was always full of evil and death from the beginning.

His father was an abusive man, and his mother was a tiny submissive woman. Mrs Mudgett would do everything her husband commanded and this was the way that Holmes would always expect women to behave.

School life was good to Mudgett, with his natural intelligence, charm and handsome looks he was able to influence most people and dreamed of a life as a doctor. By puberty Mudgett had developed a hobby of killing and dismembering stray animals. He was fascinated with anatomy and would often conduct experiments on his prey.

He left school at sixteen and married Clara Lovering at the age of eighteen in 1878. His hopes of becoming a doctor were soon dashed when he was expelled at twenty-four, from University of Michigan Medical School after he was discovered stealing cadavers.

In 1886, Mudgett moved to the upper-class area of Inglewood Illinois - changing his name to the better sounding Dr Henry Howard Holmes.

Dr Holmes
The newly dubbed Dr Holmes walked into Dr E Holton's chemist holding the advertisement that had been placed in the window asking for a pharmacist. Holmes introduced himself to Mrs Holton, the druggist's wife. She explained to Holmes that her husband was terminally ill and she was struggling to keep the store running. She would do the prescriptions she knew and for the others she would wearily traipse upstairs to ask her husband.

Dr Holmes saw his opportunity. He took a script from Mrs Holten and promptly dispensed it for her. Mrs Holton hired Holmes on the spot. Holmes, with his dapper persona brought in more customers than the little chemist had before and it thrived with Holmes as the pharmacist and Mrs Holton assisting. Then the inevitable happened and Dr Holton passed away.

Mrs Holton could not bear to leave the premises. She felt that her husband was always close by if she stayed. Dr Holmes came up with an idea. He offered to buy the Pharmacy from her, giving her a monthly salary so she could stay. The idea sounded great and the two entered into an agreement.

However Holmes defaulted on his payments pretty soon and the two ended up in court over the matter. But before the case was concluded, Mrs Holton disappeared. According to Dr Holmes she could not bear the pain of being in the place her husband had died and moved to California. Mrs Holton was never seen or heard from again.

The Castle
With the profits from the pharmacy, Holmes began the construction of his Castle across the street from the drug store. During the construction of the three storey building Holmes routinely hired and fired hundreds of contractors, claiming their work was not of his standard.

He also refused to pay them any money, and when he was taken to court over non-payment he sort continuance after continuance until the other party gave up in frustration.

The real reason behind Holmes' constant firings where so none of the contractors would get an idea of the purpose of the building with it's secret rooms, staircases that went nowhere and hidden passageways. He did not want them asking questions about the sealable rooms with gas jets or the room with an enormous kiln with a cast iron door. The large vats in the floor that would be filled with quick-lime or acid. The secret chutes that led to rooms of torture. And his favourite; the basement with it's dissection table and surgical tools and implements.

Once the building was complete Holmes moved the pharmacy into the first floor.

In 1887, while still married to his first wife, Holmes married Myrta Belknap. The marriage was not a happy one, with Myrta not able to stand Holmes' ways and would often berate him in front of customers, causing the good doctor great embarrassment in the neighbourhood. To stop her interfering, Holmes sent her, pregnant, to his parents, where she remained. The couple never bothered to get a divorce.

Holmes was always interested in making money. He always devised new 'get rich quick' schemes to make money. Once he tapped into the town water supply and sold it mixed with a little vanilla essence as a cure-all tonic he named Linden Grove Mineral Water. The authorities quickly stepped in and Holmes stopped selling the water - but he was not punished for the scam.

The local medical schools also knew they could rely on Dr Holmes to supply them with fresh cadavers. If he was ever short of cash he would murder a customer and sell the body for $25 to $50 each.

In 1890, at the tender age of thirty, Dr Holmes was quite prosperous. His new chemist on the bottom level of the Castle was attracting more and more business with it's polished wood panelling, frescoes and arched ceiling - it was the epitome of class.

Next to the pharmacy Holmes opened a jewellery store, a restaurant and barber as well as a business manufacturing soap and one of the first coping services in Chicago.

With so many business dealings Holmes needed a manager to help him. Enter Ned Conner. Ned was a job-to-job drifter who dragged his wife Julia and daughter Pearl with him to each job he held. When he saw the advertisement for a manager, he applied for and got the job. He thought his problems were over - the job paid well and seemed permanent. Conner introduced Holmes to his wife and daughter.

Julia
Holmes was instantly stunned by the beauty of Julia, a 6 foot tall red-haired green-eyed woman. Holmes instantly fired his current cashier and hired Julia.

Julia could not believe her luck. She rang and invited her eighteen-year-old sister to visit her in Chicago. Gertie was as beautiful as her sister and quickly caught Dr Holmes' eye. He showered the young woman in gifts and affection. Holmes even told Gertie he would divorce his wife to be with her.

Gertie was shocked by his proposal and hastily left Chicago. Holmes rebounded quickly from Gertie's rejection by returning his attentions to Julia. After drinking heavily one night Ned was confronted by his friends who told him of the dalliances of his wife with Holmes and Ned stormed home to speak to his wife.

He told Julia that Holmes did not love her, she was only his second choice after Gertie rejected him. Julia made further accusations back at Ned until the couple decided to separate. Ned stayed in another room in the Castle for a while before moving out permanently. On his departure he told Julia he wanted a divorce.

Julia was deeply in love with Holmes and subsequently became pregnant with his child - a fact that Holmes did not like. The doctor told his lover that he would only marry her if she aborted the pregnancy. Being a mother to Pearl already and feeling the unborn child inside her, Julia could not face the prospect and continually put the procedure off.

After further insistence by Holmes, Julia agreed that he could perform the procedure. Holmes put Pearl to bed and then carried the hysterical Julia down to his makeshift operating theatre in his basement. Neither Julia nor Pearl were ever seen alive again.

Dr Holmes had one of his lackeys clean off the dismembered body of Julia and removed all the flesh leaving only the bones. The skeleton of Julia was sold to a medical school for $200.

Benjamin Pitezel

Benjamin Pitezel, another of Holmes' lackeys, hung off his every word and did everything asked of him, soon giving his life for Holmes. The two men came up with an insurance scam where they could share in $10,000.

The plan was that Pitezel would take out a life insurance policy for $10,000. Holmes was the beneficiary. Pitezel would disappear to Philadelphia, Holmes would get a corpse, disfigure it, then with the help of Pitezel's children he would have the body identified as Pitezel and claim the $10,000.

The plan worked brilliantly and Holmes claimed the money. However Holmes was fearful when the police became interested in him. He torched the Castle and fled Chicago with one of the Pitezel daughters with Mrs Pitezel following behind, presumably to meet up with Benjamin in Philadelphia. What Mrs Pitezel did not know was that Holmes had murdered Benjamin.

In the burnt out skeleton of the bizarre building, authorities found the remains of over two hundred people. A warrant was issued for Holmes and he was arrested in Boston in 1894 and extradited to Philadelphia.

While in prison Holmes shared a cell with a shady character called Marion Hedgepeth. Hedgepeth would continually boast about his escapades. To get even Holmes told Hedgepeth about the murder of Pitezel for the insurance money. And that Pitezel was not the first.

Hedgepeth told the authorities.

Murder charges

Holmes was charged with the murder of Benjamin Pitezel and confessed to the murder, he told the police how he had burned the man alive despite "the victim's cries for mercy and his prayers, all of which upon me had no effect".

At the castle the police began the tally. It was suspected that many of the 50 guests who stayed at the Castle during the 1893 Chicago World Fair fell victim to Dr Holmes Castle. Also at least 100 typists and secretaries were murdered there. One after another would fall victim to the doctor's charms and murderous lust by responding to the never-ending ads placed by Holmes.

Three of the Pitezel children were also located. Alice and Nellie had been stuffed into a trunk and gassed. Their brother Howard was poisoned, burned, dismembered then buried.

On October 28, 1895 Holmes pleaded not guilty to the murder of Benjamin Pitezel and sent to trial. At his trial on November 4, 1895, Holmes was convicted of first degree murder and sentenced to death.

Holmes enjoyed the notoriety he gained from the trial. Giving many reporters access to himself and began writing his own memoirs. He signed a statement concerning the murders of a further 27 people, adding to his infamy.

He was hanged on May 7, 1896 at Moyamensing Prison.

Fritz Honka

A fire at 76 Zeiss Street in Hamburg, Germany on June 17, 1975, led to the discovery and arrest of serial killer, thirty-nine-year-old Fritz Honka.

Honka lived in the attic apartment, but with the fire spreading through the building, fireman wanted to evacuate everyone and went from door to door ensuring everyone was leaving, however they found the attic room was locked. Wanting to ensure that no one was inside they made the decision to break the door down. The fireman were horrified to discover the remains of four women, including the chopped up limbs of fifty-four-year-old Anna Beuschel dumped in a corner of the room. Police confirmed that the four victims were each last seen at the Golden Glove bar in Hamburg. The other victims were named as Ruth Schult, 52, who's upper body was still missing; Gertrude Braeuer, 42, for whom only the torso was present, her limbs were discovered four years earlier thrown into a nearby yard and Freda Roblick, 57, whose body was completely mummified.

At first Honka claimed memory loss when asked why the women were in his apartment, but he soon confessed to the murders. Honka described how he chose his victims. He always used the Golden Glove bar as a place to meet women, but his chosen female had to meet his requirements, which were that they had to be shorter than he (Honka was 5'4") and have no teeth, he was terrified of damage to his genitals during oral sex. Honka would escort the lady back to his apartment where, after sex, he would strangle then rape his chosen victim and leave to rot in the flat.

For his crimes Honka received a life sentence and died in prison on October 19, 1998.

I

Javed Iqbal

Javed Iqbal, the murderer of at least one hundred boys, was sentenced to one of the more unusual death sentences meted out in any Pakistan Court. The killer was to be strangled to death, chopped into one hundred pieces and dissolved in acid.

The same fate that befell his victims.

Iqbal was arrested for the murders after he confessed to 100 killings in a letter to police. When arrested at his home, two bodies were found in a vat of acid.

Piles of clothing were found at Iqbal's home for the families of missing boys to sift through. Many families recognised shoes and clothes worn by their children when they were last seen.

At trial, the man pleaded not guilty to the six-month killing spree, but was found guilty of all one hundred murders. Judge Allah Baksh Ranja's unusual sentenced was cheered on by the victims' families. The families saw the sentence as closure, knowing that Iqbal had dissolved the bodies of their children in acid, leaving nothing for burial.

Yet in a twist of fate, Iqbal escaped the gruesome death by killing himself in his Lahore prison cell on October 9, 2001. Beside the dead prisoner was his partner in crime fourteen-year-old Sabir.

The two had apparently taken poison and died during the night.

Colin Ireland
Murder by the book

Colin Ireland enjoyed taunting police when each murder was reported in the media. He yearned to be as famous as any of the American serial killers.

According to the FBI Handbook *Whoever Fights Monsters* by renowned FBI profiler Robert Ressler, a serial killer had to kill at least five to become well known and classed as a serial killer.

Colin had read the book and used it as his killer's manual in his quest to become a serial killer. He meticulously planned each murder as he set out to become famous. . He even stated in a phone call to police

> "I have got the book, I know how many you have to do..."

He told police that he enjoyed the thrill of the notoriety the killings gave him once caught.

Like contemporaries Lake and Ng, Colin Ireland was also a fanatical survival enthusiast who enjoyed the thrill of the hunt as well as the kill.

Coleherne Pub in London's Earl's Court district was to be the hunting ground for the killer. Ireland chose gay sado-masochistic men as his victims as they were willing to get tied up. Also, he believed that the public would feel less sympathy for them.

Peter Walker

On March 9, 1993, Colin met his first victim, forty-five-year-old Peter Walker. The theatre director invited Ireland back to his flat where they could get a little more acquainted away from the crowds at the pub. Little did Walker know but Ireland had brought with him a cord, knife and a pair of gloves.

At the flat, Ireland told Walker to lie naked on the bed before tying him down and whipping him. The shackled man could do nothing as Ireland placed a plastic bag over the man's head and suffocated him.

Watching the papers for two days, without any mention of the murder, Ireland decided to show police the way to the dead man.

He rung the local newspaper and the Samaritans Charity to ask if someone could let out the dogs trapped inside the man's flat.

With his first kill complete and in the papers, Ireland found it easier to kill the next time.

Chris Dunn

On May 29, of the same year Ireland struck again. At the pub he picked up thirty-seven-year-old Chris Dunn and the pair returned the victim's flat. Back at Dunn's flat Ireland tied his victim to the bed, this time though, he used handcuffs. He then proceeded to beat the man with a belt and then tortured Dunn with a cigarette lighter against his genitals. When he was done torturing the victim, Ireland strangled him.

Perry Bradley

The next victim, Perry Bradley, was also picked up by Ireland at the Coleherne Pub on June 4, 1993. The two men retired to Bradley's flat, where Bradley fell asleep, Ireland had doubts about killing the man, but then decided it "easier to kill him" and strangled him with the cord he brought with him on all his killings.

Ireland was starting to get a little cocky, knowing he was getting closer to the notoriety of a serial killer. Victim number four would be murdered only a few days later on June 8, 1993.

Andrew Collier

Thirty-three-year-old Andrew Collier was picked up by Ireland at the pub and the men returned to Collier's house. Wondering around the house talking to Collier he discovered that Collier was in fact HIV positive, Ireland became enraged, how dare he not let Ireland know or even offer sexual protection. Ireland killed him in the same manner as the others. Collier was tied down on his bed, beaten with the belt then strangled. Ireland also killed Collier's cat by breaking its neck before leaving.

The investigations weren't going as well as Ireland had hoped; he had wanted to see the murders across the front page of all the papers but to no avail. So he began to taunt police with anonymous phone calls. But used vital clues pertinent to the murders to show they were linked. He was disappointed after reading in the papers that they considered him an animal lover by asking someone to let out and feed Walker's dogs, So he told them that at his most recent murder, he killed the cat to show they were wrong. When police found Collier and his cat, they were in shock to learn they were indeed chasing a serial killer who was targeting gays.

Emmanuel Spiteri

Victim number five was killed within a week of Collier. This time on June 13, Emmanuel Spiteri was picked up by Ireland and taken back to the victim's flat. The forty-two-year-old man was tied up on the bed, beaten and tortured. Ireland was impressed b the man's strong will but killed him in the same manner as the others.

This time however Ireland was not so lucky to get away with murder. A video surveillance camera had picked up the two men as they walked along Charing Cross station together. Fearing he would be charged with murder, Ireland approached the police and said that the two men had met up with another man before adjourning to the man's flat.

However, the phone calls police had received from the killer, matched the voice of Ireland and his fingerprints were all over the crime scene.

He was charged with the man's murder and soon after admitted to the other four murders as well.

Ireland was sentenced in December 1993 to five life sentences and told he would never be released from prison.

According to some sources Ireland killed again in prison but the case was not pursued. The murder was committed while Colin was in Wakefield Prison, Yorkshire. Two weeks after, he was moved to Whitemore Prison, Cambridgeshire.

J

Jack the Ripper

In Victorian England during the late 19th Century there was a string of murders that were committed by person or persons unknown. Today, over 120 years later the murders still capture the imagination of professional and amateur sleuths alike.

The Victims
Mary Anne Nichols

August 31, 1888 is considered the date of the first of the Jack the Ripper murders. At the time of the murder forty-three-year-old Mary Anne (Polly) Nicholls was divorced from her husband William and had five grown children. She was poor and had gone into prostitution to try and make ends meet; however it cost her her life.

At 11.30pm Polly was seen walking along Whitechapel Road, Whitechapel. An hour later she was seen leaving the Frying Pan pub in Brick Lane. She was quite inebriated as she slowly headed toward the doss house at 18 Thrawl Street. However, although she had earned 20d that evening, she had spent it all on alcohol and a new bonnet. She was turned away from the doss at 1.20am, and she yelled she'd be back.

At 2.30am the woman stumbled drunkenly along Whitechapel High Street; it was the last time she was seen alive.

Her body was found on Bucks Row at 3.40am by PC John Neil and Dr Llewellyn was called to pronounce the woman dead. Her skirt was hitched up and her throat was cut, however it would be later in the night, when her body was fully examined that the extent of her injuries were realised.

Dr Llewellyn's report stated:
- 5 teeth were missing (two were already missing)
- Her tongue was lacerated
- She had a bruise on the right side of her jaw - assumed to be from a thumb being pressed to her throat, the left side had a longer bruise from the rest of a hand being pressed against the woman's throat. - summating that she had been strangled before any other injuries where made.
- There was a four inch cut along the left side of her neck
- An eight-inch circular incision was made around her throat, cutting all the tissue and organs to the vertebrae.
- She had a criss-cross pattern of cuts across her abdomen
- There was little blood on her clothes or skin.

Annie Chapman

Annie was found shortly before 6.00 am on Saturday 8th September in the backyard of 29 Hanbury Street. Her throat had been savagely cut and her body had been viciously mutilated. Organs had been removed from her abdomen in a manner that suggested that her attacker had anatomical knowledge. "Dark Annie" aged 47, was suffering from a degenerative disease and wandered the East End Streets penniless following the death of her husband in 1886. Cruelly treated by life, Annie had two daughters, one of whom died in 1882, and a son who was crippled. Living off earnings as a prostitute and selling matches and flowers, Annie was a street hardened rogue.

Yet she was easily overcome by her murderer who slit her throat in Hanbury Street.

Elizabeth Stride
Elizabeth Stride was born Elizabeth Gustafsdotter in Sweden in 1843. She came to London in 1866 and married John Thomas Stride three years later. In 1884 her husband died after many unhappy years and subsequent breakdown of their marriage. By now Elizabeth was working as a prostitute and lived at 33 Dorset Street. She had many convictions for being drunk.

The month of her murder Elizabeth moved in the lodging house at 32 Flower and Dean Street.

On the day of her murder she had started the day with money. After cleaning the rooms of the lodging house she was paid 6d, which she took to go and get drunk. She left the house at 6.30pm and went to Queen's Head public house for half an hour before returning home to comb her hair.
She left the rooms again and went to the Bricklayers' Arms Pub where she remained until 11.00pm. She was then seen leaving with a young man.
She was seen walking with the same man towards Dutfield's yard around 11.45pm, and later, at 12.30am, when a police constable saw her still talking to the man.

At 12.45am, Israel Shwartz saw the woman being pushed to the ground near the yard but was frightened off by another man. It was at 1.00am when Louis Diemshutz came into Dutfield's Yard with his horse. When his horse refused to continue into the yard, it was then that the man saw the body of Elizabeth on the ground. The alarm was raised. Elizabeth had only just been killed, it is theorised that the killer may have been still in the yard watching the discovery.

Dr Bagster Phillips was called to the scene. He later reported:
"The body was lying on the near side, with the face turned toward the wall, the head up the yard...The right arm was over the belly. The back of the hand and wrist had on it clotted blood. The legs were drawn up with the feet close to the wall. The body and face were warm...the throat was deeply gashed, and there was an abrasion of the skin about 1 1/2 inch in diameter...there was a clean-cut incision on the neck. It was 6 inches in length...death is undoubtedly from the loss of blood from the left carotid artery and the division of the windpipe."

Phillips claimed that the woman had been grabbed from behind, thrown down face first before having her throat slit.
Witness' claims of the victim eating grapes with her attacker and of a grape stalk found in Elizabeth's hand were false.

Catharine Eddowes
Catharine Eddowes was a-year-older than Elizabeth when she died. She was born into a large family and appeared to have gone to school until she was thirteen - when her mother died.

By 1863, she had moved in with Thomas Conway and by all accounts married the man. She had TC tattooed on her arm. The couple had three children before the relationship broke down.

Catharine also lived in Flower and Dean Street lodgings for some time but on the night she died she had been residing at Shoe Lane Workhouse.

On the day she was murdered, Catharine's first stop was at a pawnshop to hock a pair of shoes. She left them under the name of Jane Kelly. She had breakfast and tea with John Kelly her common-law husband of seven years.

She went off to earn money and was seen again at 8.30pm, walking drunkenly along Aldgate High Street. She was arrested shortly after for imitating a fire engine and lying down in the middle of the street. She gave her name to the arresting officer as "Nothing".

She was released from Bishopsgate cells at 1.00am and gave her name as Mary Ann Kelly. She left the cells saying "Good night old cock".

She was seen again at 1.35am chatting to a man in the Church Passage entry to Mitre Square.

At 1.45am PC Edward Watkins entered Mitre Square and found the body of Cathy Eddowes. Beside the body were three boot buttons, a mustard tin with two pawn tickets in it - one for the boots, the other for a man's shirt, and a thimble.

Her body was seen by Dr Frederick Gordon Brown who commented on the injuries as:

"The body was on its back, the head turned to left shoulder. The arms by the side of the body...both palms upwards...left leg extended in a line with the body. The abdomen was exposed. Right leg bent at the thigh and knee.
The throat cut across...The intestines were drawn out to a large extent and place over the right shoulder - they were smeared over with some feculent matter. A piece of about two feet was quite detached from the body and placed between the body and left arm.
The lobe and auricle (outside part) of the right ear was cut obliquely through...there was a quantity of clotted blood on the pavement on the left side of the neck round the shoulder and upper part of the arm...
Body was quite warm. No death stiffening...No blood on the skin of the abdomen or secretion ... on the thighs. No spurting of blood on the bricks or pavement...no blood on the front of the clothes...a piece of the deceased's ear dropped from the clothing (when she was undressed at the mortuary)...
The face was very much mutilated. There was a cut about a quarter of an inch through the lower left eyelid, dividing the structures completely through. The upper eyelid on that side, there was a scratch through the skin on the left upper eyelid, near to the angle of the nose. The right eyelid was cut through to about half an inch. There was a deep cut over the bridge of the nose, extending from the left border of the nasal bone down near the angle of the jaw on the right side of the cheek. This cut went into the bone and divided all structures of the cheek...
The tip of the nose was quite detached from the nose by an oblique cut from the bottom of the nasal bone to where the wings of the nose join on to the face. A cut from this divided the upper lip and extended through the substance of the gum...another oblique cut...on the right angle of the mouth as if the cut of a point of a knife. The cut extended an inch and a half, parallel with the lower lip... There was on each side of cheek a cut which peeled up the skin, forming a triangular flap...two abrasions...under the left ear. The throat was cut across to ... six or seven inches...all deep structures were severed to the bone, the knife marking intervertebral cartilages... All these injuries were performed by a sharp instrument like a knife and pointed. The abdomen...the front walls were laid open from the breast bone to the pubes...the incision went upwards...the liver was stabbed...[and] was slit through by a vertical cut...[The cut down the middle of the of the abdomen, stopped at the navel, went around it then continued in a straight line] There was a stab...on the left groin...and a cut of three inches going through all tissues making a wound of the perineum......the thigh was a cut extending ... down the inner side of the left thigh and separating the left labium forming a flap of skin up to the groin....there was a flap of skin formed from the right thigh...the cut[s were] made after death and there would not be much blood on the murderer. The cut was made by some one on the right side of the body kneeling below the middle of the body....the left kidney carefully taken out and removed. The left renal artery was cut through. I should say that someone who knew the position of the kidney must have

done it...I believe the wound in the throat was the first inflicted. I believe she must have been lying on the ground."[16]

Yet the killer was not finished, at 2.55am PC Alfred Long found the now famous Goulston Street Graffito on the fascia of the doorway of 108-19 Wentworth Model Dwellings.

On the ground below the writing was a piece of Catharine Eddowes apron.

The writing said:
The Juwes are the men That Will not be Blamed for nothing.

However by 5.30am the writing was erased before being photographed.

Mary Kelly

The last Ripper victim. Mary was murdered in her lodgings at 13 Miller's Court sometime after 4 am on the 9th November. This was the most savage and gruesome attack. Her entire body was horribly mutilated, her face hacked beyond recognition.

Dr Thomas Bond's (Police Surgeon to A Division) report on Mary Jane Kelly
The body was lying naked in the middle of the bed, the shoulders flat, but the axis of the body inclined to the left side of the bed. The head was turned on the left cheek. The left arm was close to the body with the forearm flexed at a right angle & lying across the abdomen. The right arm was slightly abducted from the body and rested on the mattress, the elbow bent & the forearm supine with the fingers clenched. The legs were wide apart, the left thigh at right angles to the trunk and the right forming an obtuse angle with the pubes. The whole of the surface of the abdomen and thighs was removed and the abdominal Cavity (sic) emptied of its viscera. The breasts were cut off, the arms mutilated by several jagged wounds and the face hacked beyond recognition of the features. The tissues of the neck were severed all round down to the bone. The viscera were found in various parts viz: the uterus and Kidneys with one breast under the head, the other breast by the Rt foot, the Liver between the feet, the intestines by the right side and the spleen by the left side of the body. The flaps removed from the abdomen and thighs where on a table. The bed clothing at the right corner was saturated with blood, and on the floor beneath was a pool of blood covering about 2 feet square. The wall by the right side of the bed and in a line with the neck was marked by blood which had stuck in a number of separate splashes.

Post Mortem Examination
The face was gashed in all directions the nose, cheeks, eyebrows and ears being partly removed. The lips were blanched and cut by several incisions running obliquely down to the chin. There were also numerous cuts extending irregularly across all the features. The neck was cut through the skin and other tissues right down to the vertebrae the 5th and 6th being deeply notched. The skin cuts in the front of the neck showed distinct ecchymosis (blood pooling under the skin - like severe bruising). The air passage was cut at the lower part of the larynx through the cricoid cartilage. Both breasts were removed by more or less circular incisions, the muscles down to the ribs being attached to the breasts. The intercostals between the 4th, 5th and 6th ribs were cut through and the contents of the thorax visible through the openings. The skin and tissues of the abdomen from the costal arch to the pubes were removed in three large flaps. The right thigh was denuded in front to the bone, the flap of skin, including the external organs of generation and part of the right buttock. The left thigh was stripped of skin, fascia and muscles as far as the knee. The left calf showed a long gash through skin and tissues to the deep muscles and reaching from the knee to 5 in above the ankle. Both arms and forearms had extensive and jagged wounds. The right thumb showed a small superficial

---

[16] pp44-47, Begg, Paul, Fido, Martin and Skinner, Keith, *Jack the Ripper A to Z, The* (Headline) 1992

incision about 1 in long, with extravasation of blood in the skin and there were several abrasions on the back of the hand moreover showing the same condition. On opening the thorax it was found that the right lung was minimally adherent by old firm adhesions. The lower part of the lung was broken and torn away. The left lung was intact: it was adherent at the apex and there were a few adhesions over the side. In the substances of the lung were several nodules of consolidation.[17]

Suspects
The suspects in the Ripper case has become an incredibly long list over the years from the future king of England to a serial killer incarcerated in America and include:

- Kosminski,
- Montague John Druitt,
- Michael Ostrog,
- Dr Francis J. Tumblety,
- Sir William Gull,
- Walter Sickert,
- The Masons,
- Prince Albert Victor, Duke of Clarence
- Dr Cream (see chapter in this book on this suspect)
- George Chapman (see chapter in this book on this suspect)

Also a diary purportedly written by James Maybrick, claiming to be the killer has also surfaced in recent times.

The Letters
Like many killers, it is claimed that "Jack" wrote to the media and police incessantly. Included here are two of the letters that are more widely accepted to have come from the killer.

Dear Boss,
I keep on hearing the police have caught me but they wont fix me just yet. I have laughed when they look so clever and talk about being on the right track. That joke about Leather Apron gave me real fits. I am down on whores and I shant quit ripping them till I do get buckled. Grand work the last job was. I gave the lady no time to squeal. How can they catch me now. I love my work and want to start again. You will soon hear of me with my funny little games. I saved some of the proper red stuff in a ginger beer bottle over the last job to write with but it went thick like glue and I cant use it. Red ink is fit enough I hope ha. ha. The next job I do I shall clip the ladys ears off and send to the police officers just for jolly wouldn't you. Keep this letter back till I do a bit more work, then give it out straight. My knife's so nice and sharp I want to get to work right away if I get a chance. Good Luck.

Yours truly
Jack the Ripper

Dont mind me giving the trade name

PS Wasnt good enough to post this before I got all the red ink off my hands curse it No luck yet. They say I'm a doctor now. ha ha
----

---

[17] pp57-63, Begg, Paul, Fido, Martin and Skinner, Keith, *Jack the Ripper A to Z, The* (Headline) 1992

Dated 29 October 1888
Old boss you was rite it was the left kidny I was goin to hopperate agin close to you ospitle just as I was going to dror mi nife along of er bloomin throte cusses of coppers spoilt the game but I guess I will be on the job soon and will send you another bot of innerds
Jack the Ripper.
O have you seen the devlle with his mikerscope and scalpol a lookin at a Kidney with a skide cocked up.

Jack the Stripper

Talk about an unknown killer murdering London prostitutes and you would automatically think of Jack the Ripper, but this was not 1888. This was 1960's London; the killer was similarly unknown as his Victorian counterpart and was dubbed Jack the Stripper.

At approximately 4.42am on June 17, 1959, police car number 54 made its nightly patrol travelling alongside the Thames at Oakes Meadow. The driver stopped the car and indicated to his partner the figure of a woman sat hunched at the base of a willow tree. The two policemen left their vehicle to get a closer look. As they approached the woman did not move. She sat against the tree, her blue and white striped dress ripped at the front and wearing no underwear. No other articles of clothing were present.

Doctor Robert Teare reached the scene early in the morning and gave his initial assessment of manual strangulation as the cause of death. His subsequent autopsy confirmed strangulation with the killer using his thumbs to press down on the unknown victim's windpipe. Dr Teare reported that the woman was killed no later than 2am on the morning that she was found. Fingerprints of the dead woman were taken, but no match could be found in police records. Looking for help in the case, a death mask was made of the unfortunate woman and photos placed in the media.

The next morning June 18, 1959 prostitute 'Big Pauline' came forward and identified the victim as fellow prostitute Elizabeth Figg (aka Ann Phillips, 21) who worked the Notting Hill area. Elizabeth's death was put blamed on one of the Johns as the investigation stuttered to a stop.

The frivolities of November 5, 1963, Guy Fawkes Night, were over and the local authorities looked to clean up the open ground between the Thames and Mortlake Road, where joyous people had celebrated with a huge bonfire. Three days later on November 8, 1963, Patrick Dineen, driving a mechanical digger, began to clear the debris. After a few minutes he uncovered the headless, heavily decomposed body of a woman. An autopsy was performed at the School of Forensic Medicine, Guys Hospital, London but no cause of death could be determined due to the decomposition. The police file of known missing women held many of their fingerprints and within this file Professor Keith Simpson was able to match the dead woman with twenty-two-year-old prostitute Gwyneth Rees using only a partial thumbprint. Gwyneth had not been seen since August 1963, when she was renting a basement room in Battersea.

On February 2, 1964, brothers George and Douglas Capon were sailing on the Thames near West Hammersmith Bridge, about to take part in a race, when they spotted a naked body floating in the water nearby. A group of people managed to drag the body to shore. The body was that of a female with panties, assumed to be her own, in her mouth and her stockings around her ankles. The body was taken to the mortuary in nearby Fulham Road for an autopsy to be carried out by Doctor Teare. His report stated that the unknown woman had died from drowning which meant she was alive when she entered the water, two or three days previously. But no clue as to her identity was found. As with the first victim, Elizabeth Figg in June 1959, the police utilised the media to help solve the identity of the latest victim. On the day the picture made the evening newspaper a name was put forward. She was believed to be Hannah Tailford (also known as Theresa Bell) a thirty-year-old prostitute who worked around the Bayswater Road, but again the investigation quickly dried up.

Two months passed after Hannah Tailford was found dead when, on April 8, another body was found. Irene Lockwood, a prostitute who worked the Bayswater Road, was found naked and dead, floating in the Thames by the river police. The body was discovered approximately 300 yards from the previous body. Irene, also known as Sandra Russell, was last seen three days earlier having a heated row with an unknown man. The autopsy discovered that Irene had also died from drowning and at the time of her death was four months pregnant. Nineteen days after Irene was found dead, Kenneth Archibald, a caretaker at the Holland Park

Tennis Club, walked into Notting Hill police station and confessed to Irene's murder. The case went to the Old Bailey where Kenneth pleaded not guilty. After 55 minutes of deliberation the jury brought down their verdict of not guilty. Kenneth later admitted he made up the confession,, whilst depressed.

While Kenneth Archibald was in custody awaiting trial, the fifth victim of the series was found. On April 24, 1964 Christopher Parnell found the nude body of a young female alongside the Beechams Sports Ground where he worked. Police raced to the scene to find the body dumped on a rubbish heap, her head positioned face down on her stretched out arms. The body was completely nude without any jewellery present. Fingerprints were taken which resulted in the identification of twenty-two-year-old Helene Barthelemy, a known prostitute who, like the others of the 'trade' went under several aliases. Doctor Teare once again performed the autopsy and reported that Helene had been dead for two days and that cause of death was manual strangulation. Doctor Teare noticed that virtually the whole body was covered in soot like substance, samples of the dirt were taken and when placed under a microscope it revealed that the dirt contained specks of metallic paint of various colours. Doctor Teare deduced that wherever Helene had been, it was close to where spray painting was taking place.

Three months passed after the murder of Helene Barthelemy with no arrests and another victim was found. At 5.30am on July 14, 1964, George Heard looked out of his bedroom window into Berrymeade Road. In the driveway of the house opposite George could just about make out in the darkness what looked like a tailors dummy. Annoyed that someone would dump his or her rubbish in his neighbourhood, George went down to look. As George neared he could see it was not a tailors dummy, but the nude body of a woman in a sitting position with her legs crossed and the torso slumped forward. Detectives identified the woman as Mary Fleming (also known as Mary Turner) who was reported missing on July 11, 1964.

During the investigation officers discovered that three hours earlier, George had heard a vehicle pull up in the road, stop for only a few short moments, then drive away again. As Berrymede Road is a dead end he thought nothing of it, assuming that the driver had not realised the road layout. Shortly before that, a van was witnessed in Chiswick High Road. The driver attempted to get something out of the back of the van, but drove off at speed after noticing he was being watched.

Doctor Teare performed the autopsy but was unable to determine the cause or the time of death. He did, however, discover flecks of paint on the body. When tested against those found on Helene Barthelemy they were found to match. The laboratory reported that the colour and type of the paint was of the type used by car manufacturers. This gave detectives the idea that the killer may work at or near a vehicle repair shop.

Frances Brown was another London prostitute; the money she earned working the streets meant that she could look after herself, her three children and her boyfriend Paul Quinn. On October 22, 1964, she left her home for an evening of business but never returned. On November 25, Dennis Sutton found her nude body on waste ground behind a car park in Horton Street, Kensington. Her body was covered with rubble, her head with a large dustbin lid. The autopsy confirmed cause of death as asphyxia due to pressure on the neck. Verdict – murder by persons unknown.

As they entered into the new year, despite seven victims, there were still no suspects in the case when on February 16, 1965 an eighth victim joined the list. Len Beauchamp, an electrical fitter, was walking to work when he saw the feet of a woman under bushes at the roadside. She was later named as Bridget O'Hara a twenty-seven-year-old Irish prostitute. She was last seen getting into a car at 9pm on January 11, 1965. The autopsy on Bridget confirmed that manual strangulation was the cause of death.

However, the location of where Bridget's body was found presented detectives with a vital clue. She was found on the Heron Industrial Estate and on that estate is a spray paint shop. Air samples taken from around the estate appeared to match samples taken from the most recent victims. Further detailed samples gave a more specific location as to where the victims' bodies were stored before disposal. An electrical transformer building gave the quality of sample that authorities were looking for. The building was situated directly opposite from the paint shop. The commander in charge of the investigation, Detective Chief Superintendent John du Rose, made the transformer building the focal point of the investigation. All vehicles entering and leaving the estate were to have their vehicle registration numbers noted, particularly noting were those that entered the estate in the early hours of the morning. Estimations put the number of potential suspects at anything up to 7000 people.

DCS John du Rose once again turned to the media to aid in the case, this time by manipulating the facts to his advantage. The media quoted that the list of suspects was at twenty, a few days later the figure dropped to ten. John du Rose believed that by doing this he could put pressure on the killer. The media soon quoted the number of suspects had now dropped from 6, then 3.

In June 1965, a police officer doing house calls on potential suspects visited a house just as a hearse arrived to take away a body. The man, whose name was never released, had committed suicide days earlier leaving a note stating he could not take the strain any longer. The suspect was a 45-year-old security guard on the Heron Industrial Estate; part of his rounds included the transformer building and paint shop.

Convinced that this was the killer the investigation was scaled down the following month, no more victims were found and within a year the case was no longer investigated.

Delfina and Maria de Jesus Gonzales

The sister killing team of Maria and Delfina de Jesus Gonzales of Mexico are two of the worst serial killers in history. Between them, the women murdered at least ninety-one prostitutes from 1955-1964.

The Gonzales women owned a profitable brothel in Guanajuato, Mexico, they offered the best time for any gentleman who came looking for a girl for the night. However any prostitute, working at the bordello that did not satisfy, was dispensed of by poison administered by the killer madams.

To keep up a steady bevy of hookers, the women would procure young girls through the classifieds, or abduct them from the streets. Yet it all came to a halt when Josefina Guuierez, was arrested by police for attempted kidnapping while at procuring new recruits for the brothel

Josefina told police how a lot of women, and wealthy customers had disappeared.

The sisters were arrested and the bodies of eighty women, eleven men and a handful of babies were found buried around the bordello's outskirts.

Matthew Johnson

In June 1999, it was claimed that when Matthew Johnson met LaDawn Roberts he took her to an abandoned building in Hartford, Connecticut and beat her to death. Johnson was never charged with the murder of the young woman, yet the MO of the Robert's killer was so similar to that of Johnson, that he remains the prime suspect in the case.

Aida Quinones also died in a similar manner in April 2000. The woman had been picked up by Johnson while working as a prostitute. She was raped and left for dead, under the bridge of the I-84; having had her head beaten into a bloody pulp. Thirty-three-year-old Rosali Jimenez was the next woman to die at the hands of Johnson. Her body was found in a disused Hartford building on August 29, 2000. She was discovered on her back, with most of her clothing removed. Johnson had raped the woman before beating her to death. Her death was attributed to blunt force trauma; her face had been beaten to a pulp.

Semen found inside the woman's body, as well as cigarette butts left nearby, made it easy for police to trace her killer.

Alesia Ford was found in similar circumstances. She had been raped and beaten to death and was later found in an abandoned building in July 2001. DNA found with her body matched that of Johnson and he was arrested in September 2001.

He was also the suspect in four other similar murders during the same period.

The Killer
Matthew Johnson was one of twelve children brought up in a poor family. Many of his siblings went on to abuse drugs and alcohol, yet Johnson attempted to remain clean. He was a troublemaker at home and school and was removed from the family home and put into a state home at his mother's request.

As a seventeen-year-old, the man was first sent to prison for armed robbery and assault. He spent less than a year in jail before being released. In 1982, as a nineteen-year-old, he murdered a security guard during the robbery of a church and was again sent to prison.

Again Johnson spent little time behind bars.

Once he was released, Johnson began beating up prostitutes. He was charged and sentenced to time in prison several times for attacks or for abducting women, including a two-hour rape of one of his victims. Yet was always released to attack again. However by the beginning of the new millennium his DNA, like others had been placed in a sexual offenders bank.

It would lead to his arrest in 2002 for the murders of three women.

It took the jury only a few hours to find Matthew Johnson guilty of the murders of three women in Hartford. All three women, Aida Quinones, Rosali Jimenez, and Alesia Ford, had worked as prostitutes when they met Johnson. At his trial in March 2003, it was discussed that Johnson had taken the women to a secluded place where, after having sex with them, he proceeded to crush their skulls before dumping them.

Russell Johnson

In London, Canada, twenty-year-old student, Mary Hicks, was found dead in her bed. Her death was not considered suspicious as no signs of foul play could be found. The official cause of death was attributed to a reaction to a prescribed drug.

It was a similar story following the discovery of forty-two-year-old Alice Ralston, found lying dead in her bed during November 1973. A reaction to a prescription drug was also recorded as the March 4, 1974 cause of death in the case of Eleanor Hartwick.

In August 1974, Doris Brown was also found dead in her bed in the city of Guelph, the pathologist put her death down to Pulmonary Edema.

On December 31, 1974, Diane Beltz was found murdered in her bedroom again in the city of Guelph, she had been strangled with her own underwear, and then raped after death. Louella George was found dead, via strangulation, in April 1977.

The murder of Donna Veldboom, 22, ended the sequence of murders as the police recognised the name of Russell Johnson, a known sex offender, living in the same building as Donna. Further checks on Johnson revealed that he previously lived in the same building as murder victim Louella George. Johnson was subsequently arrested and charged with three murders. At his trial the jury found Johnson not guilty by reason of insanity and was despatched to the psychiatric ward of the Ontario Mental Health Centre. After the trial, police announced, but did not clarify, that evidence existed which linked Johnson to the four deaths recorded in 1974.

Harold Jones

On February 5, 1921, in Abertillery, Wales, eight-year-old Freda Burnell failed to return home from the local oil and seed store, where she had gone on an errand for her father. Greatly concerned for his daughter, Mr Burnell went to the store to look for her. Fifteen-year-old Harold Jones was serving behind the counter and admitted that the young girl had come in, he had served her, and then she had left. Freda's father returned home hoping that she would soon return safely.

The next day Freda was found dead in a lane near the store. The post mortem revealed that Freda had been strangled after receiving a blow to the head. Her killer had also attempted to rape her. A search of the area uncovered blood and signs of a scuffle in a barn. The barn was part of the store's business and so authorities again asked Jones what he knew. He denied knowledge of the bloodstains and denied having been near the barn the previous day. Despite the lack of evidence linking Jones to the crime, he was arrested for Freda's murder.

At the trial, held in Monmouth, Jones pleaded not guilty. The jury believed his version of events and gave a verdict of not guilty on June 23, 1921.

Two weeks after the teen's release, on July 18 1921, eleven-year-old Florence Little was last seen playing by herself outside the house of Harold Jones before she vanished. When questioned, Jones confirmed that he had seen the girl outside his house but denied knowledge of her whereabouts. A routine search of nearby houses ended when a trail of blood was found in Jones's house. Authorities followed the trail into the attic where the body of Florence Little was found with her throat severely cut.

Jones quickly confessed to Florence's murder. This was followed with a confession to the February murder of Freda Burnell. Given Jones's young age he was sentenced to be held at his Majesty's pleasure.

K

Yasutoshi Kamata

The first murder committed by Yasutoshi Kamata occurred in May 1985. The middle-aged man abducted forty-six-year-old housewife Fusae Azume and took her to his apartment in Nishinari Ward, Osaka, Japan. The man was facing financial difficulties and planned to ransom victims for money. However, the man ended up strangling the woman to death in the apartment before he could continue his plan.

In June 1985 he struck again, abducting and strangling nineteen-year-old student Midori Chinen in Nishinari Ward.

The killer did not strike again until January 1987, when he abducted nine-year-old Kumiko Tsujikado on her way home from school. Kumiko was strangled to death on a roadside in Sumiyoshi Ward. Kamata also attempted to extract 30million Yen from the little girl's parents and school as ransom.

After the little girl's murder, Kamata found himself in prison for a brief period of time on unrelated charges of theft. He was released in 1991 and began killing once more.

Forty-five-year-old Kazue Wada of Naniwa Ward was the next victim. The bar worker was strangled to death by Kamata in July 1993 before being cut into pieces and strewn through the nearby mountains.

In Naniwa Ward again, Kamata killed for the fifth time. Thirty-eight-year-old Kimiko Nakana was killed in March 1994 and like Kazue the year before, she was dismembered and her remains scattered through the mountains.

The killer was arrested soon after Kimiko's murder and was tried in two separate trials for the five murders. He was found guilty and sentenced to death on March 25, 1999.

On March 28, 2001 sixty-one-year-old Kamata appealed his sentence. The Osaka High Court upheld the death penalty decision.

Edmund Kemper

Edmund Kemper II and Clarnell had an extremely stormy marriage and Ed walked out on the family in 1957 when Edmund Kemper III was nine.

According to the younger Ed Kemper, he was traumatized by his mother from an early age. Clarnell Kemper raised her son and two daughters on her own, and little Edmund was subjected to severe discipline.

Clarnell Kemper, Ed's mother began locking her son in the basement once he had started puberty in fear he would molest his sisters. Kemper spent a lot of time thinking about murdering his mother while he sat in the still, dark, damp cellar. Left alone for hours and days at a time, the boy did not know what he had done.

He claimed both his sisters and his mother constantly put him down, especially about his mammoth height. His personality became withdrawn and he had very few social skills. In his early teens, Kemper killed two of the family cats. Clarnell found the remains of one, minus the head, in the garbage can, while the remaining dismembered pieces of the other were in Edmund's closet. His animal dismemberments where also combined with his fantasies of sex and violence.

Clarnell grew sick of the teenage Edmund, and she shipped him off to his father and stepmother, who in turn shipped him of to live under the strict discipline of Ed and Maude Kemper, Ed's paternal grandparents. It was in August 1963, and his grandmother did not want to have to deal with the boy. Little did she know they would be together for such a short time.

Grandma and Grandpa Kemper

On August 27, 1964 as Maude Kemper sat at the kitchen table Edmund was loading a rifle to go out onto the farm for some target practice. His grandmother hissed a warning at him, and Kemper just stopped in the doorway. Something inside him snapped. He turned towards his grandmother, levelled the rifle at her head and shot her dead.

After wrapping the head in a towel, he moved her body up to the bedroom where he slashed and stabbed her with a knife. Before too long, Ed Kemper I pulled into the driveway. According to Kemper, to save his grandfather the torment of seeing his dead wife, Ed quickly met him at the door and also shot him dead. Kemper cleaned the kitchen as best he could before calling his mother in a state of confusion. She told him to call police. So the young Kemper rang the authorities and waited.

A court-appointed psychiatrist diagnosed Edmund as paranoid and psychotic, and the Youth Authority committed him to Atascadero State Hospital. He entered the facility on December 6, 1964. He was not yet sixteen-years-old.

Kemper stayed at Atascadero for a little over five years. During his time he was taken under the wing of the research director Dr Frank Vanasek and became a trusted inmate among staff.

During his sessions with psychiatrists and psychologists, Kemper began to get an understanding of psychology and was quick to learn what the doctors wanted to hear, not what he was actually thinking about or feeling. This new gift enabled him to dupe authorities later during his killings.

Kemper also became an eager listener of serial sex offenders. He would spend most nights fantasizing about the crimes they had told him about, and noted that the only way they were caught was by being identified by the victim. So Kemper decided the victim must not be allowed to live.

He was soon allowed to rejoin society, doctors believing he was no longer a threat - even though there was certainly a chance that his explosiveness may resurface.

But mainly it was due to his tempestuous relationship with his mother. Even though it was suggested the two be kept apart for their own safety. Kemper moved back in with Clarnell after a short stay with California Youth Authority.

Kemper was now 21, a double murderer and free.

Kemper's release
The Kempers lived in an apartment in Aptos and Kemper's mother had an administration job with University of California. Ed had looked up to the wardens at the detention centre and attempted to join the police force. Unfortunately his height made him ineligible. However it did not stop him hanging out and drinking with local police at the bar called the Jury Room across from Aptos Courthouse. He was known to all as "Big Eddie" and was well liked by all as a gentle giant.

The closest job he could get to law enforcement was as a flagman on the highways, this meant with the money he received he could leave his mother's apartment. He moved in with a friend in Alameda and purchased a 1969 Ford Galaxy sedan.

He would often spend his spare time cruising the highways, thinking about the sex crimes of his fellow inmates at Atascadero. Kemper then started to act out his fantasies by picking up young women hitchhikers, and using his knowledge of psychology, would get them to quickly trust him.

He also got a sticker from his mother's job at the University for his car; he knew that girls would accept rides from fellow students. After about 150 hitchhiker pickups, Kemper knew he was ready for the next step.

On Sunday May 7, 1972, Kemper prepared for murder. He placed a hunting knife, rope, a plastic bag, handcuffs and a Browning 9mm automatic pistol under his car seat and set out to find victims. By 4 pm he thought he would need to try again later, but then saw two teenage girls thumbing a ride.

Mary Ann Pesce and Anita Luchessa
Mary Ann Pesce and Anita Luchessa, happily accepted Kemper's offer for a lift. They were on their way to see a friend at Stanford University and wasn't sure of the way. Kemper used this to his advantage. He drove them away from where they were headed; both girls unaware of their fate, until Kemper drove down a side road.
Mary asked Kemper "What do you want?"

Kemper stopped the car, pointed the pistol at the scared eighteen-year-old women and replied coolly, "You know what I want."

Mary tried to keep her wits about her and used the skills taught at school about talking to your attacker. Kemper knew the skills too and quickly changed it around. He forced the terrified Anita into the boot of the car, and then returned his attentions to Mary. He cuffed her hands behind her back and then tried to suffocate her with the bag. She fought him, and bit holes through the bag to allow her to continue breathing. Kemper soon overpowered the woman by stabbing her twice in the back and once in the chest. Kemper then grabbed her by the chin and slashed her throat.

Knowing that Anita would've heard the struggle from the car's trunk, he decided to kill her post haste. He opened the boot and began stabbing her.

Knowing his flatmate was not at home, Kemper took the bodies back to his room in Alameda. He undressed both bodies and took Polaroid photos before dissecting them and decapitating the bodies. He took and destroyed all the possessions they had with them, before burying the body parts in the bush around Santa Cruz. The heads he kept as trophies, in his closet.

Once the heads began to rot and smell he threw them into a ravine.

To Kemper's advantage no one was looking for the two girls. For now they were just assumed to be roaming the country, as some teenagers are known to do.

The photos Kemper had taken were enough for the next few months to satiate his sexual urges. A broken arm he suffered after a motorcycle accident also prevented him from killing for a while.

By September though, Kemper's homicidal urges where beginning to surface once more.

Aiko Koo

Late in the afternoon of September 14, 1972, Aiko Koo was trying to get a ride on University Avenue Berkeley. When the friendly looking Kemper offered her a lift she was relieved, until Kemper turned the car around and headed away from her destination of San Francisco. She began screaming, so Kemper thrust the pistol into her ribs and told her to stop it. He used the ruse that he was suicidal and needed desperately to talk to someone because he was so lonely.

Once he had her at a secluded clearing in the woods he successfully suffocated the tiny-framed woman into unconsciousness before raping her and strangling her.

Kemper bundled the body into the boot, and drove to a nearby bar for a beer and sat and savoured the killing.

Late that same night he took the body to his apartment disguised in a bundle of blankets. He dissected the corpse and again scattered the remains around Santa Cruz woods, and kept the head with him in the boot of the car.

On September 15, Kemper had a follow-up evaluation by a board of juvenile psychiatrists, where he was declared mentally stable and had his record of the double homicide of his grandparents sealed. Little did the experts know that Aiko's head was in the car. After the assessment, and still being out of work due to his broken arm, he reluctantly moved back home with his mother.

With his juvenile records sealed Kemper could buy his own gun. Kemper bought himself a .22 Ruger automatic with six inch barrel and wanted to try it out.

Cindy Schall

In the cold of winter eighteen-year-old Cindy Schall was happy to accept the lift from Edmund Kemper on the evening of January 8, 1973. The young man was large but the university sticker on his car made Cindy feel a bit better about accepting the ride to her class across the College campus at Santa Cruz.

However before Cindy could even thank Kemper, he had a gun out and pointed at her, but the killer giant attempted to allay the girl's fears by claiming he was suicidal and lonely and just needed to talk to someone.

The pair drove for hours, Kemper told Cindy of his problems with his overbearing mother and his shyness and lack of success with women. Cindy tried to help Kemper the best she could considering Kemper had a gun poked into the girl's ribs.

Kemper pulled the car over into a secluded area in the township called Freedom. He told Cindy to get into the boot of the car. As she did, Kemper aimed the gun at the young woman and pulled the trigger. Cindy collapsed into the car's trunk dead. Kemper closed the boot and drove home.

In the dark, Kemper removed the corpse from the trunk and took it to his room at his mother's home. He had sex with the corpse before dissecting the body in the bath, taking copious amounts of photos of the process.

Kemper hid the woman's shirt and ring as mementos of the murder before piling Cindy's body, except her head, in garbage bags and dumping them in the ravine in Santa Cruz. He kept Cindy's head in his closet.

When Cindy's body was found the next day Kemper decided to hide the head. So he buried the eighteen-year-old's head in the front garden. It was placed at an angle under the earth where it looked up at the Kemper home. Kemper was to say later that his mother always liked people looking up to her and this was his way of doing that.

Rosalind Thorpe and Alice Lui
Another row a month later between Kemper and Clarnell sent him out onto the road in a rage. He took his gun with him. Rosalind Thorpe was coming out of a lecture and contemplating how to get home when Kemper drove by. It was too wet for her to ride her bike home.

Seeing the campus sticker on his car, Rosalind gladly accepted Kemper's offer a lift. Then as they were chatting Kemper spotted Alice Lui hitch-hiking further along. Alice jumped into the backseat of the car, and the trio continued on their way.

Kemper reached into his jacket, grabbed the gun, put it to Rosalind's temple and fired. Alice began screaming as Kemper leaned over the seat and fired at Alice twice. The killer missed the woman both times before grabbing her and shooting her in the head. She stopped moving and assuming she was dead, Kemper continued on his way. Then Alice began a guttural moan, which drove Kemper mad, like the *Tell-tale Heart* in Edgar Allen Poe's novella. He was beginning to feel weak and sick. The reality of his murders where beginning to take their toll.

He stopped the car once more, to shoot Alice. This time she was dead.

When he arrived home around 11pm, his mother was still up, so he left again to buy cigarettes. He grabbed his hunting knife and drove to a secluded spot and hastily decapitated both bodies.

The following day he transported Alice's body to his room where he had sex with the headless corpse. He then cut off the hands and threw both bodies into the ravine and the heads and hands into a canyon ironically called Devil's Slide.

Another serial killer, Herbert Mullins was also killing in the same area, and Kemper was getting cautious, he did not want to be blamed for any of Mullin's murders.

By April 1973 Kemper's life was falling apart. He packed up all the evidence of the murders into a case, along with his gun and tossed the case into ocean. The stress was becoming too much, he was suffering intense pain from stomach ulcers and severe headaches. He knew the killings had come to a climax. He thought maybe a murderous rampage maybe the way to go: to go out in a blaze of glory but that thought soon subsided.

The Ultimate Victim
On April 20, 1973 Good Friday, Kemper sat drinking beer into the night beside his mother, wondering what he should do. By 4am, he decided what he had to do. Kemper crept into his mother's room. She was awake and asked if he needed to talk. Even Clarnell knew something was deeply disturbing her son. He said no, but reappeared shortly with a hammer and knife in his hands.

She was asleep as Kemper brought the hammer down onto her skull with full force over and over. Anger raged through his body as blood began to pour from the woman's head wounds. Kemper stopped briefly and realised his mother was still alive, though barely. Kemper rolled Clarnell onto her back and sawed into her throat, until she was decapitated. He took out her larynx and tried to destroy it in the garbage disposal, but it jammed. He told police later, that even in death she was still yelling at him.

He was no longer in control; the killing had not calmed him at all. He went out for some beers before coming home to decide what to do next. He called a friend of Clarnell's, Sally Hallett, and said he was doing a surprise dinner for his mother and would like her to attend.

Her final words when she sat down at the table was, "let's sit down, I'm dead". Kemper strangled her and decapitated Sally's lifeless body. He had come to the end. He could go on no longer.

The Telephone Call
After the final murders, he left on his last car ride as a free man, to Pueblo, Colorado. Twenty-five-year-old Edmund Kemper got out of his car and called the police in Santa Cruz. He told them he had killed six women.

The officer on the line didn't believe him and told him to call back later, so he did, and he still didn't have any success in convincing the cop on the other end of the line.

So he called again and again. Each time he gave more details on how he had killed each victim and what he had done with the bodies.

Finally Santa Cruz police sent a Colorado police cruiser to pick him up. Kemper sat and waited for his arrest. The police in Santa Cruz could not believe that "Big Eddie" who drank with them at the bar across from the police station, was the man they had been hunting.

Kemper's confession was long, articulate and complete in every detail. He had spent many hours fantasizing about each and every detail of the killings.

As a child Kemper had fantasized about his own execution. Often he would enact his death, by asphyxiation.

Kemper was charged with eight counts of first-degree murder on October 25, 1973.

On November 8, 1973 he was found guilty of his crimes and sentenced to life imprisonment in California Medical Facility at Vacaville. (No death penalty was available at the time in California).

Bela Kiss
The Bodies in the Barrels
By 1916, the property of 17 Rakcoczi St, Cinkota in Hungary had been empty for two years. With the world at war it was near impossible to find the previous occupants or owners. So the District Court decided to sell the property. The property was quickly bought by blacksmith Istvan Molnar and his wife and family.

The family moved in shortly after and began renovating the neglected house. Molnar was particularly interested in clearing out the workshop so he could fit his own tools and hardware. The workshop was in complete disarray, there were seven large sealed oil drums in one corner, on top of those was a large pile of old timber and building supplies.

The man tried to open one of the heavy drums but it was tightly sealed shut. Molnar thought he'd come back to them later as he had plenty to do around the house. He told his wife about the drums, about how heavy they were and that they were sealed shut. His wife suggested that he should open the drums as they may contain valuable petrol.

So once again Molnar returned to the workshop and tried to open the drums. It took several attempts with a wrench before he opened the first drum. The blacksmith instantly wretched at the smell permeating from drum. He ran outside vomiting from the smell of decay.

His wife came to see what was wrong and looked inside the open drum and fainted.

Inside the oil drum was the naked corpse of a woman. She had been shoved into the drum feet first and then squashed down inside before the drum was sealed airtight. The seal preserved the body.

The police arrived and quickly unsealed the other drums. As suspected, they all contained the remains of women. The dead women were all middle-aged and were not on the criminal records files, so investigators turned their energies to finding the previous tenant.

According to neighbours, the previous occupant had always kept to himself and no one had even known his name. They believe he had gone to fight in the war but were unsure.

The detective in charge of the case, Geza Bialokurszky believed the women had all disappeared in or around 1913 and compiled a list of missing woman from 1911-1915. The list began as a lengthy compilation of 400 names. But that was quickly whittled down to fifteen after those who were older or younger than the seven bodies were taken off the list. The remaining fifteen names all had one thing in common. They had no living relatives.

So Det Bialokurszky began the arduous task of tracking down the women on his list.

One woman on the list was thirty-six-year-old Anna Novak. Anna had suddenly left her employment as a cook in 1911. Her boss found it strange as the woman had been a reliable worker before she disappeared and when she did go, she left all of her belongings and her identification papers behind in a trunk at the restaurant.

The advertisement
In the trunk owned by Anna Novak Det. Bialokurszky found a page from the *Pesti Hirlap* newspaper. On it was an advertisement that Anna had circled.

Widower urgently seeks acquaintance of mature warm-hearted spinster or widow to help assuage loneliness mutually. Send photo and details, Poste Restante Central PO Box 717. Marriage possible and even desirable.

With the identification papers and fingerprints taken off the trunk's locks, the police were able to identify Anna as one of the women in the drums.

The next port of call was the post office to see who had owned the post-box in the advertisement. According to the postmaster, the box was owned by a man named Elemer Nagy of 14 Kossuth St, Pestszenterzsebet. Police thought they had their man and raced to address only to find it a vacant block. Det. Bialokurszky knew he was dealing with no ordinary killer. This one was cunning and clever.

Det. Bialokurszky headed to the newspaper, *Pesti Hirlap*, to search their archives for the advertisement they had found in Anna's possession. Det. Bialokurszky found twenty inserts of the advertisement over the years and tracked down the name of the account holder. The account was made out to Elemer Nagy and gave a different address to those already investigated. However, this was also a false lead. The address belonged to a funeral parlour. The killer was laughing at the police.

So now Det. Bialokurszky went public with what he had. He published the signature of Nagy in the hope that someone may indeed recognise it.

Immediately after the signature was published, police received several calls. One was from twenty-seven-year-old Rosa Diosi. She told Det. Bialokurszky that the man they seek was known as Bela Kiss. She had been the man's mistress until he had gone to war. The last she heard was that he had been captured and was incarcerated in a Serbian Prisoner of War camp.

Rose went on to say that though the man seemed meek and mild he was sexually insatiable; she could never please him no matter how many times a day they had sex. She said she had met him through an advertisement in *Pesti Hirlap*. Many other women told police a similar story about meeting Kiss through the advertisement. However, many had short-lived relationships with Kiss. He would take everything they had of value and leave.

Bela Kiss

Checking with the army they found that Bela Kiss had been conscripted into the armed forces in July 1914. They had a photo of Kiss on file. With knowledge of his sexual conquests, police showed the photos around known prostitute areas. Many of the girls recognised Kiss immediately.

Kiss had pawned almost everything he had taken from the women and spent the money on prostitutes.

Another woman on Det. Bialokurszky's list was identified through the pawned items. Maria Tooth was one of the earliest victims of Kiss. She had fallen in love with the swindler and wanted to get married. Kiss quickly dispensed of her by killing her and putting her in a drum.

Det. Bialokurszky believed that Kiss had probably killed more than the seven women and other residences where Kiss had lived were also investigated. Bialokurszky was right. Another five bodies were recovered.

Though the manhunt continued for many years, Kiss was never found. It is suspected he was killed during the war, but no one was sure.

L

Donald Lang

Donald Lang is one of the only deaf, mute serial killers known.

Donald Lang was born on January 15, 1945 in Chicago and due to illness he lost his hearing at a very young age.

Lang's family was unable to pay for special education, so he never went to school. He was never taught sign language so he made up his own, or would draw what he wanted. As a teenager Lang got a job working on the docks in Chicago. He was a hard worker and was a well-liked employee despite his handicaps.

By November 1965 things began to change. Lang's mother had died the week before and the man began to spend more time in bars, drinking all night and cohorting with prostitutes. On November 11, 1965 Lang picked up Ernestine Williams, a thirty-seven-year-old prostitute in Romeo's Tavern in Chicago's South Side. In his own sign language, the man touched the woman's crotch then held up all ten fingers. Ernestine agreed to the man's offer and together they left the bar.

The next morning Ernestine was found in a nearby stairwell by a woman putting out her rubbish. The woman had been beaten then stabbed to death. Witnesses in the bar from the previous night were able to easily identify the deaf man as the woman's last date.

Lang was arrested and attempted to explain to police what had happened. He used a stabbing motion to try and explain what happened to the woman. A lawyer specialising in deaf and mute clients was called to help decipher what the man was trying to say without luck. The police however believed that the stabbing motion was as good as a confession and charged Lang with murder. He was sentenced to an institution for the deaf before being released again, serving only a brief sentence.

In July 1972 Lang was back working the docks in Chicago and still had a desire to kill.

On July 25, 1972 Lang and thirty-nine-year-old prostitute Earline Brown checked into the seedy Viceroy Motel together. After two hours, Lang left the building, but Earline was not seen to leave. The next couple that used the room found her stuffed inside the closet. She had been raped, beaten and strangled.

Again Lang was quickly identified and arrested on July 29, 1972 for the murder. He had blood on his clothes and large scratches across his face that helped provide police with further evidence of the deaf man's involvement. Lang also drew a crude picture of the woman and then crossed it out, as if to say she had been removed.

Lang was sent to trial and found guilty of Earline's murder. He was given a life sentence in a special treatment facility. Though only ever charged with the two murders, there are several others he was suspected of committing.

Posteal Laskey

After Boston was able to breathe a sigh of relief with the arrest of Albert De Salvo, it was Cincinnati's turn to suffer a series of strangulation murders, stretching between October 1965 and December 1966.

The first murder occurred on the night of December 2, 1965, when Emogene Harrington was strangled to death in her home with a plastic clothesline. The murder was linked to the attempted murder of a sixty-five-year-old woman on October 12, who was beaten and raped. Her attacker attempted strangulation with a clothesline, but for some reason left before completing the attack.

Fifty-eight-year-old Lois Dant was raped and murdered on April 4, 1966. Two months later, on June 10, Jeannette Messer was found dead in a local park, she too had been raped and strangled. The murder of Mrs Carl Hochhauser was linked to the same killer, when her daughter found her beaten, raped and strangled body on October 12, 1966. Eighty-one-year-old Rose Winstel was beaten and strangled to death in her home on October 20.

In December, Cincinnati police announced the arrest of Posteal Laskey, for the murder of thirty-one-year-old Barbara Bowman. Barbara got into the stolen cab driven by Laskey on August 14, 1966. She was later found dead having been raped and strangled; her body had also been run over; probably by Laskey's ride.

In 1967, Laskey was found guilty of Barbara Bowman's murder and sentenced to death on the electric chair. The death sentence was abolished five years later, leaving Laskey to serve a life sentence. No other murder charges were raised against the suspect, however Cincinnati noticed that no further strangulation murders occurred after Laskey's arrest.

In March 2002, Laskey was denied parole for the ninth time following a twenty-minute hearing.

Fernando Leyva

Fernando Hernandez Leyva was arrested on March 24, 1999 on the suspicion of murdering 137 people, kidnapping six other people and a long list of robberies.

The large, overweight man denied the charges when he appeared in a Mexican court in April 1999, yet said that he had kidnapped a journalist, and had murdered a police officer.

He was found guilty of the police officer's murder and sentenced to thirty years in prison.

While in prison he attempted suicide by hanging himself, however his weight ruled against him, and the rope broke.

Leyva had a long list of previous convictions, and he was incarcerated in 1982 for robbery but managed to escape from prison by digging a tunnel under the prison wall. Another prison sentence, for murder, was cut short when again the man escaped custody again.

Wendall Lightbourne

The island of Bermuda was the scene of a multiple murder case during 1959. The first victim was seventy-two-year-old Gertrude Robinson who was found dead on March 7, 1959 on her banana patch. She had been beaten to death and raped. Two months later, on May 9, fifty-nine-year-old Dorothy Pearce was found dead in her bedroom. Like Gertrude, Dorothy had been beaten to death and then raped.

The Bermudan police were struggling to solve the murders and made the call to Scotland Yard in London for assistance on the case. Two detectives were despatched to take charge of the investigation. Fingerprints from the two crime scenes were available, but despite an extensive check across the island, including tourists, the double killer could not be found and the detectives returned to London.

On July 3, 1959, barely days after the departure of the two officers, forty-nine-year-old Rosaleen Kenny was attacked as she lay on the bed, but her attacker ran off as her screams woke the neighbours.

Dorothy Rawlinson had lived on the island for four months having moved from England. On September 27, Dorothy took a trip down to the nearby beach. The following day police began a search after she was reported missing by Anne Sayers. Officers at the beach found her clothes, bike and personal belongings half buried in the sand. A rock stained with blood nearby suggested that they were looking for a body. There suspicions were confirmed the following day when Dorothy's body was found floating in the water, showing the signs of a bludgeoning attack.

A shopkeeper came forward with a description of a man who entered his shop on the day of Dorothy's disappearance. The shopkeeper described him as 'clearly nervous' and had been in the sea as his clothing was very wet. The customer was identified as Wendell Lightbourne, and was soon arrested. When questioned, Lightbourne admitted he saw Dorothy on the beach, but when pressured he confessed to her murder.

At his trial, Lightbourne was found guilty of the murder of Dorothy Rawlinson and sentenced to death. His sentence was however later commuted to life to be served in England.

Michael Lockhart

Michael Lockhart murdered two little girls in 1987 before gunning down police officer Paul Hulsey Jnr who was attempting to arrest the killer in Beaumont, Texas in March 1988.

The first victim of Lockhart was sixteen-year-old Windy Gallagher. Lockhart tore the clothes from her lower body, tied her hands behind her back and brutally raped her before stabbing her twenty-one times. There were four stab wounds to Windy's neck and a further seventeen wounds to her breasts and abdomen. The killer had also pulled her intestines out of the wounds in her stomach. The killer left her to be found by her sister in her home in Griffith, Indiana in October 1987.

Three months later, fourteen-year-old Jennifer Colhouer was raped before being stabbed by her killer. Lockhart had left the teenager bleeding to death in her home in Land O'Lakes in Florida in January 1988.

Two months later, officer Hulsey attempted to arrest the man in Beaumont, for speeding in a stolen car when Lockhart gunned him down.

The killer was quickly apprehended by other officers and told police that he would have continued on a country wide killing spree if he had not been caught.

At his trial Lockhart was found guilty of murder and sentenced to death.

On December 10, 1997 Michael Lockhart was executed in Texas for the death of Officer Hulsey. Had he escaped the death penalty in Texas, he had had two more death sentences awaiting him in Florida and Indiana.

As Lockhart was executed, the crowd of police officers outside the prison applauded.

M

Maoupa Cedric Maake

On March 16, 2000, Maoupa Maake was sentenced to 1,345 years in prison for the murders of twenty-seven people, the attempted murder of a further 26 people and for more than a dozen rapes and armed burglaries. In total the man was found guilty of over 130 charges.

Most of the murders occurred in Wemmer in Johannesburg, South Africa, where the killer lived.

After the sentencing the cocky killer, who had slept during most of his trial, including his sentencing, told the waiting media that he would appeal his sentence and be out of prison in two years.

The wiry thirty-six-year-old killer's MO was to watch couples having sex in their cars in secluded areas. He would pounce, killing the male before raping and killing the female occupant.

The first victim was an unidentified woman whom Maake raped and murdered in April 1996. Then, from October 1996 to April 1997, the man robbed three houses and eleven stores in Wemmer before murdering a young couple in their car. The female victim was raped before being killed.

As 1997 continued, so too did the killer's rampage. Between May and July, Maake attacked two taxi drivers and nineteen other people including Jerry Naidoo on July 11, 1997. Jerry was in a parked car with Charlotte Ndlovu when Maake happened upon them. He shot Jerry dead and pulled Charlotte from the car. He bashed and kicked the woman, calling her names such as "clitoris" and "bitch" before making her hail a taxi. The killer planned to use Charlotte as lure, so he could rob and kill the taxi-driver. When a taxi came, Charlotte jumped inside and the car sped off.

Maake returned to robbery again. He attacked thirteen shopkeepers and three homeowners between August and December 1997. Most of the attacks were in the early hours of the morning.

In December 1997, he was arrested and charged with a total of 133 crimes after attempting to pawn a pair of boots and a bike belonging to Gerhard Lavoo - who was killed by Maake on November 28, 1997.

Maake was also found guilty of the bludgeoning murder of seventy-four-year-old Harjivan Daya, whom Maake had killed with blows from the man's own hammer and the rape and murder of a fifteen-year-old school girl. Maake had shot the girl between the eyes. Some of the victims were stoned to death, others shot, and others stabbed.

The black man also did not kill within any racial boundary. Some victims were black, others white, others Asian.

To date the killer is still locked behind bars.

Ronald Macon

On September 11, 2003 Ronald Macon Jnr was sentenced to three life terms for the bashing murders of three women, a further 30 years was added to the killer's sentence for the rape of an elderly woman. The defence had argued against the death penalty for Macon, claiming he was HIV-positive and had a significantly shorter life span.

The first of Macon's victims was forty-three-year-old Angelnetta Peeples. Angelnetta had sex with Macon and the pair together drank alcohol and smoked crack before Macon lost control. The man become furious and beat Angelnetta to death with a rock in the alley at 118 E. 45th St. on the south side of Chicago on February 18, 1999.

The next victim was thirty-five-year-old Linda Solomon, who was strangled by Macon after the pair had sex. She was then bashed to death with an electrical box at 5907 S. Damen Ave, Chicago on April 4, 1999. At the time, Macon was under the influence of drugs and alcohol.

The final victim was Rosezina Williams on June 21, 1999. The pair had sex at 6847 S. King Drive, Chicago but when she attempted to leave, Macon grabbed her by the throat and strangled her into unconsciousness. The killer than tied Rosezina's hands and feet together with shoelaces before using the strap of a bag he was carrying to choke her to death. He then dumped her body in an alleyway on at 416 E. 69th Street.

In all three deaths, Macon claimed that it was the influence of crack cocaine and alcohol that caused him to fly into a rage and kill the women. Macon claimed his anger stemmed from growing up in a volatile environment. He was beaten as a child by his father, and witnessed him shooting his mother during an argument.

At the time of the murders, several different investigations were being run on several different strings of murders. The three women murdered by Macon were classed as the "pattern D" murders. The murders could be grouped together due to DNA evidence Macon had left at the scenes.

Had Macon been sentenced to death, he would have been the only man on Death Row in Illinois, after Governor Ryan commuted all prisoners death sentences to life terms earlier in 2003.

David Mahlanga

David Mahlanga sought to mete out his revenge on the Swaziland authorities for sentencing him, (wrongly in his opinion), to a twenty-year sentence for rape.

Mahlanga murdered thirty-four women over a two year period as he took his revenge that ended with his arrest in August 2001. The victims were all buried in shallow graves around the Malkens area of Swaziland. As only two victims were ever officially reported missing, and the fact that the murders continued for many years, there may be an unknown total number of other victims.

Simon Majola and Themba Nkosi

On May 21, 2002 Simon Majola and Themba Nkosi were sentenced to prison for the rest of their lives for the murders of eight people between April 29, 2000 and February 7, 2001.

Simon Majola was sentenced to eight life sentences and another 422 years for further crimes, while twenty-two-year-old Themba Nkosi was sentenced to five life sentences and an extra 375 years added to his sentence for the robbery and assault charges.

The pair were responsible for the murders of eight people who were stopped on the side of the road by the killers. The victims were then robbed before being beaten and tied up and strangled then thrown into the Bruma Lake in Johannesberg.

The bodies were found after the lake was drained and dragged in February 2001.

Nkosi had only assisted thirty-four-year-old married father Majola with five of the murders.

John and Sarah Makin

Horace Murray

Before the days of child care it was hard for an unmarried or widowed woman to work and look after her children. It was this type of predicament that people like the Makins preyed on.

An advertisement in the Sydney Newspaper read that a Miss Amber Murray was looking for a "kind person to take charge" of her baby boy, Horace Murray, for a small fee, with adoption as an option, while she tried to work in order to make ends meet. Amber was a young woman who had given birth to her son out of wedlock on March 30 1892. By June 23, 1892, when she placed the advertisement, she was finding it difficult to juggle work and a baby on her own. Little did she know that by placing the advertisement she had signed her baby's death certificate.

A kindly looking man answered the advertisement. Mr J Hill wrote to Miss Murray and offered to adopt the baby into his family for a meagre £6. Mr Hill told Miss Murray of his plight. His wife had lost a baby boy recently and was in a very melancholy state. He believed little Horace would be a perfect addition to his loving and caring family.

Amber Murray was comforted by this idea and headed to the George Street, Sydney address. At the door, Amber was greeted by John Makin, whom she believed to be Mr Hill. Makin's daughters took Horace and fussed over him, easing any feelings of apprehension Miss Murray had.

Miss Murray paid the man 10 shillings to look after Horace until she was sure that she would allow the family to adopt her son. She was given a receipt in the name of Makin's alias Mr J Hill. Miss Murray said she would enjoy dropping by often to see her little baby boy. She was devastated by having to give her baby up for adoption but hoped it was for the best interests of her 3-month-old baby boy.

Makin arrived at the same time every week to see Miss Murray at her place of employment and collect the 10 shillings to look after Horace. One day the man had terrible news for the young woman, he told her that the family would be moving to Hurstville, west of Sydney and would forward her their new address when they settled. Amber Murray was saddened by the news. Hurstville was a fair distance to travel at the time and she was worried that she would never see her little boy again. She was right.

The Makins did not go to Hurstville; they remained in inner Sydney, moving to Macdonaldtown swiftly one night before again changing their lodgings to another house in Chippendale.

Miss Murray was to never see her baby alive again. She tried to contact the family at the George Street house, but was informed they had moved away without leaving a forwarding address.

The Discovery

On October 11, 1892 builders were renovating a house in Burren Street Macdonaldtown. While digging in the garden one of the plumbers, James Hanoney, uncovered the skeletal remains of two infants. Instantly suspicion was laid on the previous occupants, the Makins. Neighbours who witnesses the commotion in yard of the house were quick to point out that the couple had at least six children residing in the house.

Soon after the discoveries in Macdonaldtown, the George Street residence was also excavated. Three babies were uncovered in that yard also. A third yard yielded two more tiny corpses.

In the 1890's birth survival rate was indeed low and there was no reason to believe the babies had been murdered. With five women of childbearing age in the house, it was possible that the babies had been their own. But there was always the probability that the family were baby farmers.

Both John and Sarah Makin were arrested along with their four daughters, Florence, 17, Clarice, 16, Blanche 14 and Daisy 11. The four older Makins were remanded in prison while autopsies and coronial inquests were held into the death of the seven babies.

The Babies

The decomposition of all but two of the babies made it difficult to establish identities or cause of death. However, sources claimed that the babies were pierced through the heart with knitting needles when they were no longer needed.

Two of the babies however could be identified. One of them was Horace Murray, the other was the baby of Horace Bottomley and Minnie Davis.

The most damning evidence against the Makins came from their own daughter, Clarice. She told the inquest that she was often asked to go and sell baby clothes at pawn shops around the area. Several of these items were recovered and three of the parents who had given their babies to the Makins identified them as belonging to their babies.

Why had the Makin's "adopted" these babies only to kill them? It became obvious that they were taking the babies and selling them to wealthy childless couples. When they had babies that they could not sell they would kill them.

The trial was called the 'Trial of the Century' at the time and the courtroom was often packed with the public as well as the press. The newspapers covered the story closely and the sentencing of Sarah and John Makin was front-page news.

Said the trial judge, Mr Justice Stephens at sentencing of John Makin to death:

You took money from the mother of this child (Horace Murray)...having bereft it of life, you buried this child in your yard as you would a carcass of a dog...you were engaged in baby farming in its worst aspect...you were carrying on the hellish business of destroying the lives of infants for the sake of gain"

John Makin was hanged for his part in the murderous campaign. His wife Sarah received a milder sentence. She was sentenced to life imprisonment. She was released in 1911 after serving 19 years in prison.

Martha Marek

Martha Marek's career as a Black Widow serial killer began with the help of her husband, who was ironically the first victim.

In 1932, Emil Marek convinced his wife Martha to help him gain $30,000 fraudulently from an insurance company. He asked his wife to cut off his leg as he had insured himself and would say that the leg was severed in a tree lopping accident.

After a great deal of persuasion, Martha Marek decided to help her husband in the scheme. After Emil had drunk a large quantity of whisky for courage he told his wife to get an axe.

Martha took an axe from the yard in their Vienna home and struck the man's leg. The axe badly damaged Emil's leg but did not sever it. It took another two blows of the axe to finally cut the leg off. Though in excruciating pain, Emil was pleased with Martha's work and set in motion the plan to con the insurance company.

Emil contacted his insurer who sent a doctor to examine the man's wounds. The doctor was not convinced by Emil's story that he had severed it whilst cutting down a tree. The company on the doctor's advice refused to pay the man's claim. The drastic plan had failed.

Emil was now out of work and poor. He was unable to work due to his injuries, but he would not have to wait long before his suffering was over. Martha Marek was furious with her husband for having failed in his attempt to get $30,000 from his insurance company. She had a new baby daughter and the family needed money.

Martha decided to get the insurance money herself. By July 1932 Emil died, his death certificate claimed he was suffering from tuberculosis, however in hindsight, it is believed he died at the hands of his wife.

This time the insurance company paid the policy. Martha inherited $30,000 once her husband was dead. The plan seemed too easy, and a month later, after insuring her baby daughter, she too died. Martha again received a princely sum.

The next person to die was an elderly family member. Martha had gone to nurse the old woman who was rather frail. Before the woman died, Martha insured her for a large sum, and also had the woman's will changed to ensure that Martha would inherit the house. Once the financial plans were in place, Martha killed the old woman.

Martha decided that she could continue her successful campaign of receiving insurance policies by taking in lodgers into her now empty house.

The first lodger to die was Felicitas Kittsteiner. The man had been concerned for his well being for quite sometime and suggested to his family that Martha was poisoning him. He claimed to have felt sick every time he ate something she had made. The family dismissed the man's rantings -until he died.

The Kittsteiner family checked into the man's claims and found that before his death, Martha had insured her lodger for a large sum, with herself as the beneficiary.

The evidence was overwhelming and the family took their suspicions to police. The body of Felicitas Kittsteiner was exhumed, so too were the bodies of Martha's husband, baby daughter, and elderly relative.

Traces of the poison thallium were found in all four bodies. Martha Marek was immediately arrested in Vienna in 1938 and faced trial for the murders of all four victims.

She was found guilty and sentenced to death; the death penalty having been reinstated earlier by Hitler.

On December 6, 1938 Martha Marek became the first woman in Vienna to be executed in more than thirty years. She was put in a wheelchair and wheeled from her death cell, in a catatonic state, to the guillotine.

At the platform, the executioner had planned to tip the chair forward with Martha's doll-like body falling into place on the chopping block. However, on the platform Martha began fighting with her guards, and attempted to flee.

She was quickly subdued and tied down; the guillotine's blade swiftly severed her head. A far better job than she had done six years earlier to her husband leg!

Richard Marquette

On June 21, 1961, the FBI made the unusual step of making their 10 most wanted, the 11 most wanted. The cause of this change was the criminal career of twenty-six-year-old Richard Lawrence Marquette. It began in June 1956 with the attempted rape of an unnamed female. The charges were dropped, thus releasing Marquette.

In August 1957, he received an 18-month prison sentence for the attempted robbery of a service station in Portland, during which he beat the attendant. After his release, Marquette returned to his hometown of Portland.

On June 5, 1961, Joan Rae Cradle disappeared during a shopping trip. Her body was found three days later and had been dismembered to such a degree that it took a further 6 days before she could be identified. Officers traced her path to a bar and the company of Marquette, who had now fled the area. For this he was placed on the FBI's list.

On June 30, officers arrested Marquette in Santa Maria, California after the manager of an employment agency recognised him from the wanted posters. Marquette confessed to Joan's murder, describing how he strangled her after an argument about his sexual ability and described how he dismembered the body. Marquette received a life sentence in December 1961 for the murder, thanking the court after the sentence was read out.

Marquette was paroled having served only 12 years of his life sentence, but he was not reformed. In April 1975 in Salem, Oregon, Betty Wilson became Marquette's second victim. She suffered the same fate as Joan Rae Cradle and was dismembered after her murder. Marquette was soon arrested and again charged with murder, once again receiving a life sentence.

Marquette was linked to a third dismemberment murder soon after his release in 1975, but no charges were made.

Kenneth McDuff

After concreting all day with friend Roy Green, Kenneth McDuff and Green went out for beers and burgers on August 6, 1966. Later in the evening they happened upon eighteen-year-old Robert Brand, his cousin sixteen-year-old Mark Dunman and Robert's girlfriend, sixteen-year-old Edna Sullivan parked near Baseball field in Guadalupe County

Green later told police what happened that evening:

> *"We rode around the baseball park and wound up on a gravel road. He [McDuff] saw a car parked there, and we stopped about 150 yards in front of it. He got his gun and told me to get out. I thought it was all a joke. I just didn't believe what he said was going to happen. I went halfway to the car with him, and he went on. He told the kids in the car to get out or he would shoot them. I went on up there and he had put them in the trunk of their car.*
>
> *He drove his car back to their car, and he told me to get in his car and follow him. I did, and we drove for a while across the highway we had come in on, and he pulled into a field. I followed, and he said that the field wouldn't do, so we backed up and went to another field. He got out and told the girl to get out. He told me to put her in the trunk of his car. I opened the trunk and she climbed in. It was then that he said that we couldn't leave any witnesses, or something like that.*
>
> *He said 'I'm gonna have to knock 'em off', or something like that. I got really scared. I still thought he was joking, but I wasn't sure. They were on their knees, begging him not to shoot them. They said, "We're not going to tell anybody". I turned towards him and he stuck the gun into the trunk of where the boys were and started shooting. I saw the fire come out of the gun on the first shot, and I covered my ears and looked away. He shot six times. He shot one twice in the head, and he shot the other boy four times in the head. A bullet went through a boy's arm as he tried to stop the fire. He tried to close the trunk, but it wouldn't close. He then told me to back up his car. By that time I was almost dying of fright, and I did what he said. He got in the boy's car and backed it into a fence, and he got out and told me to help him wipe off the fingerprints. I wasn't going to argue with him. I was expecting to be next so I helped him...We wiped out the tire tracks and got into his car and drove off another mile and turned off on another road and he stopped, and he got the girl out of the trunk and put her in the back seat.*
>
> *He told me to get out of the car, and I waited until he told her to get undressed. He took off his clothes and then he screwed her. He asked me if I wanted to do it, and I told him no. He asked me why not, and I told him I just didn't want to. He leaned over, and I didn't see the gun but thought he would shoot me if I didn't, so I pulled my pants and shirt off and got in the back seat and screwed the girl. She didn't struggle or anything, and if she ever said anything I didn't hear her. All the time I was on top of the girl I kept my eye on him. After that he screwed her again'. Edna was raped by McDuff several more times, before asking me for something to kill the girl with. I gave McDuff my belt but McDuff had other plans.*
>
> *He told the girl to get out of the car. He made her sit down on the gravel road, and he took about a three-foot piece of broomstick from his car and forced her head back with it until it was on the ground. He started choking her with the piece of broomstick. He mashed down hard, and she started waving her arms and kicking her legs. He told me to grab her legs and I didn't want to, and he said 'It's gotta be done', and I grabbed her legs, and held them for a second or so, then let them go. He said 'Do it again', and I did, and this time was when she stopped struggling. He had me grab her hands and he grabbed her feet and we heaved her over a fence. We crossed the fence*

> *ourselves, then he dragged her a short ways and then he choked her some more. We put her in some kind of bushes there."*

This statement was given the next day to police.

Though being sentenced to three death sentences for the murders of Robert Brand, Mark Dunman and Edna Sullivan, Kenneth McDuff was released on parole on October 11, 1989. It was rumoured his mother bribed the parole board after his death sentences were commuted to life, even though the killer had been sent to the chair twice before, being reprieved at the last minute each time.

He would go on to kill several more times.

Three days after being released from prison Kenneth McDuff murdered for the fourth time. His victim was thirty-one-year-old Sarafia Parker. The pretty black woman was raped and strangled before being dumped on 1500 block of East Avenue N, Temple, Texas. She was found within 24 hours.

After making death threats to a young black boy, McDuff was returned to prison, only to be paroled again on December 18, 1990.

On October 10, 1991, Kenneth McDuff picked up prostitute Brenda Thompson in Waco. The pair went to a secluded spot where McDuff bound the woman's hands, in preparation for rape. A police car pulled up beside the car in the dark, and Brenda began kicking the windscreen to get the officer's attention. She broke the windshield and McDuff sped off, narrowly missing the officer.

He eluded police and drove to deserted Gholson Road, where he tortured Brenda to death. Her body was found on October 3, 1998.

Seventeen-year-old prostitute Regenia Moore became Kenneth McDuff's sixth victim on October 15, 1991. The pair were apparently dating when they had an argument at a Waco Motel.

The pair drove off together to a secluded area off Highway 6. Once out of sight, McDuff stripped the woman of her clothes. Bound her arms and legs and pushed her to the ground. He leaned on her stomach and bent her legs awkwardly to the left breaking them as he went.

Her mutilated body was found in a sinkhole in Tehuacana Creek on September 29, 1998 after an informant gave information.

While washing her car at an Austin carwash on December 29, 1991, twenty-eight-year-old Colleen Reed was abducted in broad daylight by Kenneth McDuff and accomplice Alva Worley.

Worley later told police what happened to Colleen.

> *"I remember he told her to take her clothes off, so I don't know if he untied her. He was telling her, "all you have to do is fuck". He was trying to put it in her head that if she would just fuck, she would be turned loose. She was saying she would do what she was told. She was trying to buy time. That's what she was trying to do. Mac had his shirt off, and I believe he had his pants down. I do not know if the kid was facing up or down when he raped her. I remember he made her give him a head job. I remember that because he almost choked her. Mac had hit her several times in the head when he first got in the back with her. He was forcing her head down on him, and she was choking. I was just driving, and when I got to the Stillhouse Hollow exit, I decided to get out there to go to my sister's house. Mac was just sitting there at Stillhouse. I pulled over near the spillway, near the*

trailer houses there. I moved over to the passenger seat, and Mac got the keys out and popped the trunk. He pulled her out of the back seat, and put her in the trunk. She was quiet at that time and he had to force her into the trunk. That was the last time I saw that girl or heard anything about her. Mac drove to my sister's house...Mac broke her neck after he tortured her some more with the lighted cigarettes. He snapped her neck, and it sounded like a tree limb breaking, then he threw her, like a sack of potatoes, into the trunk of his car."

Colleen was dumped at a childhood fishing spot known to McDuff. Her body was found after McDuff's arrest.

Twenty-two-year-old prostitute Valencia Joshua was last seen alive knocking on the Waco dormitory door of Kenneth McDuff on February 24, 1992. She was raped, tortured and strangled by McDuff soon afterwards.

Her decayed body was found by bushwalkers on March 15, 1992 at the James Connally Municipal Golf Course that was behind the University campus.

Twenty-two-year-old Melissa Northrup was abducted by Kenneth McDuff at 4 am on March 1,1992 from the Quik-Pak Convenience Store, Waco where she worked. She knew McDuff, who had worked there previously.

After raping the girl, he cut her body open, and dumped it into a gravel pit in Dallas where it was found on April 26, 1992.

After watching America's Most Wanted, Gary Smithee rang Texas police to tell them that a work-colleague, Richard Fowler, looked like Kenneth McDuff. It was soon discovered that "Richard Fowler" was already in custody on charges of soliciting a prostitute. Fingerprints confirmed that Fowler and McDuff were indeed one and the same. He had been released and police began a surveillance of the man.

He was arrested while trying to make a run for it at his company's garbage collection point.

On June 26, 1992 Kenneth McDuff was charged with the murder of Melissa Northrup.

Kenneth McDuff was found guilty of the murder of Melissa Northrup on February 16, 1993 and two days later was sentenced to death.

After failing several avenues of appeal, Kenneth McDuff was scheduled to die on November 17, 1998 at The Walls Prison, Huntsville, Texas. His mother missed the opportunity to see her son one more time after arriving late. His final meal was two T-bone steaks, five fried eggs, vegetables, French fries, coconut pie and a single coke.

At 5.44pm the pre-med injection was administered to McDuff and he was led to the clinical room where he would take his last breath. At 6.08 pm he was strapped to a gurney and the needles were inserted into his arms. The killer's final words were "I'm ready to be released. Release me."

The toxins were released into McDuff's veins. He was pronounced dead at 6.26pm. He was 52.

Michael McGray

On May 1, 1985 Michael McGray, a transient, was travelling through Nova Scotia when he spotted seventeen-year-old Elizabeth Gale Tucker (known as Gale) hitch-hiking to work. McGray travelling with another man who has never been named. The men picked up the teenager and drove to a secluded area where McGray demanded oral sex.

When Gale refused, McGray punched her and then stabbed her to death. He then raped her dead body before dumping her in the woods in Digby County, Canada.

Over sixteen years later on May 29, 200, the killer finally pleaded guilty to the murder of Elizabeth Gale Tucker.

Yet the murder had not been an isolated one for the man. Though it was the first murder committed by the killer, it would be the final one to be added to his tally. McGray, at the time of his trial for the murder of Gale was already serving concurrent sentences for the murders of five other people, as well as almost a dozen others that the man claimed he had killed in both Canada and the USA.

Four days before pleading guilty to Gale's murder, McGray had also pleaded guilty to the murder of eleven-year-old Nina Hicks in Moncton in1998. The man had been charged with the murders of both Nina and her mother Joan, yet had always denied killing the little girl until May 25, 2001. Joan Hicks had had her throat slit her by her killer. Nina was found hanged in the closet of her home.

He was also serving time for the murders of two gay men in Montreal in 1991. Robert Assaly was stabbed to death in his home on March 31, 1991. The other victim, Gaeten Ethier was murdered the day after. McGray has also been sentenced to prison for the stabbing murder of taxi-driver Mark Gibbons in 1987.

At the time of writing McGray is still waiting to be charged with the murder of James Beyea in 1986. McGray has confessed to killing him.

Gennadiy Mikasevich

Gennadiy Mikasevich was born in 1947 in Polotsk, Byelorussia, USSR and went on to kill an unknown number of people during the 1970's and 1980's. Like the story of Andrei Chikatilo, several innocent men were tried, convicted and executed for the killer's crimes.

His MO was to drive around Polotsk in his volunteer policeman uniform and offer victims a lift home. He would then drive to a secluded place and strangle them with his scarf; sometimes leaving hand-written notes signed "Patriot of Vitebsk" at the scene.

As a volunteer police officer, he would question suspects in the murders and haul them in for charging over the murders. In total, four men where found guilty of Mikasevish's crimes.

Yet as time continued and more murders occurred, police turned to the letters left at the scenes and with a small red car seen at many sites. They investigated handwriting samples of red car owners and after an arduous task they found Mikasevich's handwriting matched that on the killer's letters.

The killer was arrested and interrogated until he confessed to the murders of at least two dozen people, yet the real tally could have been double that.

He took police to where he had hidden the personal effects of many of his victims.

Mikasevich was found guilty of the murders and sentenced to death. His execution, by a single shot to the back of his head, occurred sometime between 1985 and 1988.

Ivan Milat
The Backpacker Killer is arrested
On September 19, 1992 a bush walker, hiking through the Belanglo State forest stumbled across the remains of a young woman in a shallow grave; it was obvious that she had suffered multiple stab wounds in a frenzied attack. The discovery shocked the residents of nearby Berrima.

Police identified the corpse as that of Joanne Lesley Walters of England who went missing while backpacking along the Hume Highway with her friend, Caroline Clarke. So what had happened to Caroline? It wasn't long until police knew the answer to that question. The following day police found the remains of Caroline. She was only a few metres from where Joanne had met her brutal end. She had been shot over ten times through her head. The discovery of the two bodies would only scratch the surface of a more cruel and sinister plot of death and destruction.

Thirteen months after the discovery of Joanne and Caroline, police uncovered the bodies of Deborah Everist and James Gibson who were found in similar circumstances. Parts of the skeletal remains of Deborah were found in two shallow graves, she had been stabbed, and her jaw and skull fractured. James had more serious blows with stab wounds shattering his bones.

Then one after the other the remains of Simone Schmidl, Gabor Neugebauer and Anja Habschied were found. All in shallow graves, all with sickening injuries. Simone had been cowardly stabbed in the back a number of times. Six bullets shattered the skull of Gabor and if that wasn't enough he was also strangled as if to finish him off. The most horrific injuries were those inflicted on Anja. She had her head severed from her body in one bloody strike. Also the stabbing blows to her body were so fierce that she, like James, had chips knocked out of her bones with each strike.

The murders had caused such an outcry that a murderer had to found and fast.

While police kept searching the ghostly forest floor, the families of the dead backpackers sat waiting for the right lead to come along. Six months later it did.

In the early hours of Sunday May 22, 1994 a man was arrested at his Eaglevale home. He was to go down in the history books as Australia's worst serial killer.

Ivan Milat was arrested on charges of armed robbery and possession of firearms. Though police refused to say whether they had a suspect for the "Backpacker Murders", the media knew that something was important about Ivan Milat. Within a few days Ivan Milat was charged with the seven brutal murders and one attempted murder of British backpacker Paul Onions.

Who is Ivan Milat?
On December 27, 1944, Ivan Robert Marko Milat was born to his Croatian born father Stephen and his Australian born mother, Margaret. He was the fourth child in an extremely large family of fourteen. The family nicknamed the young boy Mac, though none of them can actually remember when the name originated. The family lived in a small suburban three bedroom yellow weatherboard house in Guildford. Out of the ten boys most of them, including Ivan, went to Patrician Brothers High School in the South-Western Sydney area of Liverpool. The younger members of the family attended the local schools in Guildford.

While at school Ivan played football, but with the school politics what they were, you either performed to a high standard or you got your butt kicked for not pulling your weight. School was a sort of stoic environment, which obviously helped build the character of the boys. Most of the Milat boys did not stay at school for very long. Stephen worked seven days a week yet it still was not enough to feed the family of sixteen. The choice of the Milat boys was either to go out and get a job and help with the bills and board or get out and fend for yourself. Therefore Ivan left school at the age of 15. He found work in road and construction gangs, doing odd jobs of digging foundations here and helping out there. He had jobs all over Sydney.

Ivan's father was strict but fair. If any of the children got into strife, he would whack them to the ground. He would ensure that rules were laid down up front. But, once the problem was over with, that was the end of it. It would never be brought up in conflict again. Ivan, like his brothers got on well with their father. Ivan was a devoted son who always paid his share of the board and kept the weatherboard house neat and tidy.

Ivan also took special care of his younger brother David, who at a young age, lost his arm and suffered irreparable brain damage in a car accident. He looked after his parents as well whenever he was home.

Ivan and some of his brothers enjoyed shooting and became familiar with many different firearms from a very early age. They remember knowing a lot of people that kept guns; it was just such a common thing in Ivan's life.

Ivan Milat got a job with the Department of Main Roads (known now as the Roads and Traffic Authority) at Central Asphalt, at Granville; he even got his brother Wally a job there. Ivan's employers were so impressed by his work that he was made the leading hand. He worked on the construction gang for about fifteen years until all of the employees were retrenched. Ivan, due to his extensive experience was quickly hired by Readymix, where he still worked when arrested.

Ivan met his wife in the late seventies. They married and bought a house in the western Sydney suburb of Mount Druitt. They divorced during the early eighties, and since the divorce Milat had a few relationships.

After being retrenched in mid-1992 Milat received a huge pay-out from the Department of Main Roads which he used as part of the deposit on a home he built with sister Shirley Soire in Eaglevale. The house would be the last for Milat.

Milat was an impeccably neat and friendly person who got on well with the children in the street, even letting them ride his minibike and go-kart. He was always washing his car and attending to his perfectly manicured lawn. So it came as a surprise when he was arrested for the murders.

That was until small pieces of his violent past came to light. In 1971, Milat was charged with raping a young backpacker. When released on bail, Milat fled to New Zealand to avoid the charges. He was rearrested in 1974 when he arrived back in Australia. Previous to the rape charge, Milat had criminal convictions reaching back to 1968

The Murders
Deborah Everist:
Deborah's body was very much a skeleton when it was discovered on October 5, 1993, three and a half years after her death. This made it very hard for scientists to obtain accurate information on the exact cause of death, or in this case, what injury caused her death. She had suffered at least one stab wound, though it was evident that there were several "slicing" injuries detected on Deborah's upper skeleton. But due to the advance state of decay, test were unable to determine if Deborah suffered more fatal stab wounds. Her skull had been fractured. This may have been afflicted after her death, but it has not been determined. Her jaw was also broken; this could have been inflicted by her killer punching her until she was unconscious. This would make it easier for him to kill. Both Deborah and James were found in shallow graves in the Belanglo State forest. They were covered only with leaf and stick debris.

James Gibson:
Due to the time lapse between his murder and the discovery of James' body a lot of crucial evidence had decayed or been lost. However James' skeleton did provide detectives with the modus of which James was slaughtered. The autopsy indicated that James had suffered multiple stab wounds. Most of James' sickening wounds were in his chest and upper back. The ferocity of the blows had left some of James' bones severed clean in half, other signs on his decayed skeleton of the attack were chip marks left by the swipe of the murderers' knife. It was obvious that it was the work of a madman, however what people didn't know was that as more bodies were found it was evident that the murderer was getting a "taste" for it so to speak. One of the victims was to be decapitated, two were said to have been sexually assaulted. The black floppy hat that James was wearing in the publicity photo spread all over the media was found near his murder site. It was the clincher that helped his parents to identify him as one of the two skeleton found that day.

Simone Schmidl:
Simone's pitiful remains were an all too familiar calling card of the Backpacker murders. She, like many of the other victims, had suffered multiple stab wounds to her upper back. A cowardice act, in any terms. Like the others, she was found in a shallow grave in Belanglo State Forest, covered with stick and leaf debris. Her body was discovered on November 1, 1993, after her disappearance in January 1991. The time delay between her body being discovered and her death meant that a lot of the evidence that would have helped convict someone for the crimes had deteriorated. Three days later two more bodies were found, taking the death toll to seven.

Gabor Neugebauer:
Gabor and his travelling companion girlfriend Anja Habschied were found propped up against trees in Belanglo State Forest on November 4, 1993. This seemed to suggest that Milat (like many serial killers) wanted to be caught. He was becoming good at his "work" and though he had for years eluded police, it is as though the two German backpackers were left uncovered and in a sitting position against fallen logs in the forest as a sort of tease for police. Milat was becoming cocky, yet still careful enough to conceal the bodies for nearly two years. Gabor had been shot six times in the head, three shots to the left side of his skull and three shots to the rear base of the skull. Forensic evidence also suggest that Gabor was strangled, maybe as a sadistic last effort to kill him, even though the six shots alone would have been more than sufficient. Inside Gabor's mouth was a rag. He also had a piece of cloth tied around his face as a gag. Obviously there was a struggled between the 21-year-old and his attacker. The gun used to kill Gabor was identified as Ruger 10/22. Pieces of a Ruger 10/22 and a homemade silencer were found in a wall cavity at Ivan Milat's house.

Anja Habschied:
The murder of Anja Habschied was by far the worst. Before the discovery of Anja's body, police knew that the murderer's modus operandi for death was by shooting and stabbing (though there is also evidence that he strangled at least one of his victims). With the common cause of death, police were able to link all six victims to the same person or persons, however the murder of Anja Habschied was a far cry from the wounds inflicted on the other "Backpacker" victims. Anja had had her head severed from her body in one violent blow. It sicken forensic scientists to know that it would have taken great force to do such horrific damage in the one strike. Anja's headless body was also missing the lower half of clothing. This evidence does suggest that she too may have been sexually assaulted but unfortunately due to the time lapse of almost two years between her murder and the discovery of her body, there is not enough evidence for forensics to be one hundred percent sure. Some clothing was found later the same afternoon; it was believed to belong to Anja and Gabor. Because it had almost completely decayed into the forest floor, it is difficult for police to be absolutely certain. At the time of writing Anja's head has not been found, police believe an animal had probably carried it off.

Joanne Walters:
On September 19, 1992 Joanne Walters was the first of the murdered backpackers found. She was found in a shallow grave in Belanglo State Forest only partly covered with debris. Like the murder of Gabor Neugebauer, Joanne had been gagged; and for some unknown reason she had two more pieces of cloth covering her face. Joanne had suffered multiple stab wounds to the upper half of her body, both to her chest and back. Police are certain that Joanne was sexually assaulted.

Caroline Clarke:
Caroline was found the day after Joanne on the September 20, 1992. She, like the other six murdered backpackers, was in a shallow grave. She had been shot ten times in the head. The first three shots entered her head on the right hand side through the red sweatshirt that covered her head. Two more shots entered the left side towards the back of her skull, and three shots entered at the base of her skull at the rear. The last two shots were the worst of all; they entered her skull through her forehead. If the ten horrible gunshots weren't enough she was also stabbed in the lower back. There is enough evidence to support the thought that Caroline was also sexually molested.

Ivan Milat was found guilty of all four murders and the attempted murder of Paul Onions and sentenced to life imprisonment.

The On-Going Investigation
Since the incarceration of Milat, police have continued to try and link him to a number of other unsolved murders that have occurred along the eastern coast of Australia, to no avail. He has been brought before several coronial inquests and trials without being charged with any further crimes.

The killer continues to maintain his innocence.

Zola Jackson Mqomboyi

Another example of the recent spate of South African serial killings is the case of Zola Jackson Mqomboyi.

On October 27, 2003, Judge Wilf Thring handed career criminal Mqomboyi a sentence of 120 years for the murders of two men and three women in addition to the rape of a female teenager. Judge Thring described the crimes as 'chilling'.

The five victims were discovered; buried in shallow graves, near the Mfuleni and Eerste Rivers after their suspect lead authorities to the gravesites. Mqomboyi killed the five adults between September 2000 and January 2001 using an axe, which he also used to remove their hands and feet.

Bilal Musa

Bilal Musa and his wife, Susan Ibrahim, 31, posed as salespeople or journalists to persuade their victims to let them into their houses. Once inside, they killed and robbed the inhabitants.

The crimes were committed in various Middle East cities between 1994 and 1998.

In April 1999 Musa was convicted of 12 counts of murder and robbery. The court sentenced him to death on seven counts of murder, but did not explain why the other five cases did not warrant the death penalty.

For the related robberies, Musa received a combined sentence of life in prison with hard labour.

The court convicted Ibrahim of being an accomplice to the murders and robberies. She was sentenced to death on one murder count, but an appeals court commuted the sentence to life in prison. She was also sentenced to life imprisonment with labour for the robberies.

The couple fled to Libya in 1998 but were arrested and extradited to Jordan in October 1998.

N

Arnfinn Nesset

Curare.

Curacit is a muscle relaxant derivative from the poison curare. Curare is a potent neurotoxin[18] that when used in large doses, can cause death from asphyxia. The "skeletal muscles become relaxed and then paralysed...[it interferes with] the transmission of nervous impulses...during curare poisoning, the victim is very much awake and aware of what is happening until the loss of consciousness. Consequently, the victim can feel the progressive paralysis but cannot do anything to call out or gesture."[19]

In a nursing home environment the drug would be used in very minute doses to help with the healing of broken bones, relaxing the muscles and skeleton around the wound to speed recovery in the elderly.

Yet, it was the large quantities, being bought by Orkdal Valley Nursing Home in Norway that alerted an employee in 1981 that the higher number of deaths may not have been pure coincidence.

The Arrest

The employee did not know what to do about his discovery. The home's administrator Arnfinn Nesset had ordered the large quantities and further investigation proved that since the Nursing Home opened in 1977 it had suffered a high rate of patient deaths. The entire time Nesset had been ordering the muscle relaxant in great amounts.

Instead of going to police with his concerns the nursing home worker told a journalist of his concerns.

The journalist investigated the story further and went to the police with his story. Arnfinn Nesset was immediately arrested by Norwegian police and questioned about the large amount of drugs he had ordered. The middle-aged balding man told police that it had been purchased to kill a feral dog that had been seen around the nursing home. Police did not believe his story and after further questioning the man began to confess to a string of murders at the home.

Nesset confessed to the murders of twenty-seven patients from May 1977 to November 1980 telling the arresting officers;

> "I've killed so many I'm unable to remember them all."

Police began to investigate all of the patient deaths at the three hospitals where Nesset had worked over the previous 20 years as a nurse. Yet even with a list of a further 62 possible murders, they were unable to charge Nesset. Curacit is undetectable in a dead body after an extended period of time.

The Trial

When his trial opened in October 1982, Nesset was charged with the murders of 25 of the patients at the Nursing Home, as well as charges of embezzlement and forgery after robbing many of his victims.

He pleaded not guilty and the defence claimed the killer suffered mental insanity and instability. He suffered from schizophrenia and had claimed to enjoy the pleasure of watching the victims die. Certainly this was not the motive of a sane man, the defence claimed.

---

[18] Wikipedia (2003)- Curare
[19] ibid

The trial ended on March 11, 1983 with Nesset being found guilty of 22 of the murders. The mild looking killer was sentenced to the maximum penalty available – twenty-one years incarceration, and has since been released under an assumed name.

In total, police believe that Nesset may have slaughtered up to 138 patients over a 20-year nursing career.

Dennis Nilsen

Dennis Andrew Nilsen was born on November 23, 1945 to Betty and Olav Nilsen. Betty was from Frazebrugh, Scotland and had met Olav, a Norwegian soldier in a cafe in England in 1940. Olav had moved to Scotland after the German invasion in 1940. The couple were married in 1942.

Dennis was the couple's second child of three. But despite being married, Betty and Olav did not live together most of the time.

Betty lived with her parents - Andrew and Lilly Whyte - and rarely saw Olav who seldom visited. After eight years the couple divorced.

Betty and her two sons and daughter remained at the Whyte's residence. The Whytes were a deep-seated sea-faring family, and had been for many generations. The community were all of a similar background and there was a lot of in breeding resulting in a history of mental illness in many of the families; including the Whytes.

Dennis' grandparents were a strong influence on the young boy. They were strict but loving grandparents and Dennis quickly developed their argumentative nature and stern independence.

The family was also incredibly religious. Lily would not allow cooking on Sundays and did not approve of any self-indulgent pleasures such as cinema, radio or drinking of alcohol.

The lack of entertainment and enjoyment made Dennis withdrawn, he became sullen and moody, keeping mostly to himself. But if he did speak to anyone, it was usually his grandfather Andrew, whom Dennis idolised.

When Andrew died at sea in 1951 his body was transported home and was placed in a coffin on the dining room table.

Dennis was not told of his grandfather's death until he was told to come and see him - dead on the kitchen table.

So at the tender age of six, seeing his grandfather's corpse had a lasting effect on Dennis. From that moment on, Dennis always associated love and death as part of the same.

Without his grandfather around, Dennis withdrew even further into his own world. He had few friends and kept to himself at school. He felt different to the others at school and as he began puberty he found he preferred males to the girls that the others talked about.

In 1961, at the age of 15, he left school and immediately enlisted in the army. He was given a position in the catering corps where he was quite popular.

He travelled with the army to Europe and the Middle East. During his years with the catering corps he became a dab hand with a knife and could dissect meat with precision.

In the army, Dennis was happy for a while, he even had a close friend. Dennis was a good photographer and persuaded his friend to pose for photos in the battlefields like a fallen soldier. It was the closest Dennis was to the action at the time.

At the age of 21, Dennis was out of barracks after dark one evening in Aden, where the British forces were fighting against Arab terrorists. Being out at night was not advisable.

Being quite intoxicated, Dennis caught a taxi back to barracks but fell asleep on the way.

When he woke, he found himself naked and in the trunk of a car. Keeping his wits about him, he played dead as someone opened the trunk. As his captor grabbed him and tried to drag him out, Nilsen hit the man over the head with the car wheel jack, knocking the man unconscious. Dennis quickly dressed and returned to barracks. The incident spooked him. He found himself panicky and nervous. He had nightmares of being raped, tortured or murdered.

By the age of twenty-six Nilsen left the army disillusioned over their treatment of others. He quickly joined the police force in 1972.

As police constable Q287 Nilsen was assigned to Willesden Green police station. But the police service lacked the mateship of the army. He disliked the roughness used by some of the other officers when interrogating suspects.

So with barely a year on the job, Nilsen resigned.

The next position that Nilsen held was with the Jobcentre interviewing applications for vacant positions. He became quite popular with the applicants and, with his keen interest in unionism; he became the secretary of the public service union branch.

His free time was spent in pubs in Soho and Camden Town, where he would date men.

He yearned for companionship and always felt lonely and isolated.

Back in his professional life he became increasingly more political, often participating in demos for workers' rights, but he was still a meticulous worker though somewhat erratic. His demeanour would change from gentle and meek to hot-tempered in a short period of time.

In 1975, Nilsen met David Gallichan outside a pub. The two men hit it off instantly and they moved in together the next day. Making their little family complete with a dog named Bleep and a cat.

Unfortunately, the relationship did not last as long as Nilsen would have hoped and the men parted ways.

By 1978 Nilsen again felt isolated and continued his search for companionship. He met men in pubs regularly but nothing ever came of it. He felt even worse after spending Christmas 1978 home alone.

On New Year's Eve Nilsen met up with a young Irish man at a pub. The two men returned to Nilsen's apartment at 195 Melrose Avenue in London to continue drinking and see the New Year in together.

The men drank heavily and fell into bed, both falling asleep almost instantly. When Nilsen woke during the night he panicked that the fun would stop and the young man would leave, leaving Nilsen alone once more.

Nilsen spotted one of his ties on the floor and, instantly, the answer came to him. Nilsen grabbed the tie and straddled the man's chest. He looped the tie around the Irishman's throat and pulled tight. The victim woke instantly and struggled with Nilsen who just pulled tighter on the tie.

The man fell to the floor and went limp, but he still made shallow gasps for air. Nilsen went and got a bucket of water from the kitchen and held the Irishman's head in the water until he was sure the man was dead.

The following day Nilsen took the body to the bathroom, and washed it and dressed it before putting the corpse back into his bed and slept beside it.

The next morning Nilsen knew he had to hide the body. Under the floorboards was a good temporary solution but the rigor mortis had set in making the body difficult to move. When the rigor subsided, Nilsen undressed and bathed the body again placed it in his bed, and laid down next to it and masturbated.

The man's death - though fulfilling sexual fantasies for Nilsen - also scared him. He expected to be arrested at any moment. But the police never came.

After a week of living with the corpse, cleaning it, sitting and watching TV together, he put it under the floorboards where it remained for eight months. Then in August 1979, he wrapped it in a curtain and put it on a bonfire in the back garden.

In October 1979, Nilsen brought home another date. Chinese student Andrew Ho. The two men ended up having an argument at the flat, and Nilsen produced a tie and wrapped it around the man's neck. Ho quickly put up a fight and managed to escape the killer's hold. Ho reported the incident to police who subsequently interviewed Nilsen about the assault. However the police chose not to pursue the complaint.

December 3, 1979 was the next murder.

Kenneth Ockenden, a Canadian tourist met Nilsen in a pub in Soho in December. The two men chatted freely and Nilsen agreed to show Ockenden around London that day before Kenneth returned to Canada.

By early evening the men returned to Nilsen's flat for something to eat. As the night progressed, Nilsen knew the fun would come to an end and Ockenden would leave soon. The two men were incredibly drunk by this stage and Ockenden relaxed in a chair listening to music on the headphones.

Nilsen went over to him and put the headphone cord around Ockenden's neck and pulled it tight. As the two men struggled and fought, Nilsen's dog Bleep barked frantically, however the neighbours never came to check to see if there was anything wrong.

Once Ockenden was dead, Nilsen sat calmly, poured himself another drink and listened to the music piping through the headphones.

Later, Nilsen bathed and dried the body and placed the man in his bed and fell asleep cuddled up to him. The next day before leaving for work, Nilsen placed Ockenden's body in the cupboard.

After work Nilsen retrieved the body from the cupboard and took Polaroid photos of it in various positions before propping the dead man's body in bed with him so the two could watch TV together. When Nilsen was ready to sleep he wrapped the body in carpet and placed it under the floorboards.

The family of Ockenden reported him missing within days and Nilsen panicked He had been all over London with the man before he killed him in his apartment. Any second, he thought, police would be knocking at his door. However no one ever did.

Nilsen now believed his fantasies and lust could take control. It seemed he was not destined to be caught. And for several more years he was right.

In May 1980, sixteen-year-old catering student Martyn Duffey was the next to die at Nilsen's hands. The two had been drinking together before retiring to Nilsen's apartment where the two of them collapsed into bed. Duffey fell asleep immediately and Nilsen straddled him and strangled him into unconsciousness. Nilsen then dragged the lifeless body into the kitchen where he filled the sink with water and immersed the young teens head until he was no longer alive.

> *"I then lifted him into my arms and took him into the room. I laid him on the floor and took off his socks, jeans, shirt and underpants. I carried him into the bathroom. I got into the bath myself this time and he lay in the water on top of me. I washed his body. Both of us were dripping wet. I somehow managed to hoist this slipping burden on to my shoulders and took him to the room. I sat him on the kitchen chair and dried us both. I put him on the bed but left the bedclothes off. He was still very warm. I talked to him and mentioned that his body was the youngest I had ever seen. I kissed him all over and held him close to me. I sat on his stomach and masturbated. I kept him temporarily in the cupboard. Two days later I found him bloated in the cupboard. He went straight under the floorboards."*

On August 7, 1980 Nilsen met his next victim twenty-seven-year-old Billy Sutherland in a pub near Piccadilly Circus. Sutherland was a Scottish ex-con and was covered in tattoos. He considered himself heterosexual and had a girlfriend in Edinburgh but when he travelled around he lived day-to-day and would accept money for sex with men.

After the two men had spent an evening together drinking - going from pub to pub, Nilsen grew weary and was quite drunk when he decided to go home. He did not want any company but Sutherland would not leave.

Sutherland asked Nilsen if he could stay the night as he had nowhere else to sleep. Nilsen found the request inconvenient, but let the Sutherland come home with him anyway.

Nilsen was not in the mood for any company and killed the man for being a nuisance.

Over the next six months Nilsen killed another seven men. All of them remain unidentified. Most of them were more than likely transients and those who would do anything for a warm bed for the night. Nilsen would kill those who had little chance of being reported missing. Drifters and tourists usually were his victim of choice. Those with little or no family contact. This ensured that Nilsen's killings would continue undetected.

Nilsen's next victim fitted this description perfectly. Twenty-four-year-old Malcolm Barlow had no family - his parents were dead and he had no close friends. Most of his life he had been in care due to medical handicaps. He had severe epilepsy and was on strict medication. Barlow was also always in trouble with authorities and would drift from place to place to avoid prosecution.

Barlow and Nilsen met quite by accident. Barlow was unwell and leaning against a brick fence a few doors away from Nilsen's apartment building, when Nilsen walked past on his way to work. Nilsen thought the man looked quite ill and stopped to offer him a cup of tea back at his flat.

Once inside the flat, the killer assessed the man's health and contrary to his usual habits, called the man an ambulance. Barlow was admitted to hospital for several days, due to asthma and was given medication to help manage his failing health.

A few days later, on September 18, 1980, Barlow returned to Nilsen's flat to thank him for his caring good nature but Nilsen was not home. When Nilsen returned from work he found the man sitting on the front steps of the apartment building. Nilsen was not in the mood for the unexpected company but let Barlow in to the flat anyway.

Nilsen poured himself a drink but did not off the visitor any knowing he would be on medication. The young man asked for a drink and continued to insist until Nilsen gave in and poured the man a scotch. Barlow ended up having a few glasses of scotch.

An hour later Nilsen could not arouse the comatose man. Not wanting to call an ambulance again and arouse suspicion, he decided to strangle Barlow to get him out of the way. Nilsen then covered the man's lifeless body in garbage bags and shoved him under the kitchen sink, as there was no longer room under the floorboards.

By December 1980, Nilsen knew he had to get rid of the bodies that he had accumulated throughout the tiny flat. He collected all the bodies together in the small kitchen and sat on the floor with a butcher's knife. His knife skills from the army now came in handy. He cut up the bodies into smaller, manageable pieces and filled garbage bags with the body parts.

The internal organs were put into two bags that he threw over the fence at the end of the garden. The rats, birds and flies devoured the lot in less than two days - half of the evidence was gone. Nilsen built a giant bonfire in the gardens of his Melrose Ave flat. He concealed most of the bags of body parts in rolled up discarded carpet. Nilsen was even clever enough to mask the telltale smell of the burning human bodies with an old tractor tyre he put on top of the makeshift funeral pyre.

In October 1981, Nilsen moved into an attic flat at 23 Cranley Gardens. He thought that by not having floorboards or a garden to conceal his victims that he may be less inclined to continue his murderous campaign. That was not to be.

Nilsen murdered John Howlett at the new flat in March 1982. Howlett was a transient and had always been in trouble with police. The man had met Nilsen several times in the local pubs and one evening the two men returned to Nilsen's new flat together.

Howlett was tired from the alcohol, but Nilsen felt like a few more, so while Howlett retired to Nilsen's bed for the evening, Nilsen sat alone with his thoughts and a few more glasses of scotch. Nilsen soon decided to join the man in bed, however it was murder that he wanted. Nilsen took with him to the bed, a strip of upholstery and quickly had the strap around the sleeping man's throat. As Howlett struggled, Nilsen pulled tighter. After an immense struggle Howlett hit is head on the headboard of the bed and went limp. Nilsen thought the murder was over and went to fix himself another drink before starting his usual ritual with the body. But Bleep the dog's incessant barking from the bed made Nilsen rush back in. Howlett was alive and attempting to sit up on the bed, not knowing what had exactly transpired.

Reverting to his tried and true formula Nilsen dragged the semi-conscious man to the bathroom and drowned him in the sink.

Graham Allen was the next of Nilsen's victims. He was so insignificant to Nilsen that he cannot even remember how or when he had killed the man, except he had first made an omelette.

The final victim was a punk drug-addled drifter named Stephen Sinclair. Sinclair met Nilsen on January 26, 1983 while trying to scrounge enough money to live another day.

Nilsen felt pity for the young man so he bought him a hamburger and took him home. After a few drinks at the flat Sinclair slumped down into one of the chairs - he was unconscious.

Nilsen explains the events of the murder during his arrest:

> "I picked up one of his wrists and let go. His limp arm flopped back on to his lap. I opened one of his eyes and there was no reflex. He was deeply unconscious. I took the ligature and put it around his neck... I took each loose end of the ligature and pulled it tight.... He stopped breathing. His hands slowly reached for his neck as I held my grip. His legs stretched out in front of him. I held him there for a couple of minutes; He was limp and stayed that way. I released my hold and removed the string and tie. He had stopped breathing."

On February 2, 1983 Jim Allcock, one of the tenants of Nilsen's apartment block noticed that the toilets and drains were backing up. The plumber that came said he would return the next day as the main street sewer needed to be looked at as well.

By February 8, when no work had been done, Michael Cattan of Dyno-Rod Plumbing Co was asked to come and look at the problem that was worsening. Cattan found disgusting putrid lumps of a greyish-white substance blocking the pipes coming from the house into the main sewer.

However darkness was falling and the plumber told Jim Allcock he would return at first light the next morning. Cattan called his supervisor and told him about the substance he found in the drains and told him he suspected it to be flesh.

Nilsen had seen Cattan come and inspect the drains and knew he had been found out. Nilsen had been disposing of his victims by flushing their cut up parts down the toilet. He knew he had little time to remove the offensive lumps blocking the sewer before the plumber returned with the police.

Nilsen cut-up the decapitated body of Sinclair and placed the pieces into garbage bags which he added to the other rotting corpses in his cupboard. He sprayed air-freshener around the room and hung mothballs in the robe to attempt to hide the smell.

During the night Nilsen cleared out the lumps of flesh from the main sewer, collected it in garbage bags and traipsed up and down the stairs to throw the bags over the back fence. What Nilsen didn't realised was that the other tenants spent the night listening to Nilsen trekking up and down the stairs.

When Cattan arrived the next morning he found that most of the flesh had been cleared away. Most of the tenants were quick to raise their suspicions with the plumber about Nilsen's midnight activities.

The police were called and small pieces that Cattan was still able to collect from the drain were taken for analysis and confirmed as human in origin.

The police then waited for Nilsen to return that afternoon from work to ask him about the body he had discarded in the drain.

Nilsen told the police they would find the rest of it in his cupboard in his flat. One officer walked up to the wardrobe and the smell emanating from it was enough evidence to arrest Nilsen and take him in for further questioning.

On the way to the police station one of the officers asked Nilsen:

Are we talking about one body or two?

To which Nilsen replied a-matter-of-factly:

Fifteen or sixteen since 1978.

On further questioning Nilsen gladly spoke of the murders he had committed. He was almost happy to finally be caught and unable to kill again.

Nilsen was remanded in custody for seven days from February 12, 1983 before being transferred to Brixton prison in March to await his trial. The trial of Nilsen opened on October 24, 1983 in No 1. Court at the Old Bailey. The Judge presiding was Mr Justice Croom-Johnson. The courtroom was silent as chief administrator of the Court Mr Michael MacKenzie began to read out the charges of murder to Nilsen.

To each charge he was asked

"How say you Nilsen, are you guilty or not guilty?"

To which Nilsen replied

"Not guilty".

The entire court knew that Nilsen was guilty of each murder but what was in question was the man's frame of mind when he killed each victim.

The prosecutor, Mr Allen Green, stated that Nilsen had killed with full awareness and deliberation and was therefore guilty of each murder.

The defence council Ivan Lawrence claimed that Nilsen suffered from such abnormality of mind as to substantially hinder his responsibility for his acts and therefore only guilty of manslaughter.

The trial followed these preliminary ideas for days. Going back and forth arguing whether Nilsen was in possession of his full faculties when he murdered the men.

Yet the evidence heard may never had happened. Nilsen had wanted to plead guilty to the murders but was counselled against it by the defence.

So after several days Nilsen changed his defence counsel and changed his plea at the same time. However the trial was already in full swing and continued to its conclusion. On November 3, 1983 the members of the jury retired to consider their verdict.

The following day they returned their findings. Nilsen was found guilty of six murders and two attempted murders. There was insufficient evidence to pursue the other ten murders. The judge sentenced Nilsen to life imprisonment, with the recommendation that is should mean no less than twenty-five years.

He began his prison sentence at Wormwood Scrubs before being moved to several other prisons for his safety.

Robert Nixon

Known as 'The Brick Moron', teenager Robert Nixon used a brick to beat to death a cocktail waitress in Chicago in 1936. After fleeing from Chicago, Nixon next appeared in Los Angeles where he broke into homes in order to steal.

Those who tried to protect their house were beaten to death with his favourite weapon, a house brick. At least five people died from being bludgeoned to death by Nixon between 1936 and 1938.

Nixon was arrested after he left fingerprints on a brick, that he left at a murder scene. For the murders of five of his victims, Nixon was sentenced to death and executed in the electric chair at Sing Sing prison on June 15, 1939.

Gordon Northcott

Gordon Northcott was executed on October 2, 1930. The man, along with his mother, was responsible for the deaths of brothers, twelve-year-old Lewis Winslow, ten-year-old Nelson Winslow, as well as an unidentified third boy in Wineville, Canada. All three victims had been sexually assaulted prior to death.

Northcott began his last day on earth screaming, he was terrified of the hangman's noose and kept asking if it will hurt. He had to be dragged up the stairs to the gallows. His last words were "A prayer -- please, say a prayer for me." Then the trap door opened.

O

Mohammed Omar

Sixteen women were raped and murdered by Mohammed Omar in Yemen over a period of five years. The man, who had been a professor of medicine at the Sanaa University had turned his office into a killing room. According to some reports, the killer's actions were known to some of the other members of the faculty, who turned a blind eye to the killings.

Once arrested and sent to trial, the fifty-two-year-old killer confessed to the crimes in May 2000. The victims included eight of his students and the killings had taken place from 1995 to January 2000.

During the killer's confession he also claimed to have murdered many more women in Sudan, Lebanon, Chad and Kuwai

Anatoly Onoprienko

The arrest

On April 16, 1996, thirty-seven-year-old Anatoly Onoprienko was arrested at his girlfriend's house in Zhitomir, Western Ukraine. His arrest ended "The Terminator's" reign of terror in which he was reported to have murdered over 40 people. The manhunt involving 2, 000 police and more than 3,000 troops eventually lead to Onoprienko's arrest following an anonymous tip-off. Investigators feared the tally of victims would go even higher than 52, as a gap in murders seemed too long.

Onoprienko was found with a 12-gauge shotgun that could be linked to bullets found at one of the murder scenes. He was also in possession of jewellery and electrical equipment belonging to several of his victims. Onoprienko's girlfriend was wearing an engagement ring that he had stolen by cutting off one of his victim's fingers.

Anatoly Onoprienko had worked as a sailor and had studied forestry at university before his arrest. He was known to authorities and was on an outpatient program of a local psychiatric hospital department.

When Onoprienko was arrested, he confessed to eight of the killings spanning the years 1989 to 1995, yet denied all other murders police had linked to him. In total, police believed Onoprienko might have killed up to 52 people, almost equalling the tally of fellow countryman Andrei Chikatilo.

The Rampage

Onoprienko began his murderous campaign in 1989, where he and accomplice Serhiy Rogozin robbed and killed nine people. He later claimed that he had been hearing voices since the age of seven when his brother had sent him to an orphanage after his mother had died.

Onoprienko's first human victims were a young couple, standing by their Lada car on a motorway:

> *"I just shot them. It's not that it gave me pleasure, but I felt this urge. From then on, it was almost like some game from outer space."*

He said he had derived no pleasure from the act of killing.

> *"Corpses are ugly,"* he said with distaste. *"They stink and send out bad vibes. Once I killed five people and then sat in the car with their bodies for two hours not knowing what to do with them. The smell was unbearable."*

Onoprienko then continued his rampage alone in late 1995. In the next six months he murdered forty-three people. In March 1996, police began to panic as the number of bodies rose. When eight entire families were brutally murdered in their homes, a manhunt was launched across western Ukraine. Many of Onoprienko's victims lived in remote villages in the Lvov region near the border of Poland.

On one occasion he confronted a young girl who was huddled on her bed, praying. She had seen him kill both her parents.

> *"Seconds before I smashed her head, I ordered her to show me where they kept their money,"* he said.

> *"She looked at me with an angry, defiant stare and said, 'No, I won't.' That strength was incredible. But I felt nothing."*

He blew the doors off homes on the edges of villages, gunning down adults and battering children with metal objects. He stole money, jewellery, stereo equipment and other items before burning down the houses.

On January 2, 1996 he murdered a family of four before robbing them and burning down their house in the Ukraine. After fleeing the scene he saw a man beside the road taking a rest from his travels. The killer shot him dead before continuing on his rampage.

On January 6, 1996 the killer shot dead four car drivers while travelling along the highway between Dnieprovskaya and Berdyansk. On January 17, 1996 Anatoly Onoprienko broke into the Pilat Family home and shot all five members of the family dead. He robbed the house and set it alight. Two people, Kondzela, and Zakharko who came to see what was happening at the house were also shot dead.

On January 30, 1996 Onoprienko broke into one home and shot dead a young mother, her two sons and a male friend before setting the house on fire.

Anatoly Onoprienko committed his worse murder on February 19, 1996. He broke into the home of the Dubchak family. He shot the husband and son to death and killed the wife and daughter by clawing their skin from their bodies with a hammer.

The Bodnarchuk Family were visited by Onoprienko on February 27, 1996. The killer shot dead the parents and then hacked the two daughters to death with an axe.

Novosad Family was shot dead by Onoprienko on March 22, 1996. They were the killer's last murders. He set the house on fire after looting it.

Pyotr Onoprienko called Ukraine police on April 7, 1996 after evicting his cousin Anatoly Onoprienko from his house. A few weeks earlier the man had discovered that Anatoly had hidden several guns under the house. As Onoprienko left the house he told Pyotr that he would come back and kill his family in April and now Pyotr was worried. Anatoly was a violent man and had known that he had shot someone before.

Onoprienko's blood lust climaxed with a three-month massacre in early 1996 where he began the systematic slaughter of families in the Ukrainian villages of Bratkovichi and Busk. Army and special forces where mobilised in the areas to try and assist those still living in the region as well as trying to catch the man dubbed "The Terminator".

Police used a tactic of blockading the area trying to capture the killer, however Onoprienko easily slipped through the police trap and moved to nearby villages to continue his killing spree.

The murderer had a pattern and signature to his method. He would pounce on secluded houses on the fringes of villages. Before dawn Onoprienki would sneak into the house and round up the entire family before shooting them all dead with a 112-gauge shotgun at point-blank range. The house would then be set alight before "The Terminator" fled the scene. The killer would also murder anyone who crossed his path during his rampage. Onoprienki showed no remorse, as he wiped out entire families in cold blood, battering children and raping women after shooting them in the face.

Onoprienko's Trial
At his trial in November 1998, Onoprienko stated he felt like a robot driven for years by a dark force, and argued he should not be tried until authorities determine the source of the force.

Hundreds of spectators watched the trial unfold and bayed for the killer's blood. He had devastated many villages throughout the Ukraine and the towns' people wanted their own revenge.

> *"Let us tear him apart,"* shouted a pensioner at the back of the court just before the hearing started, her voice trembling with emotion.
>
> *"He does not deserve to be shot. He needs to die a slow and agonizing death."*

At his trial Onoprienko was silent. The court asked him if he would like to make a statement to which he replied with a shrug of his shoulders, and a quiet spoken

> *"No, nothing."*

Informed of his legal right to object to the court's proceedings, he growled

> *"This is your law, I consider myself a hostage."*

Asked to state his nationality, he said:

> *"None."*

When Judge Dmitry Lipsky said this was impossible, Onoprienko rolled his eyes and replied:

> *"Well, according to law enforcement officers, I'm Ukrainian."*

Onoprienko's co-defendant Sergei Rogozin, accused of helping in the first nine murders, did speak and proclaimed his innocence.

Onoprienko had his lawyers attempt to use the insanity defence, rambling inanely during police interviews about conspiracies against him by the CIA and Interpol, unknown powers and future revelations. However psychiatrists ruled him fit to stand trial.

> *"I perceive it all as a kind of experiment,"* Onoprienko said of the conspiracies against him.
>
> *"There can be no answer in this experiment to what you're trying to learn."*

Onoprienko was found guilty and sentenced to death but was not executed due to the Ukraine's pledge as a member of the Council of Europe to suspend capital punishment.

After his trial Onoprienko said:

> *"I have never regretted anything and I don't regret anything now...I love all people and I loved those I killed. I looked those children I murdered in the eyes and knew that it had to be done,"* he said. *"For you it's 52 murders, but for me that's the norm."*

Though Onoprienko had remained completely silent during court hearings, when it came to the media he was naturally verbose. The daily newspaper *"Fakty"* published a long interview with Onoprienko from his jail cell in Zhitomir where he was quoted as saying

> *"Naturally, I would prefer the death penalty. I have absolutely no interest in relations with people. I have betrayed them."*

The misunderstood killer added that he was shaken by people's indifference to his crimes. As he slaughtered his victims in one village,

> "people screamed so loudly that they could be heard in neighbouring villages. But nobody came to help them. Everybody went into hiding, like mice."

During an interview with a *London Times* reporter Onoprienko reminisced about the murders he had committed.

> "The first time I killed, I shot down a deer in the woods,"

he said, in a flat monotone, as if reading from his curriculum vitae.

> "I was in my early twenties and I recall feeling very upset when I saw it dead. I couldn't explain why I had done it, and I felt sorry for it. I never had that feeling again."

> "To me killing people is like ripping up a duvet... Men, women, old people, children, they are all the same. I have never felt sorry for those I killed. No love, no hatred, just blind indifference. I don't see them as individuals, but just as masses."

Onoprienko's crimes caused such revulsion in Ukraine, that the Ukrainian President considered temporarily lifting a moratorium on capital punishment to execute him. Instead the serial killer's sentence was commuted to 20 years in jail, a term that outraged most Ukrainians.

Telling a reporter after his sentence:

> "To me it was like hunting. Hunting people down,"

> "I would be sitting, bored, with nothing to do. And then suddenly this idea would get into my head. I would do everything to get it out of my mind, but I couldn't. It was stronger than me. So I would get in the car or catch a train and go out to kill."

Some experts view the fact that he grew up without parents and was given up to an orphanage by his elder brother as a clue to his destruction of entire families. Strangely, his most vicious spree coincided with the time when he moved in with the woman he intended to marry and with her children - towards whom, she claimed, he was always very loving.

Onoprienko, however, claimed he was possessed.

> "I'm not a maniac," he said, without a hint of self-doubt. "If I were, I would have thrown myself onto you and killed you right here. No, it's not that simple. I have been taken over by a higher force, something telepathic or cosmic, which drove me.

> "For instance, I wanted to kill my brother's first wife, because I hated her. I really wanted to kill her, but I couldn't because I had not received the order. I waited for it all the time, but it did not come.

> "I am like a rabbit in a laboratory. A part of an experiment to prove that man is capable of murdering and learning to live with his crimes. To show that I can cope, that I can stand anything, forget everything."

Onoprienko insisted he should be executed claiming:

> *"If I am ever let out, I will start killing again," he said. "But this time it will be worse, 10 times worse. The urge is there.*
>
> *"Seize this chance because I am being groomed to serve Satan. After what I have learnt out there, I have no competitors in my field. And if I am not killed I will escape from this jail and the first thing I'll do is find Kuchma (the Ukrainian president) and hang him from a tree by his testicles."*

P

Carl Panzram
The Confession
During his final prison stretch in the late 1920's, Carl Panzram confessed to twenty-one murders,

> "In my lifetime I have murdered 21 human beings, I have committed thousands of burglaries, robberies, larcenies, arsons and last but not least I have committed sodomy on more than 100 male human beings. For all these things I am not in the least bit sorry".

The Person
Panzram was born on June 28, 1891 to Prussian migrant parents in Minnesota. Carl Panzram was always in trouble. Police knew his name from quite early. When he was eight he was convicted for drunk and disorderly conduct. Then again three years later, when a string of burglaries landed him in reform school, he retaliated by burning the place down.

He left the institution at age thirteen and headed home, filled with the knowledge that would last him a lifetime –

> "how to steal, lie, hate, burn and kill"....

He went home to his mother, who was grieving over the drowning death of her favourite son and ignored Panzram's homecoming, so the teenager moved on again.

He ran away to pursue a transient life, where he was gang raped by four hobos on one occasion.

> "I cried, I begged and pleaded for mercy, pity and sympathy, but nothing I could say or do could sway them from their purpose. I left that box a sadder, sicker but wiser boy...".

The bums seemed to have taught Panzram another valuable lesson:

> "I had learned that a rectum could be used for other purposes than crepitating".

He also joined the army for a short stint; he was drunk when he enlisted which may account for his un-army like behaviour that culminated in a court-martial and three years at Leavenworth.

In 1911, after his release from prison, Panzram travelling with a companion attacked a railroader. The men robbed him of $35.00, bound his arms and legs, and stuffed a sock in his mouth.

> "I figured that as I had such a good chance as that, I would commit a little sodomy on him... He is still there, unless the buzzards and coyotes have finished the last of him long ago."

Panzram kills
At one point during his trips Panzram killed a young boy. In his own words he explained what happened:

> "I sat down to think things over a bit. While I was sitting there, a little kid about eleven or twelve-years-old came bumming around. He was looking for something. He found it too. I took him out to a gravel pit about one quarter mile away. I left him there, but first committed sodomy on him and then killed him. His brains were coming out of his ears when I left him, and he will never be any deader."

Travelling around the world -- South America, Europe, Africa and US – Panzram left a trail of corpses in his wake.

With proceeds from one of his many robberies Panzram bought a yacht, named the John O'Leary, a name he would adopt himself, and lured ten sailors aboard with the promise of free bootleg liquor. However, after the sailors drank themselves into oblivion, Panzram raped them, slit their throats and dumped them all overboard.

Later, in West Africa, he hired eight native guides to help him hunt crocodiles. Instead, he killed his hired hands, sodomized their corpses and fed them to the hungry reptiles "for sport."

Panzram's arrest

When he returned to the United States in 1928, Panzram was arrested for a string of burglaries and sentenced to 20 years in prison. Once incarcerated, Panzram vowed he'd "kill the first man that crosses me" and did.

Robert Warnke, a civilian laundry man was in the wrong place at the wrong time, Panzram took an iron bar and smashed the man's skull in.

He was sentenced to Death Row for the murder, where he befriended jailer, Henry Lesser, who listened intently to Panzram's story (and would later published it).

Even when human rights organisations tried to have his life spared, Panzram would retort:

> *"I prefer to die that way, and if I have a soul and if that soul should burn in Hell for a million years, still I prefer that to a lingering, agonizing death in some prison dungeon or a padded cell in a mad house... The only thanks you or your kind will ever get from me for your efforts on my behalf is that I wish you all had one neck and that I had my hands on it... I have no desire to reform myself. My only desire is to reform people who try to reform me, and I believe that the only way to reform people is to kill' em."*.

Finally he got his wish and was due to be hanged on September 5, 1930.

Bitter to the end, Panzram went to his maker with a curse on his lips:

> *"Hurry up you Hoosier bastard"*, he snarled at the executioner preparing the noose. *"I could hang a dozen men while you're fooling around"*.

Eusebius Pieydagnelle

During 1871, Frenchman Eusebius Pieydagnelle stabbed to death six people, in each case he confessed to experiencing a 'blissful orgasm' as he murdered them. His confession in court claimed that when he was growing up in Vinuville, the butcher's shop opposite gave him great excitement. Against his father's wishes Pieydagnelle became an apprentice at the shop and revelled in the blood that he began to drink. He took to slaughtering the animals with intense pleasure, but soon it was not enough.

Pieydagnelle's father refused to accept his son becoming a butcher and had him removed from the apprenticeship. Pieydagnelle became severely depressed; he needed to have the sensation of fresh blood back on his skin so he became a killer.

His first victim was a fifteen-year-old girl whom he said he could not resist. His sixth and final victim was the owner of the butchery, Mr Cristobal.

At his trial in 1871, Pieydagnelle requested to be sentenced to death as he wanted death and could not commit the sin of suicide. The request was granted.

Dr Marcel Petiot

During March 1944, the house at 21 Rue Le Sueur, Paris, had been pouring thick foul smelling smoke out of the chimney for five days.

On the evening of March 11, Jaqcues Marçais had had enough of the stench and went across the street to complain to the owner of the building, Marcel Petiot. Jacques found a note pinned to the door indicating that Petiot would be away for a month, so Jacques called the police.

Two officers Joseph Teyssier and Emile Fillion, arrived at the house. After trying the door and various windows and failing to gain access to the house, the officers asked the neighbours where Petiot was staying. The officers telephoned Petiot from a nearby café. Petiot requested that nobody enter the house and that he would be there within 15 minutes.

Half an hour later Petiot had still not arrived, so the fire department was called. Fire Chief Avilla Boodringhin managed to open a window and climb in. Once inside, he followed the smell and smoke to the basement and found the origin of both.

Minutes later the fireman returned to the front door clearly in a shocked state. In the basement he had found two large stoves, one was alight. On the door of the stove was a severed human hand, on the floor lay two skeletons along with various other bones including rib cages, skulls and jawbones.

Outside Petiot arrived on a bicycle, but claimed to be his brother Maurice. When Petiot was asked about what the fireman had discovered, Petiot explained that he was the head of a resistance movement and that the bodies were those of Germans and of French traitors. Parts of Paris were still under German rule and the police officers amazingly accepted the story of a French patriot and let him go.

The police commissaire was called however, to view the discovery at Petiot's home. Next to Petiot's medical consultation room a large pile of quicklime was found. Mixed in with the lime officers found large quantities of bones and flesh. In a second room, a manure pit was found with a block and tackle above it, within the pit further remains could be seen mixed with quicklime. In the basement of the outhouse a sack was found which contained the left hand side of a human body without the head.

More body parts were left scattered on the floor of the basement. Further discoveries were found in the outhouse. Parts of the building were suspicious in their design; a triangular room with 8 iron rings were fixed to one wall. Part of another wall had a hidden spyglass, which was positioned such that the iron rings could be seen. The triangular room had two doors, neither of which had a handle on the inside, when one of the doors was finally opened it had a solid brick wall on the opposite side. The commissaire left the building horrified by the grisly discoveries, but puzzled as to how and why the unknown victims were killed.

The next day the German authorities, now aware of the find, insisted that the French police arrest Petiot. However, Petiot could not be found and when the detectives reached his temporary home, they discovered that he had actually left less than half an hour before their arrival. But considering that the French police considered Petiot a hero after telling them who the victims were, it was questionable how much effort was being put into the search for him.

Gravediggers from the local cemetery were hired to clear the body parts from the house and sift through the pits of lime. Eventually a report by forensic experts, Doctor Albert Paul, Doctor Léon Dérobert and Doctor René Piédelièvre, concluded that at least 10 bodies were found in the basement of the main house and in the outhouse. But other evidence suggested that many more victims had met their end in the house.

Yet no evidence could be found that could determine the cause of death of any of the victims. The report noted that whoever completed the murderous task had taken great care in making identification of the victims difficult. The time of death was placed at least a year before their discovery. The report also referred to nine bodies recovered from the Seine during 1942 and 1943, the bodies were dissected in a similar way to the discoveries in the latest horror.

Despite the obvious difficulties in gaining clear identification of the victims, French police believed that they were able to name two of them.

Jean-Marc van Bever had been arrested on February 19, 1942 for heroin addiction and police had the man's fingerprints on file. Petiot, working as a respected general practitioner in Paris, was charged with supplying Jean-Marc with prescriptions for the drug. With a trial date set for May 26, 1942 Jean-Marc vanished 4 days before the trial was due to begin and was not seen again. On May 22, a man fitting Petiot's description was seen walking with Jean-Marc moments before his disappearance, a claim Petiot denied. At the trial Petiot received a one year suspended sentence that was reduced on appeal.

A second, virtually identical case was discovered when French police delved into the records on Petiot. Raymonde Baudet was arrested on March 5, 1942 for forging a prescription for heroin. The prescription was originally written by Dr Marcel Petiot. Although the prescription belonged to Raymonde, she used her mother's name of Khait in the details. Petiot visited Madame Khait with the intention of using her as his defence in the case. Petiot tried to persuade her to take part in a forgery that, should the case go to court, she would be identified as a heroin addict and hence help her daughter. Petiot offered Madame Khait F1500 to help the case. On March 25, 1942 Madame Khait told her husband David that she was to collect the money and then left the house. She was not seen again. However, a letter appeared at Madame Khait's home two days after her disappearance. Written in her handwriting, the letter stated that she was going to unoccupied France until Raymonde's trial was over. Her husband accepted the letter as true.

However, Raymonde reported her mother's disappearance to police. Police Inspector Roger Gignoux investigated the case and quickly noted the similarities of this case and the Van Bever case and also noted the close ties that Petiot had in both instances. Gignoux at this point believed that both missing people were now dead.

In 1944 the police continued their search for Petiot. They tracked down his brother Maurice and questioned him on the discovery at 21 Rue Le Sueur. Maurice denied being involved with any murders. However, French police did find a link between Maurice and the bodies. Evidence was found that Maurice and a second man, Robert Massonière had delivered 400kg of quicklime to the house on February 11, 1944. Maurice was arrested on February 17 on charges of conspiracy to commit murder.

Commissioner Georges-Victor Massau began to theorise about the bodies found at 21 Rue le Sueur, and came to the theory that the victims were wealthy people who were hoping to flee the occupation and were killed, but without evidence it couldn't be proven. However word reached commissioner Massau that his imaginative theory might actually hold some truth.

Jean Gouedo, a Paris businessman, met with the commissioner to tell a story of his business partner Joachim Guschinov (a Polish Jew). Joachim wanted to escape from the Germans and used Petiot to do so. He paid Petiot F25000 to help him gain a safe passage to South America using a forged passport. In January 1942 Joachim said goodbye to his wife and left to meet Petiot, Joachim was not heard from again.

Further investigations into the claim turned up an underground escape network and Petiot appeared to be the 'arranger' in each case. Roland Porchon ran a Parisian furniture shop and confessed to police of his links to the network. He told detectives about Réne and Marcelle Marie whom he introduced to Petiot as wanting to escape. The couple however decided not to go, and when questioned by police later the Maries confirmed the story. Petiot had offered the couple an escape route costing F45000 each. After discussing the option with friends the Maries decided not to risk the plan. Roland Porchon put pressure on the couple not to report the incident, they agreed, believing that it was the resistance operating the escape route. Roland Porchon confessed in court in front of Judge Georges Berry that an associate of Petiot, Réne-Gustav Nézondet, had told him of the bodies at Rue le Sueur in June 1942. Other stories came forward linking Petiot with the disappearances of French citizens wishing to escape, but still Commissaire Massau could not find the proof he sought, nor could the chief suspect be found. The investigators looked into the man's background for clues to who their killer actually was.

Marcel André Henri Félix Petiot was born at 3.00am on January 17, 1897 in Auxerre, France, the eldest son of Felix and Marthe. At age 17 Petiot was expelled from his third school for 'disciplinary problems' and theft. A psychiatric examination of Petiot found that he was an abnormal youth and the charges of theft were dropped.

In 1916, Petiot fought in the Great War, where he suffered an injury to his foot and also suffered from a poison attack. During this time Petiot first showed indications of a mental condition that would eventually result in a discharge from the army. The military doctor diagnosed the man for discharge as suffering from a 'mental unbalance' severe depression, paranoia and suicidal tendencies.

Petiot enrolled at university, successfully achieving a medical degree in December 1921. The achievement helped him in set up his first medical practice in the village of Villeneuve-sur Yonne, 25 miles from Auxerre, where in July 1926 he was elected mayor.

Commissaire Massau continued in his search for Petiot, who had not been seen since cycling away from the house at the beginning of the case. Sightings of the missing suspect continued to trickle in to the police. He had been seen in Paris, at the Spanish border, in Belgium and also on a ship heading for South America. Then news reached Massau that a military officer named Captain Simonin had arrested Petiot in Paris.

Since Paris had been taken back from the German invaders in August it was the French army who controlled the city and had been instructed to be on the lookout for Petiot. On October 31, 1944 Captain Simonin was at the Saint-Mande-Tourelles Metro station in Paris with three fellow officers. At 10.15pm a man named Henri Valeri entered the station, he was approached by Captain Simonin and asked the time. As Valeri hung out his wrist to look at his watch, a set of handcuffs closed and Petiot was placed under arrest. It was only after Petiot was handed over to police that the subject of how he was captured came under the spotlight, as the military knew nothing of Petiot's arrest. Captain Simonin was actually a man named Soutif, a notorious undercover collaborator.

Petiot was charged with the deaths of twenty-seven people and the trial opened on March 18, 1946 at the Palais de Justice in Paris. Petiot stated that he did commit the murders that he had been accused of, however they were done for France. The victims were those of German collaborators and traitors against his country, therefore he entered a plea of not guilty. Petiot claimed to be a member of the resistance, but would refuse to implicate any other member of the movement.

The tribunal president, Michel Lesser insisted that Petiot reveal the names of the resistance comrades who assisted him in the disposing of the bodies found at his home. Again Petiot refused, stating that 'these men are heroes and are no more guilty of killing traitors than I am'. Questioning continued with how collaborators were captured. Petiot replied that collaborators were easy to spot. He claimed that his group of men would disguise themselves as German soldiers on patrol, if they came across somebody they suspected of being a collaborator; they would approach and question them. Petiot stated that it was the answers they gave that implicated them. This was the pattern for the whole trial, the state would pose questions, Petiot would reply in a flamboyant manner without actually giving any information away.

On March 26, 1945 the Chief Coroner, Dr Albert Paul, gave the account of the victims found at the house. He stated that the coroners office were able to determine that 10 bodies could be reconstructed, but with the extensive amount of remaining bones in addition to 5kg of hair, Dr Paul suggested that there were many more victims involved. Of the confirmed 10 bodies, 5 were male and 5 were female, all were aged between 25 and 50. The cause of death could not be determined in any of the victims, nor could the timing of the deaths. Various methods of murdering the victims were theorised, including the use of gas in the 'triangular' room, but no evidence could be found that presented itself as a plausible method.

The evidence for and against was concluded on April 3, leaving both the prosecution and the defence to present their case summaries. After 15 hours of case summary, prosecutor Pierre Dupin asked for the death sentence. Defence lawyer René Floriot made his plea to the jury, by questioning the flimsy evidence against his client. Floriot reminded the court that his client had admitted to nineteen of the 27 murders of which he was charged, but the prosecution had failed to prove that the victims were not collaborators. When Floriot ended his speech, the crowd inside the courtroom stood up and applauded him. The jury left to begin their deliberations.

Three hours later the jury returned and promptly informed the court that they had found Petiot guilty of 26 counts of murder and the sentence for the crimes was death. An appeal was lodged by René Floriot but was rejected on May 23.

Early in the morning of May 25, 1945 executioner Henri Desfourneaux and his assistants built a guillotine in the grounds of Santé prison. Shortly after 4.00am Petiot was woken in his cell and taken away for the pre-execution formalities. He was offered the traditional cigarette and a glass of rum; Petiot refused the drink but gladly smoked the cigarette. In an office near to the courtyard, Petiot had the nape of his neck shaved and his hands tied behind his back. Desfourneaux's assistants then led Petiot in to the courtyard where he saw the guillotine for the first time.

The executioner took the condemned man, tied his feet together, and then laid Petiot down on the table before tying him securely to it. Petiot looked up to the witnesses and said 'Gentleman, I ask you not to look, this will not be very pretty'. At 5.05am the blade dropped and Petiot's head fell from his shoulders

Thomas Piper

On May 23, 1875, five-year-old Mabel Young left her Sunday school lessons at Warren Avenue Baptist Church in Boston, Massachusetts and met with her aunt, Mrs Hobbs. After ten minutes of chatting with other parents, Mabel's aunt was ready to leave, but her niece was nowhere to be seen. A frantic search of the area did not locate the young girl, Mrs Hobbs began to panic.

A scream from the belfry of the church had several people rushing to the source. On the first floor of the tower a large pool of blood was found, nearby lay a blood stained cricket bat. Into the belfry and through a trap door the low moans of a small child in pain could be heard. In the corner of the room lay Mabel Young; her clothes were soaked with blood, her skull severely fractured above the left ear, such that the doctor could feel her brain. Mabel was carried down from the tower, where Doctor Cotting treated her at a nearby house. Unfortunately Mabel Young died at 8pm the next day. She never regained consciousness.

Thomas Piper, a bachelor in his twenties, a sexton at the church and known alcoholic, was quickly arrested for the murder of Mabel Young. The local community was shocked at the arrest but the police had good cause.

On December 5, 1873, less than two years before the murder of Mabel, Piper was arrested for a murderous attack on Bridget Landregan; her skull had also been fractured. Hours later a woman named Sullivan was found barely alive in a ditch with severe wounds to her head; she recovered after treatment. Lack of evidence in the case resulted in Piper being released, but the authorities resolved to keep an eye on the suspect. So upon hearing of the MO in the Mabel Young case, officers instantly thought of Piper.

The police searched Piper's room and found bloodied clothing. At the station Piper was questioned and soon broke down and confessed to Mabel's murder. Witnesses who saw Piper running from the church at the time of the murder backed up his confession. Other young girls at the Sunday school told of how Piper would make efforts to lure them to the belfry. In addition to the murder of Mabel Young, Piper confessed to the murder of three other women including Bridget Landregan and also to attacks on Ms Sullivan and the January 1874 attack on Mary Tynan, who died in a lunatic asylum after suffering brain damage caused by Piper's attack.

For the crimes Piper was executed on the gallows in 1876.

Rudolf Pliel

Rudolf Pliel's taste for death could probably be traced back to his childhood in Germany when he tortured a cat to death at the age of seven-years-old. As a teenage soldier Pliel witnessed the horrors of the Second World War, to which he claimed was his finest sexual experience. Then he started killing for his own pleasure.

In March 1946, Pliel murdered Eva Miehe with an axe, before dumping Eva's body in a nearby canal. Further murders followed until his eventual arrest in 1947 where Pliel confessed to twenty-seven murders across Germany using knives, axes and hammers.

Pliel's trial took place during November 1950 in Brunswick. Pliel was charged with the murders of nine people, which he complained was not enough. The state found Pliel guilty and handed out a life sentence. From his prison cell, Pliel continued to give clues to authorities as to where additional bodies would be found. He once offered his services to a mayor as an executioner and to prove he could do the job, Pliel directed him to a well where at the bottom one of his victims lay.

In February 1958, Pliel carried out a threat of suicide by hanging himself in his prison cell.

Jesse Pomeroy

Jesse Pomeroy was born on November 29, 1859 in South Boston, and was well known around the neighbourhood due to his physical disabilities. The boy had a milky eye, almost devoid of pigment but would later help victims identify their attacker. He also had a cleft palate and hair-lip. The boy was tormented by his peers and spent most of his earliest years alone or with his mother. However the boy was full of hatred and sexual desire even at the age of eleven and began taking smaller children into the woods where he would strip them and attack them before turning to murder.

On December 26, 1871 three-year-old Billy Paine was found hanging from the rafters in a disused farmhouse in Chelsea. The young boy survived the attack but had been severely beaten and covered in welts. His attacker was twelve-year-old Jesse Pomeroy.

On February 21, 1872 Jesse Pomeroy attacked his second victim. This time seven-year-old Tracy Hayden was coerced into joining Pomeroy in a disused farmhouse. The little boy was beaten badly around the face, he was stripped and Pomeroy beat the child severely with a stick. Tracy was found later by a passer-by. The little boy survived the attack.

Eight-year-old Robert Maier from Chelsea was asked by thirteen-year-old Jesse Pomeroy if he would like to go and see a circus. The boy agreed and followed Pomeroy to a disused outhouse. The little boy was stripped naked, tied up and whipped. Pomeroy masturbated as he beat the young boy then absconded. Robert was found and taken home. He survived the attack. Robert was Pomeroy's third victim and it was obvious the attacks were getting more brutal and sexual.

Jesse Pomeroy attacked another child on July 22, 1872. He asked seven-year-old Johnny Balch if he would like to earn some money by doing an errand for a rich man. The little boy happily accepted and followed Pomeroy to the outhouse at Powder Horn Hill, Chelsea. Once inside Pomeroy stripped the boy naked, tied him up, hanged him from a rafter and beat him until he was almost dead. The boy barely survived the attack. A $500 reward was offered, without success to find the culprit of the four attacks on small children over the past eight months.

With Jesse and his brother in tow Ruth Pomeroy moved from Chelsea to 312 Broadway South Boston on August 2, 1872. Jesse was the major suspect in the brutal attacks on the very young children in Chelsea, so his mother thought it best if they leave the area. Soon after the Pomeroy's move, the attacks began in South Boston.

Seven-year-old George Pratt was spirited away by thirteen-year-old Jesse Pomeroy in South Boston on August 17, 1872. The boy was offered 25c if he went on an errand. The boy was taken to an area near the Boston River where he was stripped of all of his clothes and beaten with the buckle end of a belt. Pomeroy kicked the young boy to the ground and gouged long strips of skin from the child's chest with his fingernails. As the boy screamed in agony, Pomeroy bit into little George's cheek, taking a large bite from it. He then stabbed the boy in the chest and genitals with a large sewing needle before biting the child's face again.

Somehow George survived the attack and was found a few hours later, in severe shock and bleeding profusely.

On September 5, 1872 six-year-old Harry Austin was lured to a rail bridge in South Boston by Pomeroy, where he was stripped, and severely beaten. Pomeroy stabbed the boy in both of his armpits and between the child's shoulder blades.

He then took his knife and attempted to cut off the little boy's penis. He failed in his bid, but left the boy with permanent injuries.

Only a week after the previous attack, Pomeroy attacked seven-year-old Joseph Kennedy on a vacant houseboat in South Boston Bay on September 11, 1872. He bashed the child's head against a wall before stripping the young child and beating him, breaking the child's nose, and bashing several teeth from the boy's mouth. Pomeroy also used his knife on the little boy. Joseph was cut on his face, his legs and his back. As a final injury, Pomeroy splashed salt water all over the boy's wounds. Joseph survived the attack.

Five-year-old Robert Gould was the next victim of Pomeroy's on September 17, 1872. The boy was tied to a telegraph pole and stripped. Pomeroy attempted to scalp the young boy but was disturbed by near by railway worker who come to the boy's rescue. Pomeroy escaped.

Thirteen-year-old Jesse Pomeroy was positively identified by many of his victims due to his milky eye and was charged with the attacks of nine young children and sentenced to six years at House of Reformation at Westborough on September 21, 1872.

In less than two years Jesse Pomeroy was released into his mother's care on February 6, 1874.

On March 18, 1874 ten-year-old Katie Curran went to the local store run by the Pomeroy's to buy a new notebook. She was served by fifteen-year-old Jesse Pomeroy and was never seen alive again.

A handyman found her body in the basement of the store four months later on July 18. The body had been partially burned.

After going to church on April 22, 1874 four-year-old Horace Millen remained in his church clothes when he went to buy some bread for his mother at a local bakery. On the way he encountered Pomeroy. The boy was taken to Savin Hill Beach where he was stabbed eighteen times in the chest. The little boy's throat was cut so deeply his head was almost severed from his body. His eyes were gouged out and his testicles partially removed. The young boy had put up a good struggle and his hands had been cut to pieces in the attack. However he could not survive the injuries inflicted upon his tiny body.

Two brothers found the mutilated body later that same afternoon.

On April 23, 1874, the day after the brutal murder of four-year-old Horace Millen, Jesse Pomeroy was arrested for his murder. The police tried to get a confession out of the fifteen-year-old but he refused to talk. So after several hours of unsuccessful questioning, the police took Pomeroy to see the body of Horace lying in the funeral home. The fifteen-year-old was shaken enough to confess to the boy's murder.

Five days after confessing to the murder of Horace Millen, Jesse Pomeroy was found guilty of murder at a Boston Coroner's Court on April 28, 1874.

While Pomeroy was in custody the burnt and mutilated body of ten-year-old Katie Curran was uncovered in the basement of the store on Broadway, Boston on July 18, 1874. She had been stabbed and had her chest and vagina cut open.

When confronted with the discovery Pomeroy confessed to the murder of Katie. Jesse Pomeroy was found guilty of the murder of Katie Curran in a Boston Coroner's court on July 30, 1874 and sent to trial in December.

The trial of fifteen-year-old Pomeroy for the murders of ten-year-old Katie Curran and four-year-old Horace Millen opened on December 10, 1874. It lasted a little over two months and resulted in Pomeroy being sentenced to death for the murders

The sentence was later commuted to life.

After fifty-three years in Sing Sing, Jesse Pomeroy was moved on August 1, 1929 to a prison farm, a halfway place to his release before being set free on September 29, 1932 he was 72 years of age.

Jesse Pomeroy died on October 2, 1932, just short of his 73rd birthday.

Madame Popova

In March 1909, Russian police arrested a woman named Madame Popova for a suspected poison attack. However her confession surprised everyone. Madame Popova gave details of the poison murders of over 300 husbands over 30 years. She claimed that unhappy wives would contact her about their unwanted husbands, whom she would eliminate via the use of poison for a small fee, but in many cases it would be done for nothing.

Her arrest came after one client felt remorse for her husband after his death.

For her crimes Madama Popova was executed by firing squad.

Dorothea Puente

It started with rumours of bodies buried in a Sacramento garden and a missing person, Alvaro 'Bert' Montoya. The persistence of the rumours from those who knew the potential suspect and the insistence of a check by Sacramento social workers into the house at 1426 F Street, led to Detective John Cabrera and Federal Parole Agent Jim Wilson visiting the home of Dorothea Puente on November 11, 1988.

At the time, Jim Wilson was investigating Puente for parole violation. The terms of her release of parole included a ban on renting out the rooms of her property, yet there she was operating a boarding house. Detective questioned Puente about Bert and his present location, Her reply suggested that he was 'away'. After a brief search of the house, the group went back outside and into the garden, where Detective Cabrera asked Puente for permission to dig a few holes into the earth. Puente never hesitated in agreeing.

Cabrera and Wilson began to dig random holes into the garden using their shovels, each over a foot below the surface, but nothing was found. After an hour of fruitless searching, the officers were close to calling it all off when Jim Wilson made a discovery. Buried eighteen inches below the surface, he unearthed some clothing. He signalled Cabrera over as he used the shovel's blade to open the clothing revealing a human thighbone.

Detective John Cabrera again asked Puente about Bert's whereabouts, to which she replied 'He's alive'.

With the discovery in her garden, Puente was taken away for questioning, after which the officers felt they had insufficient evidence for any charges to be bought against their suspect and so Puente was taken back home. By the time they arrived, television cameras surrounded the house.

At 8am the following day, November 12, the authorities continued with their search of Puente's garden. Puente watched from the house as the crowd of reporters and onlookers continued to grow. Forensic pathologists studied the bones that emerged from the ground and announced that the body was not that of a male, but that of a female and had been buried since April of that year. Carbrera was stunned, the dig had originally taken place in the hope of finding Bert Montoya, but here was an unknown female.

Another section of the garden was next on the list for excavation. Only forty-five days earlier a layer of concrete had been poured over a small area and it raised suspicion. Detective Cabrera believed the area might yield some further secrets. Two feet down lay a second body, which investigators initially believed was male. A third body was found at 2.30pm, buried under a recently planted sapling. Then a fourth, under an aluminium shed. However, the number one suspect was no longer around. Just prior to the second body being uncovered, Puente had asked permission to visit her nephew at the nearby Clarion Hotel, the request was granted, because she was not under arrest at the time. But Puente had not been seen since she left. Mervin McCauley, Puente's closest friend at the house, was arrested for accessory to murder, but in truth the authorities were still unsure as to what was happening.

The four bodies recovered were sent away for autopsy. Meanwhile a fifth body was found late on November 13, three feet under the earth. Early the next morning a sixth, then in the afternoon a seventh body were unearthed, which would be the last found in Puente's garden.

Dorothea Helen Gray was born on January 9, 1929 in Redlands, San Bernardino County, California, the sixth of seven children born to parents Jesse Gray and Trudy Mae Yates. Puente's life suddenly changed when on March 29, 1937, her father suddenly died leaving Trudy to raise the family. Unfortunately Trudy died the following year in a motorcycle accident on December 27. The children moved to Fresno, California to be raised by an uncle and aunt.

Puente married four times throughout her life. She also discovered a way to beat the welfare system. She set up a boarding home, taking in tenants who lived off welfare. Social workers were happy for her to help with their clients, unaware that she was stealing money from them. In 1978, Puente was arrested and charged with thirty-four counts of forgery against her tenants, for which Puente received five years probation. A psychiatric evaluation of Puente was performed by Thomas Doody MD, his report stating that Puente was a chronic schizophrenic.

At the end of her probational period, Puente returned to her previous business as a carer of the elderly. Esther Bussby used Puente's abilities as a full time carer for herself. However her frequent visits to the hospital were arousing suspicion. At home Esther fell into a coma-like state causing her to be admitted into hospital, her stay was short as she quickly recovered from the unknown illness. But once home, the symptoms returned. An investigation into the circumstances of her illness uncovered one interesting fact. Her carer, Puente was accused, but not charged, with attempted poisoning of previous husbands. Esther was moved into a nursing home, where she made a full recovery, until a visit by Puente. Blood tests were taken and high levels of a sedative and relaxant called Digoxin were recorded. Esther immediately sacked Puente. She later found that Puente had been telling Esther's friends that she had been suffering from cancer and taking donations, which were pocketed. County social worker Mildred Ballenger investigated the case and uncovered four further cases where clients of Puente had suffered unexplained illnesses. In addition, several personal items were mysteriously vanishing from their property.

In September 1981, after an attempted overdose of barbiturates, Puente was evaluated again by psychiatrist Dr Doody. He once again reported on Puente's mental health, stating that she had 'multiple physical problems'.

In January 1982, Puente was again arrested for forgery and grand theft. She was cashing benefit checks for tenants who no longer resided at her boarding house. She was granted bail. Three months later Puente was arrested again for grand theft and again it involved forged benefit checks. In May 1982, Puente visited the Zebra Club Bar in Sacramento and met seventy-four-year-old Malcome McKenzie. After a couple of drinks, the pair left to go to his apartment. A few minutes after arriving, Malcome could no longer feel his limbs, a few moments more and he fell to the floor paralysed. Puente calmly got up from her seat and went from room to room, collecting Malcome's valuables into a suitcase. Before leaving Puente, removed a ring from Malcome's finger.

A few hours later the paralysing drug wore off and Malcome reported the theft to police. Puente was arrested on May 18. In her possession were many of Malcome's valuables, 2 stolen credit cards and a plane ticket to Mexico.

At the trial in August 1982, Puente pleaded guilty to 3 felony charges. Despite her personal pleas to Judge Warren for consideration to her family's welfare, Puente was found guilty on August 18 and received a total of 4 years and 4 months. There would be no probation and her sentence was to be completed at the California Institute for Women in Frontera. On September 9, 1985, she left the facility having lost a significant amount of weight and suffering 2 strokes.

The first thing she planned to do upon her release was to return to the boarding house routine. She moved in to the house at 1426 F Street, but decided not to license it as a boarding house, thereby side stepping her parole rulings.

A tenant of Puente's was fifty-five-year-old Benjamin Fink. Ben, an alcoholic since his teens, would regularly get angry over simple things. In January 1988, in a fit of anger, Ben broke the windows in his room throwing furniture around. Puente calmly walked into his room and, using her kindly voice, persuaded

Ben to calm down and to accompany him to Puente's room where everything would be better. Ben went with Puente and would cause no more trouble in the house.

The other tenants questioned Puente about Ben's disappearance. She explained that Ben had left the house to go travelling. Other tenants complained of the 'death' smell in the house and Puente pointed out the state of the drains. John Sharp, however, did recognise the smell as he used to work in a mortuary. Ben did make a final appearance at the house; he was the fourth body exhumed from the garden.

Alvaro José Rafael Gonzáles Montoya, known as Bert was born in Guadalupe, Costa Rica on September 8, 1936 and moved with his mother, sister, niece and nephew to New Orleans in 1962 to escape his abusive father. In 1968, Bert suffered what doctors described as a 'psychotic break'and became severely paranoid, suffered visual and aural hallucinations and withdrew completely into himself. Against his will, Bert was taken to a psychiatric hospital without any successful treatment.

Upon his release, Bert hit the road as a drifter, stopping in Sacramento in 1981. Social workers took Bert on board in 1988, giving him a place to stay at the Detox Centre at 2700 Front Street in Sacramento. Bert's social workers were successful in arranging benefits for him and also found him somewhere more suitable to live. Puente was more than happy to take Bert in at her boarding home. She also helped him with his mental problems, Puente fraudulently claimed she was a registered nurse. He moved in on February 3, 1988.

Bert's happiness in his new home was short lived. On August 10, he returned to the Detox Centre saying he did not want to go back. Bill Johnson, a staff member at the centre, persuaded Bert to return to the house with him to discuss the situation with Puente. Bert told Bill how Puente would force him to take his medication, but once in Puente's presence, Bert's changed his story. Bill Johnson admitted later, after the case broke, that he failed to spot that Puente intimidated Bert.

After the meeting, Bert agreed to stay at the house. The meeting took place on August 11, 1988, the last time Bert was seen alive.

During the autumn, Sacramento social worker Judy Moise had continual difficulty in trying to reach Bert Montoya at the house. Puente's response to Judy's questions was that Bert was out, or was not available, then that Bert was away visiting Puente's relatives in Mexico. Given that Bert wasn't really capable of caring for himself nor did he easily fit into social gatherings, Judy Moise was suspicious of Puente. She insisted that Bert be back in the house as soon as possible. In November Judy threatened Puente with the filing of a missing person's report if he had not returned by November 7, a Monday. Early on that Monday morning, Judy Moise was preparing to visit the house to see Bert, when the phone rang. A man calling himself Michael Obergone told Judy that he was Bert's brother-in-law and that he had just visited him at Puente's house, the pair were now off to Utah on a business trip, despite Puente suggesting that they don't.

Before Judy could question the man further, the phone call ended. A pager message was also left for Judy giving the same story. Judy immediately called Puente demanding to know where Bert was. Puente relayed the same story that Michael Obergone had just given. Angry and very concerned for her client's welfare, the social worker filed a missing persons report.

Officer Richard Ewing responded to the report, visited the house at 1426 F Street and met with Puente. She gave him a tour of the house, to which Officer Ewing believed there was nothing amiss. However upon meeting one of the tenants, John Sharp, he was secretly passed a slip of paper without Puente noticing. Once alone Officer Ewing read the note that had written on it 'She's making me lie'. After ending the meeting Officer Ewing and John Sharp met up again allowing the tenant to speak freely. John told of Ben Fink's disappearance, late night digging in the garden and how Puente insisted that he confirmed the story of Bert's trip.

Officer Ewing made a written report about the visit to the boarding house and the meeting with John Sharp to Detective John Cabrera, who was in charge of missing persons. On November 8, Cabrera received a phone call from Judy Moise demanding to know what he was going to do about the Bert Montoya case. While he agreed that the case warranted further investigation, he felt he had other priorities to attend to. Judy Moise was not happy about this and proceeded to do some further investigating herself. Meanwhile John Sharp had quit the boarding house and entered the homeless shelter at Bannon Street

Judy Moise and Beth Valentine were called to the homeless shelter to speak to John Sharp. He told them the same story he had told Officer Ewing. Judy seemed to be in no doubt that Bert had somehow been murdered by Puente. On November 9, Judy again called Detective Cabrera, but he was not available. A check at the social security office found that Puente was receiving at least 10 social security checks at her house each month. Judy believed that Puente was cashing in the checks for herself. On Thursday November 10, Judy Moise and John Cabrera spoke again. Cabrera agreed that she should visit the station the following day and go through all her findings and suspicions with not only himself but also his senior, Detective Terry Brown along with Federal Parole Officer Jim Wilson. The meeting ended with the decision to dig in Puente's garden.

With Puente missing from the excavation scene, a warrant was issued for her arrest on murder charges. Puente was hiding in Los Angeles.

In the Monte Carlo I bar on Third Street, Los Angeles, Charles 'Chuck' Willgues, a retired carpenter, sat alone with his drink. At the far end of the bar sat an elderly lady, also sitting on her own. Charles decided that the woman did not belong in this bar on her own and so beckoned her over for some company. The pair sat down and chatted and enjoyed a drink together. Charles later recalled that somehow the conversation turned to money, more specifically what his income was. Charles was on disability payments to which his female companion politely informed him that he was able to receive over $100 a month more than he was currently receiving. The pair made a date for the next day to talk more. She then suggested that Charles phone her at her motel, the Royal Viking, at 8.30 that evening.

Charles went back to his nearby apartment, excited about his late night date, but something in the back of his mind was annoying him, something was vaguely familiar about this woman. As he sat watching the early evening news the answer came to him. He watched a report on the discovery of seven bodies in a garden in Sacramento, his date looked similar to the woman on his television screen. Charles telephoned Gene Silver, assignment editor for Channel 2 news. Immediately upon hearing Charles's story, Gene headed to meet with him at his house. The two men discussed the events of the afternoon, 8.30 rolled by and Charles made the phone call as promised. Gene pulled out a photograph of Puente to which Charles confirmed that she was his date, Gene called the police.

Shortly after 11pm, Puente heard a knock at the door of her room and got up to open it, there stood Police Sergeant Paul Von Lutlow. When asked for identification, Puente handed over a driver's license bearing the name Dorothy Johanson, the surname of a previous husband. Puente was arrested and taken to nearby Ramparts police station. In her purse she as carrying $3042. Before the night was out, Puente was flown back to Sacramento and charged with the murder of Alvaro 'Bert' Montoya.

The autopsy of the third body had taken place on November 15, 1988 by Dr Gary A Stuart. Fingerprint examination had determined that the body was that of Bert Montoya. Fingerprint analysis also identified the bodies of Dorothy Miller, 65, Leona Carpenter, 80 and Benjamin Fink. Medical x-ray comparison confirmed the remaining bodies of Vera Faye Martin, 65, James Gallop, 64 and 80-year-old Betty Palmer, whose head, feet and hands were missing. No physical cause of death could be found in any of the victims.

However a drug named Flurazepam was found in all seven cases. In overdose, the drug can cause breathing difficulties and coma.

On March 29, 1989, authorities added an additional two murder charges against Puente, those of Everson Gillmouth and Ruth Monroe.

Sixty-one-year-old Ruth Munroe met Puente in late 1981, the pair decided to try a new adventure together by leasing a restaurant. The plan was for Puente to run the kitchen while Ruth handled the stock and other items. But Puente had other ideas. On several occasions she complained to Ruth that they needed more money to keep the business open. Ruth obliged by putting thousands of dollars in thinking that Puente was doing the same. On April 11, 1982, with Ruth's husband terminally ill in hospital, Puente suggested she move into her boarding house and be with friends. Two weeks later on April 28, Ruth suddenly died. The autopsy report revealed an overdose of codeine and acetaminophen. Her death was reported as suicide. Ruth's family later found that some of Ruth's belongings had vanished and her bank accounts were drained of money. Puente denied any involvement.

On January 1, 1986, local fisherman Roy Beals was on the bank of the Sacramento River in Sutter County, when he found a coffin-like box. Obeying his curiosity, Roy opened the box to find the decaying figure of a human body, wrapped in plastic. Sickened by the sight of what he saw, Roy raced to the nearby store and told owners Marge and Marvin Horstman of his discovery. They called the Sheriff's department. Sergeant Wilbur Terry was placed in charge.

The body was taken to Ullrey's Memorial Chapel for autopsy, which was performed by Dr Frederick Hanf. The bloated body was that of a male partially wrapped in blankets and plastic, it was that of a male wearing only a t-shirt and shorts. But he could not be identified, nor could Dr Hanf find a cause of death.

Almost three years later Lieutenant Wilbur Terry heard of the discovery of bodies buried in the garden in Sacramento and thought of his unsolved mystery. The bodies in the garden had been wrapped in plastic like the body he had investigated. He contacted Sacramento police asking for details of missing persons. One name came out, Everson Gillmouth, matching the general description of the body found on the riverbank.

An investigation began into Everson's death. Detectives were looking for a link back to Puente; the wrapping of the body in plastic seemed too much of a coincidence to ignore. A link presented itself with the discovery that Everson's truck had been sold eighteen months after his body was found. The new owner of the truck was a man named Ismael Florez. Detectives questioned Ismael on December 9, 1989, he admitted knowing Puente but not Emerson. By the end of the interview Ismael admitted that Puente had asked him to build a large box, but he didn't know what it was for. Detectives believed that the box was meant for Emerson and they had their link.

Puente's next appearance was in court on April 25, 1990 for the preliminary hearing to determine if the case would go to trial. The hearing ended on June 19, 1990 with Judge Gail Ohanesian giving her verdict that there was ample evidence in all nine cases that allowed Puente to go to trial for 9 counts of murder. The defence team however were disappointed. In their opinion the prosecution had no evidence to link their client to any of the deaths of which she was accused.

At the trial, that began on February 9, 1993 in Silas, Monterey County under Judge Michael J Virga, the defence showed that in each of the nine cases, the 'victims' had not died at Puente's hands, but of natural causes. The defence suggested that Bert Montoya suffered a fatal diabetic induced coma. They had medical records proving abnormal blood sugar levels taken shortly before his disappearance. Benjamin Fink had died because of his alcoholism. Leona Carpenter was in and out of hospitals with chronic illness for many years. Vera Faye Martin suffered severe heart problems as had James Gallop, however he also suffered with an inoperable brain tumour. The defence team would also present medical records in which a doctor had written that James Gallop did not have 'long to go'. They couldn't argue however that in seven cases higher than normal levels of Dalmane or Flurazepam were found during the autopsies. John O'Mara, for the prosecution, would add that Puente had seemingly endless access to these drugs.

On April 27, 1993, previously suspected accomplice Mervin McCauley took to the stand. He admitted digging a hole in the garden after a request from Puente. She claimed it was to plant a bush. The hole was positioned in front of a religious shrine, in the exact spot where authorities would recover the body of Betty Palmer. McCauley denied any involvement in burying Betty. He denied any involvement in killing anyone.

Later in the trial, the case moved to the death of Everson Gillmouth. Dr Frederick Hanf went through his autopsy findings stating that no cause of death could be found. The defence made him admit that the death could have been from natural causes. Ismael Florez took the stand and admitted, as he did when questioned by police at the time, that he built the coffin sized box for Puente and that was all he did. Eventually on June 7, 1993, the prosecution case rested. The defence case was much shorter, lasting less than 3 weeks. Defence lawyers Clymo and Vlatin presented witnesses that gave testimony on Puente's good character; others gave testimony on the victims' medical – and in some cases mental – problems. On June 24, the defence rested and closing arguments began.

Prosecutor John O'Mara briefly went through his case identifying the links between the disappearance of each of the nine victims and the increase in money in Puente's grasp. This money gained through the forgery of their social security checks. He identified the state of Betty Palmer's body, found without her head, hands or feet, hardly natural causes. The suspicious nature of holes dug in Puente's garden for seemingly no reason. All of these points, John O'Mara argued, identified Puente as the cause in the deaths of nine innocent people and should be punished.

Kevin Clymo presented closing arguments for the defence. His main point to the jury was simple; had the prosecution, beyond reasonable doubt, proven that Dorothea Puente had murdered these people? He stated that the prosecution had failed to identify not only how these nine people died, but also who was responsible. Kevin Clymo offered that the prosecution's case was based entirely on circumstance and no hard evidence against his client. John O'Mara returned to give his final points. He reminded the jury of the last person to be seen with 'Bert' Montoya – Puente, the last person seen with Ben Fink – Puente. Vera Faye Martin was not seen again after moving into Puente's boarding house and Ruth Monroe died 2 weeks after moving in with Puente.

On July 15, 1993, it was time for the jury to begin deliberations. After 2 weeks the first indications of a decision came from the jury. They were in deadlock on all nine counts. Judge Michael Virga gave them instructions to continue their deliberations. On August 26, 1993, the jury announced a verdict in three of the nine charges, in the remaining six they were still deadlocked. Judge Virga declared a mistrial in the cases of Ruth Monroe; Everson Gillmouth; Bert Montoya; James Gallop; Vera Faye Martin and Betty Palmer. However the verdicts in the remaining three cases would stand.

The clerk of the court read out the verdicts
In the case of Leona Carpenter – guilty of second degree murder
In the case of Dorothy Miller – guilty of first degree murder
In the case of Benjamin Fink – guilty of first degree murder

Despite the guilty verdicts in three of the cases, John O'Mara was not happy. He privately questioned, as did the relatives of the deceased, how the jury could only find Puente guilty in some of the cases and not the rest. Judy Moise was devastated. It was the case of Alvaro Montoya that led everyone to Puente and the discovery of the bodies, yet the jury failed to find her guilty in that case.

The next step was to determine Puente's punishment. The penalty phase began on September 21, 1993; a sentence of death was an option for the jury. A procession of relatives and close friends of Puente took the stand and told the jury of a wonderful and compassionate woman. Psychiatrist Dr William Vicary gave his opinion. Puente was not insane but was in full control of her actions; she knew what she was doing. The defence pleaded for mercy, but the prosecutor was not looking for leniency. He demanded that the punishment fit the crime. Puente had murdered these people. He argued that Puente's punishment should also be death.

On October 13, 1993, the jury announced that they were unable to reach a verdict as they were deadlocked again. Because of this the judge announced that Puente would automatically receive a life sentence without parole to be served in Monterey Prison.

Q

Thomas Quick

Following his arrest in 1996, Thomas Quick quickly became Sweden's worst serial killer after confessing to fifteen murders across Scandinavia, claiming his first murder was when he was fourteen.

On May 28, 1997, Quick was found guilty of the 1988 murder of Yinon Levy, an Israeli tourist visiting Sweden.

Nine-year-old Theresa Johanssen disappeared from Drammen, Norway in July 1988.

In November 1997, Quick returned to the area to lead Norwegian police to her gravesite where several bone fragments were recovered. For Theresa's murder, Quick received a guilty verdict on June 2, 1988 and was to serve his time in the high security Säters Sjukhus Psychiatric Hospital.

Further murder charges followed including the 1981 murder of Trine Jensen and the 1985 murder of Gry Storvik. Quick also confessed to the murder of eighteen-year-old Olov Hogbom, who disappeared from Sundsvall, Sweden on September 7, 1983, and eleven-year-old Johan Asplund, also from Sundsvall, who vanished on November 7, 1980. Quick was convicted of Johan's murder in June 2002

R

Gilles De Rais

> *"He is nobody in the world which knows or which can understand all that I made in my life. He is nobody in the planet which can thus make"* Gilles de Rais

Gilles De Rais was born in 1406 in the "Black Tower" at Champtoce.

De Rais was 11 when his uncle, Armaury d'Craon was killed in battle at Agincourt. The death meant that De Rais' mother Marie d'Craon, who had married Guy de Rais, was the sole heir to the vast wealth of Jeanne La Sage. The marriage between d'Craon and De Rais was a political marriage culminating in the combined fortunes of three of France's wealthiest families.

Guy de Rais had changed his name from Laval to de Rais to ensure he inherited the wealth from Jeanne la Sage - the last of the de Rais family. However before la Sage died she decided to change her will and instead gave the money to Catherine de Machecoul, Marie's paternal grandmother.

Marie's father Jean d'Craon saw that problems may occur and as a promise of good faith offered Marie's hand in marriage to Guy De Rais.

Nine months after the marriage Gilles was born followed two years later by another boy Rene.

The life of the De Rais boys was quite cold and distant. The privilege class preferred to treat their sons as adults from a very young age. They were raised mainly by nurses and teachers and rarely saw their parents.

The first time he properly saw his parents was at the age of seven when he was introduced into French society.

From the age of seven Gilles was tutored in the classic arts, humanities and Greek and Latin. He was also taught warfare and the ways of high-society court. Though he was a willing student, De Rais never got used to courtly behaviour and grew up rough and only semi-skilled.

In 1415, after the feast of Epiphany, Gilles mother Marie died. The death was devastating to the young boy and within three years Gilles father also died while boar hunting. A boar turned on the man and gored him. It took Guy some time to die and the man used the time to draw up a will on how his soon-to-be orphaned sons should be raised and by whom.

The children were sent to a cousin, Jean Tournemine de la Junaudaye. Guy made it known that he did not want his father-in-law, Jean d'Craon to have anything to do with the boys after he died. The reasons for this were because De Rais gave up his family name of La Sage for the sake of the de Rais fortune only to have it snatched away by d'Craon.

However d'Craon was not going to give up that easily and contested Guy De Rais' will in mid 1416 ending with the two boys being handed over to their maternal grandfather, against the dying wishes of their father.

While being raised by their parents the two de Rais boys were kept busy being educated and tutored in the arts, but once handed over to their grandfather they were left to run free around the castle Champtoce.
Jean d'Craon was by now the second richest man in France and spared nothing when attempting to gain further wealth. He was described by many as a ruthless and cunning man.

The only attempt at education Jean tried was warfare. He taught the boys what he could and by the age of 14, Gilles began his first campaign as a squire. He would practice his new skills of sword fighting, jousting and hand-to-hand armed combat for hours. But he yearned the real battles he had heard so much about.

Jean encouraged the young man's ambition, telling him that by fighting in war, Gilles may be able to expand his own wealth and land holdings.

Continuing to scheme, Jean arranged the marriage of Gilles to Jeanne Paynel, the daughter of the wealthy and powerful Lord de Hamye of Normandy. The marriage would make the d'Craons the most powerful family in France if not Western Europe. The French Parliament knew what the marriage would mean and forbade the marriage until Jeanne was 18.

The decision angered D'Craon and less than a year later he announced the betrothal ceremony of Gilles to Beatrice de Rohan, the niece of the Duke of Burgundy. The marriage however never eventuated.

Instead, Gilles De Rais married Catherine de Thonars on the November 30, 1420, and became one of the richest noblemen in Europe. He lived extravagantly until his arrest by the Church.

On May 8, 1429, Joan of Arc and her captains, Gilles among them, fought the siege of Orléans. On July 17, the Dauphin was crowned King Charles VII, and one of his first acts was to name Gilles De Rais a Marshal of France. At the same time, Gilles formally allied himself with his cousin Georges de La Trémoille, a favourite of the new King.

Gilles' wealth and powers were immense but the man was unable to deal with all that society had given him as Joan of Arc's chief of the militia. Gilles spent money as fast as he earned it bringing his wealthy family to the edge of bankruptcy many times.

Towards the beginning of 1432, Gilles De Rais withdrew from public life and spent his time studying science and the theories of alchemy (the notion of being able to turn base things into gold) after the war had finished. Yet the man was restless. He enjoyed the sport of war and the smell of blood and wanted more.

So he ventured out and murdered children, often sodomising the corpses as he went. He would also have servants murder victims as he watched on, re-enacting battle scenes De Rais had seen during the war. At other times he would wine and dine his victims before slaughtering them.

On July 30, 1440, Jean de Malestroit, Bishop of Nantes and Chancellor of Brittany, issued the first document in the proceedings against Gilles de Rais. Based on public innuendo only, it accused Gilles of murdering children and performing sodomy and other unnatural acts with them. He was also accused of evoking, sacrificing to, and entering into compacts with demons.

At his trial, Gilles was given a list of his crimes. According to the list, during a total of fourteen years, he had seized at least 140 children, committed sodomy, murdered and dismembered them. He was also charged with conspiring with others in worshipping demons and studying the dark arts.

Gilles confessed to having once borrowed and read a book on alchemy and demon summoning and having practiced alchemy. Everything else he denied.
There were many accusations based on hearsay and innuendo. Many historians have the number of kills by Gilles as high as 140-170 but these are highly sensationalistic

The less than accurate charges included the children who disappeared during 1438. Three children disappeared in January, two in June, one in September, one in October, and one in November, for a total of eight. In 1439, seventeen disappearances are reported--two in January, one in February, three in April, two in May, one in June, three in August, three in October, and two in December. For 1440, the year of Gilles' trial, one child was stated to have disappeared in February, two in March, three in April, and one in July. The children's ages range greatly however the median was 10.

After being interrogated for several weeks by the judge in one of his torture chambers Gilles "confessed", and was put to the stake and burned on October 26, 1440.

Richard Ramirez

During the summers of 1984 and 1985, Los Angeles suffered one of the longest heat waves to hit the city. Residents left their windows open hoping for a cooling breeze, however during this period, Los Angeles also was in the grip of a killer who used the open windows to gain access to unsuspecting victims whom he would rob, rape and murder.

On June 27, 1984, Jennie Vincow, a seventy-nine-year-old mother of two, was sound asleep in her bed unaware that prowling around her apartment in Glassel Park, was an unwanted guest. Having prised his way through a window, Richard Ramirez, high on cocaine, was making his way silently through her belongings but found nothing of value.

Becoming angry and frustrated at his lack of success, Ramirez removed his 6-inch hunting knife from its sheath, raised the blade high in the air and plunged it deep into Jennie's chest. Despite Jennie screaming for help the stabbing continued. Gathering her strength Jennie attempted to escape but her attacker's strong grip over her mouth kept her down on the bed. Lifting her chin Ramirez stabbed Jennie in her throat following with a slash so deep it nearly removed her head. Although Jennie was now dead, Ramirez continued with three further deep stabs to her chest. Finally sated, the attacker picked up a radio and quickly but calmly walked out the front door and made his getaway in a stolen car, his clothes covered with blood.

At 1.20 pm the next afternoon, Jack Vincow, Jennie's son, came by the apartment to visit, as he did on most days. Jack noticed immediately that the window screen was missing and the front door unlocked which was very unusual. Entering the house, Jack found the apartment ransacked and blood smeared on the walls. Finally, he entered the bedroom and found the bloody body of his mother. Jack ran to the block manager's office and dialled 911.

At the autopsy the next day, Dr Joseph Cogan noted that in addition to the wounds to Jennie's neck and chest, there would be a number of defensive wounds to her hands and arms and a deep stab wound to her inner left thigh.

Ramirez was quiet for the next nine months until he spotted his next victim. The date was March 17, 1985 and Maria Hernandez was driving home on the freeway when the killer spotted her and decided to follow her. Maria made her way into Rosemead, eventually parking her car in her garage. Getting out of the car, Maria pressed the button to automatically close the outer door. Ramirez, dressed all in black, an AC/DC cap on his head and his newly purchased .22 gun in his hand, stopped his car, got out and walked directly towards Maria. Bending down, he entered through the closing garage door, his cap falling off. The killer pointed the gun directly at Maria's head, startling her.

The garage door finished closing, plunging the area into darkness. Maria raised her hand in defence, as Ramirez fired the gun. By some miracle the bullet was deflected by the keys held in Maria's hand. Instinctively she fell to the ground and played dead. Her attacker left her and moved on into the house, assuming he had claimed the life of his victim.

Entering the kitchen, Ramirez spotted Dayle Okazaki duck behind a counter and waited patiently until she looked up from her position of safety. Dayle crouched behind the counter in the belief that the intruder with the gun had not seen her. After what seemed an eternity, Dayle got to her feet hoping the man had gone. Standing up Dayle fell back to the floor dead with a bullet to the forehead. Ramirez left the house the same way he went in. He was surprised by the sight of Maria still alive and attempting to escape from the garage.

Again Ramirez raised the gun and pointed it at Maria, but changed his mind and instead headed back to the stolen Toyota he was driving and escaped the scene, leaving his cap behind.

Shortly after leaving Maria alive, he spotted "Veronica" Tsai Lian Yu and decided to follow her into Monterey Park, however Veronica spotted the suspicious Toyota tailing her and pulled over. Ramirez drove on. Veronica decided to stalk the stalker and followed the car. With both cars forced to stop at a red light in North Alhambra Avenue Ramirez got out of 'his' car and headed towards Veronica's. An argument sprung up between the two strangers, which resulted in the angry killer getting into Veronica's car via the unlocked passenger door. "What do you want?" questioned Veronica; the reply came in the form of a bullet in her side. Opening the door to escape, she was shot again, this time in the back. Laughing, Ramirez got back into the Toyota and drove off towards the freeway.

Jorge Gallegos, a witness to the attack raced over to find Veronica alive but her breathing very shallow. A second witness, Joseph Duenas, also raced to the scene having first dialled 911. Officer Ron Endo from Monterey police was the first on the scene and was soon joined by officer Gorajewski who kept back the gathering crowd. Ron Endo attempted to get a statement from the injured woman, when she suddenly stopped breathing. The two officers administered CPR as they waited for the medical team to arrive. Once on the scene they decided to immediately take Veronica back to the Monterey Park hospital, where Dr Richard Tenn pronounced her dead after checking her vital signs.

Maria Hernandez was in Beverley Hospital after her close call with Ramirez when Deputy Gilbert 'Gil' Carrillo visited her from Los Angeles Sheriff's Homicide Department. Gil was a friend of the family. Asking Maria about the gunman, she described him as 5'10", thin with black hair and dark, really scary eyes. Maria also offered to work with a sketch artist. Later in the week autopsies were completed on both Veronica Yu and Dayle Okazaki. Ballistics reports would indicate that it was "more than likely" that the bullets came from the same gun, but because of the poor condition of the bullet taken from Dayle, it could not be absolutely identified.

In late March 1985, a police report came into Gil Carrillo's hands of a man in black who had followed two young girls, and attempted to get them into his car. A check of the car's number plate, which the girls had noted, indicated that the owner of the car was a man named Paul Samuels. A surveillance team was put in place to monitor Samuels' activities. However they found it difficult to get some quality photos of the suspect, as Samuels became aware of being followed. Eventually the surveillance team managed to secure some photos and showed them to Maria Hernandez, who tentatively identified Samuels as her attacker. Samuels was arrested on April 2 and a search of his house uncovered, amongst other things, a .38 revolver. Samuels was put in a line up and viewed by witnesses to the crimes. None could positively Samuels as the shooter so he was released.

Whilst the police were using their resources investigating Paul Samuels, another fatal attack took place. Vincent and Maxine Zazzara were sound asleep in their single level house in Strong Avenue. At 2.00 am on the morning of March 27, Ramirez was in the yard searching patiently for a way into the residence. Eventually he managed to remove a screen and open a window. Taking off his shoes, Ramirez silently walked through into the lounge where he found Vincent asleep on the couch. Drawing the .22 weapon from his waistband, the killer neared Vincent and placed the barrel of the gun an inch from the left hand side of the sleeping man's head, just above the ear, and pulled the trigger. Vincent leapt to his feet trying to grab the intruder, but the bullet had done its damage to his brain and Vincent soon collapsed to the floor dying.

Maxine Zazzara, sleeping in the bedroom, was awoken by the gunshot as her husband's killer rushed into the room demanding to know where the money and jewellery were. Ramirez grabbed Maxine forcing her onto her stomach and tied her hands together with a necktie, taken from a nearby closet, and also gagged her. Ramirez then left Maxine on the bed and began to ransack the bedroom searching for valuables. Struggling against her bonds, Maxine managed to free her hands and reached for a gun kept under the bed. Ramirez, hearing a noise behind him spun around to find a shotgun pointed directly at him. The stand off was short as the intruder grabbed for the gun held in his waistband. Maxine, with the shotgun trained on Ramirez, pulled the trigger.

Nothing happened, the barrels were empty; Vincent had removed the bullets because young children had visited the previous weekend.

In an instant three shots fired out and Maxine was hit three times, dying instantly. Angry with Maxine, Ramirez punched and kicked the body, then ran to the kitchen and returned with a 10-inch knife. Plunging it deep into Maxine's chest, the killer attempted to cut out her heart, but failed to get through the ribcage. Angry at the failure, Ramirez opted for the eyes instead. Using a knife he cut off the eyelids and removed both eyeballs, which he then placed in a jewellery box. Returning to the body, he continued his attack, Ramirez stabbed Maxine repeatedly in the stomach, neck and pubic region. Sated, he ended the blood lust and left the house covered in blood and carrying rings and watches in a pillowcase. He also left with the family's shotgun and the jewellery box containing Maxine's eyes.

Family friend Bruno Polo arrived at the Zazzara home at approximately 8.45 that evening to drop off some moneybags from the restaurant they co-owned and he noticed that the front door was open. Ringing the doorbell and knocking on the door got no reply, so Bruno put the bags in the letterbox and left.

The next morning, concerned that there was no answer the previous day, Bruno returned to the house and again tried to contact the owners by ringing the doorbell, with no success. Bruno called their name through the open door, but received no answer. At work, Bruno mentioned his concerns to his colleague Al Persico, who agreed to follow him to the house to investigate. Reaching the Zazzara residence for the third time, Bruno not waiting for Al to turn up, entered the house. Once inside he heard the television still on and headed towards it. Entering the lounge he spotted Vincent lying on the couch. Assuming he is asleep Bruno moved closer and spotted the blood.

Suddenly realising Vincent was dead, Bruno rushed outside where he bumped into Al and told him what he saw. Disbelieving Bruno's story, Al made his way in and saw the body of Vincent on the couch. Leaving the lounge room Al headed toward the bedroom to find the horrific scene left by Maxine's killer. Al quickly joined Bruno outside where Bruno had called the Zazzara's son Peter who in turn called the police.

Homicide detectives Russ Uloth and J D Smith were the first on the scene arriving at 12.00 pm. Once there, the detectives scanned the house looking for evidence of the perpetrator. Outside multiple shoe prints were found in the dirt of the flowerbeds that surrounded the house, plaster casts were taken that revealed a size 11 ½ foot wearing Avia aerobics sneakers. At the autopsy, carried out by Dr Terence Allen, the bullet that killed Vincent was confirmed to be a .22 calibre. The autopsy on Maxine would indicate that it was the shots that killed her and the stabbing had occurred post mortem. Unfortunately, the bullets were too damaged to allow a comparison to the Veronica Yu and Dayle Okazaki murders.

Just six weeks later, Ramirez was back in Monterey Park scanning the houses looking for a lapse in security. Due to the excessive heat of the summer it didn't take long before he spotted an open window covered only by a screen. Quickly removing the screen and opening the window wide, the killer entered the home of Bill and Lillian Doi on May 14. Standing in the bedroom at the end of the bed where Bill was asleep, the killer placed a single bullet into the chamber of his newly purchased gun. The metallic sound woke Bill up. When the man spotted Ramirez he reached for the gun he kept on the nearby cabinet. Before he could get hold of his weapon a shot was fired hitting sixty-six-year-old Bill in the mouth, the path of the bullet damaged his mouth, voice box and his brain.

Ramirez reloaded his gun and tried to fire for a second time but the gun jammed. Frustrated, the killer dived across the bed and viciously punched and kicked Bill until he was unconscious. Satisfied with his work,

Ramirez made his way to the second bedroom where Bill's fifty-six-year-old wife Lillian slept. Lillian, having heard the commotion from the room next door was wide-awake, unfortunately she was an invalid and unable to go to her husband's aid.

Bill's attacker locked Lillian's hands together with a pair of thumb cuffs and began ransacking the house. In the first bedroom, Bill came round moaning in pain. The noise alerted Ramirez and the killer returned to beat Bill to unconsciousness again. Ramirez then returned to Lillian's room and raped her as she lay helpless beneath him. Finally, after completing the ransacking of the house, Ramirez left using a pillowcase to carry the valuables he found and leaving the thumb cuffs still in place on Lillian's fingers.

Bill came round again but scared the stranger would attack him again, he lay there in the silence until he was sure the man in black had gone. Once satisfied Ramirez had gone, Bill got to his feet and immediately checked on his wife before dialling 911, breathlessly pleading for help before passing out again. A few minutes later, Bill regained consciousness and again dialled 911 asking for help. At 5.04 am Fire captain Norman Case was first on the scene and with his team gave first aid to Bill until the medical team arrived.

Bill was taken to Garfield hospital however, on the way, Bill's vital signs flat lined. Arriving at the hospital at 5.13am, and despite all medical efforts, Bill did not regain consciousness and was officially pronounced dead at 5.29am. Lillian, beaten and bloodied, was able to tell police officer Bill Reynolds about the mysterious man dressed in black with bad teeth that had assaulted her. Lillian was taken to Monterey Park Hospital for medical attention. Once again detectives would find numerous shoeprints around the Doi residence: size 11 ½ Avia aerobic sneakers.

Monrovia lies approximately 20 miles northeast of Los Angeles and was the home of eighty-three-year-old Mabel Bell and her invalid sister eighty-one-year-old Florence Lang. As usual, the front door was left unlocked despite the fact it was night and they were asleep, it was May 29, 1985. A quick search of the house by Ramirez during the early hours told him that the owners were not particularly well off and he was not happy. Finding the two elderly relatives asleep in their beds, Ramirez headed to the kitchen to find a knife, but was disappointed to find none he considered sharp enough for the task ahead. Instead he picked up a hammer and returned to Florence's bedroom. He struck the unconscious woman repeatedly on the head exposing the brain. Using an electrical cord he tied Florence's hands behind her back before moving to Mabel's room.

As with her sister, the attacker struck Mabel on the head with the hammer. Mabel woke up screaming as the attacker struck her head again. Using duct tape to cover Mabel's mouth, Ramirez ripped an electrical cord from the nearby clock, stripped the cable to expose the wires, turned the power on and shocked the semiconscious woman. After ransacking the rooms of the house searching for whatever he could sell, Ramirez returned to the comatose Florence and raped her. Before leaving, the man in black took Mabel's red lipstick and drew 3 pentagrams, one on Mabel's thigh, the second on her bedroom wall and the third on the wall of Florence's room.

The next night at approximately 4.00am, Mabel and Florence's attacker entered another house in Burbank using the dog flap. Using a torch to see in the darkness, he headed directly for the bedroom and moved towards the sleeping figure of forty-two-year-old Carol Kyle. Holding a gun to her head in preparation, Ramirez shone the torch directly into Carol's eyes and shouted at her to wake up.

As Carol bolted up right, the killer demanded to know if anyone else was in the house. Carol admitted that her eleven-year-old son, Mark, was asleep in the next room. Ramirez pushed and prodded Carol towards the young boy's room and ordered her to lie on the floor. The killer dived across the bed and put the gun to Mark's head. Carol rushed in to protect her son. Angry at her actions, Ramirez handcuffed the pair together and moved them into a closet while he ransacked the house.

Finding little, he returned to Carol and demanded to know where the remainder of the valuables were. Ramirez removed the handcuffs from Carol and dragged her back into the bedroom and ordered her to show him where the jewellery was. After giving him her diamond and gold chain she wore round her neck he tied her hands behind her back and attacked Carol, forcing her to fellate him. Ramirez then raped and sodomised her before leaving the house. After a short time Mark broke free of his bindings, and called 911.

At 6.05am, officer Roger Cervenga arrived at Carol Kyle's house and was soon joined by officer Paul Barcus. The officers entered the house and finding Carol and Mark safe; they checked the remainder of the house to confirm no one else was present. Carol was then taken to St Joseph Medical Centre for a rape examination. Soon her daughter, who had spent the night at a friend's house, arrived home. Officer Barcus stayed with the children, whilst their mother was in hospital. At 7.15am criminalist Bobby Cestaro arrived and dusted the house for fingerprints but found none.

Mabel and Florence, who were attacked by Ramirez on May 29, were still severely injured and lying in their house until June 1 when the local handyman, Carlos Valenzuela, notice that something was wrong when two days newspapers had not been picked up. Concerned, Carlos entered the house to discover the injured women. The man raced to a neighbouring home and dialled 911. The fire department was first on the scene at 11.50am. Medivac fireman, Ken Struckus checked the women and found them both alive, but only just. Both Florence and Mabel were in a comatose condition and were taken by ambulance to Arcadia Methodist Hospital where Dr Michael Agron examined them. Despite the medical teams efforts Mabel died two weeks later on July 17, 1985.

Arcadia lies approximately thirteen miles north east of Los Angeles and it was there on July 2, that the next attack took place. Ramirez prowled the quiet nighttime streets looking for an appropriate house. He soon found one, lifting the screen away from an unlocked window, opened it and silently slipped in. Mary Cannon, a grandmother of five, was asleep and didn't realise anyone was in her house until the vase came crashing down on her head. Mary was beaten unconscious by Ramirez and she would not wake again. The killer took a 10-inch knife from the kitchen and plunged it deep into the left hand side of Mary's throat. Pulling the knife out he stabbed Mary again and again all over her body in a bloody frenzy. Ramirez then ransacked the house and left.

The next morning, Mary's neighbours, Christine and Frank Starich, concerned that neither had seen their elderly neighbour that day, entered Mary's house. Immediately the couple saw that the house had been ransacked and left to call the police to report the burglary – they had not seen Mary. Officer Ed Winter was first to respond. Upon approaching the house Christine and Frank relayed their findings to the officer who entered. Quickly Ed found the bloody body of Mary Cannon and reported the homicide.

Whitney Bennett was late going home. The sixteen-year-old had gone to a late night party and it was after 1.00 am on July 4 by the time she got home to her parents house in Sierra Madre. She cleaned up, and went to bed. Ramirez stood silently in the girl's room watching her as she slept, wanting to damage her. Going back outside to the stolen car he was currently driving, he retrieved a tyre iron and returned to Whitney's room. Silently, he approached and stood over her. Suddenly he clamped his hand over Whitney's mouth and struck her head eleven times with the bar, knocking her unconscious. The killer then climbed onto the bed and straddled Whitney; he took a telephone cord and began to strangle the young girl. But before he killed Whitney, he inexplicably stopped and left the house via the bedroom window. The next morning Whitney woke up with a blinding headache, unaware of the attack that had happened the night before. Finding blood on the bed she began screaming and her parents run in to find their badly beaten daughter, whom they had not seen since she left for the party the previous evening. When asked what happened, Whitney could not answer, having no memory of the night's attack.

Later that morning, 'Gil' Carrillo and Frank Salerno visited the crime scene, hoping to find the Avia shoeprint that would link this with the other attacks. One clear shoeprint was found in Whitney's bedroom. At the hospital Whitney lay unconscious in the emergency room. Eventually, the doctors came out and gave her parents news that Whitney would be ok, but would require 478 stitches to put her head back together. She remained in hospital for a total of eight days, and continued to receive medical treatment for the next two and a half years.

Two nights later on July 7, 1985, Ramirez was back in Monterey Park, searching for another house to burgle. He boldly approached the front door of sixty-one-year-old Joyce Nelson's home. Finding it locked, he tried the nearby window, which he found, unlocked. Opening it wide, he climbed in, paused, waiting for his eyes to get used to the dark. When ready, he searched through the house moving silently and soon came upon the owner sleeping on the couch. After making sure that no one else was present in the house, Ramirez returned to Joyce, placed his .22 gun to her head and shouted at Joyce to wake up, demanding to know where the valuables were. Joyce defied the killer's demands. Her refusal to answer was met with a flurry of punches to the head knocking her unconscious. After dragging the woman to the bedroom, he continued the beating, which resulted in Joyce's death. The attack ended with a heavy kick to the head so hard that it left a clear imprint of an Avia shoeprint in Joyce's head.

The same night sixty-three-year-old Sophie Dickman was woken at 3.00am by the man in black holding his hand firmly over her mouth. In a similar pattern to the previous attacks, Ramirez demanded to know where the valuables were. Sophie was a psychiatric nurse and knew how to deal with this type of person. Dragging his now handcuffed victim to the bathroom, the killer began ransacking the house, but soon returned empty handed. Angry, he again demanded to know where the jewellery was; Sophie replied that she didn't have any. Ramirez's response was a punch to the woman's stomach. Asking again for valuables, Sophie told him their location in the second bathroom. Again dragging her to his destination, the attacker claimed his prize of diamonds. He turned to Sophie, punched her in the head, dragged her to the bedroom and attempted to sodomise Sophie but failed. He then threw her onto the bed and locked the handcuffs to the bedpost before attempting to rape Sophie but failed to get an erection. Frustrated he left the house reminding Sophie he knew where she lived. Waiting until she was sure her attacker had left, Sophie dragged the bed over to the window, managed to open it and called out to her neighbour for help.

Linda Arthur was a deputy with the sheriff's office and was woken by Sophie's calls for assistance. Rushing to Sophie's aid, Linda discovered what had happened and dialled 911.

In July the Los Angeles media became aware of the serial killer loose in Los Angeles and newspapers began printing likenesses of the killer, as well as describing the murders and the victims within their pages.

On July 13, 1985 a town meeting was called by the Monterey Park police and over 2000 people turned up to discuss the case which was held at the City Council Chambers.

On July 17, the killer claimed another victim, when elderly Mabel Bell succumbed to her wounds. The autopsy report, written by Dr Sara Reddy, showed the cause of death as 'massive brain trauma'. At the time her sister Florence remained in a comatose state.

Three days after Mabel died, the killer was back on the streets prowling, this time Glendale was the target. In the fog Ramirez stood outside the modest home of Maxon and Lela Kneiding. The couple were aware of the attacks by the mysterious man in black and so locked all their doors and windows before retiring to bed. But the killer would not be stopped that night.

Cutting the glass on the rear French doors, Ramirez reaching inside, opened the lock and entered. In his hand he carried a .22 gun, in the other a large machete. Silently moving through the house, he confirmed who was at home then entered the main bedroom and turned on the lights. Maxon sat upright in the bed, as the machete swung round hitting him in the head, leaving a deep gash. Maxon pleaded for his life, Ramirez ignored Maxon's pleas, placed the barrel of the gun against his head and pulled the trigger. The gun failed to fire, but before Maxon could react, the gunman cleared the jam and fired again killing Maxon instantly. Lela screamed as the killer aimed the gun at her and fired three times. Using the machete Ramirez cut the bodies several times across the throat and upper body, leaving slashes three inches deep and six inches across before quickly grabbing whatever he could and fleeing the house.

After dropping the items stolen from the Kneidling's at his fence, Ramirez, still not satisfied with the night's work, travelled north to Sun Valley. Parking the stolen car he was driving in Charbonne Street, Ramirez moved silently along the road and stopped at the home of Chainarong Khovananth and his family. It was 4.15 am. Moving to the rear of the house he tried the sliding glass windows, found them unlocked and went inside. Immediately he found the mother, Somkid, asleep on the couch. She woke to find a hand clamped over her mouth and a .22 gun pointing at her head. The intruder told her to lay silent and still, Somkid nodded her agreement. Continuing to move through the house, Ramirez found Chainarong asleep in the main bedroom. Placing the gun just above his left ear, the gunman fired, the bullet entered Chainarong's brain killing him instantly. Returning to Somkid, Ramirez tied her up and dragged her to the bedroom where he raped her next to her dead husband. After demanding to know where the valuables were, he raped and sodomised Somkid twice more before tying her up again and leaving.

It was at 7.40 am the following morning when Maxon and Lela Kneidling were found dead by their daughter Judy Arnold. The ballistics report completed on July 22, indicated the weapon was the same as the gun used in the murders of Veronica Yu and Dayle Okazaki. The attack on the Kneidlings was reported in the media the next day and gave the attacker the name by which he would be known. "The Nightstalker."

Northridge lies 25 miles from Los Angeles and it was there that the Nightstalker made his next appearance. Finding the rear sliding doors unlocked, Ramirez silently entered the modest home of Chris and Virginia Petersen on Acre Street. He crept into the main bedroom and loaded his gun. The sound woke Virginia; she was immediately shot in the right side of her temple as she attempted to sit up. The gunshot woke Virginia's husband, Chris, and Ramirez attempted to shoot him also in the temple. Chris leapt out of bed to attack Ramirez who fired twice more, but fortunately he missed both times. Forced to escape Chris' attack, the Nightstalker fled for his car. Virginia though severely injured dialled 911. Chris then drove his wife to Northridge Hospital, where they were both treated.

Diamond Bar is a small town lying in the La Brea canyon about 30 miles from Los Angeles where Elyas Abowath had settled with his wife Sakina and their two young children, the youngest ten weeks, the other three years of age. At approximately 2.30am on August 8, 1985, the rear glass door opened and in crept the Nightstalker. Silently, he moved through the house. He reached the main bedroom where he placed the barrel of his .25 gun against Elyas' head just above the left ear and fired, instantly killing the thirty-one-year-old father. Jumping over the bed, the killer straddled Sakina and punched her repeatedly in the face and threatened to kill her. Ramirez blindfolded and gagged Sakina and punched her again in the head. The intruder then began to ransack the house and found the family jewellery hidden in a suitcase in the closet. Returning to Sakina he forced her to fellate him, then he raped and sodomised her. Suddenly sensing that something was wrong, he pulled out his gun from his waistband as the three-year-old child entered the room. Punching Sakina to the floor he grabbed the youngster and threw him on the bed. Ramirez tied the child up and put a pillowcase over his head. Returning again to Sakina he continued to beat her and demanded jewellery from her body. Finally satisfied that he had got all they had, the Nightstalker handcuffed Sakina to the doorknob and left the house with a pillowcase stuffed with valuables.

Sakina managed to pull her son close and freed him of his bindings. She persuaded the crying boy to go into the night to the neighbours house for help. At 3.43 am the doorbell of Bob and Roswitha Wilson's front door rang. Bob opened the door to find the three-year-old boy standing at the door in his pyjamas and a rope tied to his arm. Bob and his wife Roswitha ran to their neighbours' house where they found Sakina shouting for help and Elyas dead. Roswitha returned home and called the police.

At noon the following day, a press conference was called to give the press details of the fourteen linked attacks in Los Angeles County. The next morning the press was full of details of the latest attacks. Public tips began pouring into the sheriff's office by the hundreds. Composites of the Nightstalker's face was released to the public and a reward for the capture stood at $80,000. But with the public on the lookout, the Nightstalker left Los Angeles and headed north to San Francisco.

At 2.00am on August 18, the Nightstalker continued where he left off in Los Angeles. He climbed in an open window into the home of sixty-six-year-old Peter and his wife Barbara Pan, 62, in the Lakeside District of San Francisco. He moved directly upstairs, to the main bedroom and stood next to the sleeping figure of Peter. Removing the gun from his waistband, he placed it directly on Peter's forehead and fired instantly killing him. The Nightstalker then attacked Barbara, but she fought back and was shot in the head. After ransacking the house, he returned to the bedroom, took Barbara's lipstick and wrote 'Jack the Knife' on the wall along with a pentagram. The next morning the bodies of the Pan couple were found by their son on a surprise visit.

San Francisco was now aware of the Nightstalker's activities due to LAPD communiqués about the case. The mayor's office gave a press conference of their own. Unfortunately the mayor, Dianne Feinstein, gave details of the case that 'Gil' Carrillo and Frank Salerno had worked hard to keep away from public knowledge. However, on the positive side, the size of the reward was increased to $90,000.

Because of the newspaper reports on the evidence that Nightstalker wore Avia sneakers, the killer threw the shoes into the San Francisco Bay and on August 25 he returned to Los Angeles.

Back in Los Angeles, the Nightstalker stole another car, a 1976 Toyota and headed south stopping at Mission Viejo at 1.00am. Ramirez parked the car in Chrisanta Drive and walked boldly along the road towards his next target unaware that a young teenager – James Romero III, was watching him. Trying the front door and windows gave him no access, so the Nightstalker moved to the rear of the house, removed a screen from an open window and climbed in. Bill Cairns, 29, and his wife Carole Smith, 27, were asleep in the upstairs bedroom when the Nightstalker silently crept in. He cocked the gun ready to shoot.

However, the sound woke Bill from his slumber and although still half asleep he tried to get out of bed. Seeing his target move, Ramirez shot Bill in the head and moving closer to the wounded man, shot him twice more in the head, the impact knocking Bill back onto the bed. Leaping to the opposite side of the bed, the Nightstalker pulled back the covers to reveal Carole whom he punched in the face. He pulled her from the bed and hog-tied her with ties from the nearby closet. The Nightstalker continued his assault on Carole punching and kicking her whilst demanding to know where the valuables were. Ransacking the house, he found jewellery and watches. Returning to the helpless Carole, the Nightstalker dragged her to another room where he raped and sodomised her. Demanding more cash, the crying Carole directed him to where $400 could be found. Slipping the money into his pocket, the Nightstalker left by the front door.

James Romero III watched Ramirez leave, and noted down the number plate of the car the suspicious man in black was driving.

Carole Smith managed to free herself from her bonds and checked her fiancée, finding Bill breathing, Carole ran to the neighbours for help and a medivac quickly arrived and took the pair to Mission Community Hospital. Once there Bill was immediately taken into surgery. The operation successfully removed two of the bullets; the third however, was in an area too vital to be removed without causing more damage. Unfortunately, Bill suffered permanent brain damage from his injuries.

Jesse Perez, a sixty-two-year-old cab driver and small time thief, believed he recognised the man in the photo fits. The descriptions given out of the mysterious man in black was similar to a man he knew as Rick. Jesse asked his daughter, who worked at the Sheriffs office in Los Angeles, to contact the police on his behalf. At the end of August detectives Ike Angular and Mike Griggs met with Jesse Perez and his daughter to talk about his suspicions.

Nervously, Jesse told the detectives what he knew, mentioning that he had bought a .22 gun from 'Rick' for $50 on credit, which was now in the possession of a female friend in Tijuana. Jesse talked about 'Rick' being obsessed with burglary. 'Rick' also talked about an Asian couple he had killed in Monterey Park, also that he had been arrested for stealing a car and crashing it into the bus terminal while being chased by the LAPD. Jesse continued to tell the detectives of the fence that 'Rick' used. After the interview Jesse took the detectives to a garage near Dodgers Stadium owned by Felipe Salano before being driven to Tijuana to retrieve the gun he mentioned. Salano was arrested and questioned about 'Rick'. He swore that he didn't know his last name or his address. 'Rick' always called him if he had anything to sell.

With the partial number plate noted down by James Romero III, the car was soon found abandoned in a shopping centre in the Wiltshire District of LA County. The car was taken to Santa Ana where it was tested for fingerprints. One single clear print was found on the back of the rear view mirror.

In San Francisco, the authorities released pictures of the jewellery stolen during the Pan attack, in the hope that a buyer would recognise the items and come forward. Earl Gregg came forward; his mother-in-law Donna Meyer had given him a ring. Earl told SFPD detectives Carl Klotz and Frank Falzon that the ring came from Donna's friend Rick, whom he knew was a burglar. Earl agreed also that Rick looked similar to the photo fit of the Nightstalker. Klotz and Falon thanked Earl and paid a visit to Donna Meyer's house. Donna told the detectives of a jewellery box given to her by Rick in August. Rick also gave her some jewellery a few days later.

When asked how she knew Rick, Donna replied that he was a 'friend of a friend – Armando Rodriguez', and she first met Rick with Armando in El Paso, Texas. Next the detectives drove to the home of Armando in order to discover Rick's last name. Refusing to talk, Armando was taken to the police headquarters under the threat of accessory to murder. After some time in the cells, Armando gave the police the surname of Rick it was Ramirez.

At the same time as Ramirez's name was discovered, the fingerprint taken from the stolen Toyota, was matched with a record from the police files including theft and stealing a car in December 1984. The computer produced the name of Richard Munoz Ramirez. In fact the fingerprint system had only gone computerised that morning and this was one of the first checks made on the new system. The file mug shot was shown to Jesse Perez who confirmed that 'Rick' was Richard Ramirez. The next day the newspapers all had Ramirez's name and photo printed on the front page.

Ricardo Munoz Ramirez was born at 2.07am on February 28, 1960, the last of 5 children to Julian and Mercedes Ramirez. The pregnancy was difficult, Mercedes was working at a chemical plant for several years without protection from the fumes and she suffered from dizziness and nausea throughout her time there. The pregnancy however, compared to previous births, gave Mercedes such discomfort that she and Julian decided to see a specialist who insisted that in order to keep the child, she must stop working at the chemical plant. Mercedes agreed.

When Ricardo was two-years-old, an accident occurred in which a heavy dresser fell on him, knocking him unconscious for fifteen minutes. The accident left a cut on his head, which required thirty stitches.

Ricardo was again knocked unconscious at five-years-old. He had gone with his brother Robert to the local park to find their sister Ruth. Once there Ricardo spotted Ruth playing on the swing and ran toward her, unfortunately before Ruth could avoid him, the swing crashed into Ricardo's head. The cut would again require a visit to the hospital for stitches. During 5th grade Ricardo suffered his first epileptic attack. Mercedes was sent for and was advised by the school to take him to the doctors. She instead took him home.

The next day Ricardo suffered a second fit. This time Mercedes did take him to the hospital where the doctor examined her son and told Mercedes that Ricardo was an epileptic and was experiencing 'Grand Mal Seizures' which he would eventually grow out of. The seizures lessened over time and stop when he reached his teens.

As he grew older, Ricardo spent more and more time with his cousin Miguel who had recently returned from Vietnam. Miguel regaled Ricardo with stories of gun battles with the enemy whilst they both smoked pot. Ricardo had been smoking pot and breaking into houses since he was ten-years-old.

On May 4, 1973 Ricardo was at cousin Miguel's house, when Miguel and his wife Jessie argued about Miguel's lack of employment. The argument resulted in Miguel shooting his wife from point blank range into her face. Told never to mention what he saw, Ricardo went home and never said a word about what he saw to anyone. Miguel, because of his war record was found innocent by reason of insanity, and was committed to a Texas State Mental Hospital.

By ninth grade, Ricardo's school results, which had been good, began to fall. He was now playing truant, rarely staying at his parent's house, and preferring to sleep overnight in the local cemetery. Eventually Ricardo moved out of the house in July 1973 and moved in with his sister and her husband, Roberto Avala.

At 15, Ricardo got a job at the Holiday Inn doing general jobs. After three months of employment, he got hold of a master key and began using it to steal from rooms while the occupants were out. He soon realised that more valuables would be available at night when the customers were in the room asleep. Using the key, Richard crept in stealing cash, watches and jewellery while the owners slept, unaware of the intruder.

Becoming older, Ricardo realised what his desires were. One night he crept into the closet of an unsuspecting woman while she was in the shower. When the woman returned to the bedroom Ricardo clamped his hand over the woman's mouth from behind, wrestled her to the floor, gagged and tied her up. Just as he attempted to rape the woman, her husband walked into the room. Ricardo jumped up, fists flailing, but was punched to the floor and knocked out by the larger man. The police were summoned and subsequently arrested Ricardo. However, the couple lived out of state and decided to drop the charges rather than return to the state for a trial.

When Miguel was released from the mental hospital in late 1977, he and Ricardo joined up and continued their previous friendship, smoking pot and taking hallucinogens. Ricardo had gained the nickname 'fingers', because of his thieving. He was now dressing in black, breaking into people's houses and stealing their valuables. At eighteen Ricardo left El Paso for good heading for Los Angeles. Within a year Ricardo was addicted to cocaine that was paid for by the many burglaries he committed. Ricardo was being drawn deeper towards Satanism and sadism. In summer 1978, Ricardo met a young female drug addict with whom he shared some angel dust. He wanted sex but she refused and insisted he left, which he did, but returned later when she was asleep. At approximately 3.00am Ramirez entered the woman's room, leapt on the bed, gagged and tied the woman up and raped her several times before leaving.

Shortly after the final attack, Ramirez went to Tucson, Arizona hoping to visit his brother, Robert, who was not home.. Disappointed, Ramirez walked back to the bus terminal to catch a bus back to Los Angeles. At 7.25 am on August 31, 1985 the coach carrying Ramirez arrived back in Los Angeles, its passenger was completely oblivious to the fact that his face was on the front page of every newspaper. Ramirez walked through the terminal, and not one of the policemen on duty spotted the wanted man. The police were actually watching people and vehicles leaving Los Angeles, not those entering.

After exiting the bus terminal, Ramirez entered Mike's Liquor Store for a drink. Inside he noticed some elderly women whispering and pointing at him, Ramirez then saw the reason for their actions. He saw his face on the newspaper. Rushing from the store Ramirez could hear sirens in nearby streets. The store owner had called the police so Ramirez had to get away quickly. He ran towards the freeway and got on a bus. He noticed that the passengers were pointing at him as they had recognised his face and after a short bus ride Ramirez got back off the bus deciding to steal a car.

Manuela Villanueva was sitting in her car with the engine running, waiting for her boyfriend Carmello Robles to return from the nearby grocer. Ramirez saw the car and headed directly for it. Claiming he had a gun Ramirez demanded the car. Manuela refused and screamed out; Carmello heard and came running back towards the car with another man, Arthur Benavedes. Ramirez, upon seeing the two men, ran off down an alleyway. Frank Moreno was coming through the alley when Ramirez ran past and over a fence. Ramirez headed towards Hubbard Street, an area with a large community of Mexican-American citizens. Clambering over a fence Ramirez landed in the garden of Luis Munoz, who recognised the Nightstalker. Luis struck Ramirez with the tongs he was using at his barbecue. Ramirez quickly left the garden by leaping over the fence into Luis' neighbours' property.

In the back yard a Mustang car was empty and running so Ramirez got in, but didn't realise that the car was sitting up on jacks, nor did he spot the owner, Faustino Pinon, heading back towards the vehicle. Faustino spotted Ramirez attempting to steal his car and grabbed him by the neck. Ramirez again claimed he had a gun but it didn't stop Faustino reaching for the ignition to remove the keys. Ramirez ran from the car and leapt over another fence as Faustino dialled 911. Back in the street, Ramirez spotted Angela De La Torre getting into her car. Reaching Angela, Ramirez demanded the keys. Angela refused and was punched in the stomach. Ramirez took the keys and got in the car. Angela's friend Lourdes Estupinion was already in the car, but immediately got out screaming 'El Matador' (the killer). Jose Burgoin and his two sons, Jamie and Ernesto, saw the incident and ran to Angela and Lourdes' aid. Jose, after politely requesting that Ramirez get out of the car, struck Ramirez on the back of the head with a metal bar. Ramirez now got out of the car and continued down the street.

By now the neighbourhood had come out onto the street to find out what was the commotion. Ramirez was closely pursued by Jose who swung the bar at Ramirez, but missed. Another swing hit the Nightstalker on top of his head, knocking him to the ground. Sheriff's deputy Andres Ramirez arrived at the scene and was met by a crowd chanting 'we caught him'. Reaching the centre of the crowd was Ramirez, who begged the deputy to save him from the crowd. The deputy handcuffed and frisked the suspect. Ramirez gave his name, as an ambulance was called to treat his injuries. By now more LAPD officers were arriving at the scene in response to the sightings of the Nightstalker from residents of Hubbard Street. Ramirez was arrested and after being treated by the medical team was taken to Hollenbeck Station past the crowd, by patrol car who hurled insults and spat at Ramirez.

At the police station, the officers were very wary of the suspect and handcuffed his leg to the chair. Ramirez told the officers where he kept his weapons (in a locker at the bus terminal) and also said that he would rather die than spend his life in prison. Gil Carrillo and Frank Salerno arrived with no comment given to the barrage of questions from the reporters who had congregated outside. At 10.10 in the morning Gil and Frank were joined by two other detectives, Leroy Orozco and Paul Tippin, to conduct the first interview of the

Nightstalker. Ramirez's first comment was to request a lawyer. Without a lawyer present Ramirez was happy to talk about his background in El Paso, but not about his crimes.

At 10.40 the interview ended. Ramirez was fingerprinted and moved to the county jail to await arraignment. Whilst Ramirez sat waiting in the cell he cut his palm and drew a pentagram and the number 666 on the floor with his blood.

On September 3, 1985 it was time for Ramirez's first court appearance. He was shackled and bundled into a vehicle surrounded by several other police vehicles as well as a helicopter overhead. Ramirez was taken to the thirteenth floor of the Los Angeles Courthouse and placed before Judge Elva Soper. Ramirez told his public defender Alan Adashek that he intended to plead guilty to all charges. Prosecutor Phil Halpin put forward to the court the eight charges the suspect was being charged with. Included was the murder of Bill Doi; the robbery of his home and the rape of Lillian Doi. Further charges were to be filed against Ramirez in the future. At the end of the proceedings Ramirez was lead away from the courtroom once again in shackles.

On September 5, Ramirez was forced to attend a line up, however Florence Lang was still in a comatose state following the attack on her and could not attend. The remaining surviving victims did attend and quickly picked out their attacker as number two in the line up.

Ramirez's attorney Alan Adashek complained bitterly about the line up, stating that the wound that Ramirez received from the strike to the back of the head just prior to his arrest (the metal bar used by Jose Burgoin) was clearly visible, and some hair had been shaven off during treatment. He believed that this made it an easier task to identify Ramirez. In addition Ramirez's face had been in all the local newspapers. These incidents made a fair trial difficult.

On September 27, the further charges were read out in court. Phil Halpin read out an 84-page complaint. The new charges contained fourteen new murder counts and 45 other felonies including rape; sodomy; abduction; assault; unnatural acts on a minor; and robbery. Ramirez continued to demand that the public defender Alan Adashek plead guilty on his behalf. This caused arguments between the two leading to Ramirez hiring a different lawyer to represent him. On October 9, fifty-six-year-old Mexican Joseph Gallagos agreed to act as Ramirez's lawyer; the change was agreed to during a meeting with Judge Soper and Phil Halpin. But Ramirez soon changed his mind again after his sister, Ruth, persuaded him to meet with two attorneys she had confidence in. After a brief chat with Arturo and Daniel Hernandez, Ramirez agreed to allow them to represent him and not Joseph Gallagos. Judge Soper was not impressed by the quick change, but after taking it under consideration, he announced to the court on October 24, that the Hernandez brothers were to be Ramirez's attorneys. As he was being led back to the court holding cell, Ramirez stood up and held out his left palm up to the courtroom spectators. On it Ramirez had drawn a pentagram and written 666 underneath. This action prompted the famous photograph of the Nightstalker. After a short adjournment Ramirez was led back into the court to enter his plea of not guilty.

For the preliminary hearing Phil Halpin planned to use 140 witnesses to prove that they had enough evidence to allow the case to go to trial. However the defence team believed that the case against Ramirez was incorrect and in some areas illegal. The hearing itself began on March 3, 1986 in the courtroom of Judge James M Nelson. During the hearing, Sheriff's deputy Russ Uloth was called to the stand and testified about the crime scene he was called to at the home of Vincent and Maxine Zazzara.

Russ Uloth described the condition of Maxine's body, particularly the fact that her eyes were missing, when Ramirez began to cackle loudly. Once the prosecution had ended its presentation of evidence, Ramirez's lawyers decided not to offer any defence, preferring to wait until the actual trial. Phil Halpin requested that 18 charges be dropped including the abduction/molestation charges. Judge Nelson made his judgment that the prosecution had enough evidence to hold Ramirez for trial; in addition, due to the multiple murder charges Ramirez could face the death sentence. The final charge count read: 14 counts of murder; 5 counts attempted murder; 15 counts burglary; 5 counts robbery; 4 counts rape; 3 acts of oral copulation; 4 counts of sodomy all committed between June 27, 1984 and August 8, 1985.

Judge Nelson set May 21 as the trial commencement date. But as with many major trials the date was soon changed. After many delay tactics by the defence team, including a claim that the trial judge was racially biased, jury selection began on July 21, 1988. The selection itself took six months to complete. Eventually on January 10, 1989 a jury plus twelve alternates selected from an original pool of 1600 were sworn in and the trial began in the courtroom of Judge Michael Tynan.

During the trial, Ramirez wore his sunglasses that he refused to take off and laughed when witnesses and survivors took to the stand to give their testimony. He would also look around the courtroom and snarl at the spectators, including the many admirers, some of which had visited him in his jail cell. At other times Ramirez would place his fingers by his temples in mock horns and chant 'evil, evil'. Sometimes Ramirez would play around in order to relieve his boredom and at one stage managed to bring a mirror into the courtroom with him. Ramirez would sit in his chair and reflect the ceiling lights into the judge's eyes.

The prosecution eventually rested its case against Ramirez in mid April 1989 and had presented 537 pieces of evidence and 139 witnesses. Prior to the defence opening, Ramirez's lawyers, now including Ray Clark, again tried to persuade Ramirez to claim insanity but he refused. The defence began their case on May 1, after a day's delay caused by one of the prosecution witnesses, Felipe Solano, admitting that he lied during testimony in order to protect a friend. The concern was cleared up, but then the defence team requested a further delay. They announced that they needed time to decide whether a defence would be made. In fact it was Ramirez who was causing the delay. He continually claimed the trial was a farce and refused to take part saying he wanted to die.

After heated discussions with his lawyers, Ramirez had a mother to son talk with his mother Mercedes and Ramirez agreed to allow the defence case to be presented. Defence attorney Ray Clark wound up the defence's case two months after it started on July 10, allowing final summations to take place.

At the end of the summations, Judge Tynan gave his final instructions to the jury; he explained the applicable laws and how to reach a verdict on the charges. In total, Judge Tynan took two days to go through his statement. At 11.25am on July 26, 1989 the jury began their deliberations. However, as with the whole trial, the deliberations didn't go easy. One juror, Robert Lee, continually fell asleep during discussions and it lead to the remaining jurors complaining to the judge and the juror was replaced. On August 14, juror Phyllis Singletary failed to show up at the court. Later that day she was found shot dead in her apartment in an unrelated crime. She was shot dead by her boyfriend after an argument about the case, and was replaced by an alternate from the pool.

Finally on September 20, 1989 at 10.20am, the jury announced that they had reached a verdict with a unanimous decision. Ramirez was not present as they returned to court to give their verdict, instead he listened from the courtroom holding cell. Each of the counts was read out and in each case the jury found Ramirez guilty. At the defence request, the members of the jury were polled, each juror stated that they understood and agreed with the guilty verdict.

The penalty phase of the trial began on September 27, with prosecutor Phil Halpin describing the brutality of the crimes that Ramirez had committed and requested the death sentence. Ray Clark defied Ramirez and begged for mercy for his client. Prior to the penalty phase starting, Ramirez had given instructions to the defence team that they should offer no defence. He wanted to die and be in hell with Satan. Again the jury retired to begin deliberations the next day. Five days later the jury completed their discussions and returned to the court to announce their verdict at 10.20 on October 3, 1989.

Judge Tynan clearly read out the jury's verdict, a recommendation for the death penalty. As with the main trial, the judge requested that the jury confirm that the decision was made by them and was correct.

Five weeks later came the day of Ramirez's official sentencing. Before giving the sentence Judge Tynan asked Ramirez if he had anything to say. Ramirez said yes and stood to give a short speech ending with:

"You maggots make me sick".

Judge Tynan formally sentenced Ramirez to nineteen death sentences, one for each murder and six for the other crimes. In addition, Ramirez received six years for each of the remaining 32 charges to be served at San Quentin. Following sentencing, surviving victims and relatives of the deceased were given the opportunity to make statements to the court prior to the death warrants being signed, many did. When asked by the court reporters what he thought of the death sentence, Ramirez replied

"Big deal, death comes with the territory..... see you in Disneyland"

Ramirez was moved to San Quentin and given prison number E37101 and placed in cell 3AC8. Eventually he moved cells from the Adjustment Centre, where he had been since arriving at the prison, and into a cell on death row. His neighbours in death row included fellow serial killers Randy Kraft; Juan Corona and Lawrence Bittaker.

But Ramirez was not finished. He still had one more shock up his sleeve. On October 3, 1996 Ramirez married forty-one-year-old Doreen Lioy, she had been one of Ramirez's admirers since his picture first appeared in the newspapers. She had been present throughout the trial and visited him constantly throughout the proceedings.

Sid Resala
Resala – the boy and the man
Sid Ahmed Resala was born on May 14, 1979 in El Biar, in Algiers. He was an unexceptional student at school, preferring to spend his time playing basketball with friends.

Resala was raped by two different men when he was eleven years of age. He claimed that he was lured away from a group of friends and assaulted. The attacks caused the boy psychological turmoil, and by the time he was a teenager, he had begun raping girls and young women.

In 1994, the Resala family moved to Marseilles, France to escape the escalating Islamic violence of their homeland. The move unsettled the troubled young man further and by February 1995, Sid Resala found himself in prison having raped a fourteen-year-old boy at the Saint-Charles Rail Station. While in prison, Resala was brutalised by another inmate, further enraging the young man who inflicted the same pain on others when he was released in 1997.

Resala settled down for a short time and married Nadia Adbelmalek. The couple had a daughter, Sara, but Resala returned quickly back to his old ways and the violent streak was escalating.

He found himself in front of the courts for burglary and received 100 hours community service. However, he strayed once again, threatening someone with a knife, and was incarcerated once more. While in prison Resala's wife divorced him and took the couple's daughter with her to live in Amiens.

By the end of June, 1999 Resala was released from prison and began an education course in waiting tables. He travelled every weekend from Marseilles to Amiens to see his daughter, and it was during the train trips that Resala began his killing spree.

The murders
By the time of the murders at the end of 1999, Resala had been charged almost 45 times by train officials for not having a valid train ticket with him. It was just another example of the contempt that Resala had for officialdom.

On October 13, 1999 Sid Ahmed Resala attempted to rape twenty-year-old Birmingham University student, Isabel Peake who was on the otherwise empty carriage. When she fought off his advances, Resala threw her from the Brives to Paris high-speed train as it drew near to Chateauroux. As Isabel was thrown from the train she struck her head on a pylon. The train at the time was travelling at a speed of 150km per hour. The woman died instantly from the blow.

Having thrown Isabel from the train, Resala also discarded the woman's luggage tossing it from the moving train. When it was found, a search was made along the tracks and soon Isabel's body was found discarded like a rag doll, her shirt and bra torn from her body.

Resala was as person of interest as police searched for clues of the attack of the English university student. A re-enactment was staged on January 15, 2000 to ensure that the woman had been murdered and not fallen from the train and police spoke of their interest in talking to Resala who had been seen talking to the woman before getting on the train at Limoges.

Yet no further enquiries were made by police into the background of Resala and he remained free to kill again.

The next victim was thirty-six-year-old Corinne Caillaux on December 14, 1999. The mother of two young children was travelling on a sleeper train to Grasse to see her mother when she was attacked. As her five-year-old son slept in another carriage, Corrine was on her way to the bathroom when Resala pounced on the woman at around 2am. He pushed her into a toilet cubicle and raped her as she attempted to fight him off.

Resala produced a knife during the attack and stabbed the woman a total of fourteen times, her throat was cut, as well as lacerations to her face, chest and back. The killer alighted the train at Dijon soon after the attack and was seen on video surveillance on the station at Dijon at around 2.40am.

Corinne's body was found the next morning by train officials, still in the toilet cubicle. They also found a blood-covered cap, belonging to Resala near the body.

The twenty-year-old became an instant suspect and his prison photo was flashed on television screens across France.

Resala quickly fled to Portugal as police began a massive manhunt for the killer dubbed the "*Train Killer*".

On December 17, 1999 police gained a search warrant for the apartment of Resala at 51 Jules-le-Fevre in Amiens and found, in the basement, the body of twenty-year-old student Emily Basin, Resala's ex-girlfriend.

The killer continued to flee from police, as the charges perpetuated until he was arrested at Lisbon on January 12, 2000. Resala purchased a ticket to fly to the Canary Islands when Interpol arrested him.

Resala was imprisoned at Lisbon as he fought the extradition charges from France, where he was to face the three charges of murder.

He spoke often to the press, telling them how he had been high on drugs when had attacked Isabel, and had attempted to kill himself by cutting his own throat in his holding cell.

Resala dies before trial
On June 28, 2000 Sid Resala committed suicide by setting fire to his Lisbon prison cell mattress. The smoke that quickly filled his room, overcame Resala and he died from the toxic fumes given off by the supposed fire-retardant bedding. He had jammed his door shut with a bar from his bed to prevent prison guards from entering his cell.

However according to other inmates, the guards were busy watching the World Cup match between France and Portugal that had gone into over-time rather than checking on the commotion.

Angel Resendiz
The sentencing of Angel Resendiz
On May 18, 2000 the "Texas Railroad Killer" Angel Resendiz was sentenced to death for the murder of 39-year-old Dr. Claudia Benton, a geneticist who was stabbed, bludgeoned and raped in her West University home on December 17, 1998.

Forty-year-old Resendiz, was also charged with the murders of six people in Texas, two in Illinois and one in Kentucky while riding freight cars across the United States when he was found guilty of the murder of Dr Benton.

At the preceding trial, the defence counsel testified that Resendiz suffered from paranoid schizophrenia and claimed to have supernatural powers. The killer believed the murders were to please God.

Resendiz also blamed his actions on a life of glue-sniffing and head injuries sustained during childhood, such as being dropped on his head right after he was born. Head injuries sustained in childhood are often seen as a precursor to "becoming" a serial killer as an adult, and was an avenue of defence at the killer's trial.

The victims
The first victim murdered by Angel Resendiz was attacked on August 29, 1997. Resendiz attacked University of Kentucky student Christopher Maier, 21, and his girlfriend while they were walking along railroad tracks in Kentucky. Resendiz bludgeoned Chris to death with a rock, before beating the student's girlfriend. Once Resendiz had the woman under his control, he raped her before bashing her further. The attack on the young woman was ferocious, she had her nose broken and one of her eye sockets was smashed; yet she survived the attack that killed her boyfriend.

The second known victim was an elderly woman. Eighty-seven-year-old Leafie Mason was found in her home in Hughes Springs, Texas by relatives the day after her shameless murder. On October 2, 1998 Resendiz had broken into the woman's house that was near the rail-line, and bashed the woman to death with an antique iron.

Police were able to lift a partial handprint from the windowpane through which Resendiz broke in. It later helped police link the murders to the one killer.

After leaving more than a year between the first and second murders, Resendiz struck for a third time only ten weeks after the murder of Leafie Mason.

On December 17, 1998, the killer broke into the home of thirty-nine-year-old Dr Claudia Benton in West University Place, Texas. The doctor worked at the near-by Baylor College of Medicine when she was murdered and later found in her home by a colleague.

According to the killer he had only broken into the house to steal items of value but claimed to have found medical instruments that he believed were used in abortions. He claimed to have become enraged and decided to kill the occupant of the house.

Dr Claudia Benton was bashed nineteen times over the head with one her own figurines by Resendiz before he raped and stabbed her to death. Once he had killed his victim, Resendiz ransacked the home, stealing several items of value including a jewellery box and a campaign button. Items that were later to be found in the home of Resendiz's de facto wife would eventually send Resendiz to Death Row.

The Reverend Norman "Skip" Sirnic and his wife Karen were Resendiz's fourth and fifth victims on May 2, 1999. The couple, who lived in the parsonage at the Uniting Church in Weimar, Texas, were beaten to death with a sledgehammer that Resendiz found in the garage.

A parishioner of the United Church of Christ found the Rev. Norman J. "Skip" Sirnic, 46, and his wife, Karen, 47, bludgeoned to death in the church's parsonage, located near railroad tracks on May 2, 1999. Police confirmed the couple were beaten with a sledgehammer taken from the garage.

First-grade schoolteacher Noemi Dominguez, 26, died after being clubbed repeatedly in the head with a pickaxe in her Houston apartment. Relatives found her body on June 5, 1999. She had died within 48 hours of being discovered.

On June 4, Resendiz travelled to Fayette County, where he bludgeoned Josephine Konvicka, 73, to death with a pickaxe in her farmhouse in Fayette County, Texas.

George Morber Sr., 80, was shot in the head with a shotgun in his mobile trailer home in Gorham, Ill., on June 14 1999, and his daughter, Carolyn Frederick, 51, was sexually assaulted and clubbed to death with the butt of her father's rifle.

On July 15, 2000 authorities found the remains of another victim the day after Resendiz, 39, was arrested by Marion County Sheriff's detectives in Texas. The remains were those of Wendy Von Huben, a sixteen-year-old runaway from Woodstock, Ill. The decomposed remains were wrapped in a blanket and camouflage jacket, about 100 yards from the railroad tracks.

Resendiz told the detectives that he strangled Wendy eight hours after he killed her travelling companion, Jesse Howell. Jess was found slain on March 23, 1997, near railroad tracks running through Belleview, a north-central Florida town about halfway between Tampa and Jacksonville.

Resendiz told the detectives he met Jess and Wendy near Jacksonville on March 23, 1997, the day of Howell's killing. The couple caught a ride with Resendiz in a grain car, hoping to find work picking oranges.

On January 24, 2002 Angel Resendiz told police about the murders of three more people in Texas. The killer gave intimate details about the murders. The police was prone to believe his confession after they were able to link him to an unsolved murder from the details he provided.

The other two suspected victims are yet to be found.

Police in Bexar County declared in a media conference that convicted serial killer, Angel Resendiz had murdered a homeless woman in 1986. The killer had confessed to police that he had taken the woman on a ride on his motorcycle before shooting her dead at an abandoned barn.

The killer was able to prove his confession by telling police the exact clothes the woman had been wearing and where precisely she had been found in the barn. He also told them he had shot her four times using a .38-calibre gun.

Sjef Rijke

Sjef Rijke, from Utrecht, Holland, used rat poison to murder two women, with two others surviving similar attacks. The two women, Willy Maas who died aged eighteen in January 1971 and Mientje Manders who died on April 2, 1971, were both engaged to be married to Rijke and both suffered agonizing stomach pains before their deaths. The Dutch authorities were suspicious, but no autopsies took place.

A third woman, eighteen-year-old Maria Haas, married Rijke soon after Mientje's death. The marriage lasted six weeks with Maria walking out. She said she was frightened by her husband's intense jealousy.

Dutch police finally caught up with Rijke after a fourth woman, who dated Rijke, complained to her doctor of painful stomach cramps. After some tests, rat poison was identified as the cause. This was the information that led authorities to arrest Rijke on suspicion of poisoning his first two wives. Once in custody, Rijke confessed to the attacks but claimed he did not intend to see them die; he just wanted to watch them suffer. At his trial in January 1972 he received two life sentences.

John Robinson

The Arrest

At 10.15am on Friday 2, June 2000 at 36 Monterrey Lane, Santa Barbara Estates, Kansas, two police officers knocked on the door of John Robinson Snr and told him he was under arrest. He was charged with the aggravated sexual battery of two women. His wife, Nancy, was bought in for questioning but had nothing to offer the investigation.

The next day a team of detectives and forensic investigators set up base on Robinson's farm in La Cygne. The cadaver dogs quickly found five large metal barrels. When opened, the first barrel revealed a naked, blindfolded and decomposing body lying face down in the foetal position. A second barrel was opened where another decomposing body was found. The bodies were removed from the scene and taken to Dr Donald Pojman for autopsy.

Over the weekend, search warrants were signed approving a search of two storage lockers owned by Robinson in Raymore.

On Monday June 5, the task force moved in and opened locker #E2. Inside, three further barrels each marked "Rendered Pork Fat" was found. Kevin Winer of the Kansas City PD Crime Lab, opened the first barrel, and found, amongst other items, a shoe, which when picked up had a leg attached to it. Immediately the barrel was resealed. All 3 barrels were taken away for autopsy to Dr Thomas Young in Jackson County.

That afternoon John Robinson made his first appearance in court after the discoveries on his property. Wearing standard issue prison orange, Robinson was in Johnson County Courthouse where he was told that his bond was raised to $5 million. On Tuesday afternoon at another press conference, DA Chris Koster announced that each of the three barrels found in the storage locker contained a female body.

On Wednesday morning one of the bodies was identified as Suzette Trouten who has been missing since March 1, 2000. On June 12, 2000 Beverley Bonner was named as the first of the three bodies found in the storage locker barrels.

The next day, June 13, John Robinson was charged with five counts of first-degree murder for the bodies found in Kansas and Missouri. The death penalty was sought by both states. In Johnson County District Court, Kansas, Robinson was formally charged with two further counts of murder for the deaths of Suzette Trouten and Izabela Lewicka in addition to the aggravated kidnapping of Suzette. In Cass County he was charged with the murders of Beverly Bonner and the two unidentified women found in the storage locker.

The women were later identified via their dental records as Sheila Faith and her disabled daughter Debbie.

John Edward Robinson was born in the Chicago suburb of Cicero on December 27, 1943. He was born the third of five children to his parents Henry and Alberta. At twelve, encouraged by his father, he joined the Boy Scouts and by 1957 he was named Eagle Scout. He was chosen as the sole American representative to lead 120 boy scouts at the Royal Command Performance in London in front of Queen Elizabeth II. At age 21, he married Nancy Lynch, but soon left Chicago for Kansas after being accused of embezzling money from the hospital where he worked.

In 1969, Robinson was arrested for embezzling over $100,00 from his latest employer, Fountain Plaza X-Ray Laboratory. In August he was found guilty of embezzling $33,000 and received a suspended sentence and placed on probation for three years.

In 1971, after several more cases of theft from employers, Robinson set up his own business but would continue forging documents to pay for his growing family.

His forgery crimes peaked in 1975 when Robinson was caught forging signatures and letters attempting to claim thousands of dollars via a shares scam. But an investigation into Robinson's company by the US Securities and Exchange Commission led to a four-count indictment for securities fraud, mail fraud and false representation. Robinson was fined $2,500 and placed on three years probation

In 1977, in an effort to raise his public profile, Robinson invented a new award, which he claimed in its first year. He was now Kansas City's "Man of the Year". The award included tricking state senator, Mary Gant, into presenting him with a plaque. The *Kansas City Star* ran a story about the luncheon in its next edition. However, the paper received numerous protests about the false story resulting in a reporter, Mack Edwards, being sent to investigate the claims. Embarrassed, the *Star* ran another story exposing Robinson's criminal history and his guilt in the embezzlement charges.

On December 30, 1980 Robinson was fired from another job as Employee Relation Manager at Guy's Foods in Liberty, Missouri. In June the following year Robinson was charged with Felony Theft. He was eventually ordered to pay back $50,000 to Guy's Foods.

On December 31, Robinson pleaded guilty to stealing a cheque worth $6,000 and faced a possible 7 years in jail. Robinson made a deal with the prosecutor and received 60 days in jail with five years probation. His jail time was served from May 8, 1982 before being released in July.

In summer 1984, Robinson advertised for a sales representative for his company, Equi-II. Paula Godfrey, a nineteen-year-old graduate, applied for the job and was successful, with Robinson even promising her a trip to San Antonio for training. Excited about her prospects Paula told her parents about the job and her employer.

On September 1, 1984 Robinson turned up at the Godfrey house to pick up Paula for her San Antonio trip. It was the last time Paula was seen alive by her family. With no contact from his daughter for four days Bill Godfrey flew to San Antonio himself, where he discovered that Paula hadn't booked into the hotel where she was supposed to be staying. Returning back home Bill confronted Robinson at his offices and demanded that his daughter contact him within three days. After two days a handwritten letter appeared with a Kansas postmark on it. The letter, supposedly written by Paula, stated that she was safe. Bill Godfrey dismissed the letter as a fake and took it directly to the police.

A second handwritten letter posted to the Overland Park police department, again reportedly written by Paula, stated that she was OK, thanking John Robinson for all his help. It also stated that she did not want to see her family again. Again Paula's family disbelieved the letter. However the police took the letter as genuine and removed Paula from the list of missing persons.

In January 1985, Robinson was allegedly involved in the disappearance of another woman. Lisa Stasi, a nineteen-year-old mother of daughter Tiffany, separated from her husband after a short but violent marriage and was staying at Hope House, a shelter for battered women, in Kansas. Her social worker Cathy Stackpole met Lisa to give her good news of a charity organisation willing to help her by offering her a job with training and a home rent free as part of their program. Lisa went to her sister-in-law's house to await collection by the group. John Robinson soon arrived to pick up Lisa and her baby, Tiffany, and drove away,

Lisa promised to return soon to collect the remainder of her things. A few days later after staying at the Overland Park Rodeway Inn, the threesome booked out on January 10, 1985, and Lisa was not seen alive again. Fifteen years later, the baby Tiffany resurfaced as the adopted niece of John Robinson. On Friday

January 11, 1985 Robinson met his brother Donald and his wife Helen at Kansas City International Airport. Robinson handed them their newly adopted daughter Tiffany, informing them that the mother had unfortunately committed suicide recently. Donald and Helen were unaware of the true story.

On January 13, Cathy Stackpole received a typed letter from 'Lisa Stasi' dated January 10, stating how grateful she was for their help. Lisa's mother-in-law Betty Stasi received a similar letter, but Betty knew that Lisa could not type. A few days later Robinson made phone calls asking if anyone had heard from Lisa, claiming that she and her daughter had disappeared from the Inn. At the time, Robinson's probation officer, Steve Haymes, became suspicious of Robinson's business dealings after hearing rumours of illegal activities and began an investigation into their dealings.

Irv Blattner an assistant and fellow parolee to Robinson walked into the Secret Service office in Kansas City on March 19, 1985 and offered to turn government witness into Robinson's activities. The previous week the Secret Service had questioned Robinson about a $741 cheque that had been illegally cashed by a friend of Robinson. The cheque was meant for a student named James Hargrove. Blattner believed that Robinson was setting him up to be a fall guy. Special Agent John Guerber asked Blattner about any involvement Robinson had in an organization assisting young women with babies. Blattner told the agent of a plan to help pregnant women give birth, then put the babies up for adoption. At the end of the interview Blattner signed a statement giving details of Robinson's illegal activities. On March 21, at 11.55 am Robinson was arrested. He later posted a $50,000 bond and was released from custody.

The FBI was involved in the investigation into Robinson and interviewed women at the Outreach program. Agent Levin gained evidence that a building used by Robinson's Equi II business was being used as a brothel. On March 26, Robinson and his attorney, Bruce Houdek, presented at a parole violation meeting held at Missouri State Probation Office. Robinson had to answer counts of parole violations of forgery and consorting with someone with a criminal record. Robinson denied both charges, claiming it was Blattner who was responsible for the cheque and also that he was unaware that Blattner was on probation. Steve Haymes was frustrated that it was proving difficult to pin Robinson down to any crimes.

The FBI continued to keep Robinson's business at Troost Avenue under surveillance. On June 12, 1985 while Robinson was away, they moved in. In the apartments they found Theresa Williams. She thanked them for saving her from Robinson. Theresa began to relate her story to the agents. Befriended by Robinson in April 1985, Robinson led Theresa into prostitution and she agreed to allow Robinson to become her pimp.

As the relationship continued, Robinson began to assault Theresa regularly and was able to coerce her into a plot to frame Irv Blattner. Robinson instructed Theresa to write a diary with dialogue that he gave her. This diary was to culminate in her apparent murder by Irv Blattner on June 15. Robinson told Theresa that she would actually be going to the Bahamas. While the FBI was able to take Theresa away from Robinson, probably saving her life, they did not make any move on Robinson.

For three weeks following Theresa's apparent disappearance from Troost Avenue, Robinson employed a private investigator, Charles Lane, to search for Theresa. On July 10, 1985 she was found. Robinson instructed Charles to monitor the house where she was living to find out the cause of her walking away. However Lane was interviewed by the FBI and Theresa was moved, this time well away from Robinson.

On July 29, 1985 Robinson returned to the courthouse in Clay County and was found guilty of breaking the conditions of his parole on three counts. On August 21, Judge Hutcherson ordered that Robinson's probation be revoked, thereby forcing Robinson to serve the remainder of his seven year sentence behind bars. An appeal was lodged which allowed Robinson to remain on bail for $250,000 during the appeal process. In May 1986, at the appeal hearing, Robinson came away with a satisfactory conclusion. The decision was overturned, which allowed Robinson to stay out of jail albeit on parole.

But it didn't last long, In January 1986, while on bail pending his appeal hearing, Robinson was in court defending a charge of felony theft. Robinson's company Equi-II had been commissioned by Back Care Systems International to market their range of products. The plan included publishing brochures to advertise the company. Back Care Systems International became suspicious that the requested work was not being carried out. Robinson forced Irv Blattner to forge invoices, but the trick failed, landing Robinson in court.

The three-day trial ended on January 30, 1986 and resulted in Robinson being found guilty of felony theft to the tune of $3600. The District Attorney for Johnson County, Steve Obermeier, observed Robinson's criminal past and persuaded the judge to take it into account when sentencing. Judge Herbert Walton agreed with the D.A. and sentenced Robinson to 5-14 years in addition to a fine of $5000. Defence lawyers tried to appeal the decision, but the appeal was denied.

On July 10, 1986 Robinson was charged again; this time on four counts of attempted fraud on a business deal with Gerhard Kuti. Robinson offered Gerhard part ownership on a land agreement, for which he paid Robinson $150,000. He later discovered Robinson had fraudulently modified the sales agreement to read $100,000 and pocketed the remainder.

Despite the additional charges, Robinson was still out of custody and continued to run his business. In January 1987, he employed Catherine Clampitt as his secretary. The job required Catherine to travel across the country on behalf of Robinson. Catherine's family were mildly suspicious of this opportunity and warned her to be careful. In spring 1987, Catherine disappeared. She was declared a missing person on June 15. Robinson was questioned, but with no clear evidence the case was dropped.

On May 16 1987, Robinson was finally sent to the Johnson County Jail, to serve a minimum sentence of five years. He was transferred to the Kansas State Penitentiary in Hutchinson as prisoner #45690. During his stay at the facility, Robinson suffered a series of strokes, which resulted in the right side of his face being partially paralysed.

On January 23 1991, Robinson had served the minimum time at Kansas and with his good behaviour he was granted parole. However, Robinson was immediately handed over to Missouri prison officials to serve the remainder of his original sentence after breaking his parole terms. Due to his ill health after the series of strokes, Robinson's sentence was carried out at Moberly Correctional Facility. He was then transferred again to Western Missouri Correctional Centre in Cameron. There he served the remainder of his sentence before being released in the spring of 1993.

Beverley Bonner met John Robinson during his time at the Missouri prison where she was responsible for the library in the facility and Robinson was made her assistant. The two became friends, having actually met twenty years earlier, when they worked at the same company in Kansas City. Soon the friends became lovers.

Once Robinson was released from prison, he offered Beverley the job of running his company Hydro-Glo, which sold organic vegetables. Beverly agreed and Robinson set up a home in Florida. Beverley divorced her husband, Dr William Bonner, after he found out about the affair she had with Robinson during his prison sentence, and she moved to Florida to be with Robinson.

Beverley's family never saw her again. Her ex-husband received the occasional typed letter bearing her signature, telling him that the company was sending her on various assignments around the world, travelling to Australia and across Europe. William never doubted the authenticity of the letters. However he did think it very odd that in December 1995 Beverley failed to attend the funeral of their eldest son Randy. He assumed that she must have been on important company business.

In 1994, forty-six-year-old Sheila Faith was smitten with Robinson when she first encountered him on the Internet. She had been depressed since her first husband, John, died in 1991 and had been left to raise her fifteen-year-old disabled daughter, Debbie, on her own. Sheila fell deeply in love with her knight in shining armour and announced to her friends that she and Debbie were to move in with him at his home in Kansas. Her friends were shocked by the sudden decision and warned her that it sounded to good to be true, but Sheila would not listen. In the summer of 1994, Robinson arrived at Sheila's door to help them move home, Sheila and Debbie were not seen alive again.

Shortly after they left for Kansas, Sheila's brother William Howell received the first of many typed letters signed by Sheila, telling him what a wonderful time she was having. But William was suspicious and asked social security to track down his sister and niece via the social security cheques they received for Debbie's disability. However, the administrator refused to divulge such information as it was considered private. In autumn of 1994, the social securities administration received a typed letter signed by Dr William Bonner informing them that Debbie was now completely disabled and required full time care. This in turn made an increase in the cheques payable to Sheila Faith.

Born in Poland, Izabela Lewicka immigrated to America in November 1993 with her family when she was 15. At nineteen Izabela became involved in the BDSM (Bondage, Domination, Sadomasochism) scene where in 1997 she made contact with Robinson over the Internet. Within nine months of the initial contact Izabela moved away from the family home in Indiana to be near Robinson in Kansas City, where she offered herself as a permanent sex slave.

During their time together Izabela proudly told people that Robinson was her husband, whereas he would say that she was his cousin. Izabela often visited Robert Meyer's bookstore in Overland Park, and was considered a regular. She and Robert would chat about the books she was purchasing. On July 18, 1999, Izabela, on one of her visits to the bookstore, was accompanied by Robinson whom she announced was her husband as he purchased some books for her. The pair was about to leave when Izabela mentioned to Robert that she was moving away. That was the last time Robert saw Izabela. Her parents received typed letters from Izabela telling them of her adventures around the world.

Suzette Trouten had experienced the BDSM scene for several years, particularly in the Gorean practices, becoming the slave to several masters and using the Internet to find willing partners. In 1999, Suzette 'met' a man in an Internet chat room who went by the name of JR (Robinson) who described himself as a wealthy businessman from Kansas City. After several months of contact by email, JR made a job offer to Suzette to nurse for his diabetic father on a round the world trip. Suzette was very tempted by the offer, but suggested that she spend some time in Kansas meeting both JR and his father before making a decision. In October 1999, Suzette and JR met, Robinson managed to persuade some colleagues to pose as various members of his family to entrap Suzette. At the end of the five days that she was in Kansas, Suzette agreed to the job offer and on February 14, 2000 she moved to Kansas to begin her new life. For the next two weeks Suzette rented an apartment on Robinson's credit card and he visited her regularly explaining that he had some business deals to conclude before she could begin her new career. The pair had regular sex taking photographs of the moments. Suzette emailed these to her friend Crystal Ferguson. The emails between the two friends would continue long after March 1, when Suzette disappeared. The tact of the emails suddenly changed after that date. Suzette no longer talked about past friendships or events in her life. All correspondence talked of how good her life was and how happy her boss and new master made her. All the emails were signed 'Suz' a nickname she never used.

Crystal continued to receive emails from 'Suz', and she explained that because her new master was treating her so well, she wanted Crystal to experience a relationship similar to hers. Crystal was highly suspicious that it was not her friend sending the emails, and so to expose the author, Crystal decided to play along. A man named JT who advertised himself as a stern but fair master soon contacted her. Crystal noticed that the email style was very similar to those from 'Suz' and hence suspected that they were from the same person. After a few weeks of playing along with her master JT, Crystal began receiving phone calls from him, and then a new contact began emailing her. A second male named Tom began emailing and offered to be Crystal's master, but again she was suspicious. Tom gave Crystal a series of phone numbers with which he could be contacted at any time. Using a police friend, Crystal had the numbers traced – each of them led back to John Robinson.

At the end of March, John Robinson called the Trouten household and spoke to Suzette's mother, Carolyn. He complained that her daughter had let him down, she had run away from him and her job, to be with a man she had only just met and that he hadn't seen her since. Carolyn's other daughter, Dawn, contacted Overland police and found that Robinson was already under investigation.

Oblivious to any investigation into his businesses, Robinson, in his many guises, continued with his emails to Crystal, attempting to persuade her to visit him in Kansas. On March 29, Detective Jack Boyer of the Lenaxa Police department contacted Crystal. The purpose of his visit was because of her friendship with Suzette. The detective explained that he was part of a task force investigating the disappearance of her friend. After discussing the case with Crystal, she mentioned the emails she was receiving from 'Suz' and the new contacts JT, JR and Tom and her suspicions. Detective Boyer agreed with her and requested Crystal to continue emailing them but pass copies onto him, Crystal said she would.

Robinson was known to stay at the Extended Stay America hotel in Kansas. In March he stayed for a few days with an unnamed woman. During their stay at the hotel the woman was only seen once, asking the hotel clerk to make four photocopies of a document. The desk clerk witnessed the document and was horrified to read that it was a slave contract. Kansas's law requires the all hotels provide a list of long stay guests to police. The hotel notified police as to the document's contents and the owner of it. The visiting detective left instructions to inform police immediately should Robinson return.

In the search for Suzette Trouten, detectives discovered that she and Robinson stayed at the Guesthouse motel in February. Forensic tests were done and bloodstains were discovered in the room they rented, but were unable to determine the source. Back at the Extended Stay America hotel an unnamed woman, from Dallas, booked in. Robinson, who soon joined her in room 120 on April 23, 2000, paid for her stay. The FBI staked out the hotel gathering evidence against their suspect.

After five days Robinson ordered his slave back to Dallas and prepared to move to back to Kansas. Robinson promised to help her with the move, but he never turned up. She tried calling Robinson but he was not contactable. He had taken a number of photographs of his slave in various bondage poses and she wanted them back. Unable to reach Robinson, she called the police. Two officers from Lenaxa interviewed the woman. After listening to her story, the detectives talked to the FBI, where for the first time they learnt of their file on Robinson that included suspicion of prostitution and white slavery.

On May 19, 2000 Robinson was again the subject in a complaint from another unnamed slave. Robinson used room 120 at the Extended Stay America. The woman told detectives that during her stay Robinson repeatedly overstepped the 'safe' mark, as with the previous women he beat her and took several photographs. When she complained, Robinson quickly left. The Lenaxa task force, followed by the FBI, interviewed the woman to gain important information about Robinson.

The task force decided that Robinson was becoming too dangerous and the decision was made to arrest him. District Attorney Paul Morris approved the arrest warrant and on June 2, 2000 detectives moved in.

The charges against Robinson were increased on July 28, 2000 when he was charged with the murder of Lisa Stasi, who had disappeared in 1985, and the aggravated interference with parental custody in the case of Robinson's 'niece' who was believed to be Lisa's daughter Tiffany.

In late January 2001, Missouri prosecutor Chris Koster, backed up the three murder charges with 56 counts of forgery. Robinson was accused of forging the social security cheques intended for Sheila and Debbie Faith. Robinson, if found guilty of the forgery charges could have faced a 382 year sentence.

Despite a last minute appeal by the defense team citing slow release of prosecution evidence, the trial of John Edward Robinson Snr began on September 16, 2002 in the Olathe courtroom of Judge John Anderson III. Robinson's case was the first in the state to potentially end with a death sentence. In all previous cases the defendant had negotiated a plea bargain in order to avoid the death sentence. The prosecution, headed by District Attorney Paul J Morrison, had charged Robinson with eight counts including the murders of Suzette Trouten; Izabel Lewicka and Lisa Stasi. Morrison had also successfully argued, prior to the trial, that although Robinson was to be tried separately for the murders of Beverly Bonner and Sheila and Debbie Faith in Missouri, they were so crucial to Robinson's activities that they could be included as evidence of an ongoing pattern.

On October 8, testimony began. Outside, in a radio station stunt, t-shirts were being sold with the phrase 'Roll Out the Barrels' emblazoned on them. For two weeks, and with the testimony of 100 witnesses, DA Paul Morrison presented his case to the jury. Robinson's wife, Nancy, testified that she knew that her husband used the alias James Turner and that he was having affairs with other women. She also admitted that Robinson enjoyed a BDSM lifestyle. Deputy Coroner Donald Pojman described how each woman was killed having received heavy blows to the left hand side of their skull. Each was instantly killed. However Izabel Lewicka did not, she somehow survived for a short period of time before succumbing to the injury.

The defence argued that the prosecution case was entirely based on circumstantial evidence. They admitted that evidence presented did link Robinson to the five women, but not to their deaths, hence the case was not proven. Patrick Berrigan, for the defence, pointed out that no other potential suspects were investigated; Robinson was the sole focus for the police investigation. Despite the fact that other unknown persons had ample opportunities to have committed the murders, the potential suspects were overlooked.

On October 28, 2002, the testimony ended and the jury filed out to begin their deliberations. The following day at 3pm, after 11 hours of discussion, the jury returned with a guilty verdict on all charges. Robinson gave no reaction to the verdict.

Three days later the penalty phase of the trial began. Under Kansas State Law the options were simple, a life sentence or death by lethal injection. To be sentenced to death, the jury must be unanimous in their decision. The defence pleaded for a life sentence, using members of the Robinson family to request mercy. Nancy Robinson once again took the stand. When questioned she accepted that her husband was guilty because the jury had found him so. The jury, however, rejected the pleas and announced their decision of death by lethal injection. Once again Robinson stood to hear the verdict and offered no response. He was taken back to his cell at Johnson County Jail and placed on suicide watch until he received his formal sentencing. Meanwhile, his defence lawyers filed an appeal against the verdict. The appeal was rejected and on January 21, 2003, Judge John Anderson III formally gave Robinson a death sentence and a life sentence for the murder of Lisa Stasi, whose body has never been found.

In March 2003, Robinson agreed to be extradited to Missouri to face a further three murder charges; those of Beverly Bonner, Sheila Faith and her daughter Debbie Faith. On April 24, 2003 Robinson pleaded not guilty to the three murder charges. Judge Joseph Dandurand set a trial date of March 8, 2004.

On October 16, 2003, Robinson returned to court to announce, via his lawyers, a change in his plea. Robinson had negotiated with prosecutor Chris Koster to give a guilty plea for the three Missouri murders. In exchange for the plea, Robinson received a life sentence. However, as part of the plea, Robinson confessed to two further murders for which he had not been charged. These two additional victims were identified as nineteen-year-old Paula Godfrey, who disappeared from Olathe in 1984, and twenty-seven-year-old Catherine Clampitt who vanished in 1987.

S

Heriberto Seda

On November 17, 1989, New York police received a letter with the opening words 'This is the zodiac'. The letter was addressed to the anti-crime department and contained a warning of 12 murders. One for each of the 12 zodiac signs. With one murder already claimed and no evidence to link it to any specific crime the police dismissed the letter as a crank.

On March 8, 1990 at 1.45am Mario Orozco was shot in the back by a mystery assailant whilst walking through Brooklyn. The bullet was lodged next to Mario's spine but he survived the attack.

Three weeks later on March 29, 1990 a drunken Germán Montenedro slowly made his way home after a row with his girlfriend. Suddenly Germán crashed to the ground, knocked unconscious as his head hit the hard pavement. A bullet had punctured Germán's left hand side cutting through his liver, and stopped on the right hand side of his body. Germán awoke in pain, but alive. He was able to reach his father's house and was taken to hospital. The man was the second survivor of the mystery gunman.

Just two days later seventy-eight-year-old Joe Proce was walking through Queens in the early hours near to his home, when an unknown man approached him. After a brief argument about money Joe turned his back and crashed to the floor having been shot. The bullet entered his lower back hitting his kidney. Joe's neighbours who had heard the gunfire called 911, and an ambulance took Joe to hospital. On June 24, 1990 Joe died in hospital.

The New York Post received a letter on June 6, addressed to the editor, it read

> *This is the Zodiac the twelve sign*
> *Will die when the belts in the heaven are seen*
>
> *The first sign is dead on March 8 1990 1:45 AM*
> *White man with cane shoot on the back in the street*
>
> *The second sign is dead on March 29 1990 2:57 AM*
> *White man with black coat shoot in the side in front of house*
>
> *The third sign is dead on May 31 1990 2:04 AM*
> *White old man with cane shoot in front of house*
>
> *No more games pigs*
>
> *All shoot in Brooklyn with .380 RNL or 9mm*
> *No grooves on bullet*

The top of the letter was marked with a large circle intersected with a cross.

It was a further thirteen days before the newspaper let the public know of the threats with the headline 'RIDDLE OF THE ZODIAC KILLER'.

Two days after the New York Post printed the Zodiac letter, a fourth shooting took place. Larry Parham was asleep on a bench in Central Park when the unidentified assailant now known as the Zodiac shot him in the chest, the bullet somehow missed his aorta and exited Larry's body via the right armpit. Due to the early hour of the day, it was a couple of hours before an ambulance was on the scene. Once again the Zodiac's victim survived the shooting. A note found at the scene contained the now familiar circle intersected with a cross.

The New York Post received a second letter from the Zodiac.

> *This is the <u>Zodiac</u> I have seen the post and you say*
> *The note sent to the post not similar to any of*
> *The San Francisco Zodiac letter you are*
> *Wrong the hand writing looked different it is*
> *One of the same <u>Zodiac</u> one <u>Zodiac</u>*

The letter went on to say

Fourth sign dead shoot in Central Park
    White man sleeping on bench with little
    Black bag shoot in chest

In addition, the Zodiac included a drawing of the original Zodiac killer taken from Robert Graysmith's book about the San Francisco Zodiac of the 1960's. In fact, New York Post journalists made contact with Robert Graysmith to ask if he had any insight into these shootings. Graysmith checked that the suspects in the original case had not moved to New York – none had.

The New York police released a wanted poster of a black man seen speaking to Larry before he was shot. In the subsequent furore, police questioned several people that 'looked like' the suspect. Astrologers predicted that the next victim would be a Leo causing panic amongst Leos.

There were no further shootings attributed to the Zodiac for over two years, until August 10, 1992 when the silence ended.

Patricia Fonti walked through Highland Park and asked passers-by for cigarettes. One particularly helpful man said he would give her some if she followed him, Patricia obliged. Once secluded, Patricia was shot. The first bullet passed straight through her, then a second bullet hit her but Patricia did not go down. The Zodiac kicked Patricia, but it still had no effect. The killer drew a knife and stabbed Patricia all over her body. She was finally dead having suffered two punctured lungs and a perforated kidney. In total, police found over 100 stab wounds on her body. Patricia was the Zodiac's first direct victim.

Ten months later on June 4, 1993, Jim Weber was shot in the buttocks, but survived the shooting.

The next victim did not. The Zodiac shot dead Joseph Diacone with a single shot fired through the man's neck at close range just before midnight on July 20, 1993.

On October 2, 1993 the Zodiac struck again. Diane Ballard was shot through the neck. The bullet missed her vital arteries but lodged in her spine. The Zodiac ran away believing Diane was dead, but she survived the shooting.

The attacks had lasted four years and three people were dead and a further six shot. The police had made no arrests and had no clues to the assailant.

On March 10, 1994 officer Brian Fleming stopped a Hispanic male on suspicion of carrying a weapon. When searched, Officer Fleming found a 3½-inch dagger and a .22 calibre zip gun.

Heriberto Seda was subsequently arrested for possession of a gun. Seda's fingerprints were taken, and he was placed in the cells to await arraignment the following day.

At the arraignment Seda was granted bail. In an error, the killer's gun was labelled incorrectly, was never tested and was destroyed. All the charges were dropped, the records sealed and his fingerprint card destroyed by order of the court. Seda was a free man after the very close call.

The New York Post received a further letter from the Zodiac on August 3, 1994 admitting to the shootings of Patricia Fonti and Jim Weber. Also included on the letter were the words

>*Sleep my little dead how we loathe them*

And

>*NYPD 0*
>*Zodiac 9*

The Zodiac then again disappeared. The NYPD, having taken fingerprints from the Zodiac letters, routinely checked them against people arrested within the area to see if there was a match. None were found. One Zodiac suspect would have his urine secretly tested in the hope of a DNA match[20]. The result was negative.

June 18, 1996 and Heriberto Seda and his half sister Gladys, known as Chachi, were arguing in their humble home because Chachi and a friend, Wilber Rios, were laughing. Seda considered that sinful and demanded that he leave. Chachi turned her back on her brother and was shot in the buttocks with a .41 shotgun. In pain, Chachi managed to escape and went to the neighbours' flat where they dialled 911 for help. Wilber Rios meanwhile barricaded himself in one of the bedrooms.

Shortly after midday, NYPD officers arrived at the scene and were greeted with shots fired from the third floor window. An exchange of gunfire between Seda and NYPD officers ensued.

Fifteen minutes into the siege, negotiations began between Seda and DS Joey Herbert. After three hours of slow talking, and no shots, Seda decided to surrender and Joey Herbert escorted him out.

When police officers entered Seda's room they discovered an array of weapons including nine pipe bombs and a crossbow.

Heriberto 'Eddie' Seda was arrested and charged with fifteen counts of attempted murder and multiple counts of possession of deadly weapons and explosives. Asked to write a confession Seda duly obliged.

He was then asked to rewrite the confession and include the shooting at the cops. Seda happily rewrote it. Once again the officer read the confession and spotted the use of symbols, including one that looked like a cross.

The arresting officer, Detective Danny Powers, talked to Joey Herbert about his suspicions. Joey read through the note paying particular attention to the handwriting and became excited, exclaiming, "This is the Zodiac".

Copies of the Zodiac letters were quickly retrieved for comparison. Seda's fingerprints were also taken, and questioning began again on the suspect.

---

[20] a DNA sample was retrieved from the saliva from the Zodiac envelopes

Joey Herbert and Louie Savarese talked to Eddie about the shoot out. Seda politely discussed it. As soon as the conversation turned to the Zodiac Seda clammed up, looking at the floor. The detectives knew they had their answer. Meanwhile the fingerprints were compared to the one left by the Zodiac.

Three experts examined the letters and concluded that the Zodiac and Heriberto Seda were the same person.

At 8.00 pm the officers told Seda to confess to the Zodiac crimes. No reply. After almost three hours of persuading, badgering and shouting, Seda came clean about the shootings, eventually signing a written confession. Seda would be charged as the Zodiac killer.

Heriberto Seda's trial began on May 15, 1998 in Queens, New York and lasted five weeks after which he was convicted of the murders of three people and the wounding of another. Judge Robert Hanophy sentenced Seda to a total of 83 years in prison.

The sentence was later increased by a further 152 years for the attempted murders.

Robert Shulman

Between 1991 and 1996 Robert Shulman murdered at least five prostitutes, mutilated their bodies and dumped them in garbage cans around New York.

Robert Shulman was born on March 28, 1954 and while still a boy both his mother and brother committed suicide. He was destroyed by the deaths and blamed himself. He never fully recovered from the tragic deaths and became an angry, morose and withdrawn man.

The first woman murdered by Shulman was Lori Vasquez, a twenty-four-year-old Brooklyn woman, in 1991. The woman's mutilated body was found dumped into a Yonkers trashcan.

The second body was also found in a bin in Yonkers in 1992. The woman's body had been dismembered making identification impossible.

For two years the killer apparently did not murder another victim. Then in December 1994, he killed his next victim. The unidentified woman's body was found dumped on the side of the road in Medford. Her face and body had been disfigured beyond recognition.

Eighteen-year-old Lisa Ann Warner's body was found in April 1995. Her body had been picked up in one of the city's garbage trucks and was not discovered until the mutilated remains were found at a Brooklyn recycling plant.

Robert Shulman picked up Hollis prostitute, twenty-eight-year-old Kelly Sue Bunting, on December 11, 1995 in Queens. Shulman took Kelly to his rented apartment, where he had sex with the woman before bludgeoning her to death. Her dismembered body was dumped in a garbage bin in Melville, Long Island.

The killer was arrested and was found guilty of the murders of the three identified women. An attempt to commit suicide failed.

On July 12, 1999 Robert Shulman was sentenced to death by lethal injection for the bludgeoning murders of three of the women in New York.

Peter Stubbe

In Medieval Germany there were werewolf trials like the witch hunts of 1600's Massachusetts. But no other trial stood out in Germany's werewolf history than that of Peter Stubbe (or Stump, Stempf, Stubb or any other variation that has been suggested over the years.)

From 1564 to 1589 Peter Stubbe stalked the villagers of Bedburg Germany. During his rampage Stubbe murdered 13 children and 2 women. Both women were pregnant when murdered.

According to testimony at his trial, Stubbe tore the flesh from the bodies of his victims before devouring their hearts and other organs.

Often limbs and other body parts were found strewn around the outskirts of the village. If a member of a villager's family went missing it was always assumed that they had fallen victim to the carnage of Stubbe. The villagers lived in fear of Stubbe for over 25 years. Most of the residents of Bedburg would not travel out of their house alone. Many of them carried protection with them at all times in case they happened on Stubbe and his accomplices.

It was decided to finally track down Stubbe. Farmers with their dogs set out to catch the werewolf. According to witnesses Stubbe was in his werewolf guise when found, but soon turned into his human form.

Stubbe did not act alone in the murderous campaign. His lover, Katherine Trompi and his daughter Beell assisted him. Beell was as depraved as her father and readily committed incest with him, resulting in the birth of a son. However the baby did not live long as Stubbe quickly ate the newborn, stopping only to note on the tastiness of the brains. He also committed incest with his sister.

During the hysterical trial of Stubbe and his accomplices, witnesses told of seeing Stubbe turn himself into a werewolf when hunting for potential victims.

After his trial in Cologne, Germany in 1589 he was found guilty of the murders of the 15 victims and was sentenced to a fate to match the severity of his crimes.

Stubbe was tied down to a cartwheel. Red-hot pincers were used to pull the skin and flesh from his body.

His arms and leg were broken with hammers before his head was severed from his body. His beaten remains were then burned at the stake along side his accomplices who were burned alive.

After his execution, a high pole was put up in the town of Bedburg, where upon they placed the likeness of a wolf and the head of Peter Stump, along with sixteen pieces of wood, to represent his victims.

Ahmad Suradji
Medicine man is arrested.
Dukun Ahmad Suradji, also known as Datuk or Nasib Kelewang, was a well-respected 48-year-old witch doctor in Medan, the capital of North Sumatra. Many trusted the man for guidance on matters such as love and money and health. However, when the doctor was arrested by police for the murders of several local women, people began to wonder about the medicine man's true powers.

Suradji claimed that he would bury young women in the sands near his sugarcane plantation. Suradji would then strangle the terrified women and drink the saliva that dribbled from their mouths.

The ritual supposedly increased the man's powers so he could help clients heal all manner of problems, from poverty to illness to love. After the sacrificial ceremony was completed Suradji would dig the dead bodies out of their murderous trench and rebury them closer to his house. All of the victims were buried in a specific pattern facing the witch doctor's house.

A Father's Vigilance
Suradji may have gotten away with the murders for many more years had it not been the vigilance of one father, whose suspicions ended on May 2, 1997 with the witch-doctor's arrest along with that of his three wives, who were sisters.

The vigilant father went to police after his daughter had gone to see Ahmad and didn't return. The police quickly descended on the witchdoctor's plantation property and quickly found the body of one of the victims in a field close to his house. The police began a thorough search of the plantation and found 41 additional bodies.

Suradji Confesses
Suradji confessed to the murders of 16 women over a five-year period, hoping that once police had found that many buried superficially around the property that they may stop looking, however police kept on digging and found evidence that at least 25 women had fallen victim to the medicine man. Police found bodies and other items, including clothing and jewellery and watches that made identification easier.

With the evidence mounting against him, Suradji quickly changed his story. He told police that over the past eleven years he had murdered 42 women, ranging in ages from 11-years-old to 30. According to the killer many of the victims had been prostitutes and so their disappearance was not immediately noticed or not reported at all.

42 bodies, 120 bodies or perhaps more?
But even the supposed body count of 42 was still low. Once the media had gotten wind of the case, another 80 families came forward with similar stories about the medicine man. So police continued their vigilance of finding more bodies.

Suradji's Method
Most of the women who had hired the doctor had required him to cast magic spells to ensure the faithfulness of their husbands or boyfriends. Neighbours said that many women sought the sorcerer's help believing they would make themselves richer, healthier and more sexually attractive to men.

Suradji's method was to charge each victim according to their needs, the price was usually around $300. Then he would take them to a sugarcane plantation near his home and bury them in the ground up to their waist, he would tell the women it was a part of his ritual. Once in the ground he strangled each woman with electrical cable. Then he drank their saliva, undressed their corpse and reburied them with their heads pointing to his home to enhance his own magical powers.

According to Suradji, he had a dream in which the ghost of his father told him to kill 70 women and drink their saliva so he could become a "dukan", or mystic healer, he said.

The End of Suradji's Campaign
During their trials, both Suradji and his senior wife Tumini denied the slayings. They later claimed they confessed under torture by the police. However, their forced confession defence fell on deaf ears and on April 27, 1998, the witch doctor was found guilty by the three-judge panel of Indonesia's worst killing spree. Suradji was sentenced to death by firing squad. Those in court cheered as the sentence was read out.

T

Bobbie Sue Terrell

Bobby Sue Terrell murdered twelve elderly patients in nursing homes in Illinois and Florida. The woman, working as a nurse on the night shift, gave the patients overdoses of insulin. She would then slice and cut herself before calling police claiming there was a serial killer loose in the homes at which she worked.

Finally, an investigation was made into the woman's background and it was discovered that she was a diagnosed schizophrenic, and suffered from the controversial Munchausen Syndrome by Proxy.

Subsequent investigations found that Terrell had murdered twelve elderly patients in St Petersburg, Florida as well as several others in Illinois during 1984 and 1985.

In 1988 the thirty-two-year-old Terrell pleaded guilty to two charges of second-degree murder and sentenced to prison for 65 years.

Sipho Thwala

Thirty-year-old South African Sipho Thwala was found guilty of the murders of sixteen people on March 31, 1999.

The killer, at the time of his trial, was the main suspect in over nineteen murders linked to the serial killing case dubbed the "Phoenix Strangler" case.

The young women victims were raped and strangled to death with their own underwear before being buried in shallow graves on the cane fields of Phoenix, Durban, South Africa.

According to evidence presented at Thwala's trial, his reason for murdering young women was revenge against his girlfriend who had an abortion. The killer's personality supposedly changed after hearing that his partner had terminated the life that he had helped create.

The killer became sad and withdrawn before turning his violent thoughts to others whom he believed looked like his girlfriend.

A body found on July 1, 1997 after the annual fires in the sugar cane fields broke the case. After further investigation more bodies turned up and police looked at other older cases that appeared to be linked. A total of nineteen cases were linked to the same killer, Sipho Thwala.

Daniel Troyer

Incarcerated serial killer Daniel Troyer is currently the prime suspect in a string of murders in Salt Lake City.

Troyer, who is currently in prison for life for the murders of eighty-three-year-old Drucilla Ovard and eighty-eight-year-old Ethel Luckau, was also imprisoned for several other similar attacks.

Eighty-three-year-old Drucilla Ovard was stripped naked and bashed and strangled to death by Troyer on July 17, 1985 in the bathroom of her home in Salt Lake City. Her ribs were broken in the attack that also left Troyer with a broken hand. When the attack occurred Troyer was on parole for the 1978 attempted rape and bashing assault of a seventy-one-year-old quadriplegic woman.

Two weeks after the murder of Drucilla, Troyer failed in an attempt to attack another elderly woman. On July 31, 1985 Troyer broke into the house of seventy-year-old Carol Nelson, with intent to assault the elderly woman. Neighbours heard commotion in the house and knowing that Carol was not home at the time, called the police who arrested Troyer. Troyer was sentenced to three years in prison for the attempted break-in.

He was paroled shortly before the attack on Ethel Luckau.

Ethel was strangled as well as suffocated on August 17, 1988. The evidence that proved to be the link between the murders of Ethel and Drucilla was semen-stained towels found at each scene.

Troyer is also suspected of the murder of sixty-nine-year-old Thelma Blodgett on July 11, 1985 only six days before that of Drucilla.

Lucile Westerman is also suspected to be a victim of Troyer, murdered six days after Ethel Luckau.

It was while Troyer was in prison for the attempted break-in of Carol Nelson's home that DNA was able to link him to the murders of Drucilla and Ethel.

He was sent to trial in August 1999 where he was found guilty and sentenced to life in prison for the two murders, however investigations continue into a further dozen murders of elderly women in the region.

Tylenol Case

Unsolved cases often spark the imagination of criminalists and laypersons alike. The case of the Tylenol product tampering was one case that, to this day, remains unsolved and people still attempt to resolve it.

If nothing else, the Tylenol case produced the first product tamper-proof casings in an attempt to prevent further cases, however many copycat poisonings have followed.

The Tylenol Serial Killer struck fear into the citizens of Chicago during 1982 when seven people died from consuming cyanide laced headache-pills.

The first victim of the product tampering case was twelve-year-old Mary Kellerman. On September 29, 1982 the young girl had woken with all the classic symptoms of a cold. Her mother gave her some Tylenol. Yet little did her mother know but she had just given her daughter a capsule filled with potassium cyanide and not paracetamol.

In less than an hour the little girl was found in the bathroom of her home where she had collapsed. Her parents rushed her to hospital where she died. At the time no one suspected that the pill she had taken had been tampered with.

Later that same day, another person was rushed to hospital barely breathing. Adam Janus had taken a Tylenol capsule after feeling a slight pounding in his head. Like the Kellerman family, he had no reason to suspect the slightly lumpy pills contained anything sinister.

Adam died later that evening from the cyanide pill he had taken.

Like most sudden deaths, Adam's family were devastated by his passing. The doctors assumed he had suffered a major heart attack but they would soon discover the source. Adam's brother and sister-in-law, Stanley and Theresa, were both overcome with grief at Adam's sudden death and the following day, both took some headache tablets from Adam's Tylenol bottle. Within hours the Janus family were mourning two more deaths.

Though the deaths of three members of the Janus family were tragic, it gave police the suspicious leads they needed to conduct further tests. The bodies of Adam, Stanley and Theresa Janus were given a full toxicological screening. In the meantime more people were dying from taking the unsuspecting pills.

After giving birth to her baby son, Mary Reiner ingested a few of the tainted Tylenol pills and soon collapsed. She was rushed to hospital, but died shortly after arriving. Another victim, Paula Prince also collapsed after taking Tylenol for a headache.

The last victim was Mary McFarland. Like the other victims she collapsed after ingesting the cyanide laced Tylenol capsules.

When cyanide was found in the blood of all three members of the Janus victims, police and paramedics began to piece together the sudden deaths around Chicago. So far all the victims had taken Tylenol capsules.

The bottles of Extra Strength Tylenol was tested from the victims' residences and found to contain cyanide filled capsules. Someone had removed the paracetamol powder from the capsules and replaced it with cyanide.

A statewide product recall was launched and Tylenol was removed from the shelves of all pharmacies and supermarkets in Illinois.

In total, the Tyenol killer had removed 7 bottles of Tylenol Extra-Strength from six stores in Chicago, and replaced several tablets from each bottle with tainted pills before replacing the bottles back in a group of stores. Most of the bottles contained 5 cyanide pills, only one contained 10 of the tainted tablets.

The bottles were placed back on the shelves of two Jewels Food stores, an Osco Drug Store, Walgreen Drug Store, Franks Finer stores and another store on the day that Mary ingested the medication.

Police arrested several people suspected of being the Tylenol Tamperer, yet no one has ever been charged with the murders. To date, the case remains unsolved.

U

Andrew Urdiales

On January 18, 1986 student Robbin Brandley was returning to her car on campus at Saddleback College, Mission Viejo, California when she was attacked by Andrew Urdiales. The man lunged at the young woman with a six-inch bladed knife. He stabbed her a total of forty-one times in the neck, chest, back and hands. Robbin bled to death at the scene. Urdiales, a marine at the time, returned to the Corps base after the attack and acted as if nothing had happened.

The second victim of Andrew Urdiales was twenty-nine-year-old Julie McGhee. The woman was abducted by Urdiales and taken to a remote area near Cathedral City. Once alone, the killer bashed the woman before raping her. Urdiales then shot Julie at close range, killing her. Once the woman was dead the killer stripped her of her clothes and jewellery making it harder for police to later identify her remains.

Julie's partially decomposed body was found in July 1988, and showed teeth marks from wild animals. There were also several .45 calibre cartridge casings found at the scene. Police were able to match them with two later murder victims, Tammy Erwin and Mary Ann Wells.

The body of Mary Ann Wells was found on September 25, 1988 in a deserted alleyway in an industrial area in San Diego. The woman, working as a prostitute, was picked up by Urdiales and driven to the industrial estate. The pair agreed on $40 as payment for sexual intercourse. Once Mary Ann and Urdiales had sex, he pulled out his .45 calibre gun and shot the woman to death and dumped her body from the car. Urdiales then took back the $40 he had given her and returned to his Marine barracks. However, the killer made two mistakes. He left a condom at the scene of the crime on which Mary Ann and Urdiales' DNA was found. Also the casings from his gun matched those found at the murder of Julie McGhee. Police were able to instantly link the cases.

In April 1989, Urdiales picked up eighteen-year-old Tammy Erwin. The killer drove her to a deserted area and demanded sex. After he raped her, Urdiales shot Tammy three times. He dismantled his gun and threw parts of it away after Tammy's murder. He knew he had left casings at the last three murders and was concerned that they would be linked. Urdiales was right to be concerned; police quickly linked the murders of Tammy, Mary Ann and Julie.

The murders were beginning to take a toll on Urdiales and he was discharged from the Marine Corps in 1991.

Nineteen-year-old Jennifer Asbenson was lucky to escape with her life in Palm Springs on September 28, 1992. The woman had been waiting at a bus stop on her way to work. The friendly looking Urdiales stopped and offered the woman a lift to work. The woman accepted and Urdiales drove her to work.

When Jennifer had finished her shift, she walked outside to find the man waiting for her. The young woman, though a little freaked out by the man waiting eight hours to drive her home, accepted the lift again. This time however, Urdiales changed. He bashed the woman before choking her until she passed out. He raped her in a secluded area, before making her get into the boot of the car. However, when Urdiales' car became bogged, the woman saw her opportunity and she escaped with her life, breaking free of the car's trunk and fleeing.

She painted a vivid picture at the trial of her attacker saying "He had a lot of rage.. showed no emotion to whatever I said. He wouldn't feel a thing for me."

The escape worried Urdiales, and for two and a half years he did not kill.

The next victim was not so lucky. Thirty-two-year-old Denise Maney was working as a prostitute in California when she was picked up by Urdiales, who was on holidays there in March 1995. The man took Denise to a deserted spot and tied the woman's hands and feet together. Urdiales raped the woman before putting the gun in her mouth and fired. The back of the woman's head exploded.

The killer then stripped off all of the dead woman's clothes to prevent identification and dumped her body in the desert.

Laura Uylaki was the killer's sixth victim. The twenty-five-year-old was picked up by Urdiales in Cook County and beaten and raped before being shot dead. Laura's hands were cuffed together and her clothes were missing when she was pulled from Wolf Lake in Cook County on April 13, 1996.

Three months later Urdiales killed again. The naked body of Cassandra Corum was fished from the Vermillion River in Livingston County. Like Laura before her, Cassandra had been beaten and handcuffed before being raped. Her ankles were taped together with duct tape, and tape covered her mouth. Urdiales cut the clothes off Cassandra before raping her and shooting her dead. He then dumped her in the river in July 1996.

Urdiales' final victim was twenty-two-year-old Lynn Huber on August 2, 1996. Her murder was an echo of Laura Uylaki's four months earlier. Lynn had been beaten and raped by Urdiales. He handcuffed the girl's hands and shot her. He had also stabbed her twenty-eight times in the frenzied attack before dumping her in Wolf Lake. Lynn had tried to fight back against Urdiales and actually broke her killer's finger.

Urdiales was arrested in April 1997 and began confessing to a string of murders.

On May 30, 2002 after a seven week trial in Cook County, Urdiales was found to be sane and sentenced to death for the murders. Urdiales is also to face trial in California for the murders of five more women and another murder trial in Livingston County, Illinois.

The defence painted the picture of Urdiales as a product of his upbringing, claiming he had been sexually abused as a child. They also claimed he was unable to control his anger due to brain damage to his frontal lobe. Urdiales had been accidentally dropped onto a concrete floor as a baby and landed on his head; the problem was then exacerbated by a car accident when he was three, when he hit his head once again. The defence lawyers claimed that due to his brain injuries as a child and another when he was a marine, he had been unable to control his anger resulting in the death of his victims.

Significant tests were conducted to confirm or deny the presence of brain injuries as claimed by Urdiales. None were found. The experts claimed that Urdiales was a sociopath, and sociopathy was not a mental illness, thereby being impossible to be insane. The fact that Urdiales had killed the family dog with a baseball bat as a child was also admitted into evidence of the man's sociopathy.

Regardless of the legal manoeuvres, it took the jury less than an hour to find him guilty of the murders of Lynn Huber and Laura Uylaki and he sentenced him to death.

V

Hans Van Zon

Born in Utrecht, Holland on April 20, 1942, Hans Van Zon was a mother's boy; polite, quiet and introverted, so it was a complete surprise when at aged sixteen he left home to live in Amsterdam. He decided to experiment with bisexuality having sexual affairs with several men, and earning money through petty theft.

On July 22, 1964 Van Zon went on a date with Elly Hager-Segov. At the end of the evening, Van Zon pretended to have missed his last train home and suggested to his female companion to let him stay the night at her flat. Once there, he persuaded Elly to make love. Later that night Van Zon wanted sex again and tried to again entice Elly, but this time she refused. So Van Zon strangled Elly then cut her throat with a bread knife. After her death he raped the lifeless body.

Three years later on April 19, 1967 Van Zon murdered another lover. Coby Van der Voort was persuaded by Van Zon to swallow an aphrodisiac; it was actually a knockout drug. As soon as Coby was unconscious he beat her to death with a lead pipe, then stabbed at the body with a knife. Van Zon boasted of the murder to a criminal accomplice of his, Oude Nol. However Oude Nol saw an opportunity to blackmail Van Zon and took it. He insisted that in order to keep his silence Van Zon was to murder people at Oude Nol's discretion.

The deal resulted in the murder of eighty-year-old Jan Donse. Jan ran a fireworks shop in Amsterdam, where on May 31, 1967 Van Zon entered the shop and beat him to death with a lead pipe. This was followed up in August with the murder of a farmer, Reyer de Bruin, who Van Zon also beat to death in addition to cutting his throat. The partnership ended when Van Zon failed in his attempt murder a woman named Woortmeyer. She notified police and Van Zon was arrested with Oude Nol.

At the trial Van Zon received a life sentence, Oude Nol received seven years as an accomplice.

Marie Velten

Over a seventeen year period, between 1963 and 1980, German housewife Marie Velten poisoned five people. Her first victims, her father and aunt, were killed in 1963 and 1970 respectively when Velten was unable to care for them. In 1976 and again in 1978, Velten poisoned two husbands purely for money. A fifth and final victim in 1980 was a lover whom Velten just decided it would be fun to kill.

Velten was arrested in 1963 and confessed to the murders. The confession led to a guilty verdict and a life sentence.

W

Hu Wanlin

Hu Wanlin was a doctor who operated in China, where a lot of patients died in his care. Unlike mercy doctors like Dr Kevorkian, who assisted terminally ill people in suicides, "Dr" Hu Wanlin's victims were murdered at the hands of a cold-blooded killer.

The number of deaths attributed to the killer may not be known, however criminologists estimate the number to be over 100.

On January 16, 2001 the doctor was sentenced to fifteen years in prison for the illegal practice of medicine that resulted in the deaths of three of his patients, though police suspected he had killed many more.

One of the deaths attributed to Wanlin was that of Wang Baoran on December 16, 1997. The man died after ingesting a concoction made by the charlatan doctor. Another patient, He Suyun died on October 1, 1998 after drinking one of Wanlin's potions.

Another victim was the former Mayor of Luohe City, China, who was suffering from cancer of the liver. The Mayor consumed a potion over four days before dying from toxicity on September 27, 1998.

The fake doctor practiced the ancient Chinese deep breathing technique of qigong that provided him with a well-publicised and profitable clinic. Yet it was his potent concoctions made with high concentrates of sodium sulphate and Chinese herbs that made the police interested in his practice. The man was incarcerated several times for the deaths of patients in his care.

Eugen Weidmann

Eugen Weidmann was born in Frankfurt-on-Maine on February 5, 1908 and grew up to join the world's rank of serial killers.

On September 3, 1937 Eugene Weidmann murdered chauffeur Joseph Couffy by shooting him through the neck on France's Paris-Orleans Road. He was last seen driving Weidmann, who had hired the man under the assumed name of Dixon, earlier in the week. The man's body was found on September 8.

Around October 9, 1937 Eugen Weidmann struck again. The killer invited Jeanine Keller on a trip to South America. Jeanine met Eugene at Fontainbleu and was never seen alive again. Her body was found weeks later in a cave.

The body of Roger Le Blond was found covered in the back of his car near the Neully-sur-Seine Cemetery on October 17, 1937. Like the other victims, the man had been shot in the back of the neck.

Eugen Weidmann was the last person ever to be executed by guillotine in public.

William Wells

William Wells murdered his wife, his brother-in-law, his father-in-law, his wife's former boyfriend and a neighbour in a killing spree that lasted 10 days.

In his trailer in Mayport, Florida, the man first murdered his wife, Irene on May 14, 2003. Wells claimed that the death of his wife was accidental. According to facts tendered to the court, Wells was "playing" with a gun; he was pointing it at her, then held it to the back of her head and fired. Wells claimed that he thought the gun wasn't loaded.

Wells' brother-in-law John McMains arrived at the trailer later that day, and found his sister dead on the floor. Wells panicked and reloaded the gun and fired three shots into the man. The final shot, to John's head, killed him.

Wells sat inside the trailer for two days with the dead bodies of Irene and John. He expected the police to come, after the loud gunfire, but they did not come. Instead, on May 16 Irene's father Bill came to the Florida trailer to chat with his daughter. Inside the trailer he found the carnage that Wells had wreaked.

Bill was shot dead by Wells, who by this time had begun taking a lot of cocaine and marijuana to cope with the situation. Instead the situation got far worse.

A friend of Irene's, Richie Reese came by the trailer the following day. Wells, by now, was out of control. He had never liked Richie, an ex-boyfriend of his wife. He lured the man inside the trailer, and killed him in cold blood.

The final victim was drug dealer James Young on May 25. The man came to the trailer to give Wells a large amount of cocaine. Wells claimed he shot him when he suspected James of attempting to steal his marijuana.

By now the police had been called, and with his four-year-old son in his arms, Wells began a stand off that lasted 12 hours. In the end Wells was arrested and charged with the five murders.

While in prison the man called a newspaper and said he was going to plead guilty to four murders and ask for the death penalty. He claimed the four murders were to hide the fact that he had accidentally killed his wife.

At a court hearing in March 2004, the man pleaded not guilty to the deaths of his wife and the others before being assaulted by another prisoner in the holding cells. Wells was head-butted several times before a guard pulled the other man off Wells.

At the time of writing Wells is still awaiting trial.

Zhou Wen

On November 28, 2003, Chinese Police in the Liaoning Province city of Anshan announced the arrest of thirty-eight-year-old Zhou Wen. The serial killer known as the Taxi Demon had been responsible for the deaths of 6 local women through June and f July of 2003. The six women, reportedly all single, had taken late night rides in Zhou Wen's taxi before being murdered and dumped on wasteland surrounding the city.

After his arrest Zhou Wen confessed to the murders claiming he had an intense hatred of women, which began when his wife had an abortion without his permission. He gave police his diary that he had written during his killing spree which detailed the location of all his victims.

When asked why he kept a diary, his answer was that he assumed he would be caught and wanted to help police to find all the bodies.

Werewolf of Chalons

A contemporary of the shape-changer Peter Stubbe, was the Werewolf of Chalons. The killer was suspected to have murdered dozens of people in France in 1598.

Little is known about the killer also dubbed the Demon Tailor, apart from him being arrested and convicted on December 14, 1598 in France.

His method of murder was to lure his young victims to his tailor workshop in Chalons. There he would subject them to rape and other perversions before slitting their throats. The killer would then slice the flesh from the bodies of his victims to eat.

A rumour around Chalons was that the killer had lured the victims to his shop as a werewolf, changing shape to avoid being recognised in his human guise.

The killer would also pounce on unsuspecting victims in the woods surrounding the area, dragging the corpses back to his home for consumption.

When a customer noticed large barrels in the killer's tailor shop, an investigation was made and bones soaking in bleach were found.

The Demon Tailor was dragged out of his store and placed before a judge on December 14, 1598. He was found guilty of killing dozens of young people and was burned at the stake; an execution method reserved for those involved in witchery.

As the flames licked higher around the killer's body, he swore and cursed at his accusers before the killer expired on the pyre.

After the killer's death the courts destroyed all records regarding the case, leaving nothing but the horror stories passed down through the generations.

Ronald West
Finally a breakthrough
In March 1999, twenty-five years after the murders where committed by the killer known as the *".22-calibre killer"*, a detective found the evidence he needed to bring the killer to justice.

A 47c stamp attached to an envelope Ronald West had sent his second wife was all police needed to test the ex-police officer's DNA against semen found at the scenes of two women he was suspected of murdering in 1970.

The file had been re-examined in the 1990's following a re-evaluation of all the cold cases in Ontario's files. Over the past several decades most of the ".22-calibre killer" case file had gone missing, yet the perfectly preserved semen samples from both crime scenes remained.

When the detective in-charge of cold cases heard about Ronald West, an ex-police officer currently serving time in prison for robbery he immediately began searching the suspect's background.

The suspect had not been on duty as an officer when the women where murdered and in fact had been holidaying in the areas where they were killed. The coincidence was too great, yet police did not have any evidence to pursue the matter further.

That was until West's second wife received a letter from him asking her to sell some of his belongings to get money for him. His wife refused and instead handed the envelope and letter to police.

When the envelope arrived on the desk of the cold case investigative officer, he could not believe his luck. West himself had licked the 47cent stamp and it had enough DNA on it to test against the semen found at the two murder scenes.

On August 29, 1999 almost thirty years after the two women were raped and murdered, Ronald West was taken from Kingston Penitentiary to Brampton Court House where he was charged with the murders of Doreen Moorby and Helen Ferguson in May 1970.

The murders
In May 1970 Ronald West murdered two women.

The killer's first victim was thirty-four-year-old nurse Doreen Moorby on May 6, 1970. Doreen was home with her twenty-one month old son in Gormley, Ontario when she answered the front door. West asked the woman if he could use her phone, he told her that his car had broken down.

West forced his way into the house once Doreen had opened the door. He threw her onto the lounge suite in her living room where he raped her before shooting her. She was shot five times in the back of her head and two more times in her back.

Before leaving the house, West picked up the gun's shell casings and wipe down the door handle. Yet he left semen inside the woman that would later be used in evidence against the killer.

Doreen's baby son slept through the attack in another room of the house.

Doreen's husband found her defiled, lifeless body shortly after the attack.

While Ontario reeled from the brutal attack, it was not long before West struck again.

Thirty-eight-year-old nurse Helen Ferguson died a week after Doreen in almost the same circumstances. Helen opened the front door of her Palgrave, Ontario house to her killer. West told the woman he had a sick child in his car and needed urgent help. Helen, being a nurse did not think twice, heading out the door only to be forced back inside by her killer.

West raped her in the front room of the house before shooting her dead. She was shot once in the head and twice in the back.

Helen's nine-year-old son, Dale, who was sick in bed with the mumps, heard the gunshots and came out to see what was happening. He saw West pick up the bullet casings and clean the doorknob as he left the house.

The young boy watched as the man fled in a tan coloured car.

Dale Ferguson gave police a good description of his mother's killer, yet it did not provide them with a suspect. The search for the murderer became one of the largest manhunts in Ontario's history yet yielded no results until 1999.

Cop turned killer
Ronald Glenn West was born in Shelburne in 1947. He lived on a farm with his parents and younger brother and was described as a quiet boy until he reached his teens.

Once a teenager, West began to rebel against the quiet upbringing he had. There were rumours of him torturing his younger brother, including once tying him up inside a barn before setting it alight. Yet it appeared that once 18, West again settled down.

In 1965, he joined the police academy, and soon graduated. He worked as a beat cop in Toronto for six years. It was during this time that he murdered the two women and had brazenly handed out the police flyers with the sketch of his own face on them.

After his time with the Toronto police, West decided to resign. He was given an honourable discharge and moved on to less legal forms of money earning and soon found himself on the wrong side of the law.

During the mid 1970s he was sentenced to time in prison in British Columbia for a series of break and enter charges and on his release he married. With his first wife he had two sons but by the early 1980's he had left his wife, taking the children with him. He never told the children why and it was not until they were adults that they were reunited with their mother.

By 1988 he had settled in Blind River with his two sons. He married another woman who took over the mothering role of the two boys. Little did West's new wife know, but he had not divorced his first wife. Instead he told her that she had died.

He worked in the local mines for a period of time, before resigning, and making money again by unlawful means. He would break into people's homes to steal money and jewellery. He spent a lot of time away from home, and refused to tell his wife where he had been. It was not long though before police could answer her questions.

The crimes that put him in Jail
One of the crimes was an attack on a 65-year-old man. West knocked on the door of the man's house where he was advertising a room for rent. He bashed the man with a wrench, before tying him up by his hands and feet. West netted a few hundred dollars in cash from the brazen attack.

In Sault Ste, he robbed several jewellery stores using a distinctive starter pistol; in total he stole over $45,000 in cash and jewellery.

In Sudbury, he beat an elderly woman, tied her up and ransacked her home. Yet he was not successful, and only found $15.

West's life was spinning out of control. His victims were able to give police a description of their attacker, as he never wore a disguise; it was only time before police caught up with him.

And catch up with them, they did. West tried to pawn the jewellery he had stolen, but made a big mistake. He used his own driver's licence as identification at the pawn shop. On June 30, 1995 police arrived at the man's door with an arrest warrant.

He was charged with the string of robberies, yet at the time the starter pistol had not been found. West was sentenced to eight years in prison for the crimes.

The trial
It was while he was in prison for the robberies that he sent the letter to his second wife that was to be his undoing. The DNA left by West on the stamp and that left during the rapes of Doreen and Helen were a match. The police had their killer.

On August 7, 2001 West appeared in the courtroom at Brampton for his hearing, and to the surprise of the families of the women he pleaded guilty to both charges. The families were of the belief that West was to plead not guilty.

The judge gave the killer two life sentences, to be served concurrently at Kingston Penitentiary

What had changed the man's plea?

The gun
Before West appeared in court for his formal pleading, his second wife had been cleaning out the home and had given a desk, belonging to West to a family member. One day there was a thud in one of the desk's drawers. When the new owner opened the drawer he found that a gun, which had been previously taped to the underside of the desk had come unstuck and fallen into the drawer. It was not the gun that had been used in the murders, but it was one that had been used in a string of robberies that West was also to be charged with.

The .22 calibre gun used in the murders was found shortly before the hearing also. West had sold it and the new owner did eventually come forward. A test of the gun proved it had killed the two nurses. West was told of the discovery and changed his plea.

More Murders?
But had Ronald West still gotten away with murder? There is a long list of murders in which the killer was now a suspect.

In June 28, 1991 Gordon and Jackie McAllister where on a driving holiday when they stopped at a rest stop just outside Blind River. They were asleep in their caravan when a policeman knocked on the door. When Jackie opened the door for the officer she was shot dead; a single shot, at close range into her chest. The elderly woman's husband attempted to outrun the shooter, but was gunned down.

Another man, Brian Major who came to investigate the noise was shot dead also.

Though wounded severely, Gordon McAllister survived the attack and was able to give police a description of the killer; it looked like West had struck again.

The two murders and Gordon's attempted murder are still officially unsolved.

There was also a serial killer loose in Ontario that police are now investigating West as a possible suspect.

Eighty-three-year-old Lillian Toussant was tied to her bed face down and her house set on fine on September 24, 1975. Six years later the killer struck again, when sixty-eight-year-old Kenneth Murphy was murdered in a fire in his home in Finch Twp, on January 8, 1981. It was only after several other fires that police reinvestigated the man's death and declared a murder had taken place.

On November 18, 1983 seventy-one-year-old Archie Collison was murdered in a log cabin in Oxford Mills. A week later Harold Davidson, 60, was shot dead inside his home in Brinston on November 24, 1983. The killer had attempted to set fire to the house by over-turning the stove, but it failed.

Two months later on February 12, 1984 the killer entered a gas station in Metcalfe. He shot Gordon Hill who was on duty at the time. The gun used was the same as that used in the murder of Harold Davidson.

Forty-eight-year-old Wallace Johnston was shot in the head in his Monkland home on May 18, 1987. The killer had shot him through a window before entering the house. The killer tried to use the oven to set fire to the house but failed once more. Once again the killer used the same MO. Fifty-nine-year-old John King was shot once in his home in Morewood. The killer set the man's house on fire using the oven on July 14, 1987.

Police linked all the killings by the murderer's MO. Most of the victims had been shot and most had then had their houses set alight, or futile attempts had been made. The press dubbed the unknown murderer the "Ottawa Valley Killer" and at the time of writing the case remains unsolved.

Chris Wilder

Christopher Bernard Wilder was born on March 13, 1945 in Sydney Australia, the eldest of four sons. His father was a US Navyman stationed in Australia. Shortly after the war the family moved to the USA, before permanently moving back to Australia settling in New South Wales in the early 1960's.

Wilder almost died twice when he was quite young. As a toddler he was found face down in the family swimming pool, and then at three-years-old, while on a family trip, he lapsed into a coma, his breathing became shallow but he regained consciousness.

When Wilder was 17, he took part in a gang rape for which he was arrested. Part of his psychiatric treatment was to have electric shock therapy.

At 23 Wilder was married, however the marriage lasted less than a week after the bride complained of sexual abuse. After graduating from college, Wilder left Australia to live in Florida, in 1969.

By 1977 Wilder's sexual frustrations were surfacing and he confessed to a psychologist that he had sexually molested a sixteen-year-old girl, forcing her to fellate him after offering her a job. Wilder was arrested after the girl called the police upon her return home.

Wilder offered to plead guilty if offered therapy to avoid a prison sentence. Yet at the trial, the jury took 55 minutes to find Wilder not guilty and made him a free man. Wilder never bothered with the therapy.

In 1980, Wilder molested a young girl. Posing as a photographer, Wilder persuaded her to pose for photographs eating a pizza for a promotion. After a few bites, the girl complained of feeling drowsy, Wilder carried her to his pickup truck and placed her in the front seat. There, Wilder began stroking the young girl's breasts, when she resisted, Wilder raped her.

After the attack, the teenager managed to remember the licence plate of Wilder's car and gave it to police. Wilder was again arrested and charged with rape. Pleading guilty to the lower charge of attempted sexual battery, Wilder received five years probation and in addition Wilder was to attend counselling with a sex therapist.

In December 1982, Wilder returned to Australia looking for work as a photographer. On December 22, two teenage girls were abducted from a New South Wales beach; their abductor forced the pair into posing for pornographic pictures. The girls, when released, handed the police the licence plate of the car, which was traced to Wilder. Arrested on December 23, Wilder was ordered to appear for trial on May 7 1983. He was given permission to return to USA on business, but only after a $350,000 bail was paid. The court case was due to begin on April 3, 1984, but he failed to appear.

Beth Kenyon, a twenty-three-year-old teacher suddenly disappeared on March 4, 1984. Her parents, William and Delores Kenyon, were extremely concerned about their daughter's welfare and phoned all the names listed in Beth's phonebook without success. A missing person's report was filed at the Metro Dade Public Safety Department, but the report was placed in a pile and forgotten about. Clifford 'Mitch' Fry was a Coral Gables police officer attached to the school where Beth worked, and he began his own investigation into the young woman's disappearance. Clifford visited Beth's home to find nothing out of the ordinary; her clothes were present and tidy. He also phoned all the numbers in Beth's directory. One of the numbers he tried was Chris Wilder. Clifford left a message on Wilder's answer phone explaining who he was and why he was calling. Clifford would not get a reply.

Bill Kenyon returned to the Metro Dade PSD on March 8, to find that no investigation had taken place into his daughter's disappearance, so he decided to take matters into his own hands. He called Kenneth Whittaker Investigative Consultants. The chief investigator, Kenneth Whittaker Snr, agreed to take the case on for a standard fee of $1000 per day, Bill agreed.

Kenneth talked to everyone that Beth knew, including family, friends and ex-boyfriends. Eventually he discovered that Chris Wilder had dated Beth two ears earlier culminating in a marriage proposal after only a few dates. Beth had turned the proposal down. Kenneth also discovered that Beth had talked to Wilder the day prior to her disappearance. Wilder denied having seen Beth recently when asked by Kenneth. However, an attendant at a gas station in Coral Gables claimed he saw Beth on March 5, buying gas when a man came in and paid for her.

When shown a group of photos, the attendant instantly picked out Wilder. When Wilder was asked to explain, he denied all knowledge, saying the attendant had clearly made a mistake. The private investigator decided to question Wilder face to face. On March 11, 1984, Ken Whittaker and Mike Fornelo drove to Wilders house to find no one there; the daily paper was still on the doormat.

On Sunday February 26, 1984, twenty-year-old Rosario Gonzalez was working at the Miami Grand Prix track. At 1.00pm she was spotted heading towards her car in the parking lot at the end of her shift.

Rosario was due to be home in Homestead at approximately 7.00 that evening, so by 3.00am her parents were hysterical. Their daughter had not even phoned to say where she was. Detectives George Morin and Harvey Wasserman were assigned to the case on Monday morning and went through the normal investigations, checking all leads, potential sightings and tips. It wasn't until George Morin got a call from Kenneth Whittaker on March 11 that the investigation took a positive turn. Whittaker told the detective about the disappearance of Beth Kenyon and that Wilder was the suspect. Whittaker also mentioned that Wilder was present at the Miami racetrack the day of Rosario's disappearance. Reaching the conclusion that Wilder may be responsible for the abduction of both girls, George Morin contacted Metro Dade PD who admitted that no one was assigned to Beth's case. Harvey Wasserman soon got a call from Clifford Fry in order to exchange notes on the two cases.

With a lack of real evidence directly linking Wilder to the disappearance of Beth Kenyon and Rosario Gonzalez, authorities had nowhere to go. Wilder continued to live his playboy lifestyle, seemingly unaffected by the investigation going on around him. On Friday March 18, 1984, Wilder packed a suitcase and said farewell to his business partner L K Kimbrell.

Three miles South of Cape Canaveral lies the small town of Indian Harbour, and the home of twenty-one-year-old Terry Harbour. On March 17, a Saturday, Terry and her friends went out to celebrate St Patrick's Day and agreed to go shopping the next day. On Sunday morning, Terry left a note for her mother letting her know where she was going and headed off to the mall. At 2.00pm Terry had not arrived home. At 5.00pm her friend Dan Bednarz was concerned and visited the mall himself to look for Terry, with no luck. At 10.30pm that evening, Terry's stepfather, Don Ferguson, drove to the mall and found Terry's locked car in the deserted car park. In the back seat was the clothes that Terry was wearing when she left earlier in the day. Meeting up with Dan, the pair waited by the car hoping Terry would turn up. At 4.30am they went home with no sign of the twenty-one-year-old, nor did she turn up for her shift at work on Monday morning. Security at the mall began questioning the staff to determine the last known sighting of Terry. 2.30pm would be the time given. At that moment she was seen wearing the clothes she had left her house in – the clothes found in the back seat of her car.

Three days after her disappearance, Terry Harbour's body was found floating face down in a creek 70 miles west of Indian Harbour in Polk County. She had been in the creek for 3 to 4 days and was identified via her dental records. A call for witnesses bought forward a woman who saw Terry in the mall on Sunday talking to a man with a camera. FBI agents presented the witness with a series of photographs of potential suspects She instantly pointed to one of them, the photo was of Chris Wilder.

March 20 1984, Tallahassee, Florida; a nineteen-year-old had just finished her shopping at Governors Square Hall. Making her way to her car, she was approached by a man wearing a blue pinstripe suit and a camera over his shoulder. The cameraman persuasively talked to the young girl about posing for photographs in the nearby park. Although flattered she politely declined the offer and turned to leave. The cameraman spun her around and punched her in the stomach, then in the face, pushed her into the car then drove off. Reaching a secluded area nearby he tied the terrified girl's hands together and put tape over her mouth. At Bradfordville, north of Tallahassee, Wilder hogtied his captive and put her in the trunk of the car.

At 8.15pm that evening, he booked into the Glenoaks Motel in Bainbridge, Georgia, where the woman was forced to perform fellatio, raped twice and tortured with the use of electrical wire attached to her legs. Taking a bottle of superglue the attacker proceeded to glue his victim's eyelids shut using a hairdryer to speed the process up, the man then sat back and watched television. Partially able to see through her eyelashes the girl made an attempt to escape. A struggle for domination took place resulting in the teenager being struck over the head with the hairdryer. Although injured she managed to reach the bathroom, locked the door and began screaming for help. Her assailant grabbed all he could and fled the room.

Bill Gaines was resting in his room at the motel when he heard a woman's scream. Quickly dressing, Bill rushed out to locate the screaming. In the corridor he crashed into Wilder running in the opposite direction. The man ran to his car, threw his belongings in the back and speedily pulled away. The screaming had now stopped and Bill returned to his room failing to find the source. At the main desk, the bell rang, the night manager looked up to find a young lady dressed only in a bed sheet, bloodstains in her hair asking for the police. She was taken to Bainbridge Memorial Hospital for treatment; the glue had fortunately not damaged her eyes. Chief deputy Bill Morris talked to the teenager about her ordeal and told the story of the photographer who abducted her.

The same day that Terry was positively identified as the body found in Polk County, another young woman disappeared; it was March 23, 1984. Terry Walden a twenty-four year old nursing student and mother of two vanished after dropping her four-year-old daughter off at school. She was last spotted at 11.30am at the Lamar University student centre. On Monday March 26, an employee of the Lower Neches Valley Authority spotted a bright jacket floating in the canal. Reaching to retrieve the garment he spotted the body of woman floating face down in the water.

The Jefferson County Sheriffs Dept and the Beaumont Police Dept searched the canal, the canal bank and nearby fields for clues. Several empty shell casings were found indicating that Terry may have been shot. However the autopsy, performed by Dr W E Korndorffer, revealed that Terry had been killed from massive blood loss as a result of three stab wounds to the chest, one wound had exited through her back. The knife had caused injuries to the woman's lungs, heart and pulmonary artery; the force of the knife attack had also fractured two ribs. The report indicated that Terry had been tied up during the attack and her mouth taped shut. Further searches of the area uncovered shoe prints to and from the bank, a piece of duct tape – believed to have covered Terry's mouth – and tyre tracks leading towards the I-90.

Jefferson County Sheriffs department held a press conference on March 29 and requested public assistance in the investigation into the movements of Terry Walden and the location of her car, an orange cougar. Several people called the hotline, but none were able to give definitive identification of the woman they saw. What the sheriff's dept did not mention in the press conference was that they were looking for a second car, a 1973 cream coloured Chrysler, purchased by Wilder. On April 6, 1984 Wilder's car was found without licence plates in Beaumont during a routine police patrol. The car confirmed to be Wilder's was removed for thorough forensic examination, which discovered numerous small bloodstains, but no weapons.

A man driving an orange cougar was spotted in Oklahoma City at the Holiday Inn South. His name, according to the credit card he used, was L K Kimbrell. The same day, March 24, twenty-year-old Suzanne Logan suddenly disappeared between the local mall and her house where she lived with her husband Brian. Concerned, Brian went to the Oklahoma PD to file a missing persons report, however the officers determined that she was probably a runaway and no investigation took place.

On March 25, at approximately 1.30pm a fisherman at Milford Reservoir near Manhattan spotted an object by a tree. As he approached he realised it was the semi-naked body of a woman clearly beaten around the head. The autopsy report indicated bite marks on both breasts, puncture wounds on her back. She had been raped and her death had been caused by a severe stab wound to the chest above the left breast. The coroner indicated in his report that death had occurred approximately one hour before the body was found. Ten days later, the body was officially identified as Suzanne Logan. The day after Suzanne's body was found, Wilder arrived in Grand Junction, Colorado.

Three days later eighteen-year-old Sheryl Bonaventura disappeared during a short shopping trip.

At 11.30am March 29, Sheryl called her friend Kristal Cesario to let her know she was visiting the Mesa Mall in Grand Junction to pick up some last minute items for their Aspen skiing trip they had planned together. By 3.30pm Sherry had still not returned home. Kristal and Sheryl's family were very concerned by her non-appearance and travelled to the mall to search for her. Immediately they found Sheryl's unlocked car in the car park. Worried for his daughter's safety, her father, Jim, visited the police station to file a missing persons report. The Grand Junction Police immediately went into action; a check on the computer returned an FBI notice to be on the lookout for Chris Wilder

A police search of the mall found that Sheryl had been spotted talking to a man by her car at approximately 1.30pm. Another young woman told the police of a photographer touting for business that she considered suspicious. In a photographic line-up she immediately picked out the photo of Wilder. The FBI was tracking Wilder's movements via his credit card use. In addition they were aware of his fraudulent use of his business partner's credit card. On the afternoon of Sheryl's disappearance from Grand Junction, Wilders card was used in a restaurant in Silverton about 100 miles south of Grand Junction. The waitress there identified the card user as Wilder and his female companion as Sheryl Bonaventura.

On April 1, in Las Vegas, the magazine *'Seventeen'* were holding a beauty contest in the Meadows Mall. Teenage girls were modelling clothes in front of the cameras as well as the judges. However, in the corner was Wilder, watching each of the girls as they sauntered down the catwalk.

Tony Korfman had expected his seventeen-year-old daughter Michelle to be home from the competition at 6.00pm. Michelle did not make it. At midnight, Tony called Las Vegas police to report her missing. A search of the mall failed to find her car, but a witness did see Michelle talking to an unknown man. Again when shown photos of the suspects, the witness quickly picked out Wilder as the man she saw.

Three days later on April 4, Wilder was in Lomita, 40 miles south of Los Angeles, searching for his next photographic subject in the Del Ammo shopping mall. Sixteen-year-old Tina Risko was reported as missing that night after she failed to return home. Tina had delivered a job application form to a store in the mall. The manager told police that a man had followed Tina from the store carrying a camera. Once again a series of photographs were shown to the manager, and again the witness picked out Wilder as the man he saw. In fact Wilder had persuaded Tina to go with him to the beach for some modelling pictures. When she asked to be taken home, Wilder produced a gun and tied up the terrified girl. That night they were in a motel in Prescotti, Arizona where Wilder raped and tortured Tina throughout the night.

In Gary, Indiana, on April 10, sixteen-year-old Dawnette Wilt was approached by a young girl who introduced herself as 'Tina Wilder' and suggested that Dawnette could be a model. Told to wait, Tina soon returned with Wilder who claimed to be a shop manager. Wilder persuaded the girl to his car in the pretence of filling in some forms. Once there Wilder produced his gun, tied Dawnette's hands and legs then covered her eyes and mouth with tape before assaulting Dawnette in the back seat of the car. The assault continued that evening in a rented room in Wauseon, Ohio, with electric shocks and rape. The next night in Rochester, Wilder again abused Dawnette with more rape and torture.

Early in the morning, on April 12, Wilder drove to woods 50 miles south of Rochester with his two captives. Untying Dawnette, Wilder marched her into the woods where, after untying her, attempted to suffocate the sixteen-year-old, Dawnette managed to prevent the attempt. Instead Wilder pulled out a knife and stabbed Dawnette in the chest and then twice in the back, he then walked away from the girl, as she lay dying.

But Dawnette was still alive, she waited till Wilder was gone, despite the deep wounds and blood loss she managed to get back to the road and flag down a passing car. Charles Larson drove the injured girl directly to Soldiers and Sailors Hospital where she was successfully treated and able to tell her story to the police and FBI.

Angry and frustrated, Wilder wanted a new car. He drove around the area looking for one that he wanted; finally settling on a Pontiac Trans Am. Tina asked the driver Beth Dodge to look at her car for a moment as she was having trouble. As Beth walked over Wilder pulled his gun and forced the unsuspecting woman inside the car. Wilder drove off to a back road, dragged Beth from the car and shot her in the back of the neck, her body was found later that afternoon.

Wilder then drove to Boston with Tina, when, inexplicably, Wilder gave his captive $300 and put her on a flight home to Los Angeles. In LA Tina eventually walked into Torrance police department, introduced herself to officer Emilio Paerels and told him her story of abduction and murder.

By April 13 Wilder was in New Hampshire on his way to the Canadian border. He had stopped in Colebrook for gas, and was still driving the Trans Am stolen from Beth Dodge. State police officers Leo Jellison and Wayne Fortier were passing the gas station when they spotted the wanted vehicle in the forecourt. Aware of the reports of the shot woman and the stolen car, the officers moved in for a closer look. Confirming the car was the one wanted by the FBI, the officers then noticed the driver of the car inside the gas station shop and recognised him as the suspect shown on the FBI wanted posters. Wilder had made the FBI 10 most wanted list on April 8. Wilder stepped outside as the officers approached in order to question him.

Wilder saw the officers and before the officers could react, Wilder got into the car and produced a gun. Leo Jellison dived into the car after Wilder in order to gain control of the weapon. The gun fired during the struggle and Leo grimaced with pain as the bullet entered into the right hand side of his rib cage, it bruised his lung and stopped near his liver. A second gunshot was fired and Wilder stiffened with pain then went limp. He was dead.

Leo Jelliman was treated at the Upper Conneticut Valley Hospital, where he was informed how close to death he was. The body of Chris Wilder was taken to Weeks Memorial Hospital in Lancaster, New Hampshire, where an autopsy was performed. The report stated that Wilder was shot twice in the chest, the first passing through his heart out via his back and striking the police officer. The second bullet also struck his heart causing cardiac obliteration.

On May 3, almost three weeks after Wilder's death, a family were on a trip on Highway 89 in Utah, during a short stop they found the nude body of Sheryl Bonaventura. Sheryl had suffered multiple stab wounds and a single shot in her chest. Eight days later on May 11, Michelle Korfmann's body was found in the Angeles National Forest, but would remain unidentified in a morgue until June 15, 1984; the cause of death could not be determined due to excessive decomposition. The bodies of Rosario Gonzalez and Beth Kenyon have never been found.

Aileen Wuornos

When writing about Aileen "Lee" Wuornos I must say that I do not believe she acted alone. I believe her girlfriend may have been involved in the murders. Many times witnesses claimed to have seen two women together; one of the identikit photos looked incredibly like Wuornos, the other one bore striking similarities to her lover.

Wuornos came from a very troubled family. She was born Aileen Carol Pittman on February 29, 1956 in Rochester, Michigan. Her father, Leo Pittman and mother, Diane Pratt had been teenage newlyweds but had separated before discovering that Diane was expecting a baby, a sister for Keith, their son.

Diane also abandoned the children leaving them with her parents. The two young children were legally adopted by Diane's parents, Lauri and Britta Wuornos on March 18, 1960, taking their new parents' surname.

Lee's (as Aileen was often called) father, Leo Pittman was a child molester and had spent most of his short life in and out of prison and mental institutions for his crimes. He never met his daughter, having been incarcerated for the rape of a seven-year-old girl very soon after Aileen's birth. In prison in January 1969, Leo hung himself from his jail ceiling bars.

As "Lee" and her brother Keith grew older, they often found themselves in trouble. On one occasion both of the children suffered severe burns when they inadvertently set themselves on fire, whilst playing with matches and lighter fluid.

As she got older Wuornos would sneak out of her bedroom window at night, in search of a different life, though usually she only found others who chose to abuse her. She would use poorly made shanties in the woods near her house to perform sexual acts with the boys from the neighbourhood for money and cigarettes, and, as she got older, drugs.

By the time she was fourteen-years-old Wuornos was pregnant. Though she had been regularly having sex with a variety of boys including her own brother, the father of the child was not known. Wuornos claimed she had been held at knife-pint and raped for six hours, producing the baby. A story that would echo in years to come.

Wuornos gave birth to her son on March 23, 1971 in a Detroit Unwed Mothers home, where it was the norm to have the child instantly given up for adoption.

Both Wuornos and her brother were quite out of control, and their adoptive mother, and real mother both were unable to handle them. In July 1971, when Britta Wuornos died of liver failure, brought on by years of heavy drinking, the two children were handed over as wards of the state.

Aileen Wuornos ran away and spent her time on the streets as a prostitute. She was charged in Colorado, but never appeared in court to face the charges. She returned to Michigan by 1973 but was often arrested for drunken behaviour and prostitution. Her brother died of throat cancer in 1976, leaving his baby sister a $10,000 insurance policy pay out. Wuornos used the cash to pay for her mounting fines and bought herself a new car, which she crashed and destroyed within a few short months.

By 1981 Wuornos was in Florida, earning meagre amounts of money for sexual favours. She supplemented her cash flow by robbing convenience stores. She soon earned herself a long list of charges, from prostitution, to disorderly conduct, armed robbery and driving under the influence of alcohol.

Then in June 1986 Wuornos met her soul mate, Tyria Moore in Daytona. It was supposedly love at first sight, across a seedy gay bar. The pair quickly became lovers and were inseparable, spending the rest of their time together, sharing in crime sprees, which suggests Tyria's involvement in the later murders.

One example of her involvement was when the pair was arrested on July 4, 1987 in Daytona for an assault on a man with a beer bottle. The two women used an array of aliases, often taking on the monikers of relatives and friends.

Wherever the women went together, they caused trouble. The women claimed that a bus driver had pushed Wuornos off his bus. They had been evicted by a landlord for destroying an apartment. The pair believed society was against them, that they were in fact the victims and Wuornos began carrying a gun everywhere she went.

With Tyria has the wife; Wuornos took the responsibility of going out to earn money. She would walk the streets, prostituting herself to earn money. The two women lead a nomadic life, moving from place to place, earning what they could from Wuornos' prostitution. That was until 1989 when the murders began.

The Murders
The first person murdered was fifty-one-year-old Richard Mallory. Richard picked up Wuornos, possibly even both women on November 30, 1989 and drove to a secluded area near Daytona Beach. Once out of sight, Wuornos and Mallory had sex after settling on a price. Wuornos produced a condom for the man to put on and the two attempted to have sex, both drinking from a bottle of Vodka during the session.

Sometime during the sex act, Wuornos produced a .22 pistol and fired three shots into the man's chest. Later Wuornos said that the man had attempted to rape her and she fired the shots in self-defence.

Wuornos dumped the man's dead body from the car and drove away. She took the money from the man's wallet and abandoned the car near Ormond Beach were it was found the next day.

Five-times married Mallory was reported missing and was not found until December 13, 1989. Fingerprints taken from a corpse found at Daytona Beach confirmed that the dead man was Mallory.

The second victim was David Spears. The forty-three-year-old man was on his way to Orlando from Sarasota to visit his ex-wife when he met Wuornos on the evening of May 19, 1990.

Wuornos murdered the man by firing two shots into his chest as she had sex with him. His naked body was found in Citrus County, Florida on June 1, 1990. The man's body had decomposed making identification difficult. By the time police had identified the body another man had been murdered.

Forty-year-old Charles Carskaddon was the next to die at the hands of Aileen Wuornos. The man was murdered on May 31, 1990 when he picked up Wuornos while on his way to see his fiancé. His body was found on June 6, a few days after the body of David Spears was located. The distance between the two dump sites was a mere thirty kilometres.

Like the previous victims Charles had been shot with a .22 gun. Wuornos had fired a total of nine bullets into the man.

She had dumped the man's body along the I-75 and driven away in his car, abandoning it in Marion County.

The next victim was murdered the day after Charles Carskaddon's body was found. Sixty-five-year-old Peter Siems was on his way to see his sister in Arkansas on June 7, 1990 when he picked up hitchhiking

Aileen Wuornos. According to Wuornos the pair pulled off to the side of the road to have sex and Peter became violent. She shot him dead and threw the body out of the car, somewhere along the highway between Florida and Arkansas. To date, Peter Siems' body has not been found.

His car, however, was found in Orange Springs, Florida. Wuornos and Tyria Moore had been driving around in the car when they had an accident. They fled the scene, leaving the car behind. A palm print was recovered from the car.

Troy Burress was murdered a little over three weeks after Peter Siems. On July 30, 1990 Troy Burress picked up Wuornos and they decided on a low $10 for sex. According to Wuornos, Troy jumped on top of her and she shot the man in the chest. As the man tried to escape Wuornos fired another shot into the man's back. Troy's body was found in Marion County five days later.

Wuornos killed fifty-six-year-old Charles Humphreys on September 11, 1990. The man had been a police officer but after retiring from the service had become a child abuse investigator. On September 11, 1990 he had been on his way home from work, when he picked up Wuornos. During an altercation with the man, Wuornos fired her gun six times into the man's body and once more to his head.

She robbed his dead body and dumped him in a secluded area, where he was found the next day. Again Wuornos stole the car and dumped it a week later in Live Oak.

By now police knew they were dealing with a serial killer, witnesses said they had seen two women at many of the scenes, or driving the stolen cars. It wasn't long before Wuornos was arrested, but another man lost his life before the serial killer was caught.

Walter Antonio was found dead in the woods near Cross City with four shots to the body with a .22 calibre weapon on November 19, 1990. The sixty-year-old had gone missing the day before. He had picked up Wuornos while out driving and taken her to the wooded area for sex.

The dead man was found naked except for a pair of socks. Wuornos stole the man's car and belongings. She dumped his clothing in a nearby county before dumping his car in Brevard five days later.

Over the next several weeks, a media campaign was conducted to find the killers of the seven men. Over and over the names and descriptions of both Wuornos and Tyria Moore were given to police. Items from the dead men also began appearing in pawnshops, and fingerprints were taken from several items. They matched those found on the stolen cars, and on a record of arrest for Aileen Wuornos.

On January 9, 1991, Wuornos was finally arrested at the aptly named biker bar "The Last Resort". Wuornos had been sleeping on a broken down old lounge outside the bar for several days before she was arrested. Tyria Moore was also arrested at her sister's home, and was given a deal of freedom if she could get Wuornos to talk about the murders via a recorded telephone line.

A week later Wuornos confessed to the murders of six men, excluding that of Peter Siems. She told police;

> "I shot 'em 'cause to me it was like a self-defending thing... I felt if I didn't shoot 'em and I didn't kill 'em, first of all... I had to kill 'em...or, it's like retaliation, too. It's like, 'You bastards, you were going to hurt me.'"

She told the police that each of the men had attempted to rape her and that she killed them in self-defence.

Over a year later, the trial for the murder of Richard Mallory opened on January 13, 1992. Two weeks later Wuornos was found guilty and sentenced to death. She hissed at the jury,

> "I was raped...I hope you get raped, scumbags of America..."

The outburst did not endear her to anyone, many in the courtroom gasped at the killer's words.

In April, she pleaded guilty to the murders of Burress, Humphreys, and Spears, and was sentenced to death on May 7, 1992.

While on death row, Wuornos was adopted by Arlene Pralle, a born-again Christian who featured largely in a documentary on the killer. She claimed she was destined to look after the killer, and wanted to break her out of prison.

After refusing to submit any further appeals Wuornos was scheduled to die in October 2002. At 9.47 am on October 9, 2002 Aileen Wuornos was pronounced dead after being executed by lethal injection, her final words were:

"I'd just like to say I'm sailing with the Rock and I'll be back like Independence Day with Jesus, June 6, like the movie, big mothership and all. I'll be back,"

Since her death, a film about her life, *Monster,* featuring Charlize Theron was released. Theron went on to win many Best Actress Awards for the role.

X

Yang Xinhai

On November 3, 2003 thirty-five-year-old Yang Xinhai was arrested by police in the province of Hebei in Canzhou, China for the murders of at least 67 people in a two year period.

He was also the chief suspect for a rash of cases in three other cities, Anhui, Shandong and Henan in China.

The motive for the killings, according to Yang, was that he had been dumped by his girlfriend and wanted to take his anger out on society.

Yang's girlfriend had left him after finding out about a prison term the man had served for rape and burglary.

Yang's method was to go to farmhouses and slaughter everyone he found. He would bash them to death. The killer used tools such as a meat cleaver and an iron hammer to murder the farming families.

Yang always wore new clothes and shoes two sizes too big to put police off his track. He travelled between the Chinese provinces on a bicycle.

He was found guilty on February 1, 2004 for the murders of sixty-seven of his victims and the rape of 25 woman after a trial that lasted less than an hour. He was sentenced to death for his crimes.

Justice was metered out quickly for the serial killer. On February 14, 2004 the killer was executed in Hehan.

The details or identities of the killer's victims were not revealed.

Y

Robert Yates

At 6.30am on April 18, 2000 Robert Lee Yates Jnr, 47, a married father of five, was arrested for the murder of sixteen-year-old Jennifer Joseph.

As Yates sat at the police station more charges of murder were added after a taskforce closed the trap around Yates. The task force had been mobilized to track the serial killer. Yates became a prime suspect when witnesses described seeing Yates' 1977 white corvette in the area on the nights that the women disappeared. Yates car was checked and detectives found enough evidence from Jennifer Joseph in the car, which led to his initial arrest.

Detectives had been on round-the-clock surveillance of Yates two days preceding his arrest.

It appeared that Spokane's serial killer grew bolder with each murder he committed. At first he relied on time and distance to separate himself from the crimes. Later the gunman grew more confident in his abilities and dumped his victims were they could be easily be found.

In the beginning, the serial killer's victims turned up miles from where they worked and where he lived. Yates' main objective was to find prostitutes to murder. Most of the victims were white, one being Asian, and they were all involved in prostitution or drugs or both, except for the earliest two murders.

Yates' style was to shoot the victims in the head with a .25-caliber gun after covering their heads in several plastic grocery bags. Investigators suggest that the bags were part of the killer's signature that helped link the murders. He dumped the bodies where they would be found in remote but well-travelled roads and in close proximity to each other. Almost all the victims had been killed elsewhere before being transported to "dump sites" where they were found.

Semen was found on eight of the bodies. Three of the victims' bodies were within 50 yards of each other, and two of the bodies were actually touching. Three victims were found with vegetation from Yates' own home on top of their bodies, which also assisted in linking Yates to the crimes.

The Murders

Susan Savage, 22, and Patrick Oliver, 21 were the first to cross paths with the Robert Yates. In 1975 the young couple were picnicking on Mill Creek, near Walla Walla, when Yates happened upon them while practicing his target shooting in the same area.

Patrick Oliver was shot three times in the head before Yates turned on Susan and shot her twice. Yates buried the couple's bodies under a pile of brush where they were found within days. It took 25 years before the families of the couple found out that they were the first victims of a serial killer, when Yates admitted he was responsible for the murders.

Twenty-three-year-old Stacy Elizabeth Hawn from Seattle was the first prostitute known to be killed by Yates around July 7, 1988. Her skeletal remains were found five months later in Skagit County outside Mount Vernon. Stacy had been shot once in the head.

Initially Hawn was listed as a possible victim of the Green River Killer, however Yates' admitted to her murder and was able to pinpoint the location she was found as well as her injuries. His confession was part of a plea bargain so he would avoid the death penalty.

Jennifer Joseph, aged 16, was found on August 26, 1997. Her body was found in an advanced state of decomposition in a small secluded spot at the corner of Forker and Judkins Roads on the Peone Prairie. She had been killed by a close-range gunshot wound to the chest. DNA was able to be extracted from semen swabs and were later matched to Yates. A sleeve button, found in the white Corvette owned by Yates, matched the shirt worn by Joseph at the time of her death. The analysis of blood smears found in the Corvette produced a match with a DNA profile generated through samples from Joseph's parents.

A man walking his dog off Hangman Valley Road found the decomposed body of twenty-nine-year-old prostitute Darla Sue Scott, on November 5, 1997. Two plastic bags that had been covering her head were also found in her shallow grave. Her cause of death was two gunshot wounds to the head. DNA found on Darla's body was matched to Yates.

A month later on December 7, 1997 the body of twenty-four-year-old Melinda L. Mercer, was found on S. 50th St. in Tacoma. She had four plastic bags covering her head and she had been shot three times.

The body of Shawn L. Johnson, aged 36, was found on December 18, 1997. Her decomposing remains were found off Hangman Valley Road with two plastic bags covering her head. The cause of death was two gunshots to the head. Semen samples taken from her body were matched to Yates.

Thirty-one-year-old Laurel Wason's body was found on December 26, 1997, in a gravel pit near the Hangman Valley Road. Her head was covered with three plastic bags and she had died from two gunshot wounds to the head. Foreign vegetation, peanut shells, packing Styrofoam and chips of broken concrete were found covering her body that matched debris found in Yates' backyard. Semen found in her body matched Yates.

Shawn A. McClenahan, 39, was also found December 26, 1997, next to the body of Laurel Wason. Three plastic bags covered her head and the cause of death was two gunshots to the head. DNA evidence from semen was matched to Yates as well as a fingerprint on one of the plastic bags. Foreign matter covering her body was also from Yates' backyard. Semen found in her body was matched to Yates.

Sunny G. Oster, aged 41, was found on February 8, 1998. Her remains were found in a wooded area in Western Spokane County and had all the hallmarks of a Yates' murder. Her head was covered with three plastic bags and she had two gunshot wounds to the skull. Yates' semen was also found on her body.

Thirty-four-year-old Linda Maybin's decomposed body was found on April 1, 1998. Her shallow grave was only 50 yards from the site of Wason and McClenahan's gravesite. Two plastic bags covered the victim's head. The cause of death was one gunshot to the head. Semen in her body was matched to Yates' DNA. Non-indigenous plant trimmings covering her body were matched to vegetation in Yates' backyard.

The next victim was found on July 7, 1998. Forty-seven-year-old prostitute Michelyn Derning was found under a bath cover by a transient in an area frequented by prostitutes in Spokane's East Central neighbourhood. The cause of the woman's death was a gunshot wound to the head. Unlike all of the other victims, she was seen alive a week before her body was discovered. The others were found weeks, or sometimes months, after they disappeared. Michelyn was not raped and was murdered where she was found.

Connie LaFontaine Ellis, 35, was found on October 13, 1998, in a ditch near the 1700 block of 108th Street South in Tacoma. Her decomposed body had three plastic bags covering her head and she had suffered only one gunshot wound to the head.

Melody Ann Murfin, 43, disappeared in 1998 and was found October 18, 2000, buried in the side yard under the bedroom window of Yates' home. Although authorities thoroughly searched the yard after his arrest, they found Melody's body after Yates provided them with a map pinpointing its precise location.

Christine L. Smith, 32, was robbed and assaulted by Yates in his van on August 1, 1998. Christine was only grazed by the gunshot to her head and managed to escape and reported the attack to police. She told the officers that she had agreed to perform oral sex for $40 in the back of Yates' van in a secluded parking lot in Spokane on Aug. 1, 1998. According to Christine, Yates was driving a black van with a bed and mattress in the back. She asked Yates if he was the "psycho killer" that had been killing prostitutes at the time. Yates actually responded by saying "he was not the killer because he had five kids and would not do that."

After several minutes when the woman had failed to arouse Yates with oral sex, he shot her in the head, nearly causing her to lose consciousness. The woman, however, struggled to stay awake and kept her wits about her as she fell backwards. Christine did not know she had been shot until a later x-ray showed fragments in her face and skull.

She contacted police again on April 18, after recognizing Yates as her attacked from his mugshot published in The Spokesman-Review. Police found bloodstains, a .25-caliber bullet casing and a bullet encrusted in the roof of a van similar to the one described by Christine that was once owned by Yates. The fragments of bullet were later removed from her head for ballistic comparison to other bullets from Yates' victims.

The Man

Robert Lee Yates Jnr. was an Army veteran who served nearly two decades as a helicopter pilot for the U.S. Army. He was the married father of four daughters and a son, ranging in age from 11 to 25 at the time of his arrest.

After dropping out of college in the early 1970s, Yates had married and enlisted in the Army on Oct. 4, 1977. Within 3 years, Yates was a warrant officer attending flight school at Fort Rucker, Ala., the home of Army aviation. He graduated with a pair of flight wings authorizing him to fly helicopters.

Yates flew the OH-58 Kiowa, and was stationed overseas in Germany during the height of Cold War tensions between Western Europe and the former Warsaw Pact. His decorations included three Meritorious Service Medals, three Army Commendation Medals, three Army Achievement Medals and a Humanitarian Service Medal for participating in a relief mission to South Florida to help clean up the devastation left by Hurricane Andrew in 1992.

He also received two Armed Forces Expeditionary Medals; one for each tour he had spent flying in peacekeeping missions with the Unified Task Force in Somalia in 1993 and in Haiti during Operation "Uphold Democracy" in 1994.

Yates ended his military career after eighteen years in March 1996 as a chief warrant officer-4, the highest rank a warrant officer could attain in the Army. He had amassed more than 5,000 hours of flight time in helicopters without a single mishap and had been awarded the title of Master Army Aviator.

He was now a civilian but did not settle well, and within months of retiring, Yates was looking to get back into the cockpit. In April 1997, the Washington Army National Guard granted his request to protect and serve while he murdered prostitutes in his spare time.

Yates was unable to fly helicopters when he first was posted into his new position as Chief Warrant Officer Yates, due to a mix-up with his medical report. At the same time detectives were working to unravel the mystery behind a growing number of bodies that were being discovered across Washington State.

Then the break came and on April 18, 2000 the killer was arrested.

On October 26, 2000 after many appalling plea bargains, Yates was finally sentenced to 408 years in prison for 13 killings. Yates was then transferred to Pierce County to face two further counts of first-degree murder of Melinda Mercer and Connie LaFontaine Ellis.

On August 13, 2002 Yates admitted he was responsible for the final two murders. He was sentenced to death. After the sentence was read, Yates read his own prepared statement:

> *I prepared this statement so that I might leave nothing in my heart that needs to be said.*
>
> *To all my victims' families, to my family and to the people in the community, to the families of Melinda Mercer and Connie LaFontaine Ellis, I know you are suffering great anguish. I find no words to comfort you, to explain, justify or soften all the evil, pain, separation and death that I've caused.*
>
> *Some things are inexpressible and inexplicable in terms of human language. The world is a frightening place, and I've made it more so for many. I've caused so much pain and devastation.*
>
> *Hundreds of people are hurting and grieving because of my acts. I let sin enter my life. I let it grow and mature until it wrought its direct consequence: death. The wages of sin bring death. Sin and wrongdoing may start small but if left unchecked, they grow into something ugly... It blinded me.*
>
> *Within myself I've had no power to defeat this full-blown sinful nature. There were times – long periods – when in between my horrific crimes, there were periods of relative calm. Nothing evil happened. But that sinful nature, which wrought so much recent violence, never really left.*
>
> *Scripture says the heart is deceitful above all things and beyond cure; who can understand? Our hearts can be deceitful beyond our own understanding, and surely mine was. I couldn't rid myself of this sinful nature. Somewhere, through all this devastation, God was knocking on the door of my heart, but I wouldn't let him in. I thought to myself, how could a God love or hear anything that was not clean. I thought I wasn't good enough to even speak to God, and if He wouldn't listen to me, then who would?*
>
> *My guilt was like a disease eating away at my soul. I couldn't share that with anyone else. Sin and guilt gnaws at our mind and causes acid to build up in our stomachs. We've all had guilt at some times in our lives. My sin and my guilt was overwhelming. It became hard to live with myself.*
>
> *Few men have ever felt the guilt I have from all the horror I've brought into your lives. I tried to cleanse myself from that guilt through denial. That only resulted in making things worse.*
>
> *I lived a double life. I stayed in denial – denial of my needs, denial that someone, somewhere could help me. Through my denial, because I couldn't face the truth, I thought I could be self-correcting,*

that if I kept it all to myself, someday it would all go away. That's denial. By my denial, I blinded myself to the truth – the truth that no one is so alone in this world as a denier of God. But that was me, alone and in denial.

Even after my arrest in Spokane in April of 2000, for a couple of weeks I persisted. I remained in denial. In May of 2000, as I started to read the word of God for the first time in over 25 years, I began to understand that someone had seen all the hideous crimes I've committed. Someone else had been there the whole time, watching each of my victims die.

God had seen it all.

That realization was like slamming into a brick wall at 100 miles an hour. It was like standing naked and ugly before the whole world. It was looking at all the ugliness inside me and exposing it for what it really was.

So the best thing that could ever have happened that April was for me to be arrested and brought to account for my actions. God had seen it all. The public and the families had seen and felt the loss and the death and the hurt caused by my actions. Now it was time for Robert Yates to open his eyes and see all that, too.

It was impossible to be in denial any longer. It was time to face the truth. When sin has deadened moral perception, the wrongdoer does not discern the defects of his character or realize the enormity of the evil he has committed. For once I listened when God spoke.

Until God's spirit working through the human agencies of law enforcement and our justice system woke me out of my spiritual blindness, I couldn't see the enormous devastation I had created, the tremendous pain and suffering I had caused. Until I came back to the love of God in Jesus Christ, I could not turn aside from my sinful nature, for the mind of the sinful man – and that was me – brings death. The mind of the man controlled by the Spirit brings life and peace. Someone needed to open my eyes.

So I turned to God. Until I turned to faith, though before in death, I saw I couldn't face the truth that finally God was bringing me to account. It was me.

I hadn't felt some of that out in Riverside. God already did it. I had to confess to him so I could admit to myself the enormity of my evil, that I needed to tell someone else who would listen and not condemn. After that I stopped the denial, stopped trying to hide the truth from my attorneys in Spokane. I told them all about my crimes stretching back all the way to 1975. That was the right way – the only way back to God.

It's been a long road back. One doesn't fall into such a deep morass of evil and climb back out in one day. Hearing the heartbreaking testimonies of all the mothers, wives, sisters, brothers and children of the lost family members I've taken from them burdens me with the incalculable loss of the unending grief and the harm that I've brought to hundreds of people. I'm so very, very sorry.

If God is the creator of this universe, then there are no unimportant people, and I took the lives of these loving, wonderful, important people from you. I feel your hurt every day and it won't go away. It never will. I've devastated your hopes and dreams. I've left you with only photographs and memories instead of warm family gatherings, cherished hugs and future happiness. The opportunity to say farewell or clear up misunderstandings was not afforded you.

Please don't squeeze back tears. Tears are part of the adjustments. Tears are jewels of remembrance, painful but glistening with the beauty of your children – children God loved so much. Children that are, as the Bible says, asleep, waiting the day when they will be called forth to be reunited with you. Please trust in that blessed hope. God is not so far from you that he is not touched by your tears. All of heaven shares your sorrow.

I believe with all my heart that there is a huge battle being waged between good and evil in this world, a spiritual battle that has allowed tragedy in this case, unexplainable evil to step forward. Why has all this evil been allowed to exist in the world? Some day God will show us. So that's why we have to trust that some day our God, who's absolutely pure, will end this struggle. When He does, the Bible promises that the old order of things will have passed away. There will be no more death or mourning or crying or pain, only the happiness and joy you long for so much this day. That's a promise from God.

Nothing I have said here today will justify or excuse my wrongs or even make sense of them. My compassion goes out to all I've hurt. There's absolutely no excuse that anyone could ever offer for the depths of pain in this room and in the lives of every person I've touched and all the tragedy I've wrought. There are so many innocent victims in all of this – families, friends and communities, my family, who had nothing to do with any of this. I'm so very, very sorry for what has happened. I and they can offer no justification for any of it. We do offer you all our sympathies and our prayers.

There are inadequate words for me to express my guilt, my shame and my sorrow for having devastated you in taking away the wonderful people, the wonderful, loving people, the warm human beings you cared for so much. It's my prayer that you will look to God to help fill the hollow I've left in your hearts.

My future is in His hands. I share your grief and always will. I'm sorry beyond what words can say. I apologize to all of you, and I thank the court for allowing me to speak.

Huang Yong

In a scene reminiscent of the Gacy home in 1978 Chicago, the bodies of 17 boys were found beneath the house of twenty-nine-year-old Huang Yong in Henan, China in December 2003

Between September 2001 and his arrest, Yong lured boys away from various Internet cafes in the province and took them home. He strangled them and buried them under his house and in his garden.

The killer was arrested on November 22, 2003 and was found guilty of the seventeen murders on December 9, 2003.

On December26, 2003 the killer was executed by a single gunshot.

Ma Yong and Duan Zhiqin

There has been a recent spate of serial killers in China. Their sudden appearance has seen many politicians and high-ranking police officers sacked or forced to resign as the citizens try to find answers.

Most provinces have been unaware of the killers until their arrests. Or the people try to get police to investigate a growing number of missing people without success.

Serial killers are definitely not unheard of China, but they have begun appearing in greater number this millennium.

China has also recently had its first known serial killer couple, Ma Yong and Duan Zhiqin.

Forty-three-year-old Ma Yong and his female accomplice twenty-year-old Duan Zhiqun were arrested in October 2003 for the murders of at least twelve women in Buji, Shenzhen, China over a five month period.

The couple posed as prospective employers and lure women, looking for work, to their home "office". Ma Yong, who called himself Mr Xie, and Duan robbed and killed the women, dumping their bodies all over the province of Buji.

When a young woman escaped from the home of Yong and Duan on October 13, 2003, the couple were reported to police and quickly arrested.

At their trial, the pair pleaded guilty to the murders of twelve young women and was sentenced to death for their crimes.

At the time of writing, both are awaiting execution.

Graham Young

Graham Frederick Young was born on September 7, 1947 at Neasby Hospital in North London. His mother, Margaret, unfortunately died that Christmas leaving his father, Fred, to look after the three-month-old baby and his eight-year-old sister, Winifred. The Young's extended family helped out, and Winifred lived at her grandmother's house and Graham with his aunt Winnie.

Fred visited his children daily and took them out at weekends. Fred soon married again and as the years passed Graham grew to despise the new 'outsider' in the family and he told friends that he hated her.

In his early school years Young's hobby was reading. He always had his nose in a book from the local library. At nine-years-old the first signs of an interest in chemistry began to show with Young having gathered some small bottles of acid and ether. His interests grew further with his reading material stretching into black magic and the Nazi movement. He begun wearing a swastika that he refused to take off. Young's parents realised that his seemingly innocent hobby was now turning into an obsession. Young experimented with mice and his acid and took part in imaginary sacrifices.

Into his pre-teens, Young chose science, particularly chemistry, as his specialist subject. He excelled in the lessons, such that he gained a free reign allowing his mice experiments to continue. Young's drawings would also leak a potential clue to his state of mind. His main topic of art was death. On one occasion Fred and Molly (his step-mother) found a drawing of coffins marked with 'mum' and 'dad'.

In April 1961, Young visited Geoffrey Reis's chemist, where he asked for 25 grams of Antimony. When asked his age, Young replied seventeen, the minimum legal age. Unsure about the customer's age, Young was thirteen at the time; the shopkeeper questioned him as to why he wanted the poison.

Young's knowledge of chemistry ensured that he was able to demonstrate a number of experiments for which he could use the chemical. Impressed with his knowledge and Young's false age of seventeen, he sold the chemical to Young. Young signed the poison register using the name of M. E. Evans also provided a false address.

Having been able to convince the chemist to sell him the poison and armed with a small amount of pocket money and an additional five shillings from a part time job cleaning floors, Young was able to regularly return to the chemist for additional bottles of the poison. Weeks later Young got into a fight with a school friend, Chris Williams. Young was jealous that Chris was spending more time with other people than with him. Chris easily won the fight over the much smaller opposition, after which Young threatened to kill Chris.

On the following Monday at school, Chris suddenly was overwhelmed with nausea and was sent home after he began vomiting. Every following Monday Chris was violently ill but no one could understand why. Young was persuading his friend to eat lunch with him, having prepared some sandwiches for the pair of them. The Williams family took Chris to the family doctor and then onto Willesden Hospital, where migraine was diagnosed. Nobody suspected poison.

Young's stepmother Molly found a bottle in his room marked as poison. She let Fred know of her find and in turn Young was banned from keeping such items in the house. The chemist who sold Young the Antimony was informed of Young's age. Young simply changed his source, changing to chemist Edgar Davies to acquire more antimony. He used the same method as with the previous chemist, by giving a false name and address.

In early 1961, Molly and then Fred suffered violent illnesses, followed soon after by Winifred. The family believed that they had been infected by a bug. Suspicion was then aimed at the boy and his chemistry set.

They theorised that he had been using teacups to mix his chemicals and failing to clean them out properly. Fred wouldn't allow this to happen and disciplined his son about playing with his chemistry set in the house. Suspicion moved onto other possibilities after the illnesses continued. Perhaps the water was contaminated. The family couldn't explain the spate of illnesses affecting them, yet it continued throughout the year. It wasn't until November 1961 that Winifred became so ill that she visited the hospital.

On April 21, 1962 Molly Young felt worse than she had done over the past year, but there was still no real explanation why. As the day went on, Molly could no longer do her regular chores and stayed at home. After lunch, Fred came home to see his son staring from the window at this wife rolling in agony in the garden. Fred immediately took her to Willesden Hospital. The doctors insisted that she stay overnight for observation. In the evening Molly told the doctors that she wanted to return home where she died.

Because of the sudden nature of her death, doctors insisted that a post mortem be carried out. Doctor Donald Teare completed his report and indicated that death was due to a 'prolapse of a bone at the top of the spinal column'. The cause of this was linked to a crash that Molly was involved in the previous year. No further investigation took place. At Young's suggestion, which his father agreed to, Molly was cremated on April 26. All evidence of the crime disappeared.

Only a few days after Molly's death, Fred fell ill. He vomited several times and suffered intense stomach pains. Winifred insisted that her father see a doctor, so Fred reluctantly visited Doctor Wills. As it was with Molly, the doctor could not find anything specifically wrong with his patient, but did prescribe a hospital visit. Fred was about to leave, when he collapsed in the office. An ambulance arrived and took Fred to Willesden Hospital.

Fred's suspicion lay directly on his son, who visited him in hospital but never said a word to his father. Instead, he was more interested in learning of the effects of the illness from the doctors and nurses. After a short stay at the hospital, Fred appeared to be improving in health and was sent home. The doctors were still unaware of the cause, when only days later, the symptoms returned. Winifred took charge of the situation and called an ambulance to take Fred back to the hospital. Initial tests on Fred indicated that he had been poisoned with either arsenic or antimony; however, it was yet to be confirmed.

The family instantly blamed Young. The following day antimony was proven to be the cause and doctors told Fred that his liver was permanently damaged and that probably one more dose would have killed him. During Fred's recovery at the hospital Aunt Winnie looked after the children, but was given strict instructions by Fred that his son was not to visit him under any circumstances.

At the school, the science teacher, Mr Hughes, heard of the sad news concerning the Young family. His own suspicions grew about Graham Young. One evening after lessons, Mr Hughes searched Young's desk and discovered several small bottles of poison and a notebook containing notes on several poisons and poisoners. Mr Hughes recalled the mystery of Chris Williams's illnesses and, making the link, went to talk to the headmaster who agreed with the suspicions. The pair decided to visit the family doctor, Dr Willis, who suggested that it was too early to point the finger at Young, but did suggest that an evaluation by a psychiatrist would help in the matter.

On May 20 the interview took place. The psychiatrist was acting the part of a careers officer to get Young to discuss his chemistry ambitions. Young proudly talked about his experiments involving poisons and his knowledge of them. After the meeting all notes were given to Detective Inspector Edward Crabbe. The following day DI Crabbe visited the family home searched Young's bedroom and discovered various types of poisons including thallium; digitalis and antimony.

Crabbe briefly spoke to Aunt Winnie and told her that he would be arresting her nephew for malicious administration of poison. As Young returned from school that day, he was greeted by the detective and instructed to empty his pockets – nothing. Then he was asked to remove his shoes – still nothing. Finally Young was asked to remove his shirt. A small vial of Antimony fell to the floor along with two other bottles which further testing would identify as containing thallium. Young was arrested and taken to Harlseden police station.

At the station Young denied everything. However in the morning, Young gave a full confession to his activities. He even admitted to where he had hidden additional bottles of poison. With this evidence Graham Young was charged on May 22 with poisoning Fred Young, Winifred Young and Chris Williams. No charges were bought against Young concerning the death of his stepmother, Molly.

His court appearance at the Old Bailey took place on July 6, 1962 in the courtroom of Mr Justice Melford Stevenson. Young pleaded guilty on all three counts. In court, a prepared statement was read out on behalf of Young that outlined the methods he used to poison his family and Chris Williams. In addition, to regularly giving his stepmother doses of Antimony.

The prosecutor Mr EJP Cussens bought up the subject of Molly Young. He re-iterated that her death was due to natural causes and not an intake of poison. However a consultant psychiatrist, Dr Donald Blair, believed that antimony may have led to the condition of her spinal column which in turn led to her death. Dr Christopher Fysh, a senior medical officer, gave the court his medical opinion of the defendant, 'Young is not suffering from a mental illness but from a psychopathic disorder, in my opinion he requires care in a maximum security hospital'. Fysh suggested Broadmoor Hospital.

Jean Southworth, acting for the defence, asked Fysh if Young had the killer instinct. Fysh replied that Young was 'prepared to take the risk of killing'. The judge handed down his sentence and under section 66 of the 1959 Mental Health Act, Young was committed to Broadmoor with an instruction that he was not to be released for a period of 15 years, without the express permission of the Home Secretary.

Young's time in the hospital was spent away from his father. Despite a few visits in the early months since his sentencing, Fred hardly saw his son. Aunt Winnie was Young's most regular visitor. Young would shy away from group contact, preferring to be on his own. His interest in Nazism continued, making his own swastika that he proudly wore on a chain around his neck. As time went on, the staff at Broadmoor became more and more confident in Young. At one point they even placed him in charge of making coffee for the staff. Almost inevitably several cups of bitter tasting coffee were found. Bleach had somehow found its way into the pot.

After his third year at Broadmoor, Young wanted to leave. The only option available to him was to petition the annual review tribunal to look into his case. His family attended the review with Fred saying that 'He should never be released'. The review resulted in rejection. Several months later, a packet of sugar soap disappeared from the cleaning room and a full tea urn was analysed just as rounds were about to begin. It contained the missing soap which would have caused severe stomach burns to any who would have drunk from it.

It was never proven that Young was responsible for the incident, though suspicion lay heavily on the teenager. After the incident Young recognised that another option for release lay open to him. Young became the model patient, using good behaviour as his route to early release.

In June 1970, the subject of Young's future was discussed at the hospital. The doctors believed that he was 'no longer obsessed with poisons, violence and mischief' and no longer a danger to others. The senior psychiatrist at the hospital, Dr Edgar Udwin, suggested that to help facilitate Young's development a stay at a family member's home for a few days would do him some good. Given that Fred would immediately refuse, they decided to approach his sister.

Winifred was unsure, but eventually decided to give her brother a chance and therefore on November 21, 1970, Young was granted leave for a week long stay at Winifred's house, where she now lived with her husband Dennis Shannon and their new born child. The couple, on Dr Udwin's advice, gave Young a free reign of the house including the kitchen. At the end of the week Young returned to the hospital, Dr Udwin was pleased to receive a good report on his patient's behaviour. The Shannon's even suggested that they would enjoy a second visit, maybe over the Christmas holiday. The request was approved and again the visit went well, Young was showing no signs of his previous obsessions and spent the time indulging in new found happiness.

Backed up by the good reports from Young's sister and by his own observations, Dr Udwin believed that Young was ready for release. In early 1971, he petitioned the Home Secretary for release. Following the ruling from Young's 1962 trial, the request was approved and Young was given a release date of February 1971. After hearing of his upcoming release, Young privately let other patients and some nurses know of his resentment of having been kept 'locked up'. Young once admitted to a nurse that he intended to kill one person for every year he spent in the hospital. However the concerns the nurse had of Young's release fell on deaf ears. Young was released from care on February 4, 1971. No one told Fred. It wasn't until a month after his son's release that a Broadmoor official finally let Fred know.

Young, before leaving Broadmoor, had gained a place at the Government training centre in Slough. On February 8, 1971 Young began a course in storekeeping, quickly making friends with another trainee at the centre, thirty-four-year-old Trevor Sparkes. The two would regularly drink together, discussing various topics. A week after meeting, Trevor confided in Young about some abdominal pains he was suffering from, confessing that his doctor couldn't help.

In the short time he had known Trevor, Young had persuaded his friend that he was knowledgeable in the field of medicine and offered him a glass of wine, convincing Trevor that it would help. For four days Trevor vomited violently and suffered pains across his whole body. He spent a four further days in the sickbay of the training centre until the pains subsided and he was able to return to work. He still believed that Young was helping him and so continued to take his advice, drinking the wine offered by Young. The pains continued, he visited his doctor and also Queen Elizabeth II hospital in Welwyn but doctors were baffled by the symptoms.

In April 1971, Young applied for the job of storeman at John Hadland Ltd in Bovingdon, Hertfordshire. Prior to his interview at the firm, Young travelled to London and visited John Bell and Croydon chemists. There he attempted to purchase antimony potassium nitrate. Young employed the same method he used years earlier, but the request was turned down. The chemist rightly informed Young that despite his impressive knowledge he did not have the written authority to purchase such substances. One week later, on April 24, Young returned to the chemist with a letter headed Bradford College London, which gave authority for Mr M E Evans to purchase antimony for experimental purposes. The chemist, Albert Kearne, handed Young the bottle and recorded his signature in the poison register, as Evans, the same name Young had used nine years previously. Meanwhile Young's interview at Hadland's had gone well, such that he was offered the job. Young agreed to start on May 10, 1971.

At Hadland's, the storeroom workers found Young to be quiet and unpredictable, he would be talkative one minute and then ignore everyone the next. Young would spend his breaks sitting reading his favourite topics of Nazism and war. Despite this, whenever topics of chemistry came up, young would suddenly brighten up and become talkative. Young's manager in the storeroom was fifty-eight-year-old Bob Egle. With Bob being a Dunkirk veteran, Young would enjoy listening to his stories of the battlefields of France which Bob enjoyed telling. The stores team would regularly help Young out with favours; rides to and from work, the occasional cigarette etc. Young would repay their kindness by fetching their cups of tea from the trolley. On June 3, 1971, Bob Egle fell ill and went home for the day, not returning until the following Monday, when his diarrhoea attacks ended.

The day after Bob returned to work, June 8, storeman Ron Hewitt began suffering from diarrhoea and stomach pains. The symptoms continued for three weeks. Bob Egle took two weeks from work returning on June 28, but on his second day back, he once again fell ill and was sent home, but he felt progressively worse. Bob couldn't sleep, he complained of numbness in his hands and feet, his back caused him pain and his headache just wouldn't go away.

Bob's wife, Dorothy, called for the doctor who diagnosed Peripheral Neuritis, an ambulance was immediately called. Bob was taken to the West Herts hospital in Hemel Hempstead, but the pain continued to get worse. He was transferred to St Albans City hospital into the intensive care unit but his condition did not improve. Bob's body was by now almost completely paralysed and his heart stopped twice. On each occasion the staff at the hospital was successful in reviving him. But on July 7, 1971 Bib Egle died. A post mortem on the body was performed two days later. The cause of death was put down to Broncho-Pneumonia in conjunction with Guillain-Barre Polyneuritis. After Bob's death Young was placed in charge of the storeroom for a probational period. But the illnesses at Hadland's was not yet over.

In September, Fred Biggs began to feel stabbing pains in his stomach and also suffered periods of severe vomiting. Fred returned to work on September 20, the same day that Peter Buck fell ill with the same symptoms, returning to work the following day.

On October 8, David Tilson was next to succumb to the mystery illness sweeping through the storeroom. After drinking a cup of tea with Young, David began to feel nauseous, but continued to work before going home for the weekend. The pins and needles David felt in his arms and legs were slowly getting worse. By Sunday his limbs were numb and he visited his doctor who prescribed rest.

On Tuesday October 12, David returned to work although the pain in his legs would not go away. On Friday Jethro Batt gave Young a ride home, as Young described how easy it was to poison somebody and get away with it. The next day Jethro was violently ill after having a mouthful of coffee made by Young. Over the weekend Jethro's legs went from numb to painful, then the pain moved to his stomach.

David Tilson felt just as bad, his chest and stomach were painful and he was struggling to breathe. His doctor sent him to St Albans City hospital for observation. Then his hair started to fall out. Jethro remained at home but he was in immense pain, unable to move easily. On November 5, he was admitted to West Herts hospital and as with David Tilson, he too was going bald. David was released from hospital on October 28 but four days later he was readmitted. In the storeroom at Hadland's only one member of the staff was unaffected by the illness, Graham Young.

Fred Biggs continued to suffer stomach pains and vomiting which was affecting everyone in the company stores, bar Young. Fred returned to work to help out with the annual stocktaking. The following day however, he once again was overcome with the same symptoms, but this time the pains were more intense. On November 4, Fred was admitted to West Herts hospital, where Jethro Batt would join him the following day. Young was now under suspicion by the staff at Hadland's. Rumours spread through the company. Young overheard Diana Smart call him a germ carrier and the next day she was off work after suffering attacks of vomiting. Fred Biggs continued to deteriorate during his time in the hospital. Several doctors reviewed his case, but could find nothing that would cause the symptoms, however they did believe Fred was suffering from some form of nervous complaint. On November 11, Fred was transferred to Whittington hospital where his condition worsened still. The skin on his face and scrotum began to peel away, he was virtually paralysed. Fred was transferred again, this time to the National Hospital for Nervous Diseases. At 7.00am on November 19, Fred died.

Panic set in at Hadland's; several employees wanted to quit. Doctors visited the factory but couldn't find anything wrong. The factory owner John Hadland returned from abroad and called in the local doctor, Dr Anderson, to talk to the staff. Dr Anderson admitted to the staff that there were three possibilities, radiation, a virus or perhaps some form of metallic poisoning. Of the three options he believed that it was an, as yet, unidentified virus working its way through the factory. One of the staff had other ideas. From the back of the room, Graham Young spoke out pointing out that metallic poisoning was clearly causing the symptoms.

Dr Anderson had privately believed that metallic poisoning could not yet be dismissed, and became suspicious of Young's statements. Speaking to John Hadland about his suspicions, John Hadland decided to secretly act. He spoke directly to Detective Chief Inspector John Kirkpatrick of Hemel Hempstead police. He detailed the illnesses and Dr Anderson's suspicions, but would not name Young as a suspect.

DCI Kirkpatrick visited Hadland's to begin an investigation. One of the first things he noticed was that the illnesses began shortly after they employed Young. He spoke to Detective Chief Superintendent Ronald Harvey for his opinion on the case. Despite his experience Harvey did not have an answer, but he was able to speak to a forensic expert who, upon hearing the symptoms, immediately gave a diagnosis of thallium poisoning. Kirkpatrick made a request that the employees at Hadland's have their backgrounds checked. Graham Young was instantly placed to the top of the list. Scotland Yard spoke to John Hadland and Godfrey Foster, the managing director, to tell them of Young's poisonous past. Officers were immediately sent out to arrest Young on suspicion of murder.

Officers visited Young's flat at 29 Maynard Road, Hemel Hempstead, but the owners didn't know where he was. They checked with his sister, Winifred. She gave the officers the address at which her brother was on holiday with his father and aunt in Sheerness. Fred Young answered the door to the arresting officers and almost instantly knew why they were there. As the handcuffs were 'snapped' onto Young's wrists, Aunt Winnie asked of her nephew 'What have you done now?'

Detective Sergeant Robert Livingstone returned to Young's flat on Maynard Road to search his room. Amongst all the German paraphernalia, he found a collection of bottles marked poison and several drawings of men with no hair. During questioning at Hemel Hempstead police station, Young boasted of how he got away with poisoning his stepmother Molly, he then suggested that doctors were failing with David Tilson and Jethro Batt by not treating them correctly.

Kirkpatrick spotted the mistake and was able to trap Young. He asked Young what poison he had used. Young however refused to answer the question but gave Kirkpatrick the antidote for it. As the interview wore on, Young could not resist boasting of his work. Eventually, using Young's arrogance against him, Detective Chief Superintendent Ron Harvey was able to gain a confession out of Young. He admitted using Thallium on Bob Egle, Fred Biggs, David Tilson and Jethro Batt, in addition to using Antimony Potassium Nitrate on Peter Buck, Diana Smart, Ron Hewitt and Trevor Sparkes.

The following day, November 22, the police were hoping for further evidence of poisoning to confirm Young's confession. The body of Fred Biggs was to undergo a post mortem performed by Professor Hugh Molesworth-Johnson. The initial observations concluded that the symptoms of Thallium poisoning were present, however traces of the metal could not be found. Fred's internal organs were sent away for more detailed analysis. Despite lack of real evidence in his hand, Ronald Harvey returned to the police station and charged Young with the murder of Fred Biggs. Young made a court appearance on November 23 to be remanded in custody awaiting trial.

Evidence on Bob Egle's murder was next on the agenda. Bob had been cremated after his death, but his ashes were buried in Gillingham cemetery. After gaining authority, Bob's ashes were exhumed and sent for testing. The results of both Bob Egle and Fred Biggs came through on the same day. In both cases Thallium poisoning was confirmed as the cause of death. Young was now additionally charged on December 3, 1971 with the murder of Bob Egle. These charges were quickly followed with charges of attempted murder on David Tilson and Jethro Batt and charges of grievous bodily harm on Diana Smart, Peter Buck, Ronald Hewitt and Trevor Sparkes. Young was then transferred to Brixton Prison.

After a delay, the trial of Graham Frederick Young began on July 19, 1972 in the St Albans courtroom of Mr Justice Eveleigh. With Sir Arthur Irvine QC acting as his defence, Young entered a plea of not guilty on all counts. After all police evidence and other witnesses had been presented, Young made an appearance at the stand. His evidence took two days and consisted mainly of prosecutor John Leonard QC verbally squaring off with the defendant.

Young's intelligence however shone through. He was able to fend off the prosecutors' questions with arrogant ease, giving confident answers to all points raised. Summing up in the case barely took an hour before the jury were given final instructions and asked to begin their deliberations. Less than one hour later, they returned.

Young was found not guilty of the charges of grievous bodily harm against Peter Buck and Trevor Sparkes, but guilty of the murders of Bob Egle and Fred Biggs. He was also found guilty of the attempted murders of Jethro Batt and David Tilson and guilty of grievous bodily harm against Ronald Hewitt and Diana Smart.

Sir Arthur Irvine called for common sense in sentencing, reminding the court that the crimes were unlikely to have been committed had Young not been released from Broadmoor early. He further suggested that a custodial sentence was inappropriate and Young should be returned to Broadmoor to continue treatment. However Young was sentenced to life imprisonment for the two counts of murder and two counts attempted murder.

In addition, Mr Justice Eveleigh sentenced Young to five years for each count of grievous bodily harm. Young was taken from the courtroom and transferred to Wormwood Scrubs and then onto Parkhurst maximum security prison on the Isle of White to serve his sentence.

Young made the headlines of the national press again in August 1990. This time however, the media were reporting his death. Graham Young had died less than a month before his forty-third birthday from a heart attack; alone in his cell in Parkhurst prison.

Z

Christopher Zidoke

January 7, 1997 saw Christopher Mhlengwa Zidoke found guilty of eight murders, five attempted murders and 5 rapes. For his crimes, Zidoke received a sentence of 140 years.

Zidoke, arrested on September 29, 1995, murdered a total of 18 people, with a further 11 attempted murders during a two year killing spree around Donnybrook, South Africa. Zidoke would enter houses, kill the males, then rape and murder the females, however on some occasions evidence proved that rape had taken place after the murder.

Anna Maria Zwanzinger
Anna Schonleben

Anna Zwanzinger was born Anna Schonleben in August 1760. By 1765 she was an orphan and moved for the next five years between different family members. At the age of 10 she was sponsored by a wealthy guardian and received a decent education.

At the age of 15 she was married to a drunken thirty-year-old lawyer called Zwanzinger. Her guardian had arranged the marriage. The couple had two children together, but it was far from a happy marriage. Anna became a prostitute at one point to support the family as her husband had become unable to work due to his alcoholism.

Anna however, still had standards, she maintained to only have had judges and men in powerful positions as her clients and lovers. She left her husband at one stage to be with a lover but Zwanzinger persuaded her back. Zwanzinger had a hold over Anna. When they finally divorced, they remarried the next day.

In 1796 Zwanzinger died, leaving thirty-three-year-old Anna to look after the two children alone. She attempted to open her own store by failed. She fell back into prostitution but became pregnant and had to stop. The baby was sent for adoption but died at an orphanage.

It was around that time that Anna began to show signs of wear and tear. Her mental stability began to waiver; she went into house service but would ignore the wishes of her employers. She felt she was above doing menial work, but needed the money. Over the next two decades she continued to do housekeeping, yet the last two years of her freedom saw her became an embittered woman who believed she should be the mistress of the house and not the maid. She poisoned several women to try to get their husbands to marry her. Little did she know she was suffering delusions and was not desirable.

Justice Glaser's death

Anna Zwanzinger had made herself a reputation as an expert knitter and housekeeper, when she was visited by Justice Wolfgang Glaser at her house in Pegnitz, Baireuth, Bavaria. He asked the now fifty-year-old woman if she would become his housekeeper. Justice Glaser went on to explain that he had recently separated from his wife and needed someone to tend his home.

On March 5, 1808 Anna became the Judge's housekeeper.

However the appointment appeared short-lived when Frau Glaser returned home to be with her husband once again, but the reunion was short-lived. Though Frau Glaser was a strong and healthy woman, she became suddenly ill on her return on July 22nd.

She suffered violent vomiting bouts, diarrhoea, pain and nausea. Five weeks later Frau Glaser was still writhing pain when she expired on August 26, 1808.

Another man dies

A month later on September 25, Anna left the Glaser's service and went to keep house for Justice Grohmann in Sanspaareil. The thirty-eight-year-old man suffered poor health and spent a lot of time in bed. Anna doted on the man and he soon became well, only to be stricken once more.

In spring, 1809 Grohmann was inflicted with diarrhoea, vomiting and severe abdominal pain. The illness lasted eleven days and he died on May 8, 1809. Grohmann's death was attributed to natural causes due to his long-term health issues. Anna was inconsolable after the man's death.

The Gebhard Family
Frau Gebhard, wife of Justice Gebhard had heard of Anna's fine skills as a housekeeper and quickly took her on after Grohmann's death. Frau Gebhard was pregnant and needed help during her confinement. On May 13, 1809, the baby was born and both mother and daughter were well.

Yet three days later Frau Gebhard became extremely unwell. She began vomiting profusely and had severe loose bowel motions. She was completely bed-ridden. On May 20, 1809 Frau Gebhard died from the illness, her last words were: *"Merciful Heaven! You have given me poison"* to Anna. However, due to Frau Gebhard's long-term ill health, no one in authority took much notice of her accusation and her death was ruled on natural causes.

By now people were beginning to suspect that it was more than mere coincidence that Anna's employers kept expiring. However nobody talked about his or her suspicions. So Anna continued her employment as a housekeeper to Bavarian Judge Gebhard.

On August 25, 1809 Justice Gebhard dined with two guests, Mr Beck and Mr Alberti. After dinner the two guests were both stricken with a similar illness to that of Gebhard's wife. A messenger who had come to the house and stayed for a glass of wine also suffered from the gastro illness.

A porter, Johnny Krause had stopped for a glass of port and only had a small sip. He noticed white sediment and had heard the gossip about Anna and chose not to drink any more from the snifter.

Yet there had been enough poison in the small mouthful to cause him a violent reaction. Others in the household also became sick. One of the kitchen maids, Barbara Waldmann became ill after a cup of coffee made by Anna. Yet again nothing was done, and no one had seen Anna put poison in any of the vessels. It was all still conjecture.

On September 1, 1909 Gebhard entertained five friends for an evening with games of skittles. All of them, including Gebhard became ill after drinking beer.

Anna is caught
At the urging of his ill guests Gebhard dismissed Anna from his service the next day. However, on September 3, 1809 Anna decided to do some last minute chores before leaving her employment. She took the saltbox from the kitchen cellar and filled it with salt from the barrel in Gebhard's room. Barbara the kitchen maid saw Anna do it. The job was actually Barbara's and she found it unusual that Anna would do it.

She then gave Barbara and another maid a cup of coffee, and the five-month old Gebhard baby some milk and a cookie. All of it laced with poison.

After Anna had left all three of them became ill. The household knew for sure that Anna was responsible and Barbara remembered the salt barrel. The police were called and the salt was tested. It contained a high amount of arsenic.

Anna was arrested shortly after and when she was searched, two more packets of arsenic were found in her possession. Police then began investigating the other deaths of Anna's employers. Frau Glaser's body was exhumed and arsenic was found in her body.

Anna confessed to all of her crimes, and was executed by a sword in 1811.

Bibliography
Books
- Appleton, Arthur, *Mary Ann Cotton,* Michael Joseph Ltd, 1973
- Askill, John & Sharpe, Martyn, *Angel of Death,* Michael O'Mara Books, 1993
- Baden, Michael, *Unnatural Death,* Sphere Books, 1991
- Baden, Michael, and Roach, Marion , *Dead Reckoning: The New Science of Catching Serial Killers.*, Simon and Schuster, 2001
- Baldens, Dennis, *The Ladykiller,* Time Life Books, 1993
- Barry, Philip Beaufoy, *Twenty Human Monsters,* Jarrolds Publishers, 1929
- Bataille, Georges, *The Trial Of Gilles de Rais,* Amok Books, 1991
- Begg, Paul, Fido, Martin, Skinner, Keith, *Jack the Ripper A to Z,* Headline, 1992
- Berry-Dee, Christopher, *Talking With Serial Killers,* John Blake Publishing Ltd, 2002
- Beavan, Colin, *Fingerprints: The Origins of Crime Detection and the Murder Case that Launched Forensic Science,* Hyperion, 2001
- Biondi, Lt. Ray & Hecox, Walt, *The Dracula Killer,* Mondo, 1992
- Black Cat, *Infamous Murders,* MacDonald & Co Ltd, 1991
- Blackburn, Daniel, *Human Harvest,* Knightsbridge Publishing, 1990
- Bland, James, *True Crime Diary,* Futura Publications, 1987
- Bland, James, *True Crime Diary volume 2,* Warner Books, 1999
- Blundell, Nigel, *The Worlds Most Horrific Serial Killers,* Sunburst Books, 1994
- Blundell, Nigel, *Encyclopedia of Serial Killers,* PRC, 1996
- Boar, Roger & Blundell, Nigel, *The Worlds Most Infamous Murders,* Octopus Books, 1984
- Brady, Ian, *The Gates Of Janus,* Feral House Books, 2001
- Braidhill, Kathy, *To Die For,* St Martins Paperback, 2000
- Brown, Malcolm and Wilson, Paul. *Justice and Nightmares: Success and Failures of Forensic Science.*, NSW University Press, 1992
- Cahill, Tim, *Buried Dreams,* Fourth Estate Limited, 1993
- Camp, John, *100 Years of Medical Murder,* Triad/Granada, 1982
- Canter, David, *Criminal Shadows,* Harper Collins, 1995
- Caputi, Jane, *The Age of The Sex Crime,* Bowling Green State University, 1987
- Carlo, Phillip, *The Night Stalker,* Pinnacle Books, 1996
- Clarkson, Wensley, *The Railroad Killer,* St Martin's Paperbacks, 1999
- Cornwell, Patricia, *Portrait of A Killer,* Little, Brown, 2002
- Crockett, Art (edited by), *Serial Murderers (True Detective Magazine),* Pinnacle Books, 1990
- Crow, Alan & Sampson, Peter, *Bible John,* First Press Publishing, no date
- Crowley, Kiernan, *Sleep My Little Dead,* St Martin's Paperbacks, 1997
- Danmore, Leo, *In His Garden,* Dell Publishing, 1981
- Davies, Nick, *Murder on Ward Four,* Chatto & Windus, 1993
- Davis, Carol Anne, *Women Who Kill,* Allison & Busby Limited, 2001
- Douglas, Hugh, *Burke & Hare,* New English Library, 1973
- Douglas, John, *Obsession,* Pocket Books, 1998
- Douglas, John & Olshaker, Mark, *Mindhunter,* Mandarin, 1996
- Douglas, John & Olshaker, Mark, *Journey Into Darkness,* Arrow Books, 1997
- Douglas, John & Olshaker, Mark, *The Anatomy of Motive,* Pocket Books, 1999
- Douthwaite, L C, *Mass Murder,* John Long Ltd, 1929
- Dumas, Alexandre, *Celebrated Crimes (8 volumes),* W & G Foyle Limited, 1895
- Dunning, John, *Madly Murderous,* Arrow Books, 1988
- Dunning, John, *Carnal Crimes,* Arrow Books, 1988

- Eddington, Joyce, *From Cradle To Grave,* True Crime, 1989
- editors of Time Life Books, *Serial Killers (True Crime Series),* Time Life Books, 1992
- Edwards, Ivor, *Jack the Rippers Black Magic Rituals,* John Blake Publishing Ltd, 2002
- Edwards, Owen Dudley, *Burke & Hare,* Polygon Books, no date
- Egger, Steven A, *The Killers Among Us,* Prentice-Hall, 1998
- Evans, Stewart & Gainey, Paul, *Jack The Ripper – First American Serial Killer,* Arrow Books, 1996
- Evans, Stewart P & Skinner, Keith, *The Ultimate Jack The Ripper Sourcebook,* Constable & Robinson, 2001
- Farr, Louise, *The Sunset Murders,* Pocket Books, 1993
- Fido, Martin, *To Kill & Kill Again,* Carlton Books, 2001
- Fido, Martin, *Jack The Ripper,* Orion Books, 1993
- Fisher, Joseph C, *Killers Among Us,* Praeger Publishers, 1997
- Fletcher, Jaye Slade, *Deadly Thrills,* Onyx Books, 1995
- Fletcher, Jaye Slade, *A Perfect Gentleman,* Pinnacle Books, 1996
- Fox, James and Levin, Jack, *Overkill,* Dell Publishing, 1996
- Freeman, Lucy, *Before I Kill More,* Pocket Books, 1977
- Fuhram, Mark, *Murder In Spokane,* Harper Collins, 2001
- Gaddis, Thomas E & Long, James O, *Panzram : A Journal Of Murder,* Amok Books, 2002
- Gaute, JHH & Odell, Robin, *The Murderers Who's Who,* Pan Books, 1980
- Gaute, JHH & Odell, Robin, *Murder - What Dunit,* Pan Books, 1984
- Gekoski, Anna, *Murder By Numbers,* Andre Deutsch, 1999
- Gibney, Bruce, *Beauty Queen Killer,* Pinnacle Books, 1984
- Glaister, John, *The Power of Poison,* Christopher Johnson, 1954
- Glatt, John, *Internet Slavemaster,* St Martin's Paperbacks, 2001
- Goodman, Jonathon (edited by), *The Medical Murders,* Warner Books, 1993
- Gurwell, John K, *Mass Murder In Houston,* Cordovan Press, 1974
- Haines, Max, *Bothersome Bodies,* Futura Publications, 1990
- Harrison, Shirley, *The Diary of Jack the Ripper,* Smith Gryphon Publishers, 1994
- Havill, Adrian, *Born Evil,* St Martin's Paperbacks, 2001
- Hazelwood, Roy & Michaud, Stephen, *Dark Dreams,* St Martin's Paperbacks, 2001
- Heimer, Mel, *The Cannibal,* Pinnacle Books, 1971
- Hickey, Eric W, *Serial Murderers and Their Victims,* Wadsworth/Thomson Learning, 2002
- Holden, Anthony, *The St Albans Poisoner,* Corgi Books, 1995
- Holmes, Ronald M & Holmes, Stephen T, *Contemporary Perspectives on Serial Murder,* Sage Publications, 1998
- Honeycombe, Gordon, *The Murders Of The Black Museum,* Arrow Books, 1984
- Hurwitz, Stephan and Christiansen, Karlo, *Criminology,* George Allen & Unwin, 1983
- Jacobs, David (edited by), *Sex Sadists,* Pinnacle Books, 2000
- James, Mike, *On Death Row,* Forum Press, 1993
- James, Mike (edited by), *Women Who Kill Viciously,* Pan Books, 2003
- Jeffers, H Paul, *Profiles In Evil,* Warner Books, 1992
- Jones, Ann, *Women Who Kill,* Victor Gollancz Ltd, 1991
- Jones, Richard Glyn (editor), *Lambs To The Slaughter,* Xanadu Publications Limited, 1992
- Jones, Richard Glyn (editor), *The Giant Book of True Crime,* Magpie Books, 1994
- Kallio, Lauri E, *Confess or Die,* Minerva Press, 1999
- Kelleher, Michael and Kelleher, C L, *Murder Most Rare,* Dell Publishing, 1999
- Kennedy, Dolores with Nolin, Robert, *On A Killing Day,* S.P.I. Books, 1994
- Keppel, Robert D, *Signature Killers,* Pocket Books, 1997

- Keppel, Robert D, *Serial Murder: Future Implications for PoliceInvestigations,* Authorlink Press, 2000
- Keppel, Robert D. with Birnes, William J., *The Riverman,* Arrow Books, 1996
- Kidder, Tracy, *The Road To Yuba City,* Doubleday & Company Inc, 1974
- Knight, Steven, *Jack The Ripper - The Final Solution,* Harper Collins, 1994
- Korn, Daniel; Radice, Mark & Hanes, Charlie, *Cannibal - The History of People Eaters,* Channel 4 Books, 2001
- Lane, Brian, *The Murder Yearbook (1991-2),* Headline Book Publishing, 1992
- Lane, Brian, *The Butchers,* Virgin Publishing Ltd, 1998
- Lane, Brian, *The Murder Yearbook (1994),* Headline Book Publishing, 1993
- Lane, Brian, *The Murder Book of Days,* Headline Book Publishing, 1995
- Lane, Brian & Gregg, Wilfred, *The Encyclopedia of Serial Killers,* Headline Book Publishing, 1992
- Lane, Brian & Gregg, Wilfred, *The New Encyclopaedia of Serial Killers,* Headline Book Publishing, 1996
- Larson, Erik, *The Devil in The White City,* Bantam Books, 2004
- Lassieur, Allison, *Serial Killers,* Lucent Books, 2000
- Lavelle, Patrick, *Shadow of the Ripper,* John Blake Publishing Ltd, 2003
- Lester PhD, David, *Serial Killers – The Insatiable Passion,* The Charles Press, Publishers, Inc, 1995
- Lewis, Jon E, *Means To A Kill,* Headline Book Publishing, 1995
- Leyton, Elliott, *Hunting Humans,* Penguin Books, 1989
- Lindsay, Phillip, *The Mainspring of Murder,* John Long Limited, 1958
- Linedecker, Clifford, *Thrill Killers,* Futura Publications, 1992
- Linedecker, Clifford, *The Man Who Killed Boys,* St Martin's Paperbacks, 1986
- Lisners, John, *House of Horrors,* Corgi Books, 1983
- Lloyd, Georgina, *One Was Not Enough,* Bantam Books, 1993
- MacKenna, Ron, *DNA and The Hunt For Britains Most Evil Killers,* Black & White Publishing, 2003
- Maeder, Thomas, *Docteur Petiot,* Penguin Books, 1980
- Mandelsburg, Rose G, *Murders In Paradise,* Pinnacle Books, 1994
- Mandelsburg, Rose G (edited by), *The Mutilators,* Pinnacle Books, 1993
- Manners, Terry, *Deadlier Than The Male,* Pan Books, 1995
- Markman, Donald & Busco, Dominick, *Alone With the Devil,* Warner Books, 1993
- Marriner, Brian, *A New Century of Sex Killers,* Forum Press, 1999
- Marshall Cavendish Publications, *Serial Murderers,* Marshall Cavendish Publications, 1992
- Masters, Brian, *Killing for Company,* Arrow Books, 1995
- Masters, Brian, *The Evil That Men Do,* Doubleday, 1996
- McConnell, Brian, *Found Naked & Dead,* New English Library, 1974
- McLaren, Angus, *A Prescription For Murder,* University of Chicago Press, 2002
- Mendoza, Antonio, *Killers on the Loose,* Virgin Publishing Ltd, 2000
- Mendoza, Antonio, *Killers on the Loose - Update,* Virgin Books, 2002
- Michaud, Stephen with Hazelwood, Roy, *The Evil That Men Do,* St Martin's Paperbacks, 2000
- Mitrione, Dan, *Suddenly Gone,* St Martin's Paperbacks, 1995
- Monaco, Richard & Burt, William, *The Dracula Syndrome,* Headline Book Publishing, 1994
- Mones, Paul, *Stalking Justice,* Pocket Books, 1995
- Motion, Andrew, *Wainewright The Poisoner,* Alfred A. Knopf, 2000
- Nash, Jay Robert, *World Encyclopaedia of Murder,* Headline Book Publishing, 1993
- NCAVC, *Deviant & Criminal Sexuality,* US Department of Justice, 1993
- Neustatter, W Lindsay, *The Mind of the Murderer,* Christopher Johnson, 1957
- Newton, Michael, *Hunting Humans – The Encyclopaedia of Serial Killers (Volume 2),* Avon Books, 1993

- Newton, Michael, *Hunting Humans – The Encyclopaedia of Serial Killers (Volume 1),* Avon Books, 1992
- Newton, Michael, *Rope*, Pocket Books, 1998
- Newton, Michael, *Still At Large,* Loompanics Unlimited, 1999
- Newton, Michael, *The Encyclopedia of Serial Killers,* Checkmark Books, 2000
- Newton, Michael, *Century Of Slaughter,* toExcel, 2000
- Newton, Michael, *Serial Slaughter,* Loompanics Unlimited, 1992
- Newton, Michael, *Bad Girls Do It,* Loompanics Unlimited, 1993
- Nickel, Steven, *Torso,* Avon Books, 1990
- Nightingale, Moira, *Cannibal Killers,* New English Library, 1993
- Norris, Joel, *The Killer Next Door,* Arrow Books, 1993
- Norris, Joel, *Serial Killers,* Arrow Books, 1990
- Norton, Carla, *Disturbed Ground,* William Morrow and Company, 1994
- Olsen, Jack, *The Man With The Candy,* Simon & Schuster, 1974
- Parlour, Andy & Sue, *The Jack the Ripper Whitechapel Murders,* Ten Bells Publishing, 1997
- Penrose, Valentine, *The Bloody Countess,* Creation Books, 1996
- Pettit, Mark, *A Need To Kill,* Ballantine Books, 1991
- Pincus MD, Jonathon H, *Base Instincts,* Norton, 2002
- Reinhardt, James Melvin, *The Psychology of Strange Killers,* Charles C Thomas, 1962
- Ressler, Robert K, *I Have Lived In the Monster,* Simon & Schuster, 1997
- Ressler, Robert K. & Shachtman, Tom, *Whoever Fights Monsters,* Pocket Books, 1993
- Ressler, Robert K; Burgess, Ann; Douglas John E, *Sexual Homicide : Patterns and Motives,* The Free Press, 1995
- Robins, Joyce & Arnold, Peter, *Serial Killers,* Chancellor Press, 1996
- Rosen, Fred, *Body Dump,* Pinnacle Books, 2002
- Rule, Ann, *Lust Killer,* Signet Books, 1988
- Russell, Sue, *Damsel of Death,* True Crime, 1994
- Sanders, John, *Forensic Casebook of Crime,* Forum Press, 2000
- Schechter, Harold, *Bestial*, Pocket Star Books, 1998
- Schechter, Harold, *Deviant,* Coronet Books, 1993
- Schechter, Harold, *Deranged,* Warner Books, 1992
- Schechter, Harold, *Depraved,* Pocket Books, 1994
- Schechter, Harold, *Fiend,* Pocket Books, 2000
- Schurman-Kauflin, Dr Deborah, *The New Predator : Women Who Kill,* Algora Publishing, 2000
- Schwarz, Ted, *When The Devil Comes to Visit,* Arrow Books, 1995
- Schwarz, Ted, *The Hillside Strangler,* Signet Books, 1982
- Sears, Richard, *Highway To Nowhere,* Harper Collins, 1996
- Selzer, Mark, *Serial Killers : Death & Life In Americas Wound Culture,* Routledge, 1998
- Sereny, Gitta, *Cries Unheard,* MacMillan, 1998
- Simpson, Lindsay & Harvey, Sandra, *The Killer Next Door,* Random Press, 1994
- Sohail, Dr K, *The Myth of the Chosen One,* White Knight Publications, 2002
- Sugden, Philip, *The Complete History of Jack The Ripper,* Constable & Robinson, 1995
- Sullivan, Terry with Mailken, Peter T., *Killer Clown,* Pinnacle Books, 1991
- Symons, Mitchell, *Criminal Records,* Headline Book Publishing, 1995
- Time Warner Books, *Born To Be Killers,* Warner Books, 2004
- Tullett, Tom, *Murder Squad,* Triad Grafton Books, 1986
- VillaSenor, Victor, *Jury : The People vs Juan Corona,* Dell Publishing, 1977
- Vorpagel, Russell, *Profiles in Murder,* Dell Publishing, 1998

- Weinstein, Bob & Bessent, Jim, *Death Row Confidential,* Harper Collins, 1996
- Whittaker, Mark & Kennedy, Les, *Sins Of The Brother,* Pan MacMillan Books, 2001
- Wilson, Colin, *A Plague of Murder,* Robinson Publishing Ltd, 1995
- Wilson, Colin & Odell, Robin, *Jack The Ripper: Summing Up and Verdict,* Corgi Books, 1994
- Wilson, Colin & Pittman, Pat, *Encyclopedia of Murder,* Pan Books, 1964
- Wilson, Colin & Seaman, Donald, *The Serial Killers,* True Crime, 1994
- Wilson, Colin & Seaman, Donald, *Encyclopaedia of Modern Murder,* Pan Books, 1989
- Wilson, Colin & Wilson, Damon, *The Killers Among Us book 1,* Warner Books, 1996
- Wilson, Colin & Wilson, Damon, *The Killer Among Us book 2,* Warner Books, 1997
- Wilson, Colin & Wilson, Damon, *World Famous Serial Killers,* ,
- Wilson, Colin & Wilson, Damon, *World Famous Gaslight Murders,* ,
- Wilson, Colin & Wilson, Damon, *Written in Blood,* Constable & Robinson, 2003
- Wilson, Paul & Simmons, James Wulf, *Murder in Tandem: When Two People Kill.* , HarperCollins, 2000
- Wolf, Marvin J & Mader, Katherine, *Perfect Crimes,* Ballantine Books, 1995
- Wolfe, Linda, *Love Me To Death,* Pocket Books, 1998
- Woods, Paul Anthony, *Ed Gein - Psycho,* Annihilation Press, 1992
- Young, Sandra Harrison & Rowland, Edna, *Destined For Murder,* Llewellyn Publications, 1995

Court Transcripts
- Howard Allen v State Of Indiana, Case No. 49S00-9207-DP-566
- Rory Enrique Conde v State of Florida , Case No. SC00,789
- The People &C., Respondent, *V.* Richard Angelo, Appellant. 88 N.Y.2d 217, 666 N.E.2d 1333, 644 N.Y.S.2d 460 (1996).

Newspapers
- Advocate, The (Baton Rouge, USA)
- Age, The (Melbourne, Australia)
- Associated Press (International)
- Bay City Times (USA)
- Belfast Telegraph (Ireland)
- Boston Herald (USA)
- Caledonian Record (USA)
- Chicago Sun-Times (USA)
- Daily News (Albany, USA)
- Daily Telegraph (Sydney, Australia)
- Detroit News (USA)
- El Paso Times (USA)
- Evening News (UK)
- Guardian, The (UK)
- Houston Chronicle (USA)
- La Crosse Tribune (USA)
- Mercury News (San Jose, USA)
- Miami Herald (USA)
- Morning Call (USA)
- Nation, The (Nairobi)
- New York Daily News (USA)
- Observer (Charlotte, USA)
- Palm Beach Post (USA)
- Post-Standard, The (Syracuse, USA)
- Reuters (International)
- San Francisco Gate (USA)
- Seattle PI (USA)
- Tribune, The (USA)
- Toronto Star, The (USA)
- Star, The (Africa)
- Sun-Sentinal (South Florida, USA)
- Sydney Morning Herald (Australia)
- United Press International
- Wichita Eagle (USA)

Websites
- www.thecrimeweb.com
- www.news.bbc.co.uk
- www.abc.net.au

Journals
- Murder in Mind
- Real Life Crimes

Index

A

Abel, Wolfgang 10, 11
Al-Hubal, Abdallah 9
Allen, Howard 12, 359
Allitt, Beverley 14
Allitt, Beverly .. 7, 14, 15, 16, 17, 18, 19, 20, 21, 22, 23
Andrade, Marcelo de 24
Angelo, Richard 25
Ann Arbor Hospital 26
Artieda, Ramiro 27

B

Baoshan, Bai 28
Barbeault, Marcel 29, 30, 31
Bashor, Donald 32
Bathory, Elizabeth 33, 35
Beck, Dieter 36
Bell, Mary 37, 38
Berdella, Robert 7
Berkowitz, David 4
Bermudez, Manuel 39
Bianchi, Ken 8
Bianchi, Kenneth 8, 40, 41, 42
Bible John 43
Bichel, Andreas 44
Bishop, Arthur 45
Black Widow 5, 218
Bluebeard 5
Bopp, Bernd 47, 48, 49
Brooks, David 92, 93, 96
Brudos, Jerome 56, 57, 58, 59, 60, 61, 62
Bundy, Carol 70, 76
Bundy, Ted 3, 4, 29
Buono, Angelo 8, 40, 41, 42
Burke, William 50, 53, 54
Butcher of Kingsbury Run 63, 65

C

Caputo, Ricardo 68, 69
Chang-Shin, Liao 78
Chapman, George 79, 81
Chase, Richard 82
Chicago Rippers 84
Chikatilo, Andrei 7, 244
Clark, Douglas 70
Clark, Hadden 86, 87, 88, 89
Conde, Rory 90

Corll, Dean 91, 92, 93, 94, 95, 96, 97
Corona, Juan 98, 99, 286
Costa, Antone 100
Cotton, Mary Ann 101, 102, 103
Cream, Dr Thomas 104, 105

D

Daglis, Andonis 108
Dahmer, Jeffrey 4, 7
Dennis, Jerome 109
Dumollard, Martin and Marie 110
Durrant, Theodore 111

F

Fish, Albert . 114, 115, 116, 117, 118, 120, 121, 122, 123, 124, 125, 126
Francois, Kendall 127, 128, 129, 130
Furlan, Mario 10, 11

G

Gacy, John 3, 4, 7, 131
Gavarito, Luis 145
Gein, Ed 146
George, Guy 148, 149, 150, 151, 152
Glover, John 153, 157, 159, 160
Golovkin, Anatoly 162
Gossman, Klaus 163
Graham, Harrison 164
Gray, Dana 165
Green, Cleo 167
Green, Samuel 168, 169
Grissom, Richard 170
Guimaraes, Edson 171

H

Hansen, Robert 4
Hare, William 50, 53, 55
Heirens, William 6, 172, 173, 176
Henley, Elmer 94, 95, 96, 97
Hillside Strangler 8
Hoch, Johann 177
Holmes, Dr Herman 178
Honka, Fritz 182

I

Iqbal, Javed 183
Ireland, Colin 184

J

Jack the Stripper 192
Jesus Gonzales, Delfina de 195
Jesus Gonzales, Maria de 195
Johnson, Matthew 196
Johnson, Russell 197
Jones, Harold 198

K

Kamata, Yasutoshi 199
Kemper, Ed 4, 200
Kemper, Edmund 200, 202, 204
Kevorkian, Dr 7
Kiss, Bela 205, 206
Klosowski, Severin 79, 80, 81

L

Lake, Leonard .... See Charles NG
Landru, Henri 5
Lang, Donald 207
Laskey, Posteal 208
Leyva, Fernando Hernandez 209
Lightbourne, Wendall 210
Lockhart, Michael 211
Lucas, Henry Lee 4

M

Maake, Maoupa Cedric 212
Macon, Ronald 213
Mahlanga, David 214
Majola, Simon 215
Makin, John 216, 217
Makin, Sarah 216, 217
Malvo, Lee 4, 5
Marek, Martha 218, 219
Marquette, Richard 220
McDuff, Kenneth 221, 222, 223
McGray, Michael 224
Mikasevich, Gennadiy 225
Milat, Ivan 226, 227, 228, 229
Mqomboyi, Zola Jackson 230
Muhammad, John 5
Musa, Bilal 231

N

Nesset, Arnfinn 232
Ng, Charles .... 7, See Leonard Lake
Nilsen, Dennis 234
Nitschke, Dr 7
Nixon, Robert 241
Nkosi, Themba 215

Northcott, Gordon 242

O

Omar, Mohammed 243
Onoprienko, Anatoly 244, 245, 246, 247

P

Panzram, Carl 249
Petiot, Dr Marcel 252, 253
Pieydagnelle, Eusebius 251
Piper, Thomas 256
Pliel, Rudolf 257
poisoner 6, 105, 106
Pomeroy, Jesse 6, 258, 259, 260
Popova, Madama 261
Puente, Dorothea 262, 267

Q

Quick, Thomas 269

R

Rais, Gilles de 270, 271
Ramirez, Richard 273, 281
Resala, Sid 287, 288
Resendiz, Angel 289
Ressler, Robert 3, 184
Rijke, Sjef 291
Robinson, John 292, 293, 295, 297

S

Seda, Heriberto 300, 302, 303
serial killer .. 3, 4, 5, 6, 7, 8, 9, 42, 48, 104, 145, 150, 153, 154, 162, 166, 168, 182, 184, 185, 203, 218, 247, 278, 289, 290, 308, 325, 337
Shipman, Harold "Fred" 4, 6
Shulman, Robert 304
Smith, George Joseph 5
spree killer 5
Starkweather, Charles 5
Stubbe, Peter 305
Suradji, Ahmad 306

T

Terrell, Bobbie Sue 308
thrill killer 4, 5
Thwala, Sipho 309
Troyer, Daniel 310
Tylenol Killer 6, 311, 312

U

Urdiales, Andrew 313

V

Van Zon, Hans 315
Velten, Marie... 316

W

Wanlin, Hu 317
Weidmann, Eugen 318
Wells, William 319
Wen, Zhou 320
Werewolf of Chalons 321
West, Ronald 322, 324
Wilder, Chris 326, 327, 328, 329, 330
Wournos, Aileen 332, 333, 334, 335

X

Xinhai, Yang 336

Y

Yates, Robert 93, 262, 337, 338, 339, 340
Yong, Ma 344
Young, Graham 345, 346, 347, 349, 350, 351

Z

Zhiqin, Duan 344
Zidoke, Christopher 352
Zwanzinger, Anna 353

COMING SOON

RIVER OF BLOOD: Serial Killers and Their Victims Volume 2
By Amanda Howard and Martin Smith

In *River of Blood*, Volume Two, Amanda Howard and Martin Smith continue their exploration of serial murder providing more cases and further insight into the mind of the serial killer, including exclusive contact between the authors, killers and the families of victims.

The second volume will include detailed biographies of historical cases such as English child killers Ian Brady and Myra Hindley, the brutal Canadian child killer Clifford Olson, Russian cannibal Andrei Chikatilo and Milwaukee's Jeffrey Dahmer.

Also included will be a chapter discussing the traits of serial killers, the way they stalk and prey on their victims. Volume Two aims to keep the reader abreast of the latest developments in the genre as well as new cases and updates of those cases already covered in Volume One.

Printed in the United States
119630LV00004B/89/A